オールド　ルーズ戦記　ボーイ

OLDBOY

publisher
MIKE RICHARDSON

editor
CHRIS WARNER

collection designer
DARIN FABRICK

art director
LIA RIBACCHI

English-language version produced by DARK HORSE MANGA.

OLD BOY Vol. 3

© 1997 by GARON TSUCHIYA and NOBUAKI MINEGISHI. All rights reserved. Originally published in Japan in 1997 by FUTABASHA PUBLISHERS CO., LTD, Tokyo. English-language translation rights arranged with FUTABASHA PUBLISHERS CO., LTD, Tokyo, through TOHAN CORPORATION, Tokyo. English-language translation © 2006 by Dark Horse Comics, Inc. All other material © 2006 by Dark Horse Comics, Inc. Dark Horse Manga™ is a trademark of Dark Horse Comics, Inc. All rights reserved. No portion of this publication may be reproduced or transmitted, in any form or by any means, without the express written permission of the copyright holders. Names, characters, places, and incidents featured in this publication are either the product of the author's imagination or are used fictitiously. Any resemblance to actual persons (living or dead), events, institutions, or locales, without satiric intent, is coincidental.

Dark Horse Manga
A division of Dark Horse Comics, Inc.
10956 S.E. Main Street
Milwaukie OR 97222

darkhorse.com

To find a comics shop in your area, call the Comic Shop Locator Service toll-free at 1-888-266-4226

First edition: December 2006
ISBN-10: 1-59307-570-7
ISBN-13: 978-1-59307-570-5

1 3 5 7 9 10 8 6 4 2
Printed in Canada

OLDBOY

volume 3

story by
GARON TSUCHIYA

art by
NOBUAKI MINEGISHI

translation
KUMAR SIVASUBRAMANIAN

lettering and retouch
MICHAEL DAVID THOMAS

DARK HORSE MANGA™

CONTENTS

第20話◉短縮ダイヤル

CHAPTER 20
SPEED DIAL

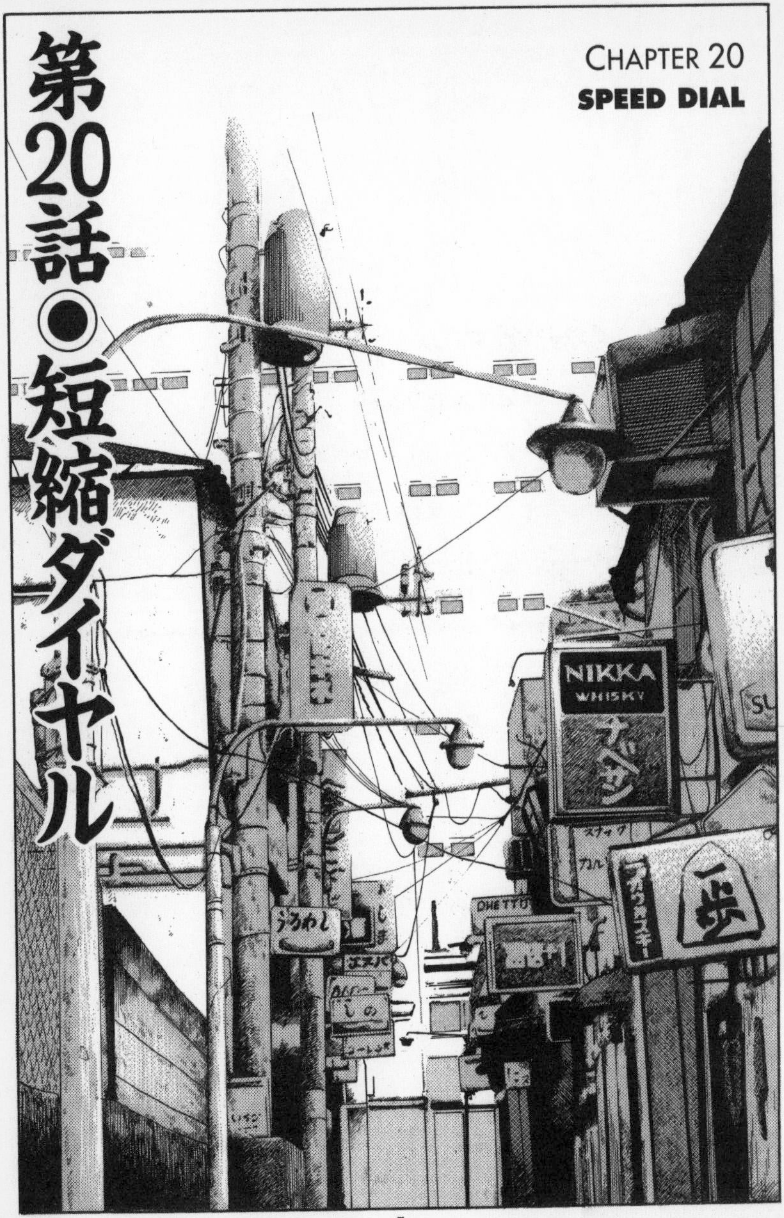
NIKKA
WHISKY

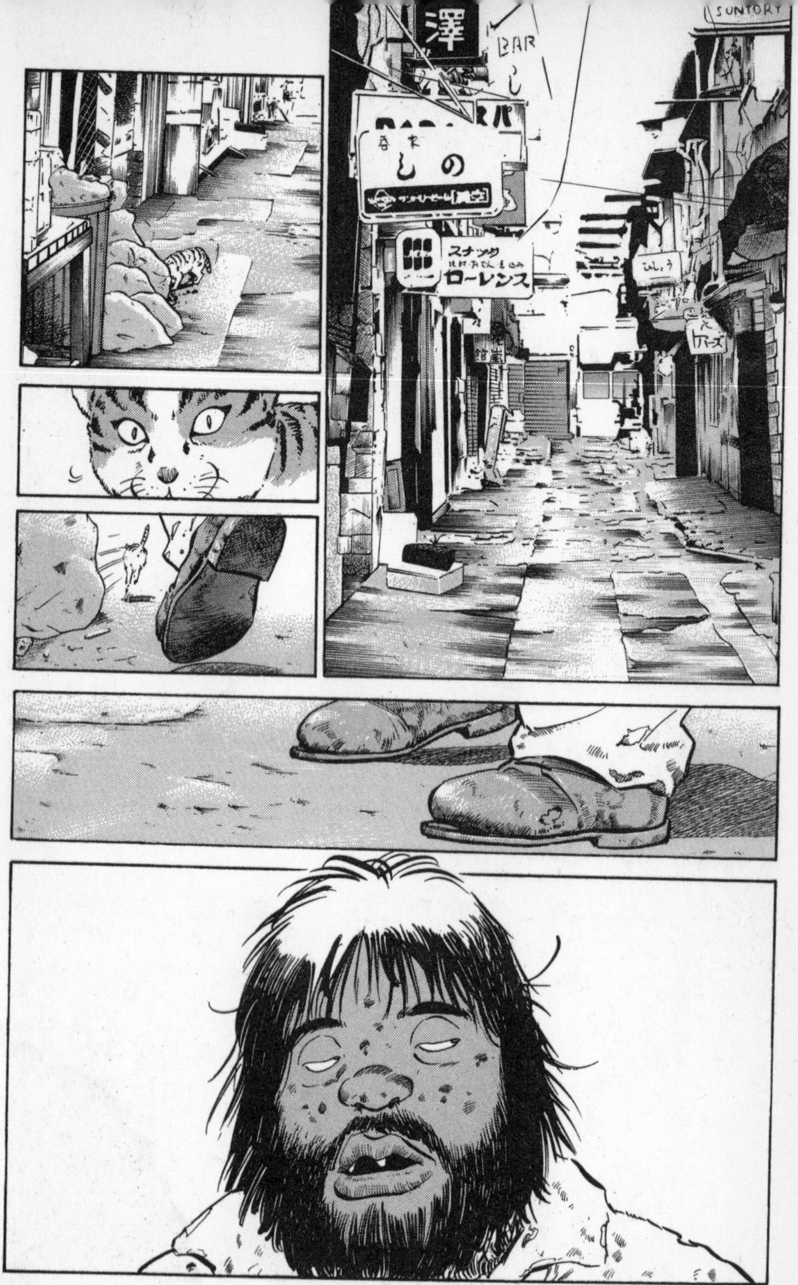
SUNTORY
澤
BAR
しの
スナック
ローレンス

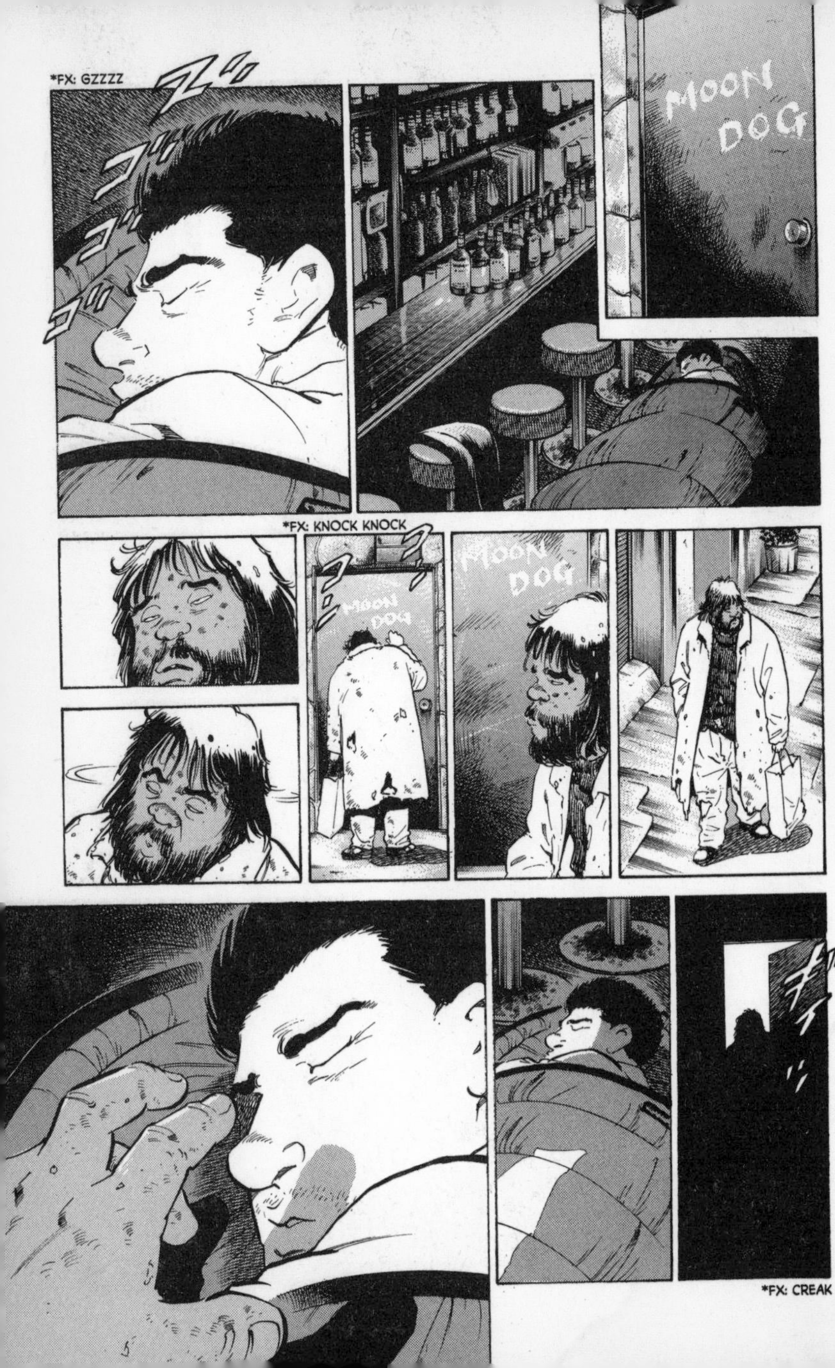
MOON DOG
*FX: GZZZZ
*FX: KNOCK KNOCK
MOON DOG
MOON DOG
*FX: CREAK

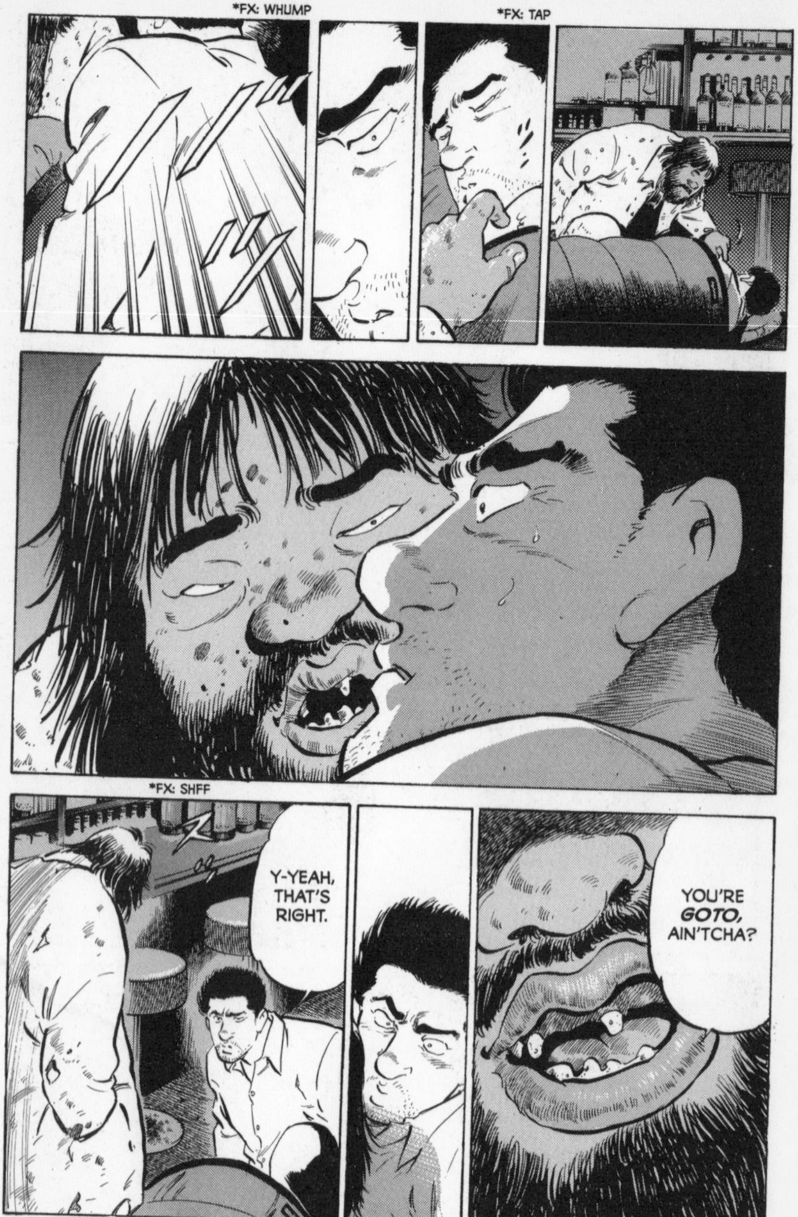
*FX: TAP
*FX: WHUMP
YOU'RE *GOTO,* AIN'TCHA?
Y-YEAH, THAT'S RIGHT.
*FX: SHFF

SOME-BODY ASKED ME A FAVOR.

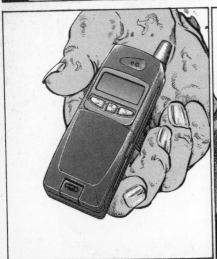

SAID... TO GIVE YOU THIS.

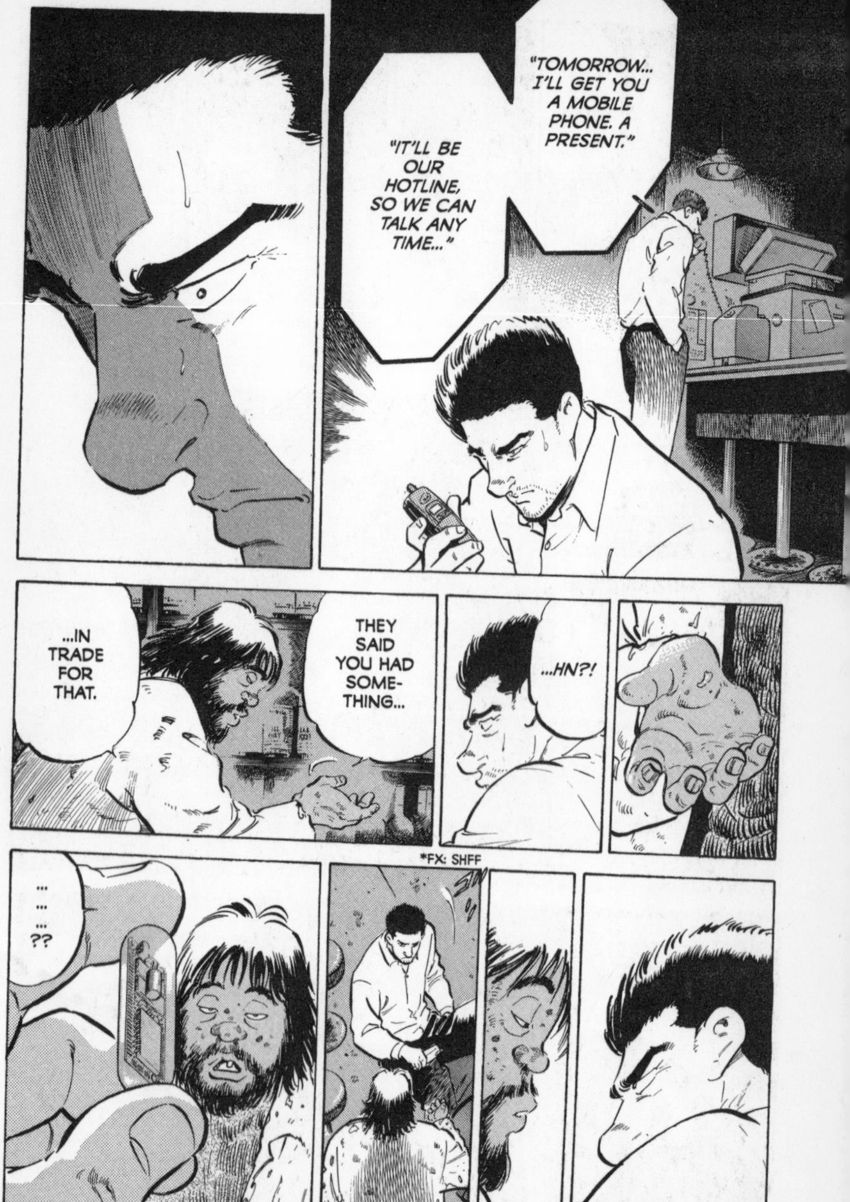
"TOMORROW... I'LL GET YOU A MOBILE PHONE. A PRESENT."
"IT'LL BE OUR HOTLINE, SO WE CAN TALK ANY TIME..."
...HN?!
THEY SAID YOU HAD SOME-THING...
...IN TRADE FOR THAT.
*FX: SHFF
... ... ??

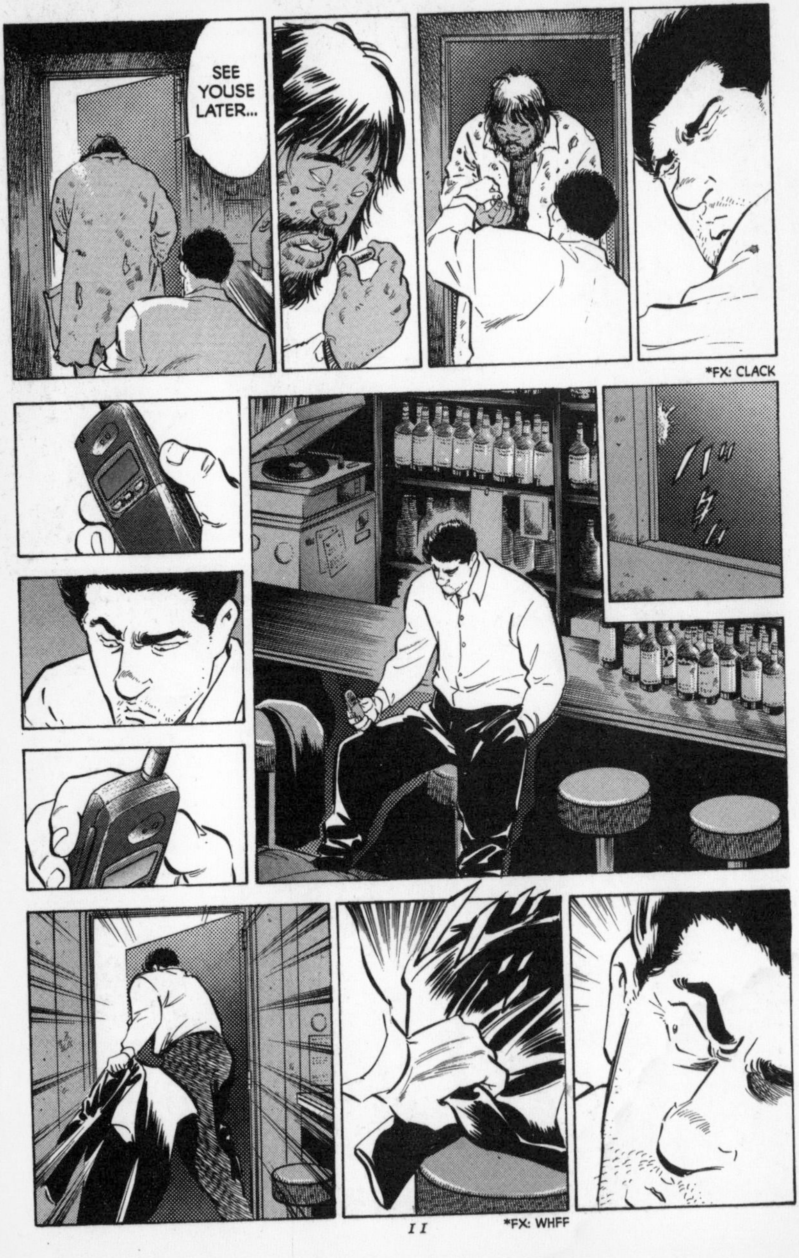
SEE YOUSE LATER...
*FX: CLACK
*FX: WHFF

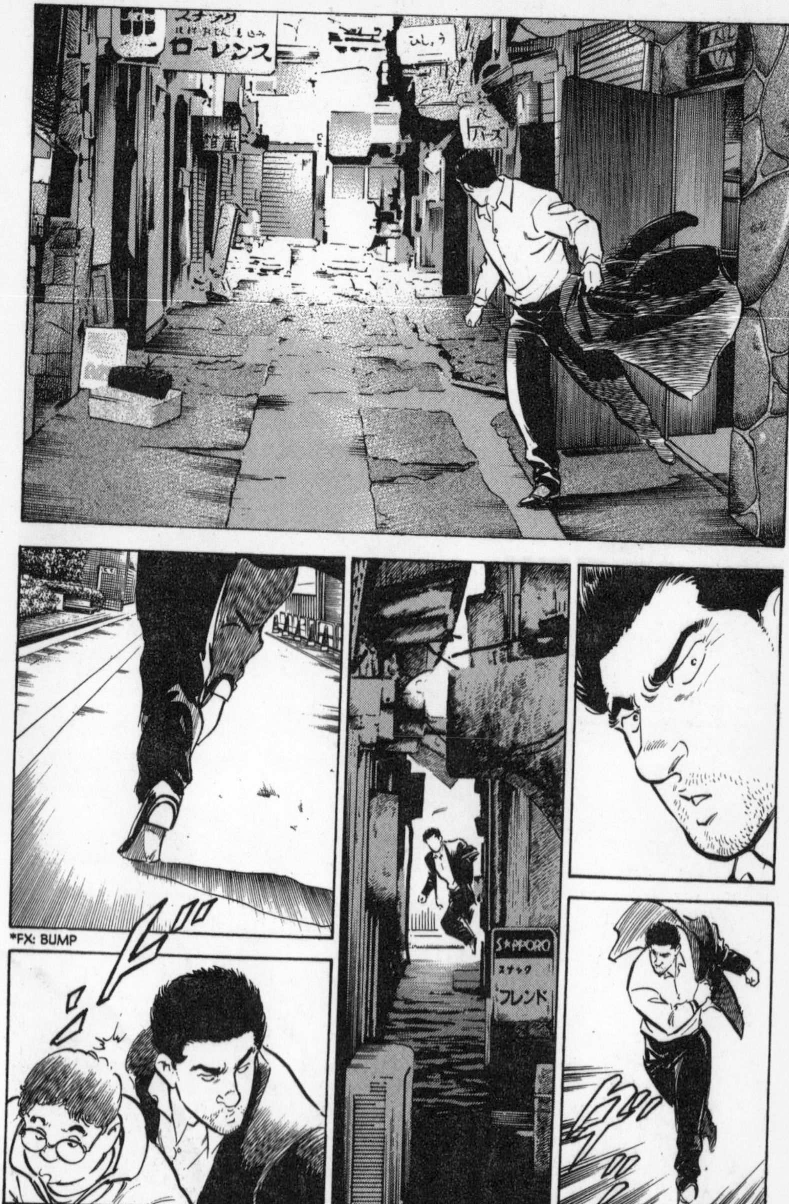
ローレンス
ひしょう
S*PPORO
スナック
フレンド
*FX: BUMP
*FX: THD

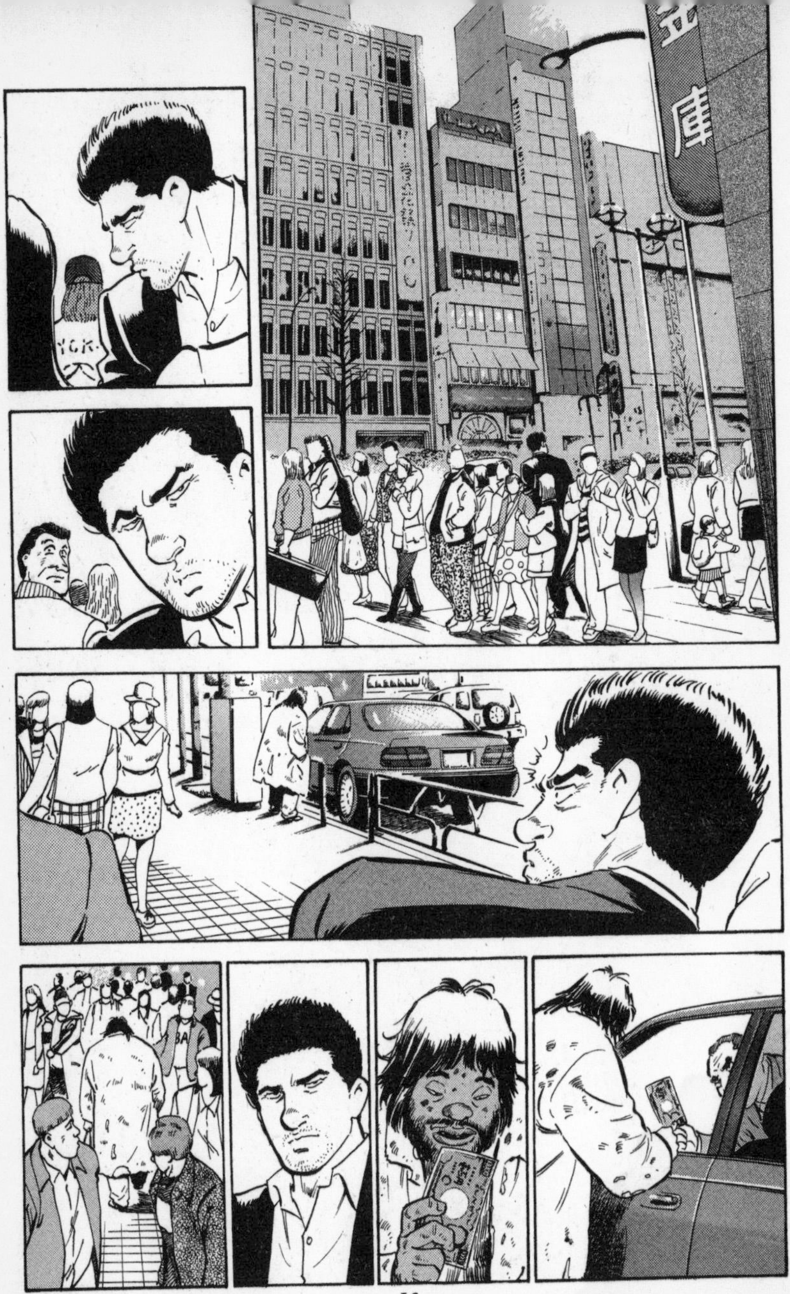
庫
YCK.

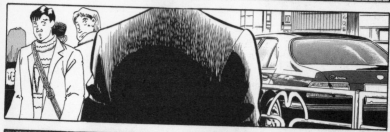

...
...
...

SORRY 'BOUT THE OTHER DAY...

...AND THANKS FOR THIS BACK.

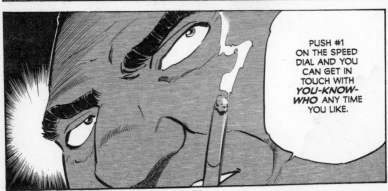

PUSH #1 ON THE SPEED DIAL AND YOU CAN GET IN TOUCH WITH *YOU-KNOW-WHO* ANY TIME YOU LIKE.

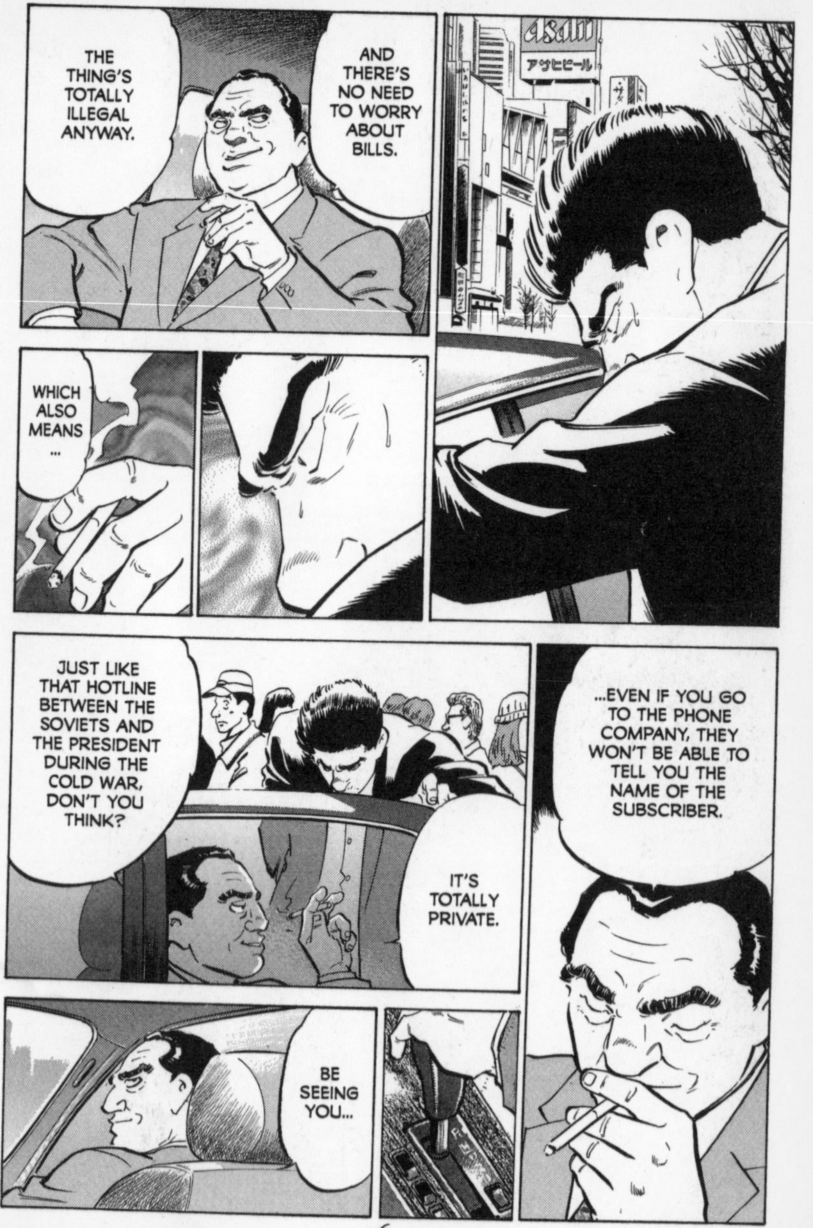
AND THERE'S NO NEED TO WORRY ABOUT BILLS.
THE THING'S TOTALLY ILLEGAL ANYWAY.
WHICH ALSO MEANS ...
...EVEN IF YOU GO TO THE PHONE COMPANY, THEY WON'T BE ABLE TO TELL YOU THE NAME OF THE SUBSCRIBER.
IT'S TOTALLY PRIVATE.
JUST LIKE THAT HOTLINE BETWEEN THE SOVIETS AND THE PRESIDENT DURING THE COLD WAR, DON'T YOU THINK?
BE SEEING YOU...

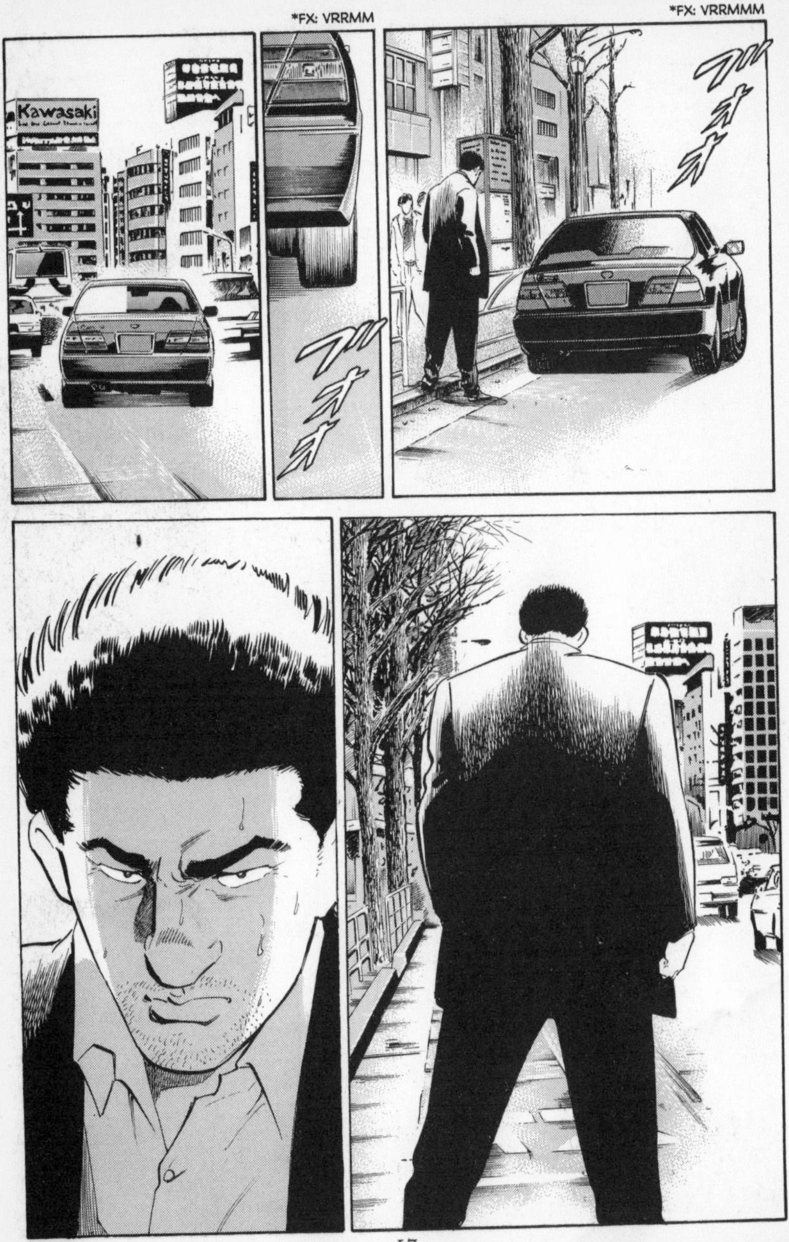
*FX: VRRMMM
*FX: VRRMM
Kawasaki

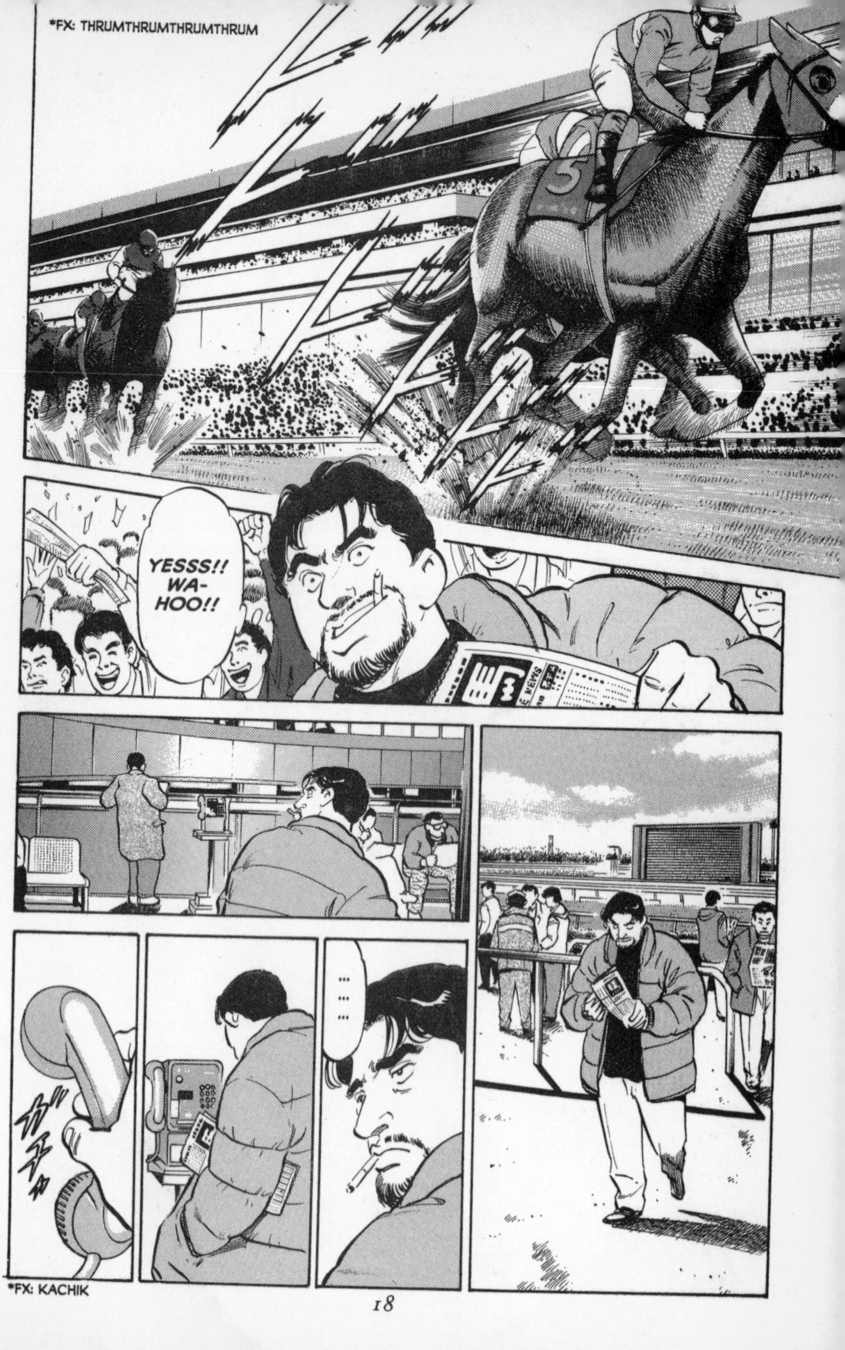
*FX: THRUMTHRUMTHRUMTHRUM
YESSS!! WA-HOO!!
...
...
...
*FX: KACHIK

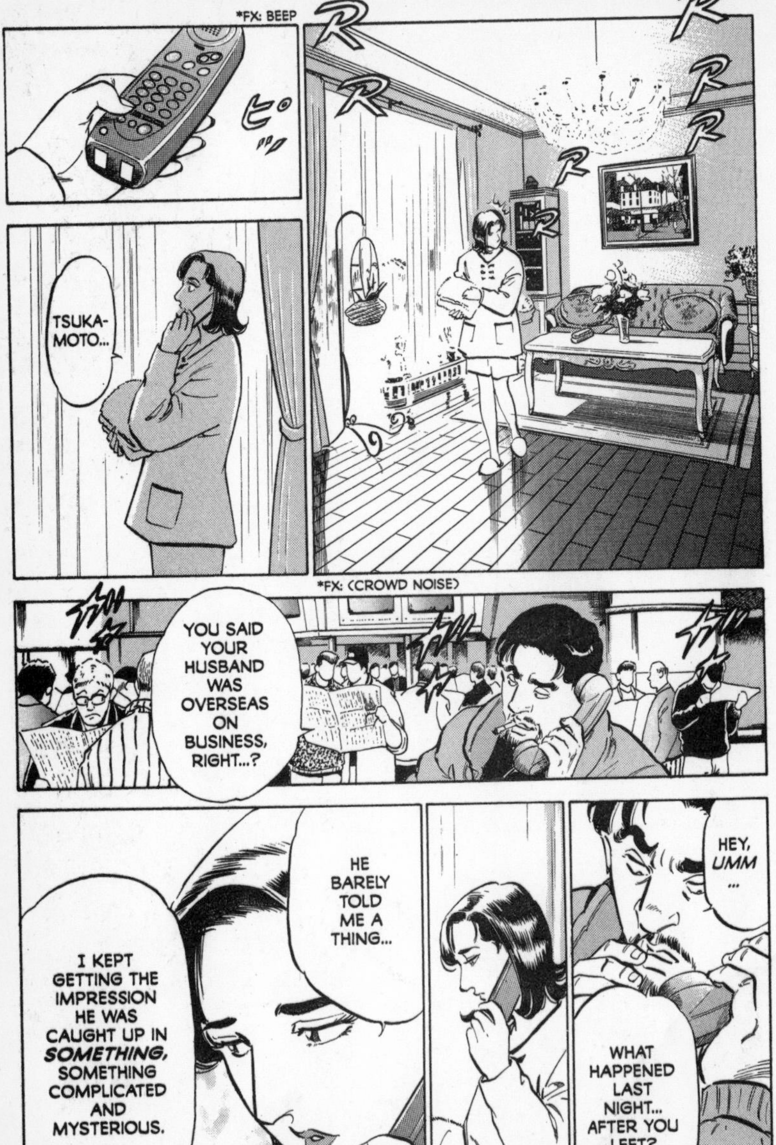
*FX: BEEP
ピ
TSUKA-MOTO...
*FX: (CROWD NOISE)
YOU SAID YOUR HUSBAND WAS OVERSEAS ON BUSINESS, RIGHT...?
HEY, UMM ...
WHAT HAPPENED LAST NIGHT... AFTER YOU LEFT?
HE BARELY TOLD ME A THING...
I KEPT GETTING THE IMPRESSION HE WAS CAUGHT UP IN SOMETHING, SOMETHING COMPLICATED AND MYSTERIOUS.

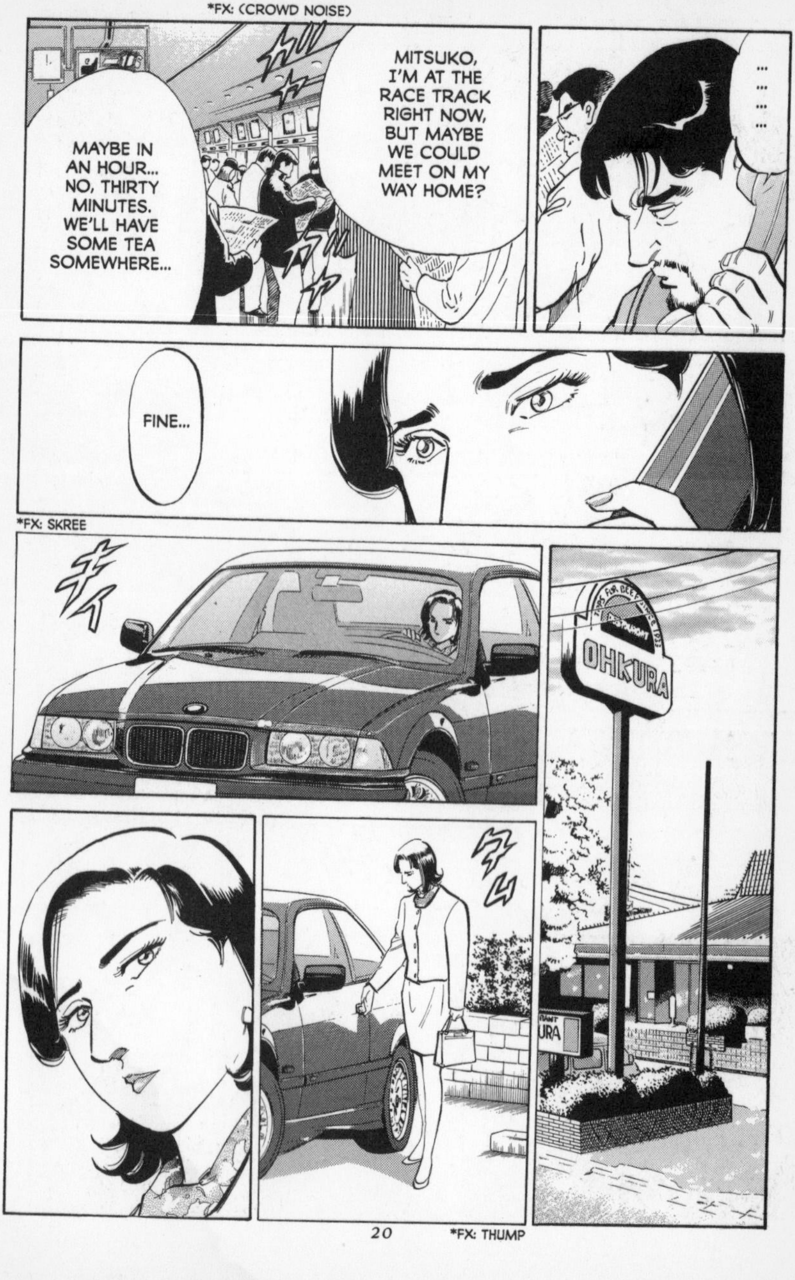
*FX: (CROWD NOISE)
... ...
MITSUKO, I'M AT THE RACE TRACK RIGHT NOW, BUT MAYBE WE COULD MEET ON MY WAY HOME?
MAYBE IN AN HOUR... NO, THIRTY MINUTES. WE'LL HAVE SOME TEA SOMEWHERE...
FINE...
*FX: SKREE
OHKURA
URA
*FX: THUMP

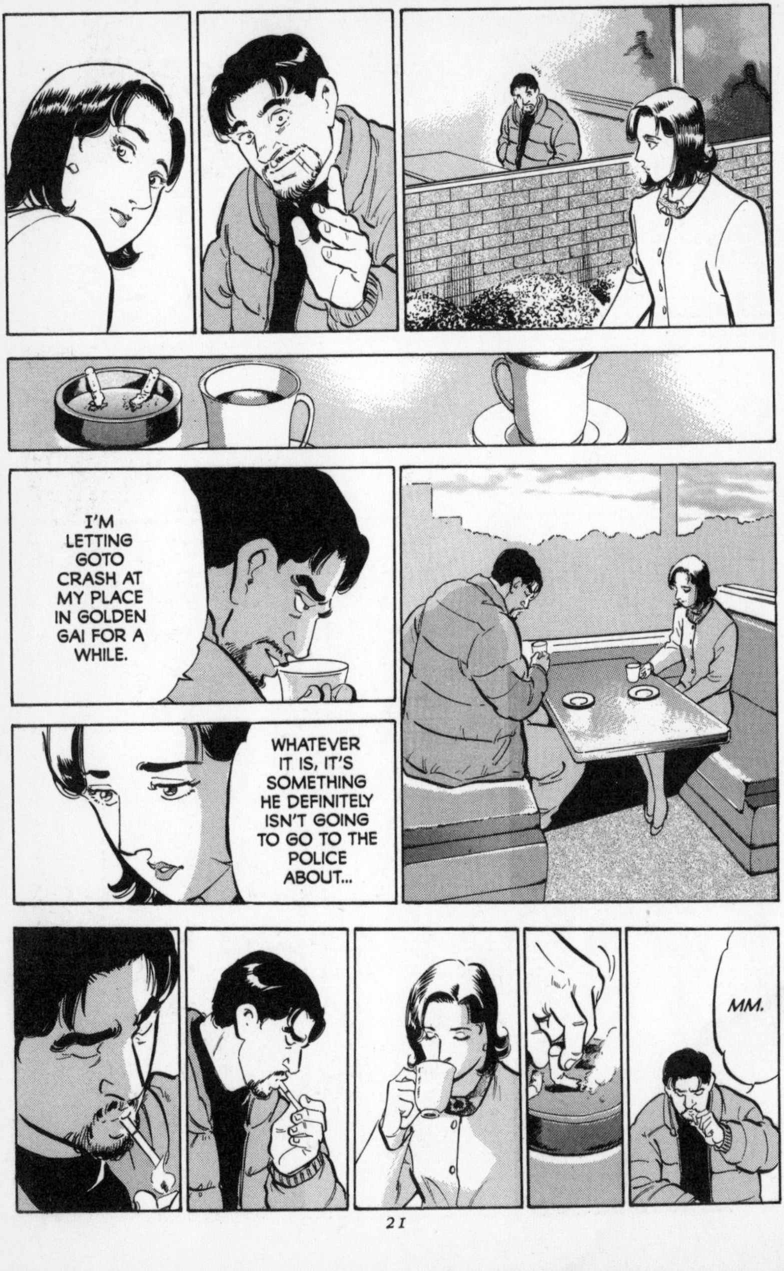
I'M LETTING GOTO CRASH AT MY PLACE IN GOLDEN GAI FOR A WHILE.
WHATEVER IT IS, IT'S SOMETHING HE DEFINITELY ISN'T GOING TO GO TO THE POLICE ABOUT...
MM.

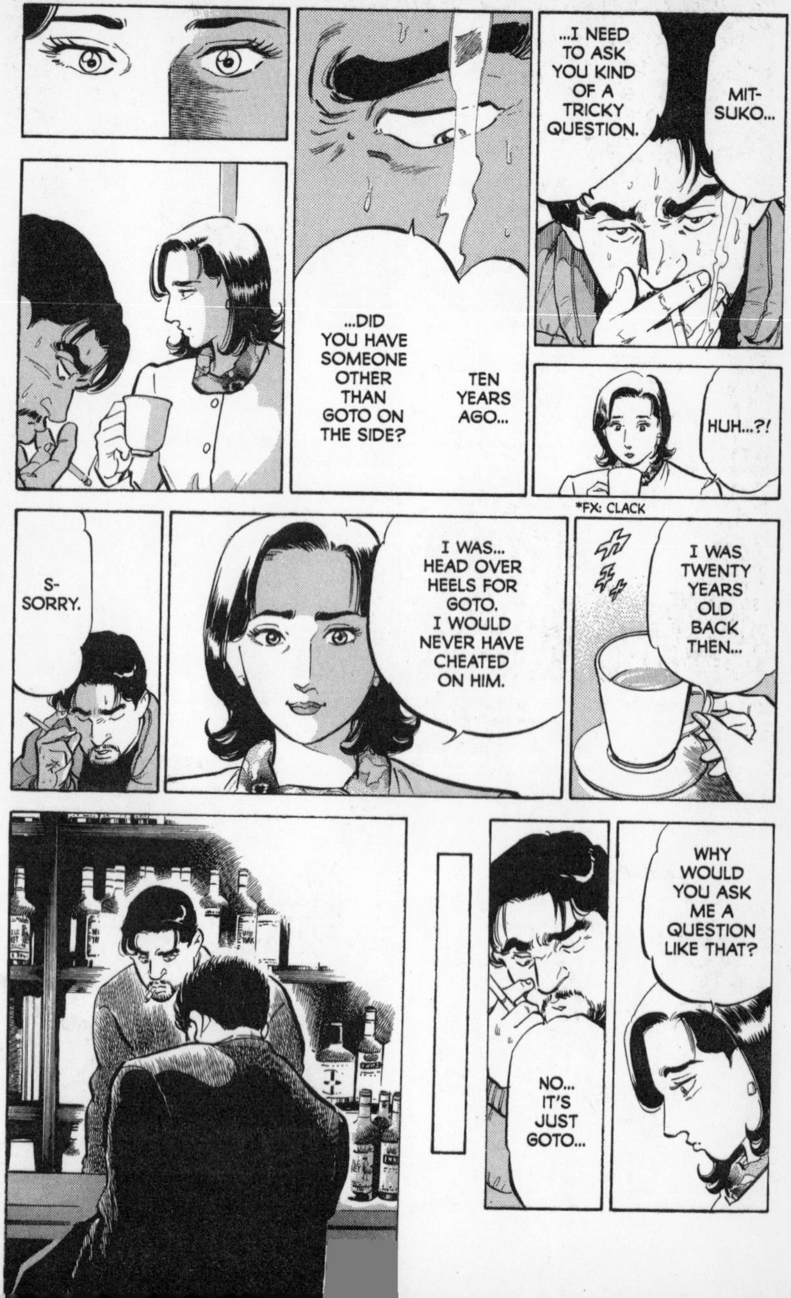
MIT-SUKO...
...I NEED TO ASK YOU KIND OF A TRICKY QUESTION.
TEN YEARS AGO...
...DID YOU HAVE SOMEONE OTHER THAN GOTO ON THE SIDE?
HUH...?!
*FX: CLACK
I WAS TWENTY YEARS OLD BACK THEN...
I WAS... HEAD OVER HEELS FOR GOTO. I WOULD NEVER HAVE CHEATED ON HIM.
S-SORRY.
WHY WOULD YOU ASK ME A QUESTION LIKE THAT?
NO... IT'S JUST GOTO...

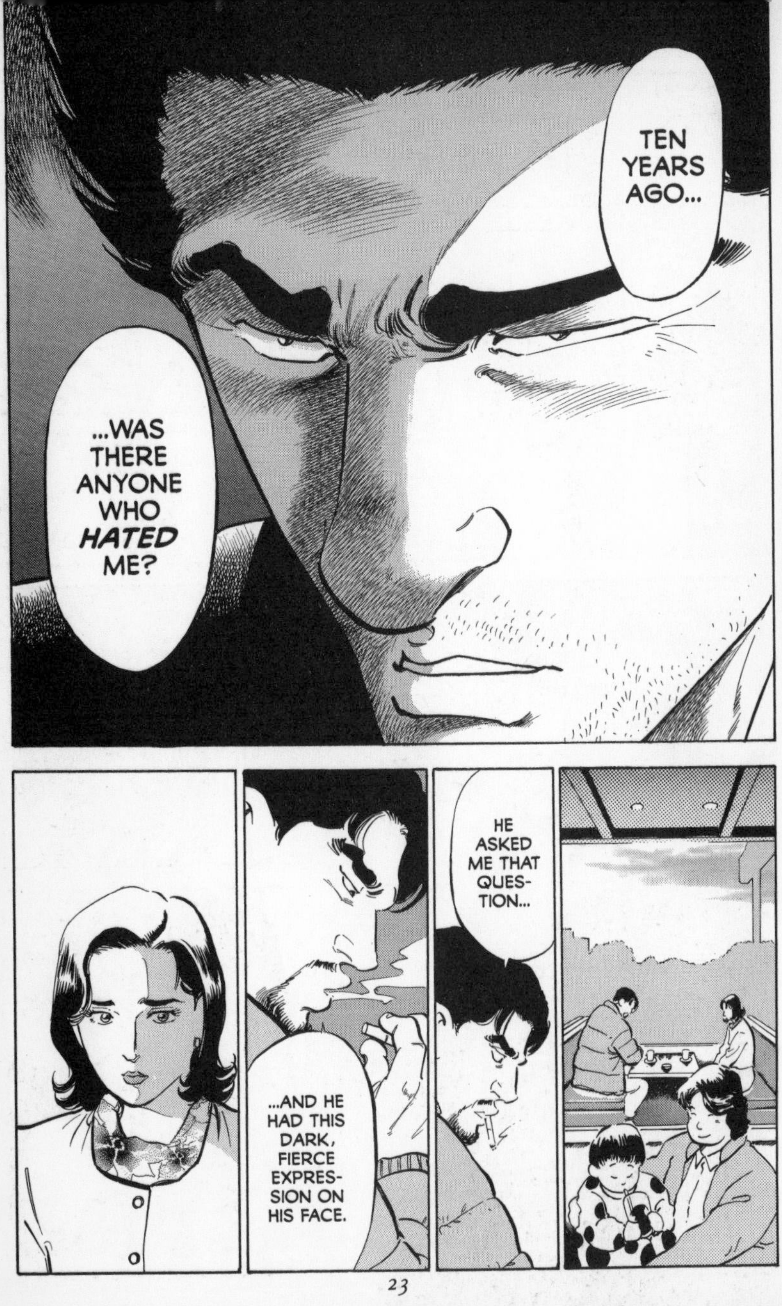
TEN YEARS AGO...
...WAS THERE ANYONE WHO *HATED* ME?
HE ASKED ME THAT QUES-TION...
...AND HE HAD THIS DARK, FIERCE EXPRES-SION ON HIS FACE.

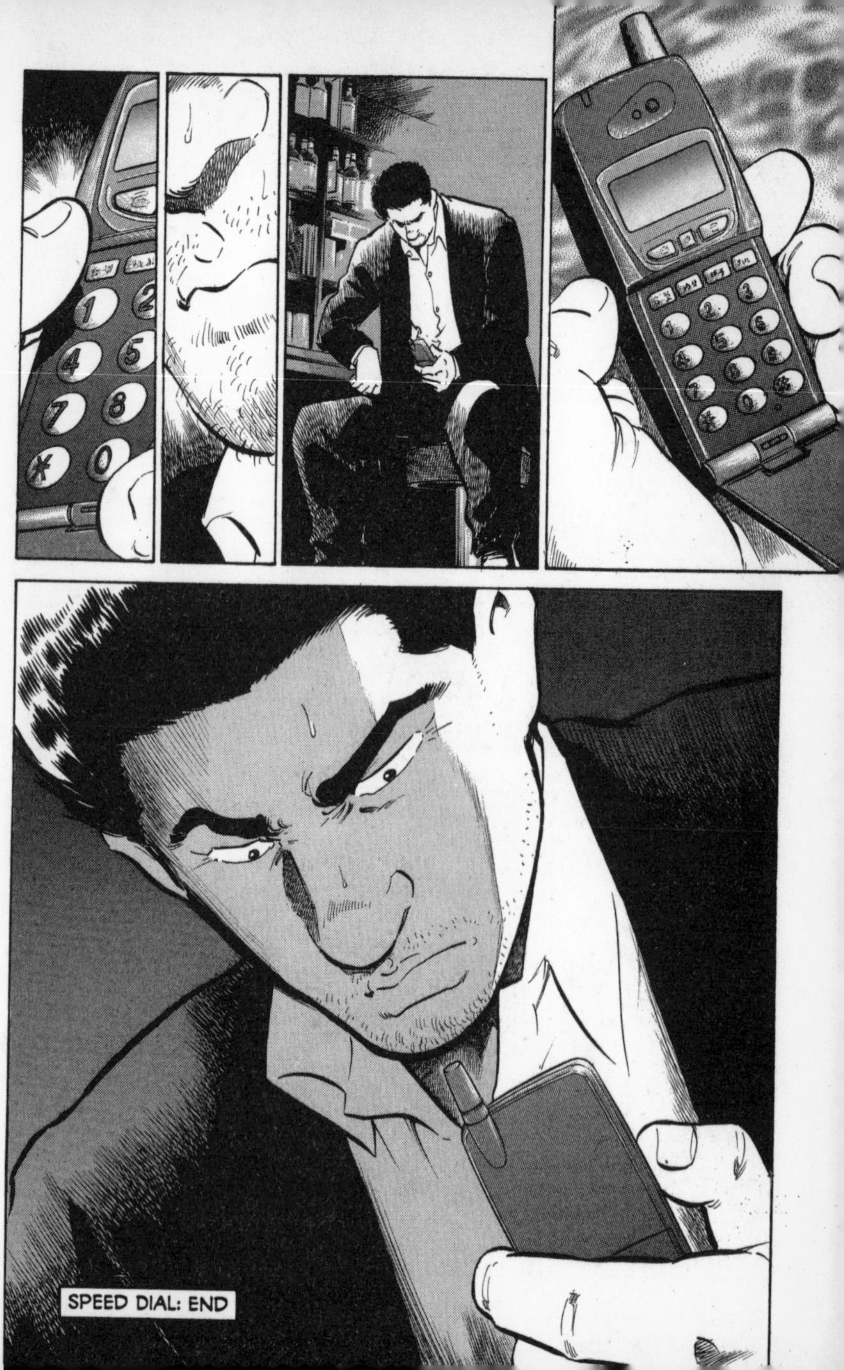
SPEED DIAL: END

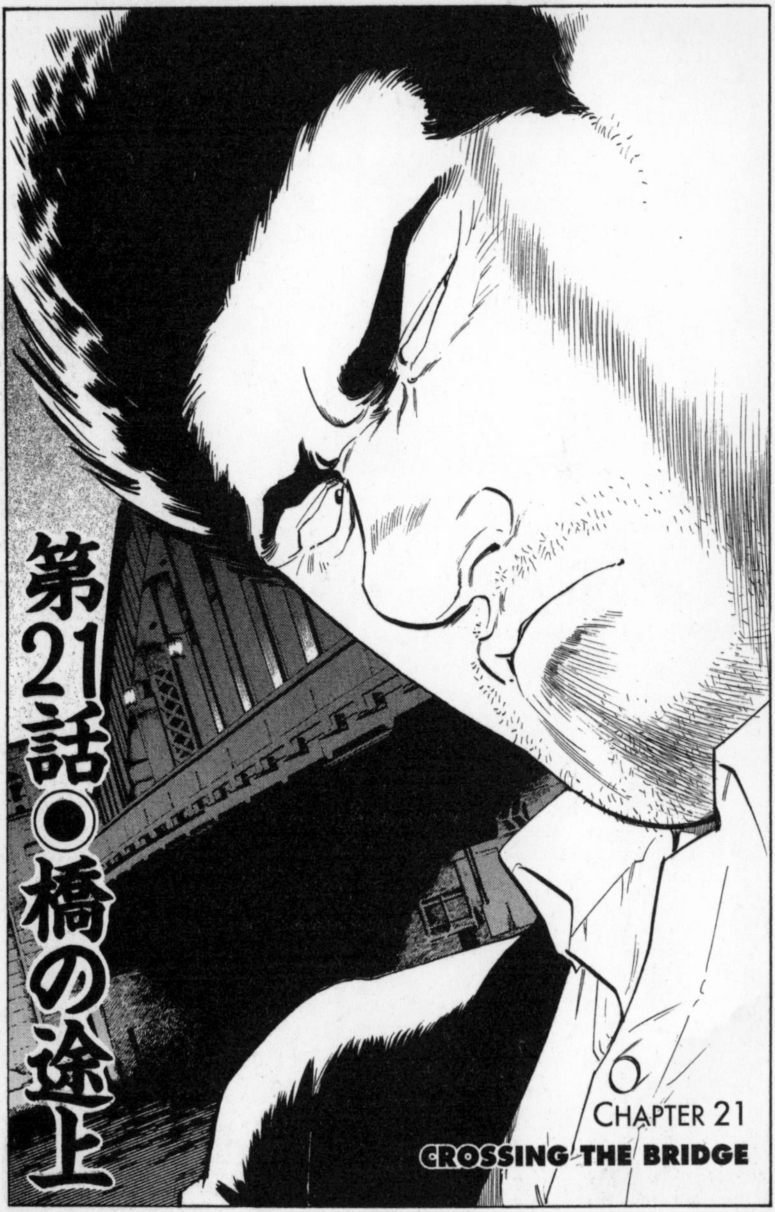
第21話●橋の途上
CHAPTER 21
CROSSING THE BRIDGE

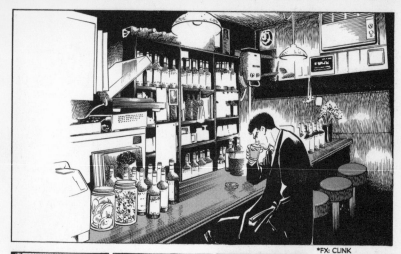

*FX: CLINK

"PUSH #1 ON THE SPEED DIAL AND YOU CAN GET IN TOUCH WITH YOU-KNOW-WHO ANY TIME YOU LIKE."

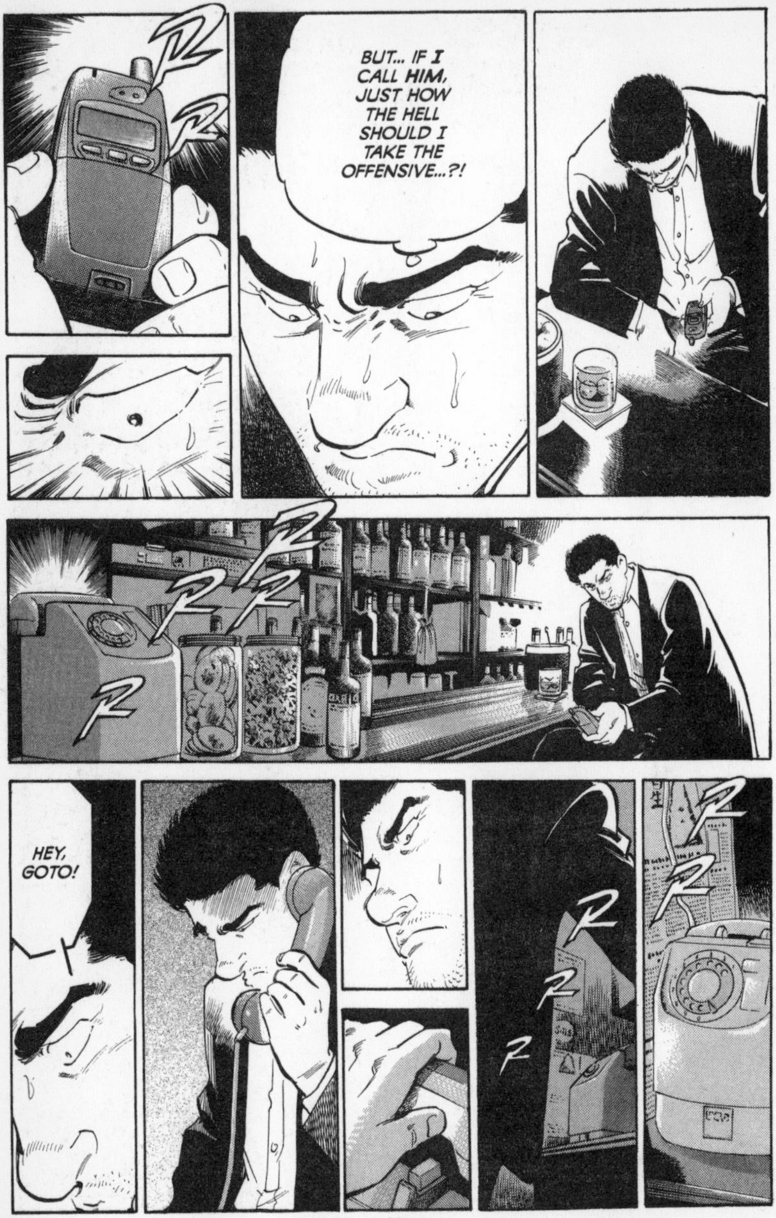
BUT... IF I CALL HIM, JUST HOW THE HELL SHOULD I TAKE THE OFFENSIVE...?!
HEY, GOTO!

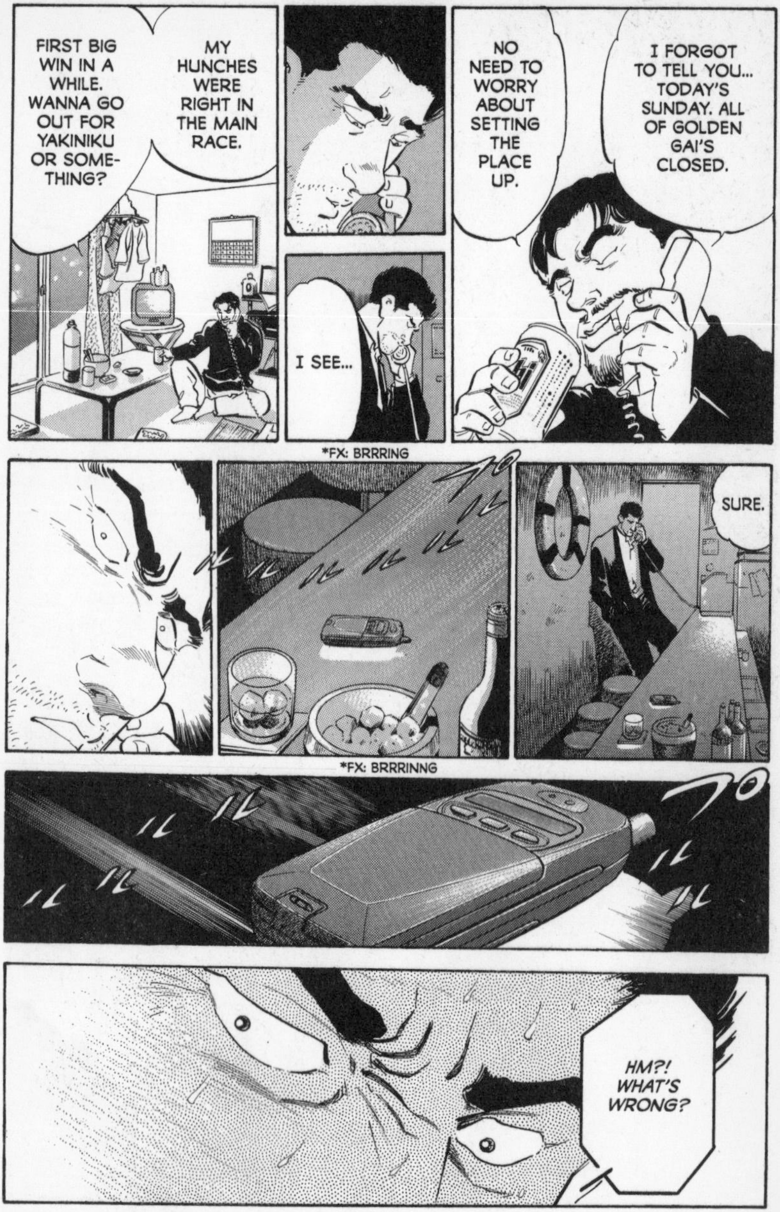
I FORGOT TO TELL YOU... TODAY'S SUNDAY. ALL OF GOLDEN GAI'S CLOSED.
NO NEED TO WORRY ABOUT SETTING THE PLACE UP.
I SEE...
MY HUNCHES WERE RIGHT IN THE MAIN RACE.
FIRST BIG WIN IN A WHILE. WANNA GO OUT FOR YAKINIKU OR SOME-THING?
*FX: BRRRING
SURE.
*FX: BRRRINNG
HM?! WHAT'S WRONG?

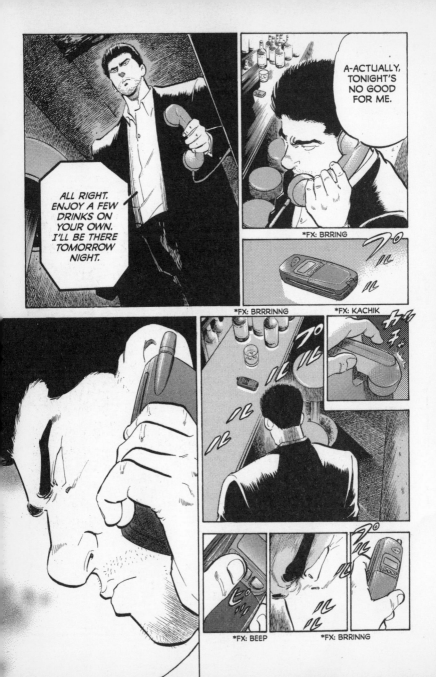

A-ACTUALLY, TONIGHT'S NO GOOD FOR ME.

ALL RIGHT. ENJOY A FEW DRINKS ON YOUR OWN. I'LL BE THERE TOMORROW NIGHT.

*FX: BRRING

*FX: BRRRINNG

*FX: KACHIK

*FX: BEEP

*FX: BRRINNG

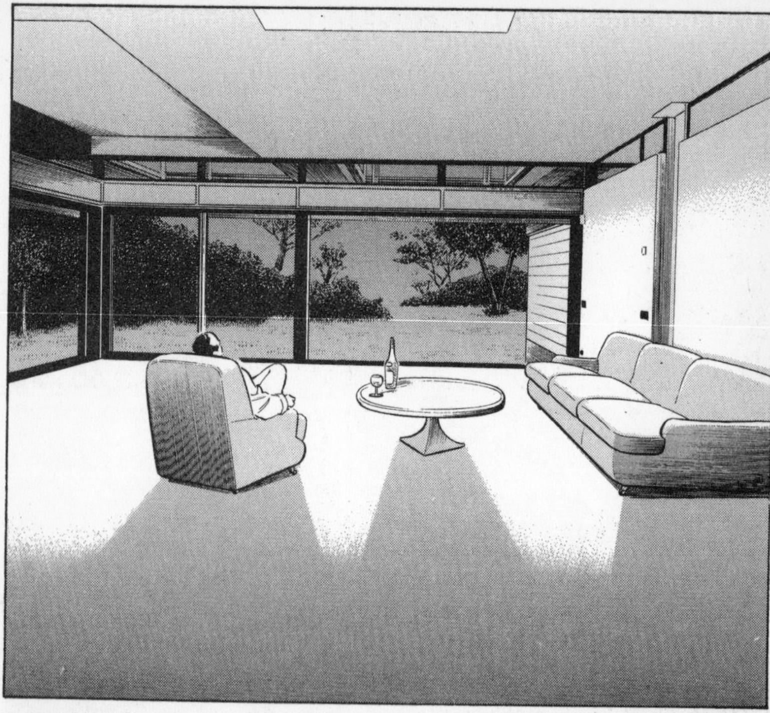

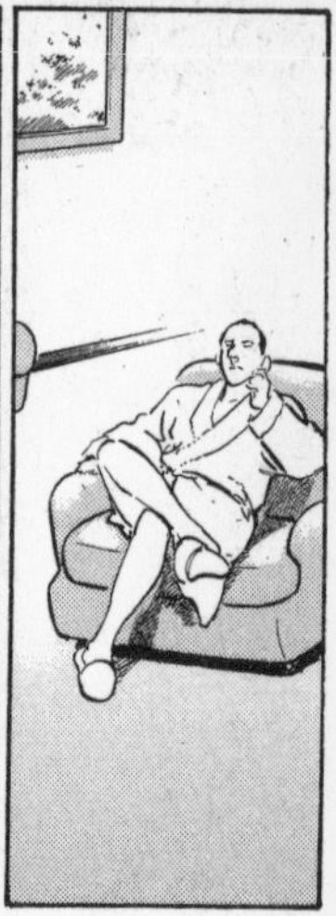

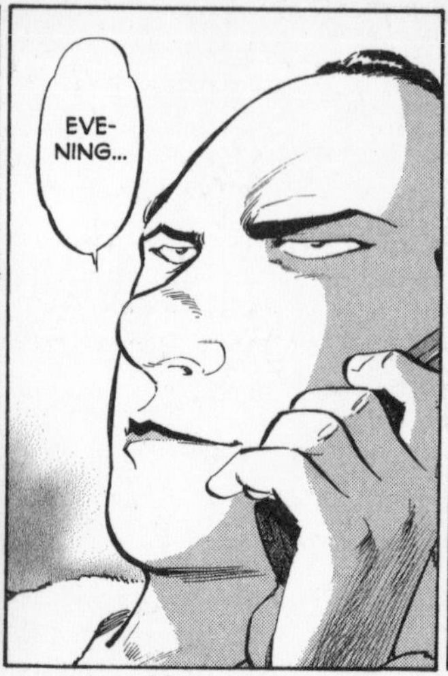
EVE-NING...

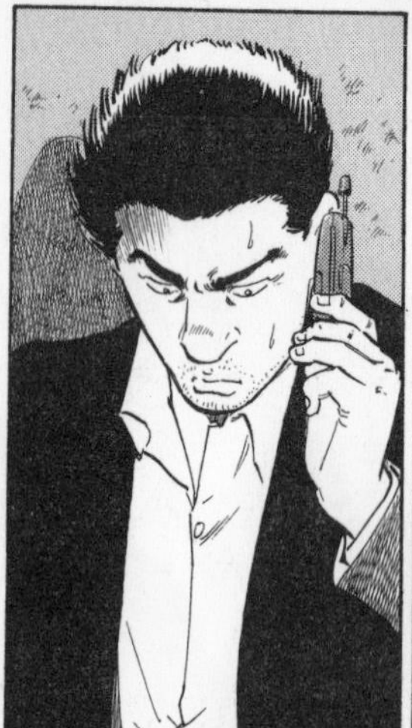

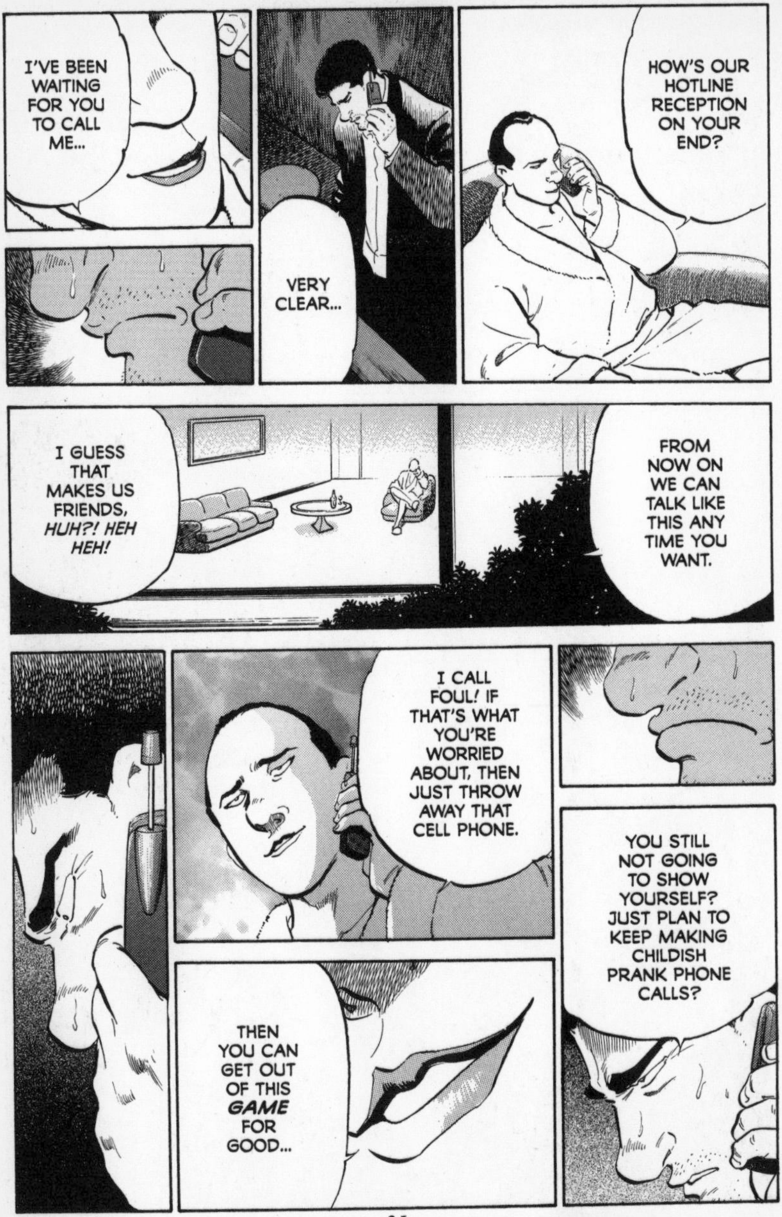
HOW'S OUR HOTLINE RECEPTION ON YOUR END?
VERY CLEAR...
I'VE BEEN WAITING FOR YOU TO CALL ME...
FROM NOW ON WE CAN TALK LIKE THIS ANY TIME YOU WANT.
I GUESS THAT MAKES US FRIENDS, *HUH?! HEH HEH!*
YOU STILL NOT GOING TO SHOW YOURSELF? JUST PLAN TO KEEP MAKING CHILDISH PRANK PHONE CALLS?
I CALL FOUL! IF THAT'S WHAT YOU'RE WORRIED ABOUT, THEN JUST THROW AWAY THAT CELL PHONE.
THEN YOU CAN GET OUT OF THIS *GAME* FOR GOOD...

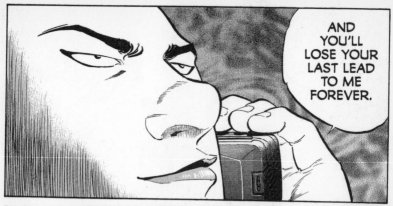

AND YOU'LL LOSE YOUR LAST LEAD TO ME FOREVER.

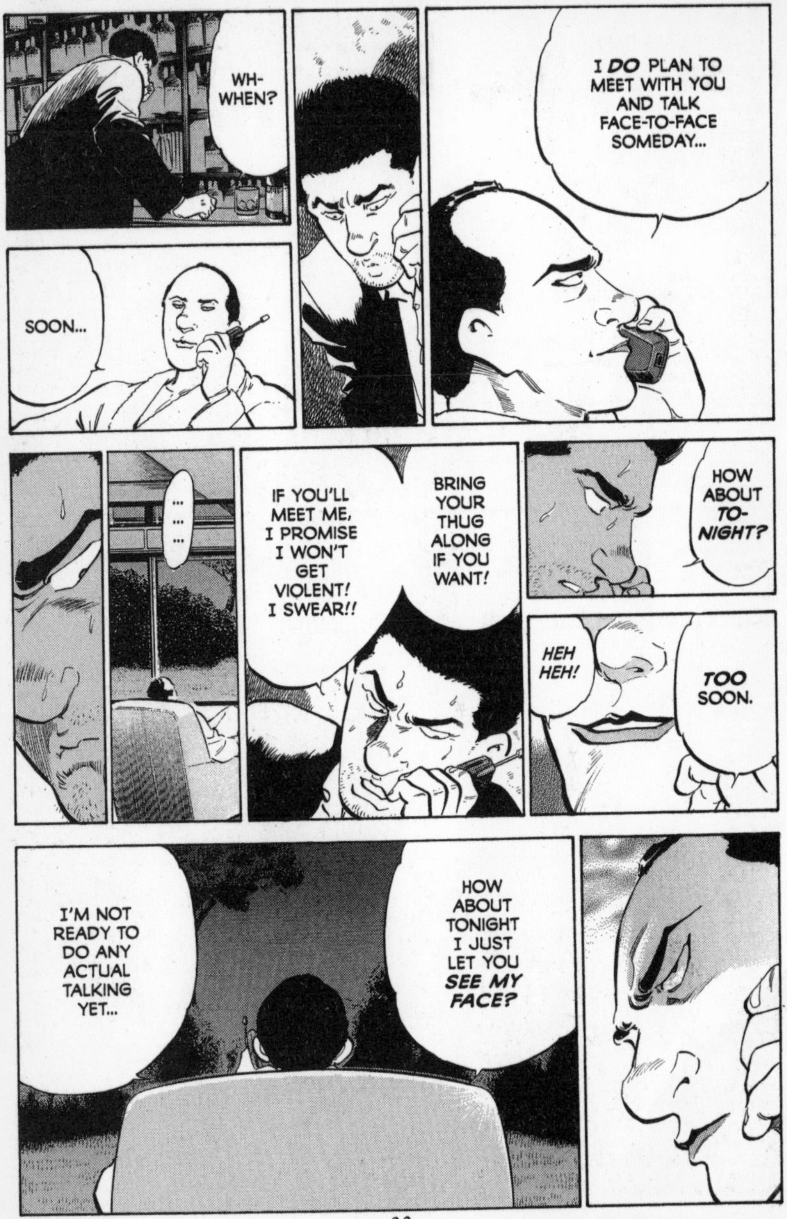
I DO PLAN TO MEET WITH YOU AND TALK FACE-TO-FACE SOMEDAY...
WH- WHEN?
SOON...
HOW ABOUT TO-NIGHT?
HEH HEH!
TOO SOON.
BRING YOUR THUG ALONG IF YOU WANT!
IF YOU'LL MEET ME, I PROMISE I WON'T GET VIOLENT! I SWEAR!!
... ...
HOW ABOUT TONIGHT I JUST LET YOU SEE MY FACE?
I'M NOT READY TO DO ANY ACTUAL TALKING YET...

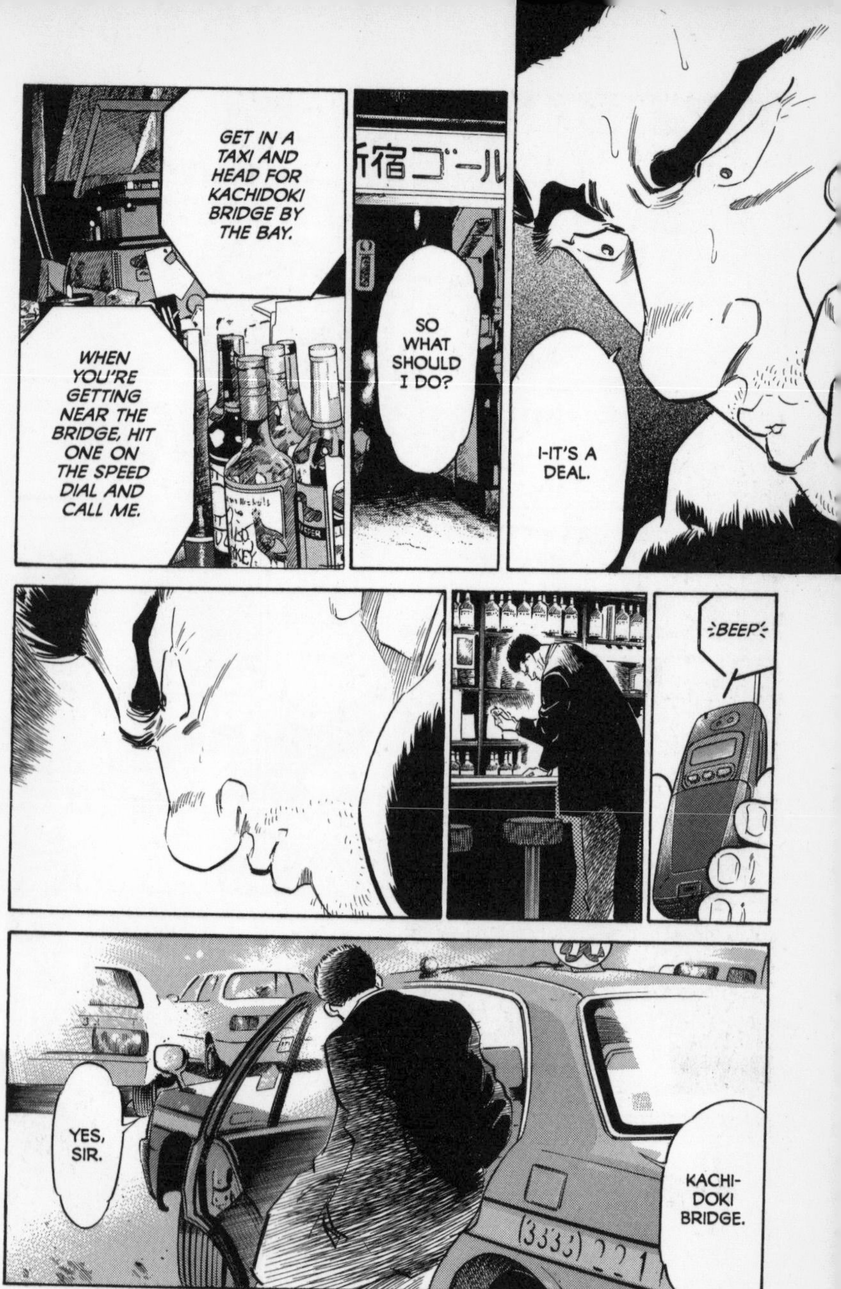
I-IT'S A DEAL.
SO WHAT SHOULD I DO?
GET IN A TAXI AND HEAD FOR KACHIDOKI BRIDGE BY THE BAY.
WHEN YOU'RE GETTING NEAR THE BRIDGE, HIT ONE ON THE SPEED DIAL AND CALL ME.
BEEP
KACHI-DOKI BRIDGE.
YES, SIR.

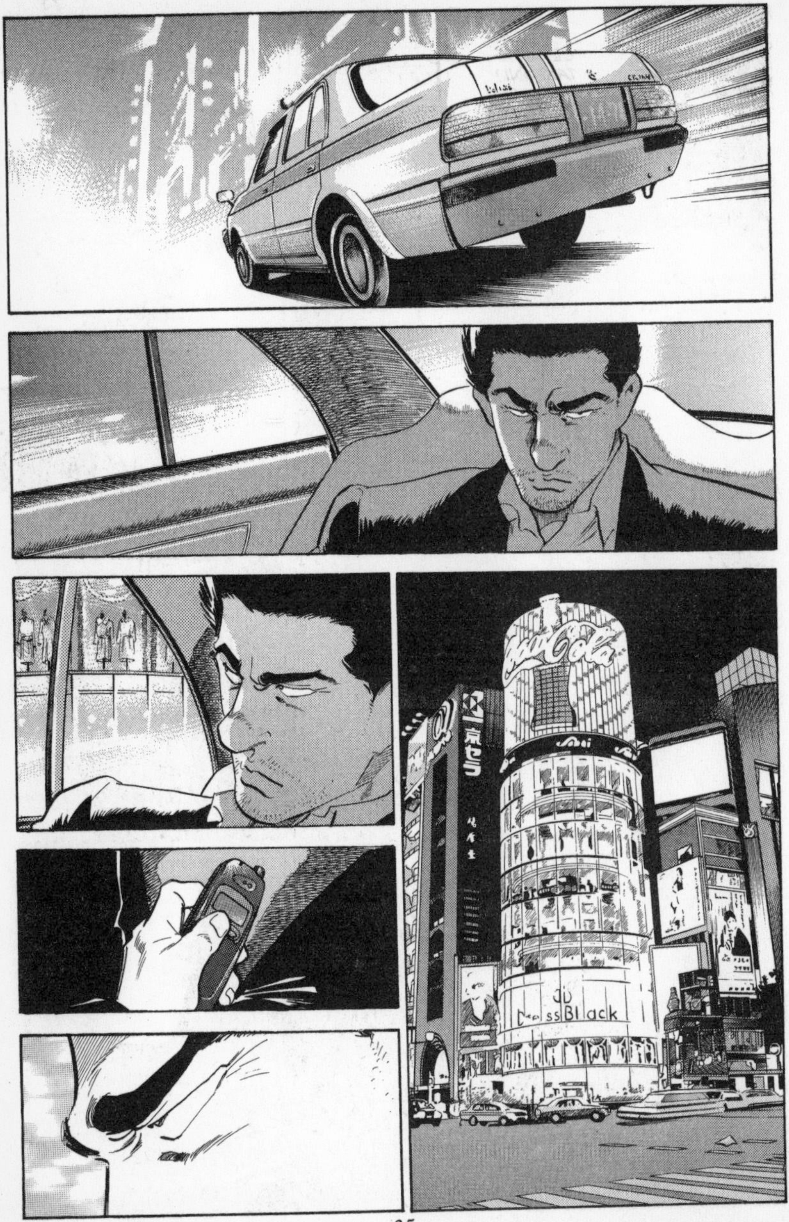
京セラ

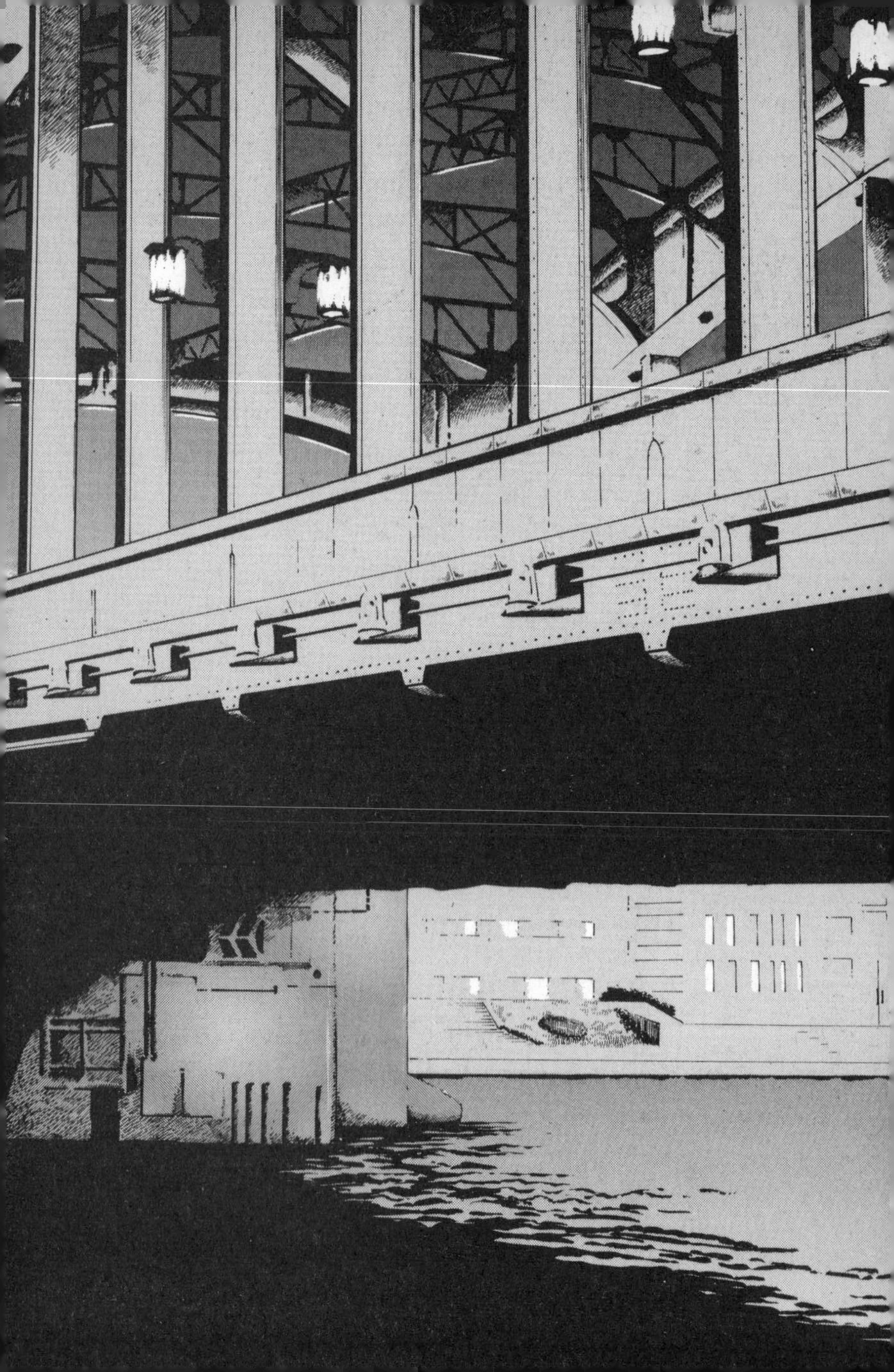

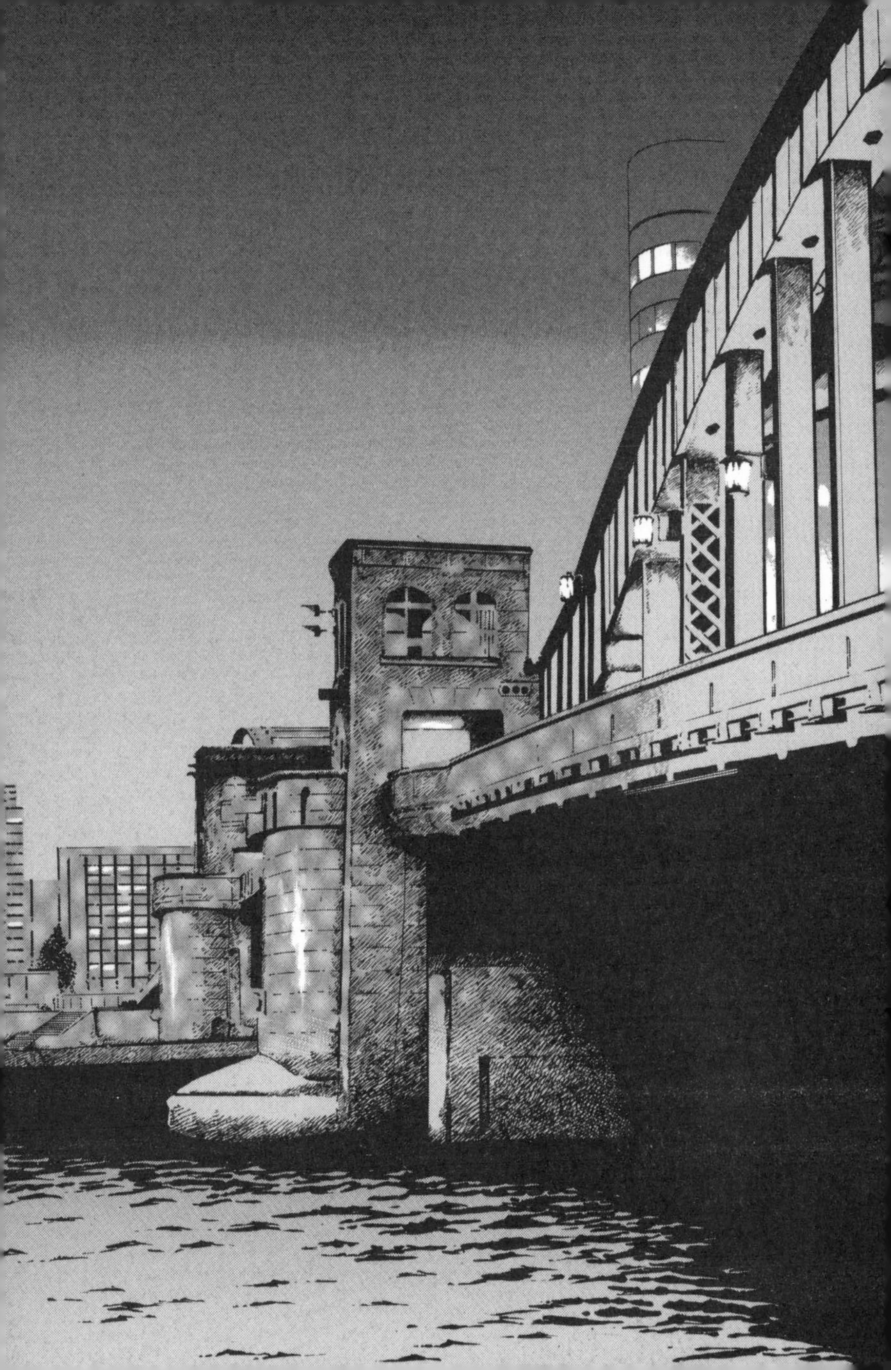

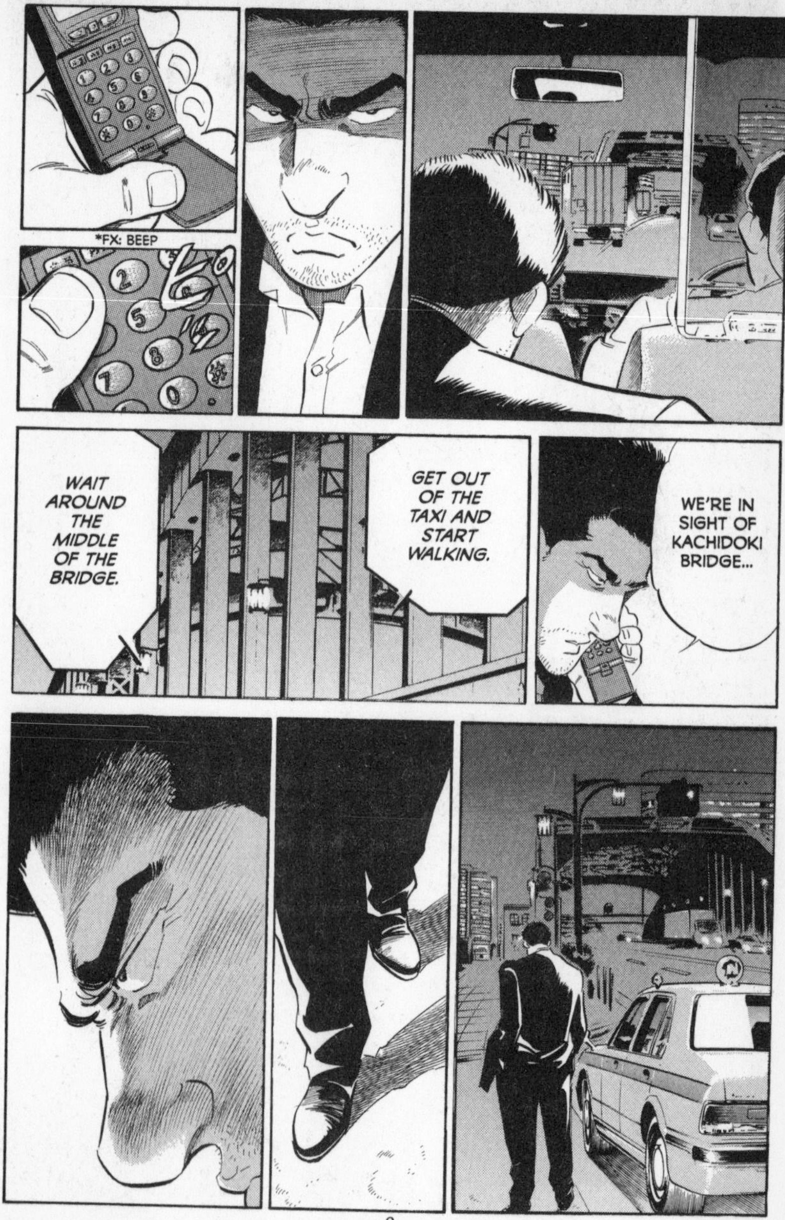
*FX: BEEP
WE'RE IN SIGHT OF KACHIDOKI BRIDGE...
GET OUT OF THE TAXI AND START WALKING.
WAIT AROUND THE MIDDLE OF THE BRIDGE.

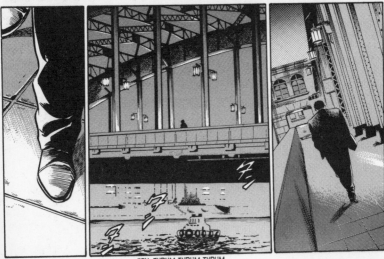

*FX: THRUM THRUM THRUM

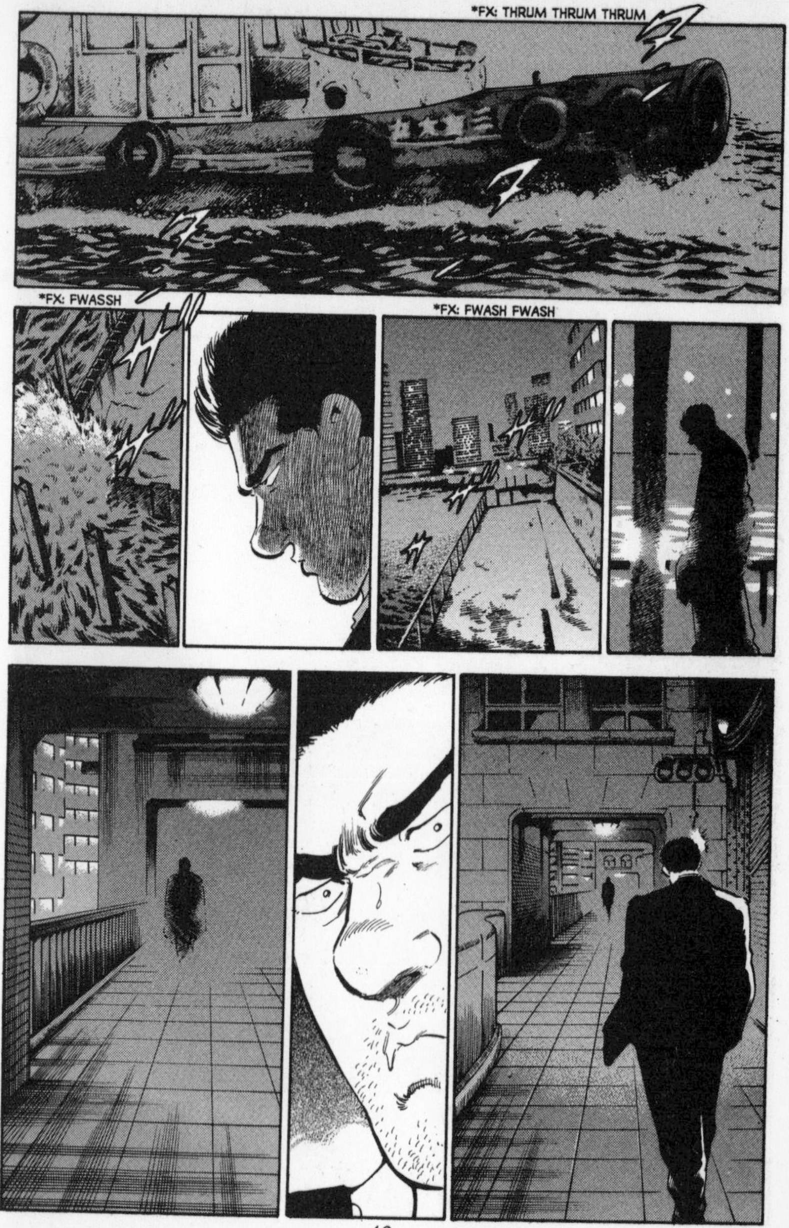
*FX: THRUM THRUM THRUM
*FX: FWASH FWASH
*FX: FWASSH

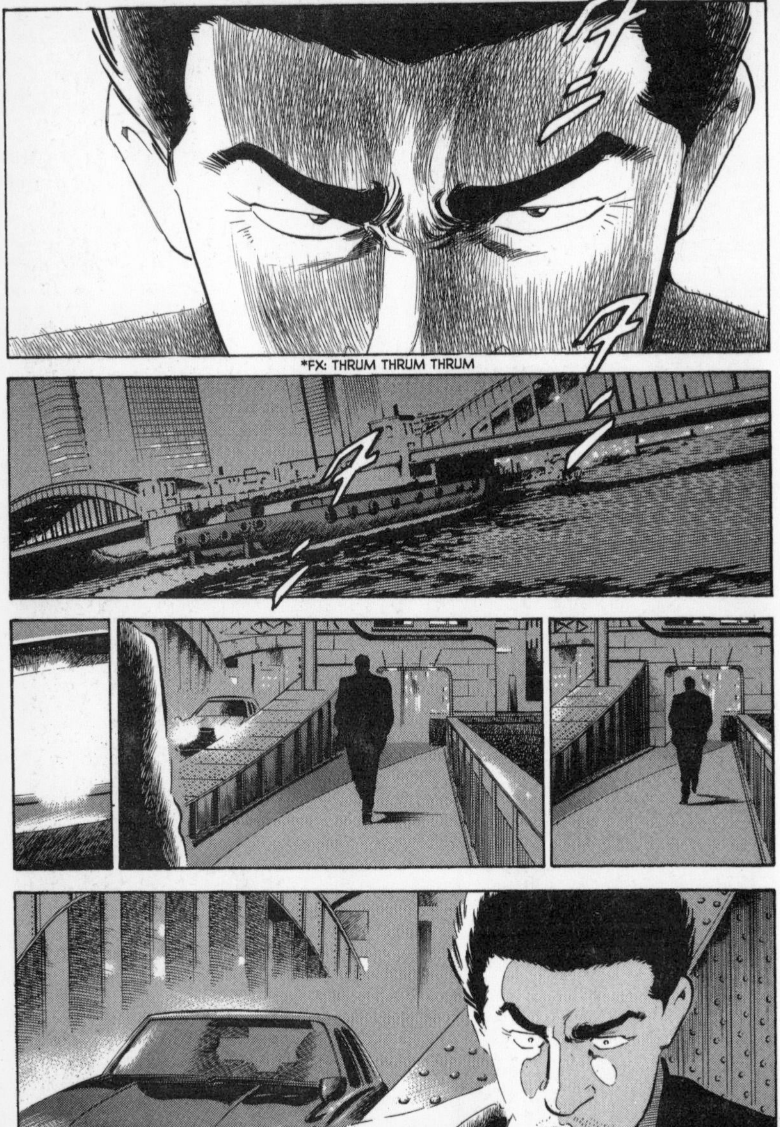
*FX: THRUM THRUM THRUM

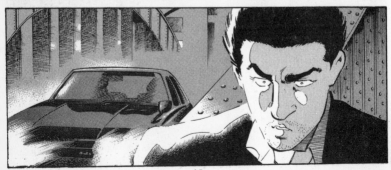

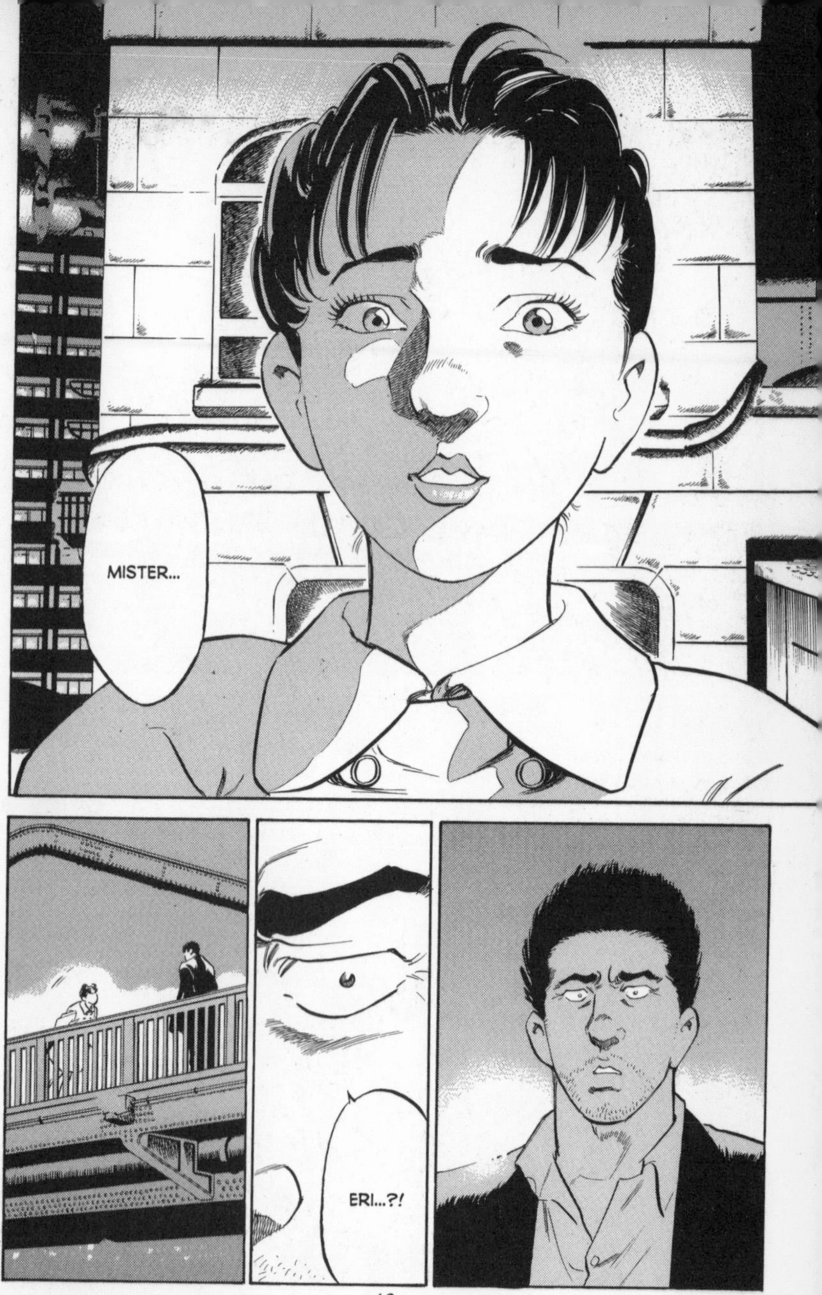
MISTER...
ERI...?!

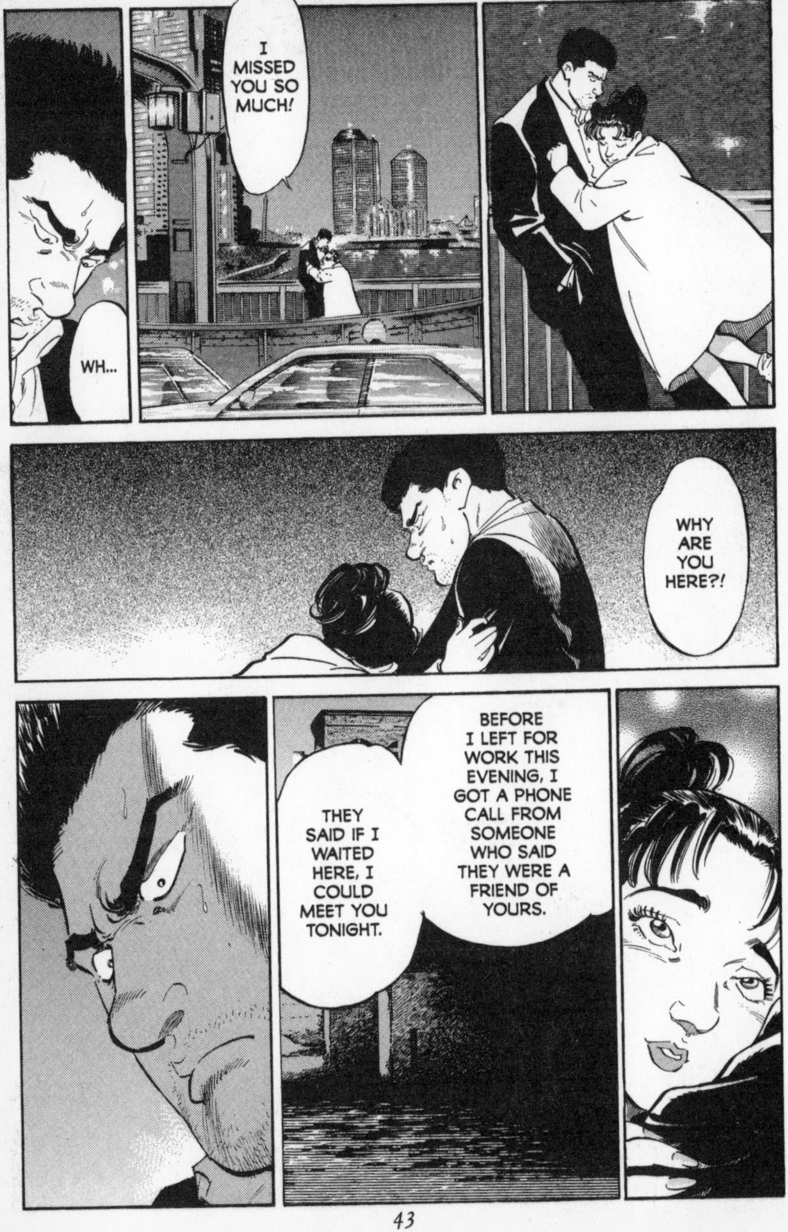
I MISSED YOU SO MUCH!
WH...
WHY ARE YOU HERE?!
BEFORE I LEFT FOR WORK THIS EVENING, I GOT A PHONE CALL FROM SOMEONE WHO SAID THEY WERE A FRIEND OF YOURS.
THEY SAID IF I WAITED HERE, I COULD MEET YOU TONIGHT.

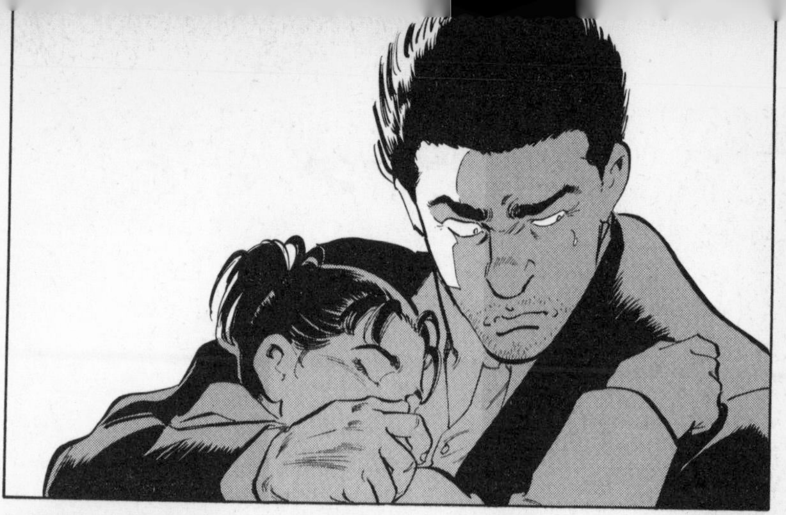

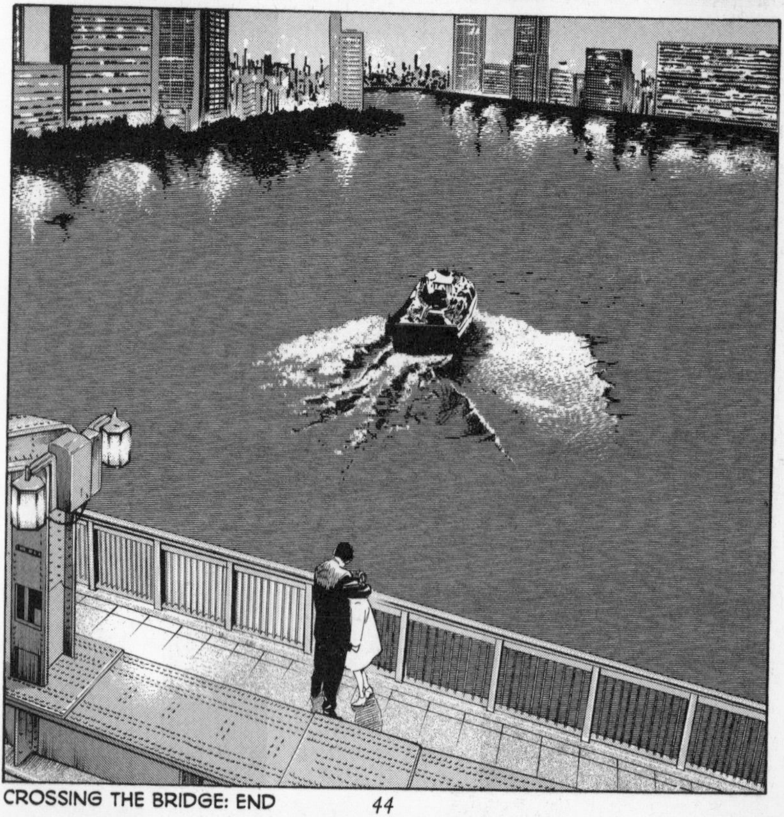

CROSSING THE BRIDGE: END

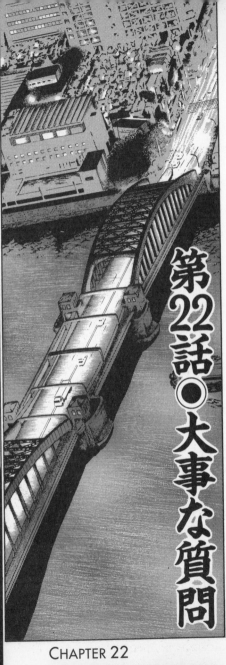

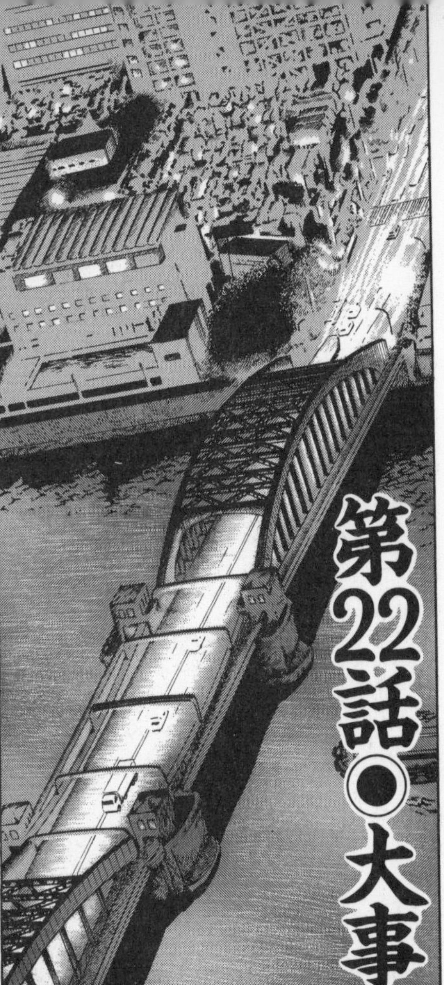
第22話●大事な質問

CHAPTER 22
IMPORTANT QUESTIONS

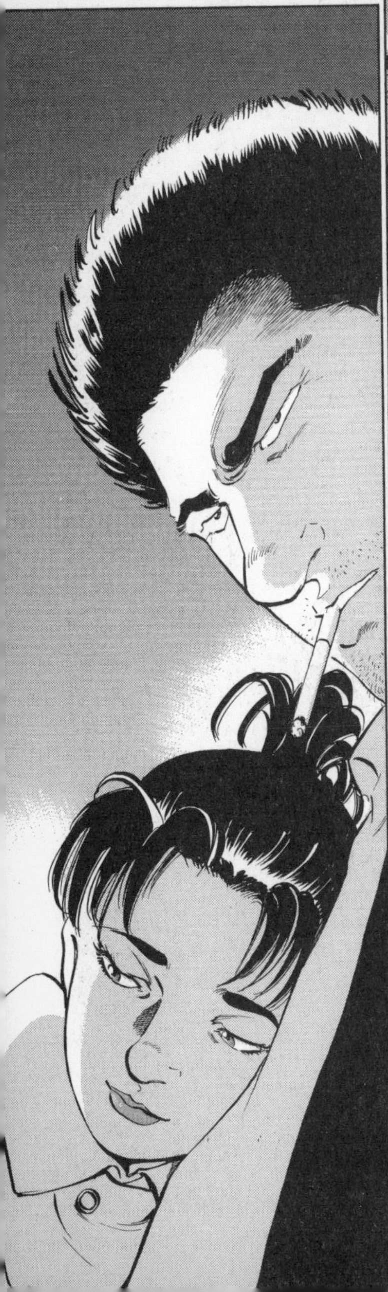

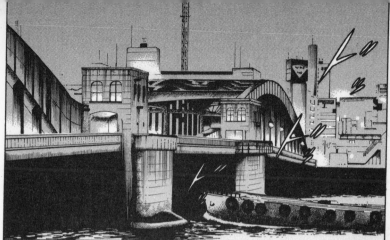

*FX: VRUM VRUM VRUM

NOW,
TELL ME
EVERY-
THING...

*FX: VRUM VRUM VRUM   *FX: VRUM VRUM

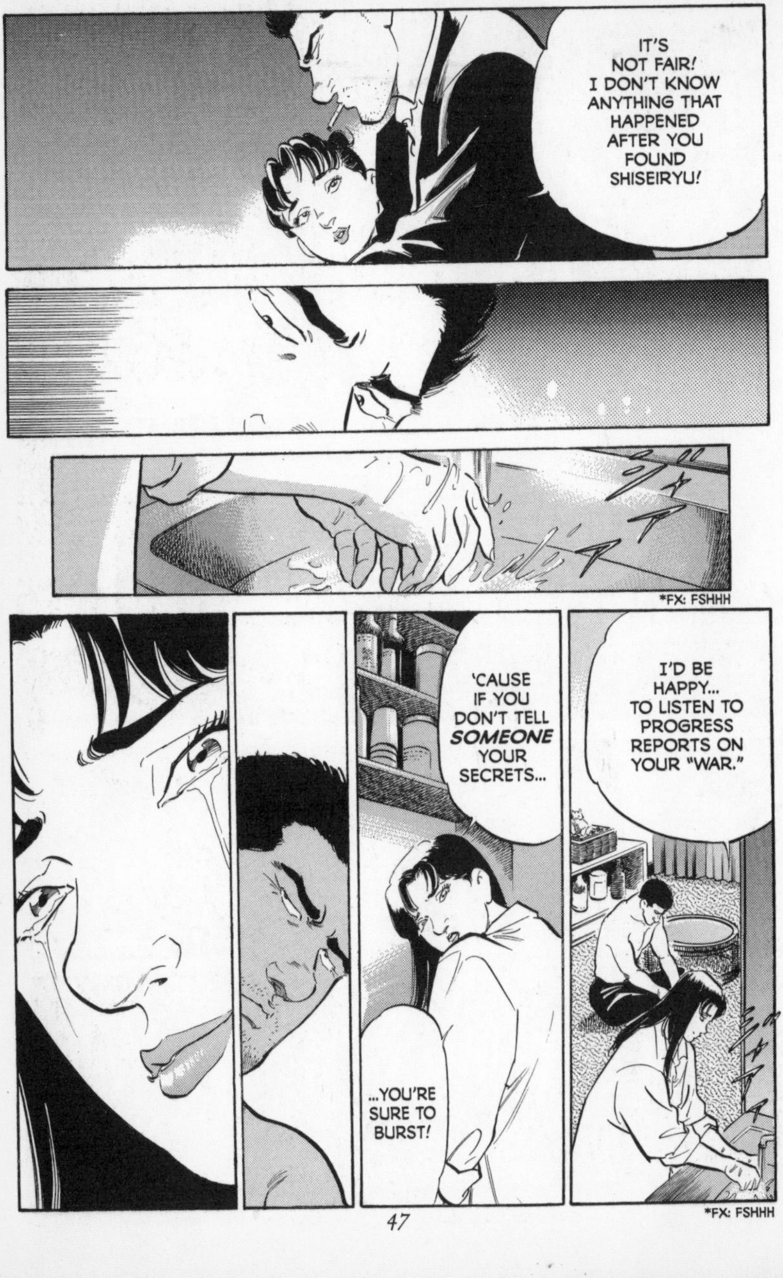
IT'S NOT FAIR! I DON'T KNOW ANYTHING THAT HAPPENED AFTER YOU FOUND SHISEIRYU!
*FX: FSHHH
I'D BE HAPPY... TO LISTEN TO PROGRESS REPORTS ON YOUR "WAR."
'CAUSE IF YOU DON'T TELL *SOMEONE* YOUR SECRETS...
...YOU'RE SURE TO BURST!
*FX: FSHHH

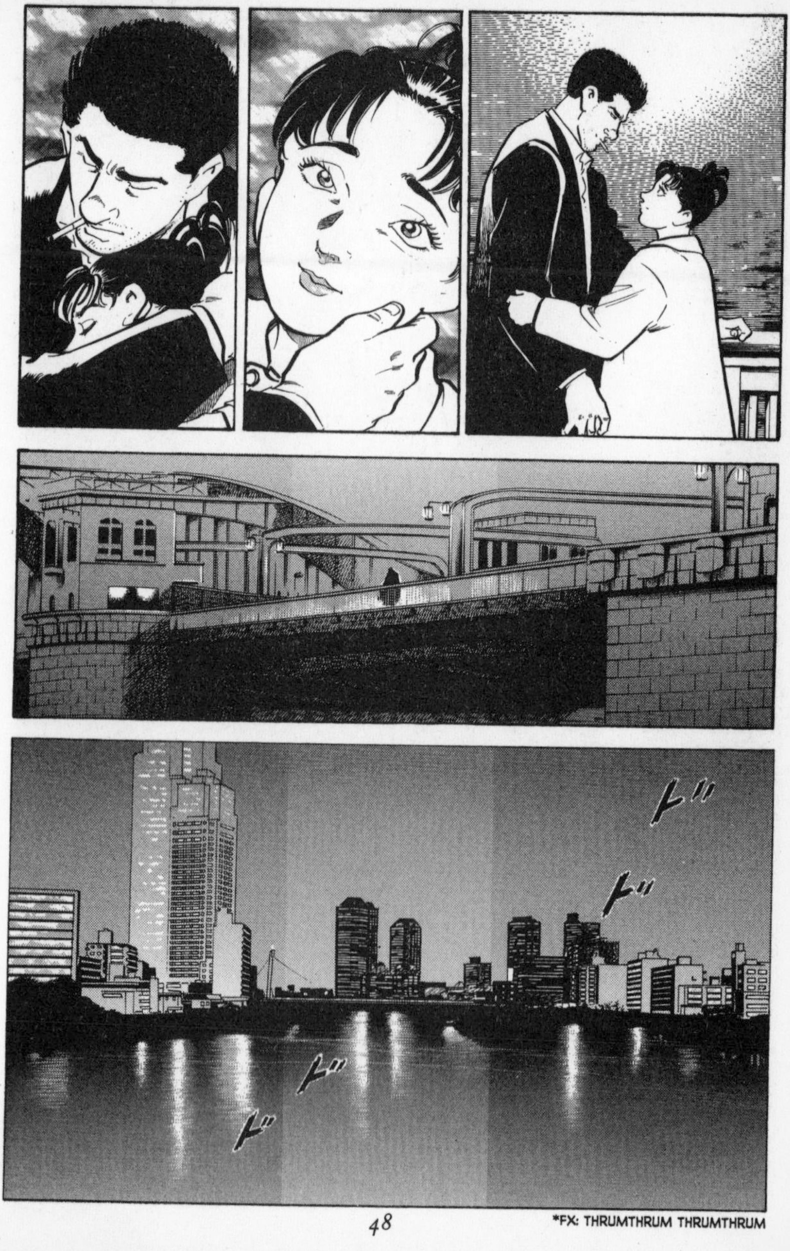
ド
ド
ド
ド

*FX: THRUMTHRUM THRUMTHRUM

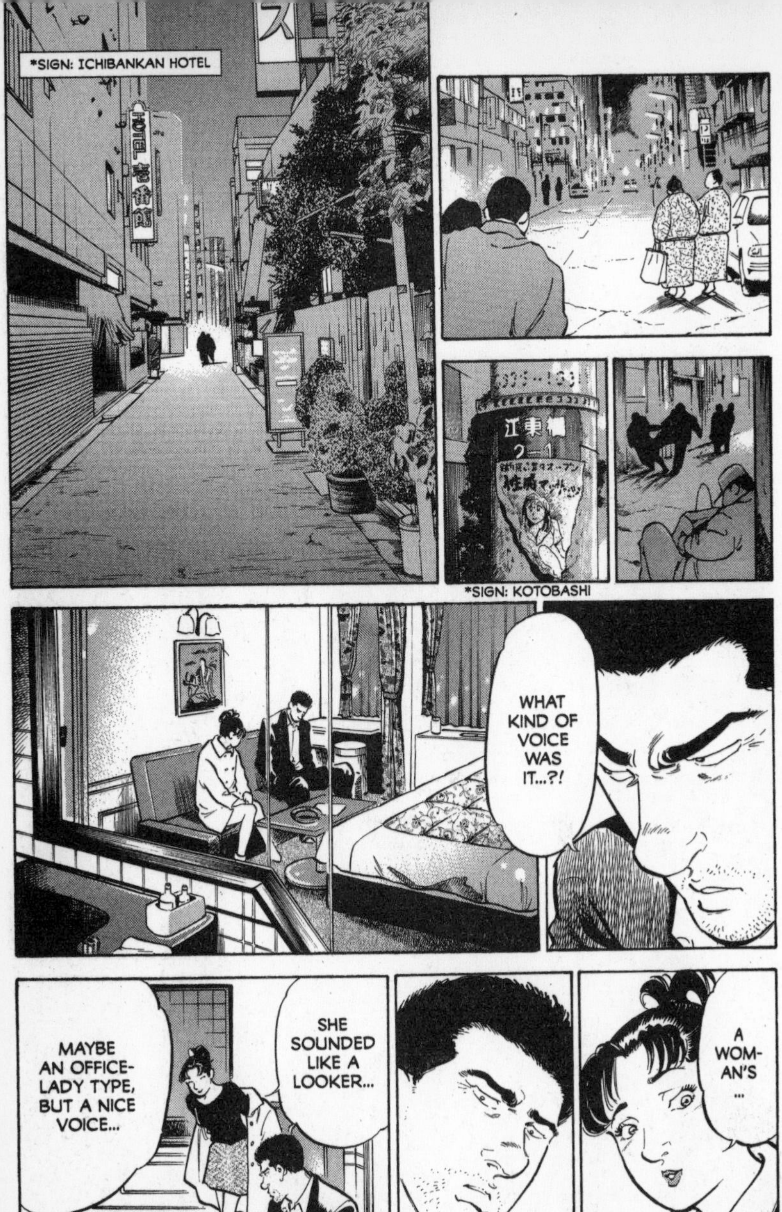
*SIGN: KOTOBASHI
*SIGN: ICHIBANKAN HOTEL
WHAT KIND OF VOICE WAS IT...?!
A WOMAN'S ...
SHE SOUNDED LIKE A LOOKER...
MAYBE AN OFFICE-LADY TYPE, BUT A NICE VOICE...

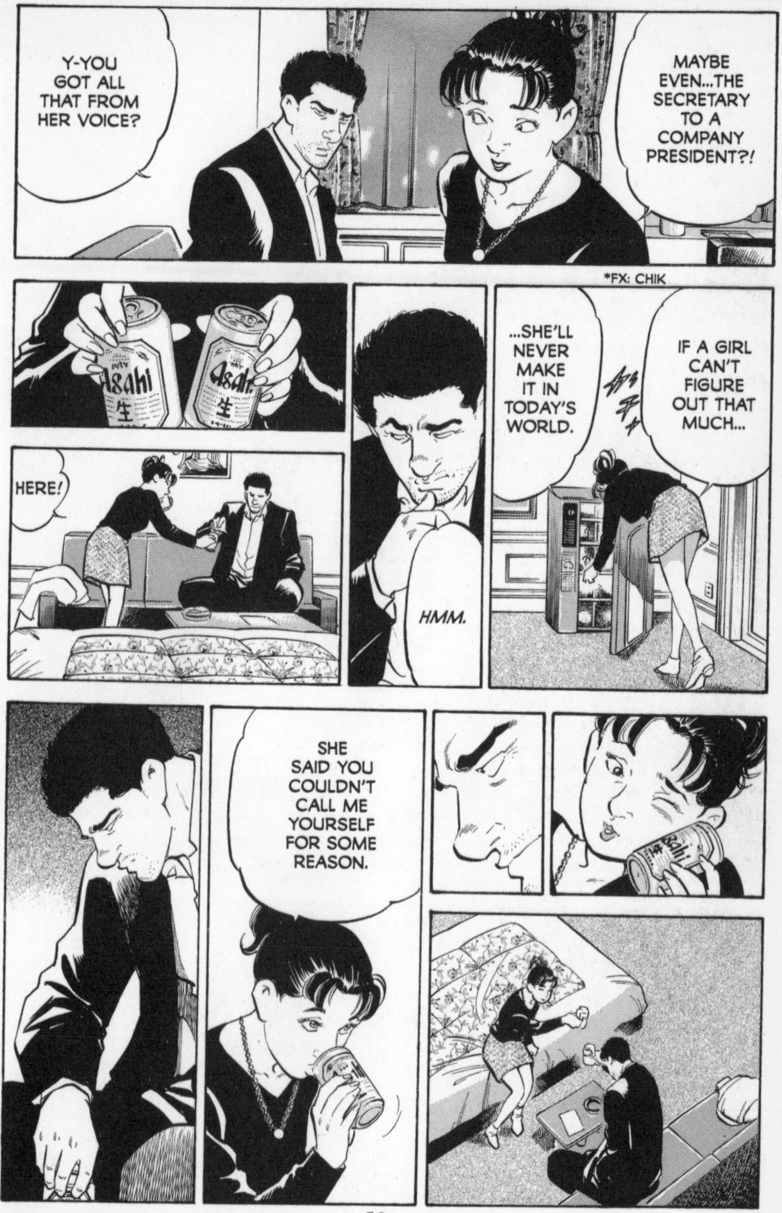
MAYBE EVEN...THE SECRETARY TO A COMPANY PRESIDENT?!
Y-YOU GOT ALL THAT FROM HER VOICE?
*FX: CHIK
IF A GIRL CAN'T FIGURE OUT THAT MUCH...
...SHE'LL NEVER MAKE IT IN TODAY'S WORLD.
HMM.
HERE!
SHE SAID YOU COULDN'T CALL ME YOURSELF FOR SOME REASON.

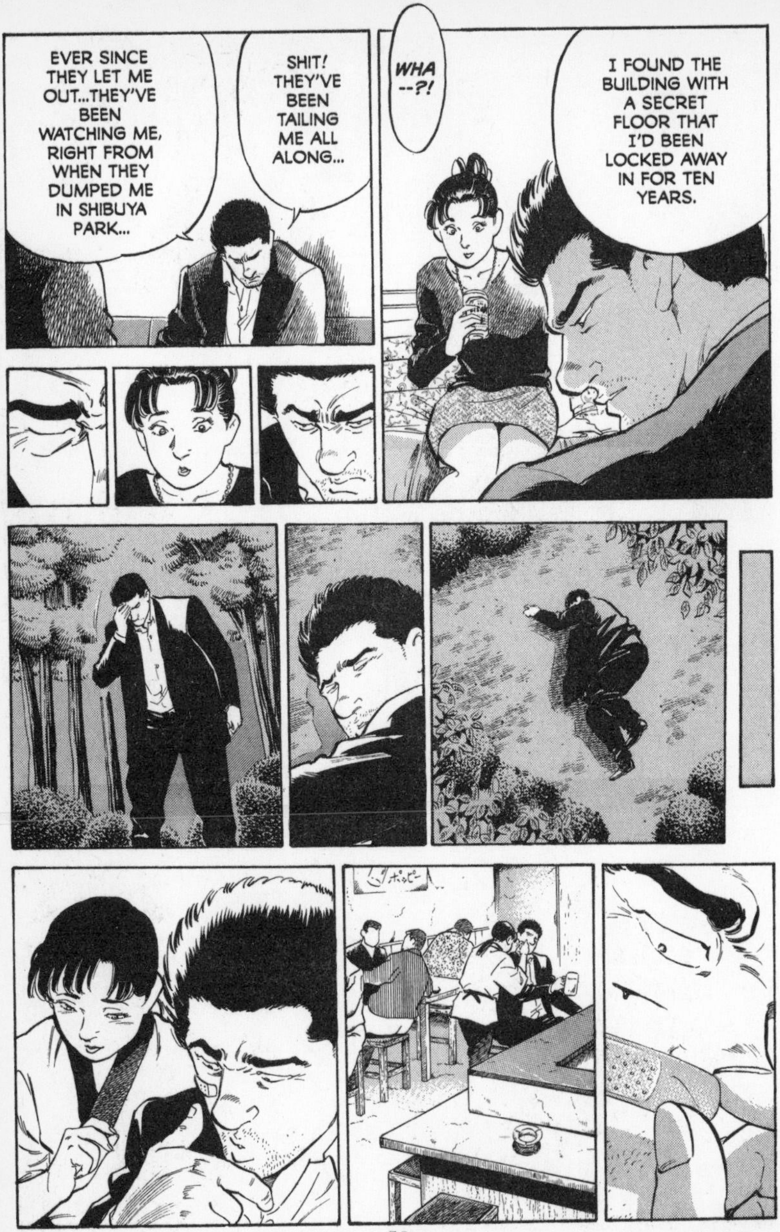
I FOUND THE BUILDING WITH A SECRET FLOOR THAT I'D BEEN LOCKED AWAY IN FOR TEN YEARS.
WHA --?!
SHIT! THEY'VE BEEN TAILING ME ALL ALONG...
EVER SINCE THEY LET ME OUT...THEY'VE BEEN WATCHING ME, RIGHT FROM WHEN THEY DUMPED ME IN SHIBUYA PARK...
ポッピー

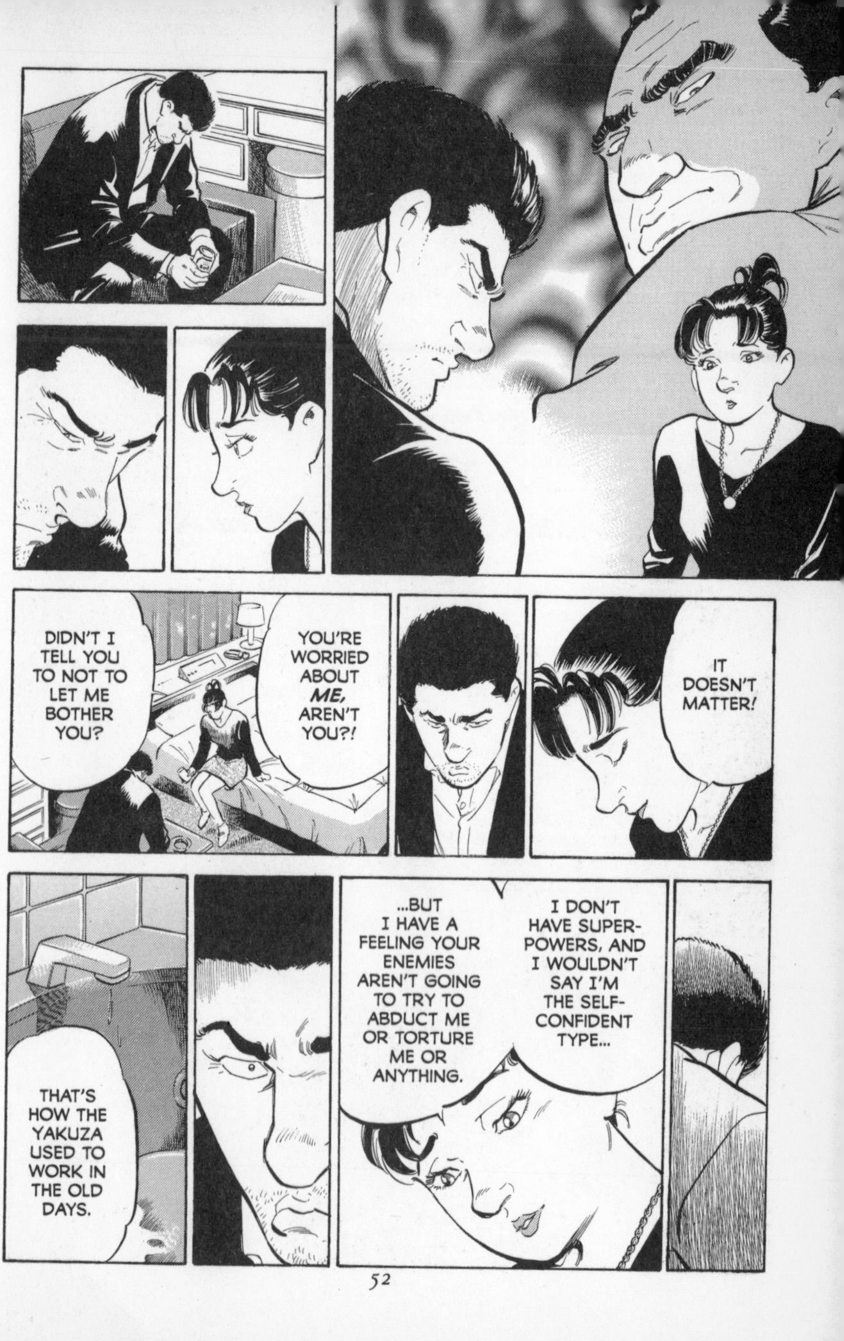
IT DOESN'T MATTER!
YOU'RE WORRIED ABOUT *ME,* AREN'T YOU?!
DIDN'T I TELL YOU TO NOT TO LET ME BOTHER YOU?
I DON'T HAVE SUPER-POWERS, AND I WOULDN'T SAY I'M THE SELF-CONFIDENT TYPE...
...BUT I HAVE A FEELING YOUR ENEMIES AREN'T GOING TO TRY TO ABDUCT ME OR TORTURE ME OR ANYTHING.
THAT'S HOW THE YAKUZA USED TO WORK IN THE OLD DAYS.

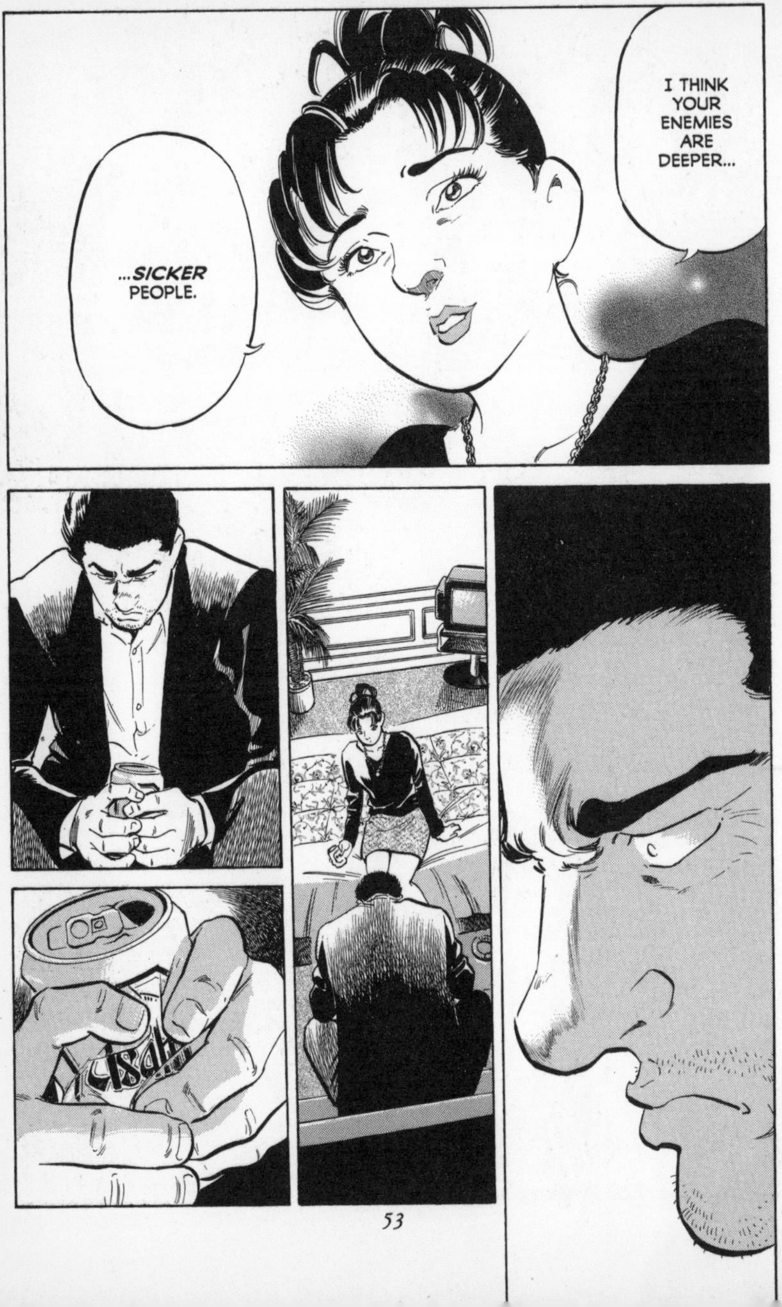
I THINK YOUR ENEMIES ARE DEEPER...
...SICKER PEOPLE.

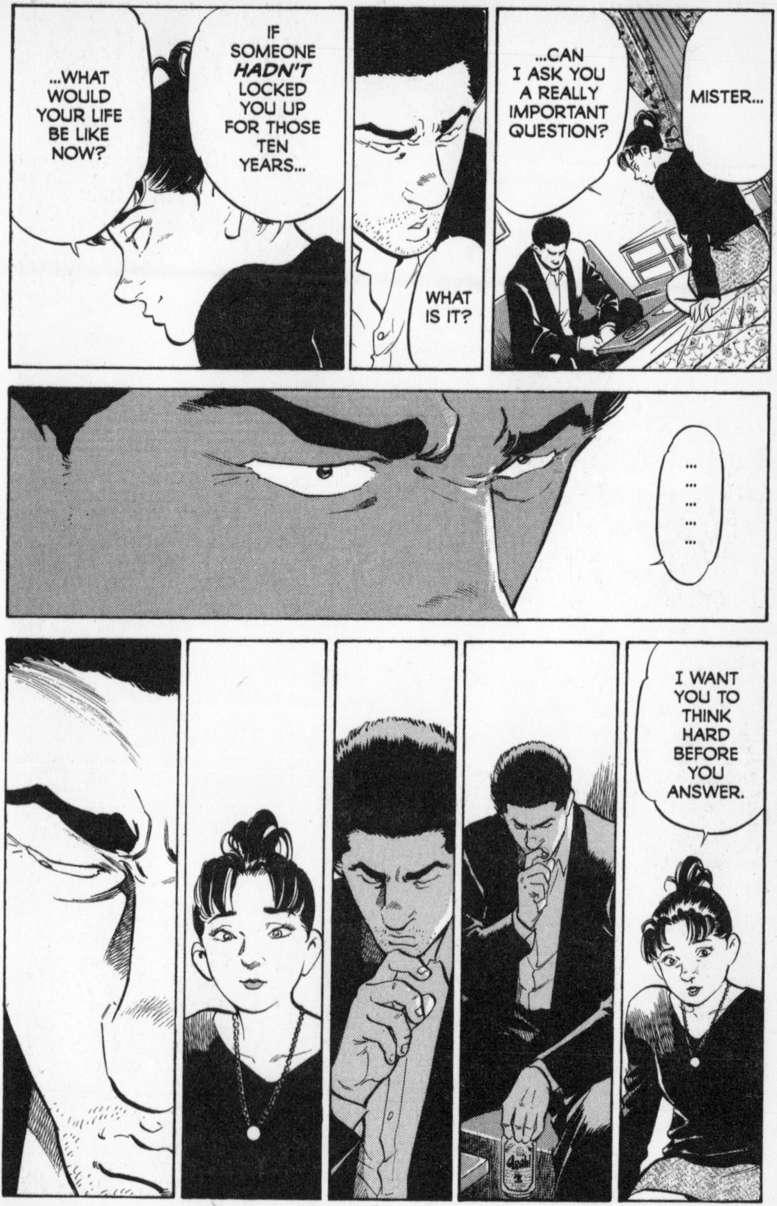
MISTER...
...CAN I ASK YOU A REALLY IMPORTANT QUESTION?
WHAT IS IT?
IF SOMEONE *HADN'T* LOCKED YOU UP FOR THOSE TEN YEARS...
...WHAT WOULD YOUR LIFE BE LIKE NOW?
....
I WANT YOU TO THINK HARD BEFORE YOU ANSWER.

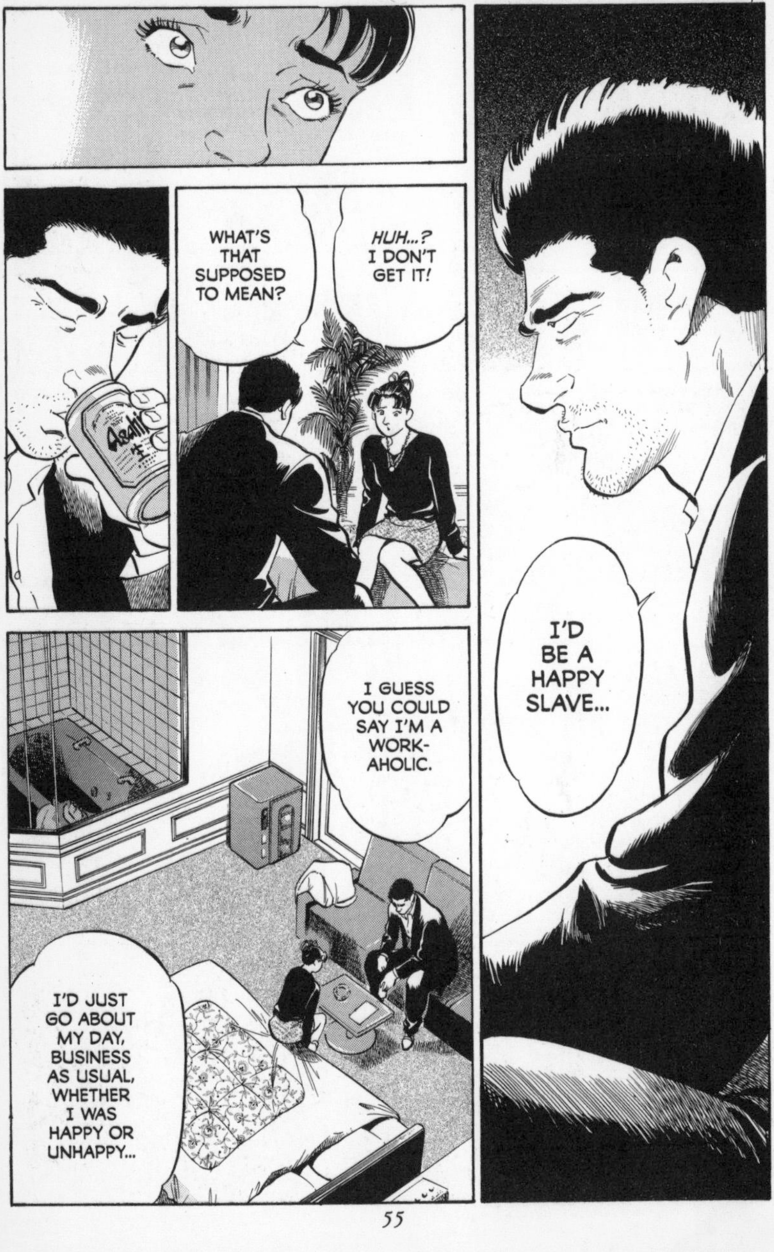
I'D BE A HAPPY SLAVE...
HUH...? I DON'T GET IT!
WHAT'S THAT SUPPOSED TO MEAN?
I GUESS YOU COULD SAY I'M A WORK-AHOLIC.
I'D JUST GO ABOUT MY DAY, BUSINESS AS USUAL, WHETHER I WAS HAPPY OR UNHAPPY...

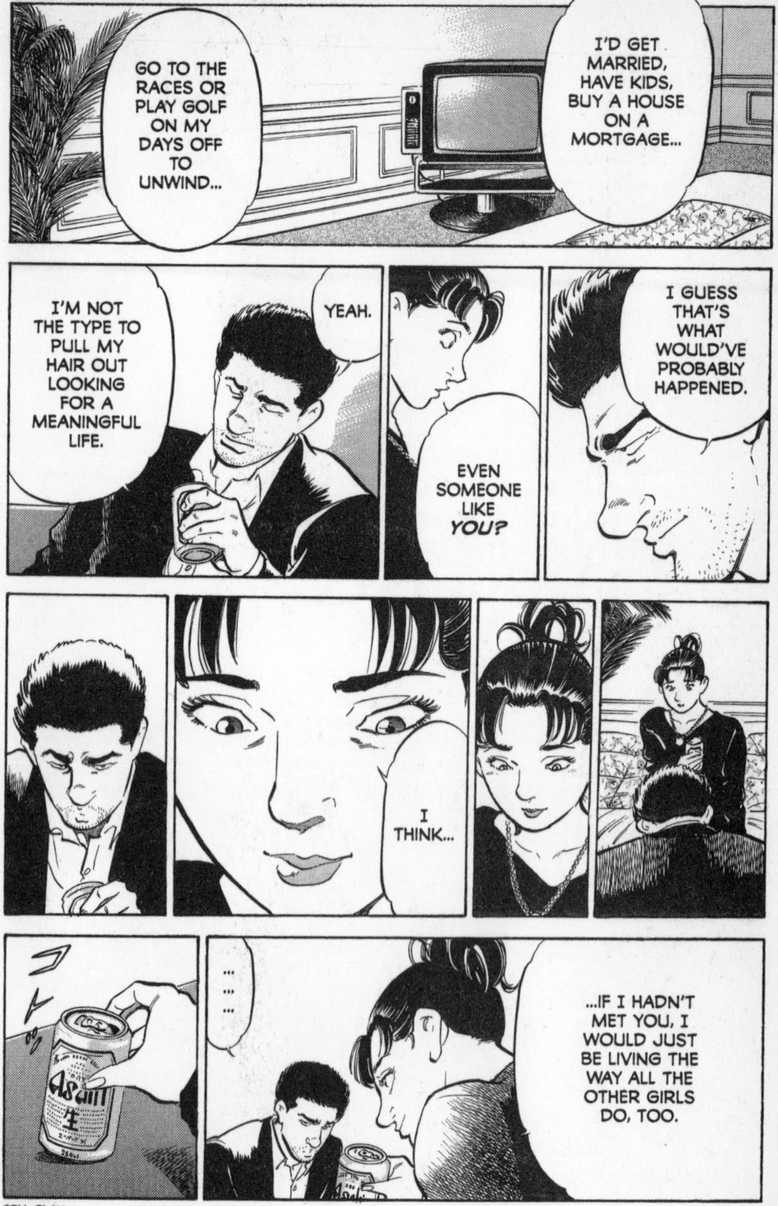
I'D GET MARRIED, HAVE KIDS, BUY A HOUSE ON A MORTGAGE...
GO TO THE RACES OR PLAY GOLF ON MY DAYS OFF TO UNWIND...
I GUESS THAT'S WHAT WOULD'VE PROBABLY HAPPENED.
EVEN SOMEONE LIKE *YOU?*
YEAH.
I'M NOT THE TYPE TO PULL MY HAIR OUT LOOKING FOR A MEANINGFUL LIFE.
I THINK...
...IF I HADN'T MET YOU, I WOULD JUST BE LIVING THE WAY ALL THE OTHER GIRLS DO, TOO.
......

*FX: CLAK

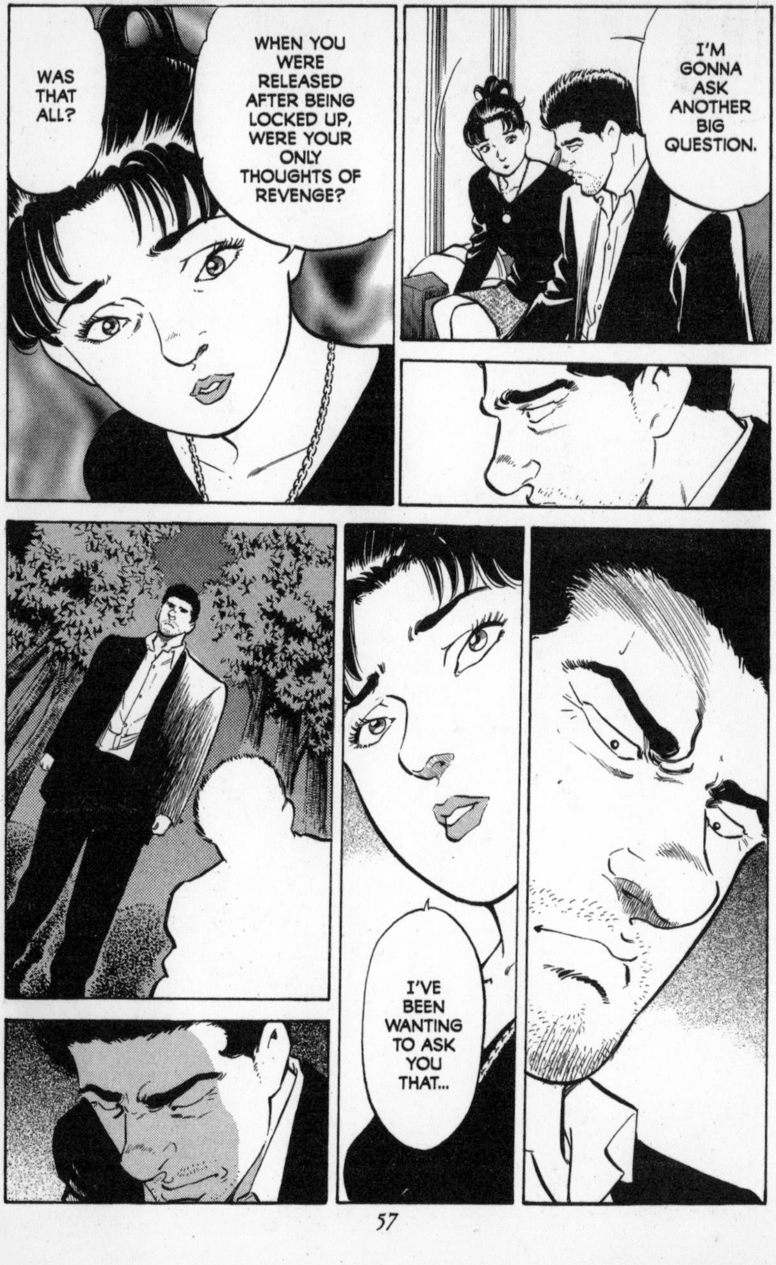
I'M GONNA ASK ANOTHER BIG QUESTION.
WHEN YOU WERE RELEASED AFTER BEING LOCKED UP, WERE YOUR ONLY THOUGHTS OF REVENGE?
WAS THAT ALL?
I'VE BEEN WANTING TO ASK YOU THAT...

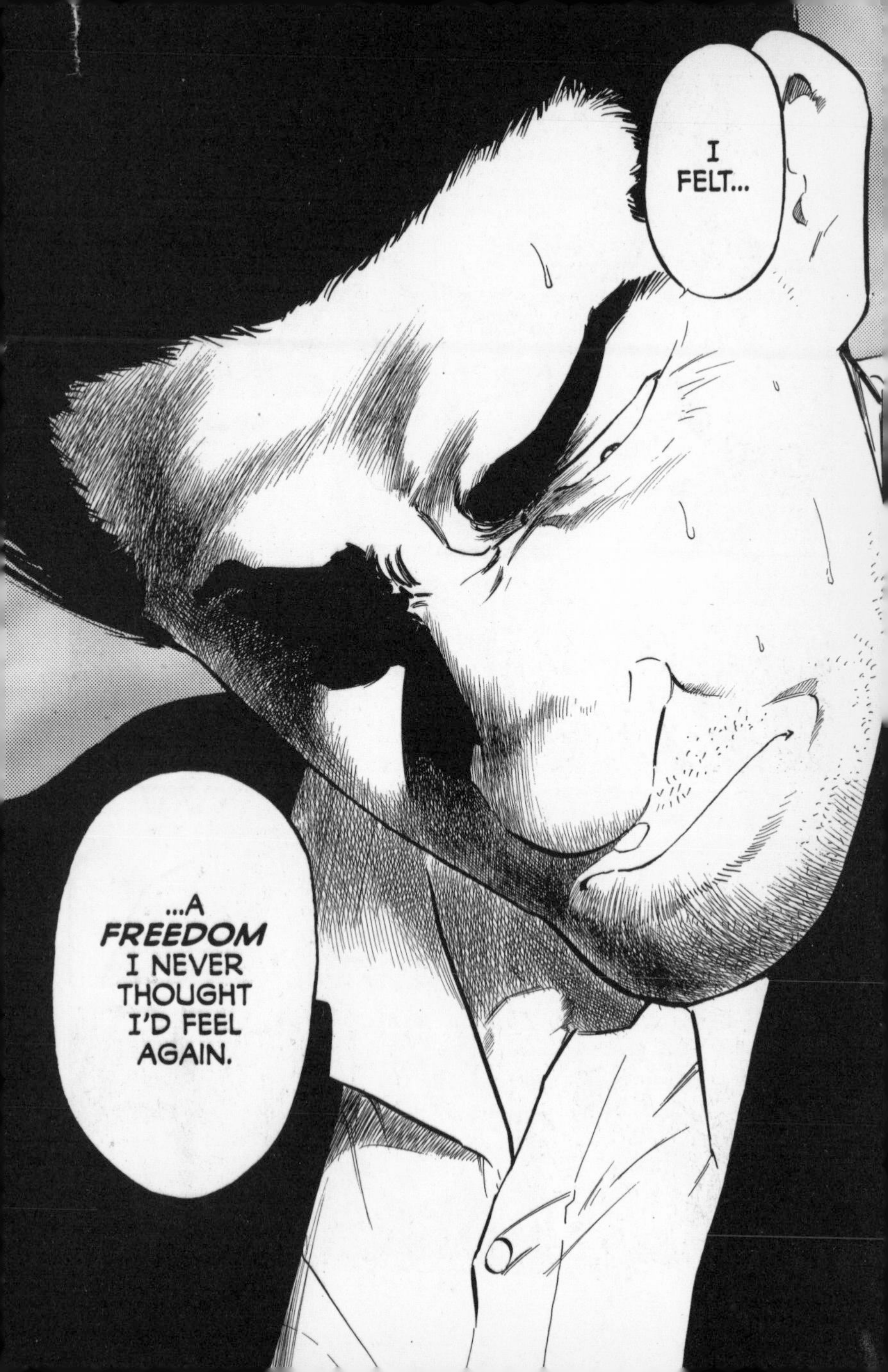
I FELT...
...A *FREEDOM* I NEVER THOUGHT I'D FEEL AGAIN.

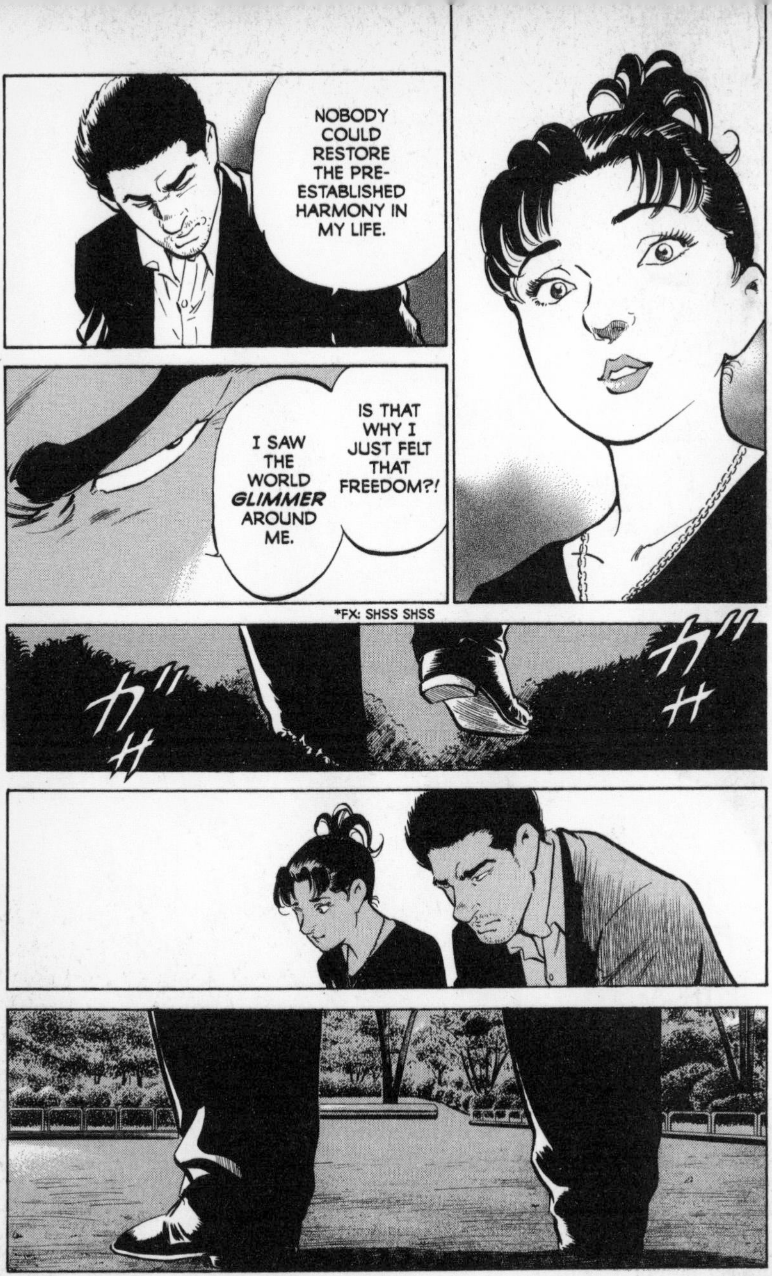
NOBODY COULD RESTORE THE PRE-ESTABLISHED HARMONY IN MY LIFE.
IS THAT WHY I JUST FELT THAT FREEDOM?!
I SAW THE WORLD *GLIMMER* AROUND ME.
*FX: SHSS SHSS
ガッ
ガッ

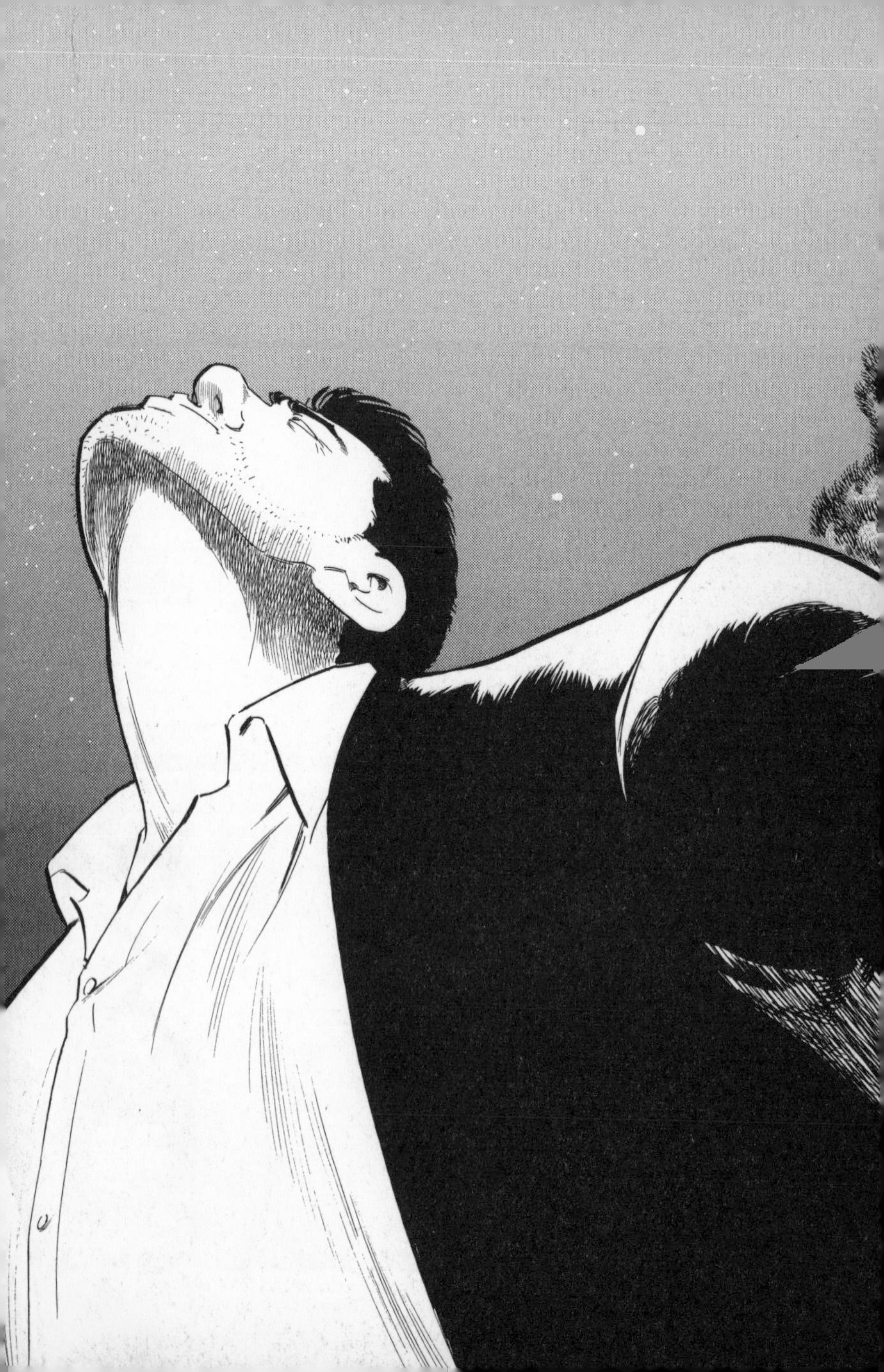

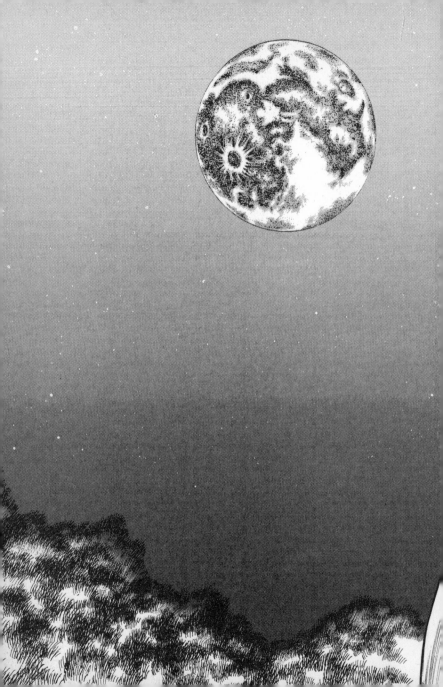

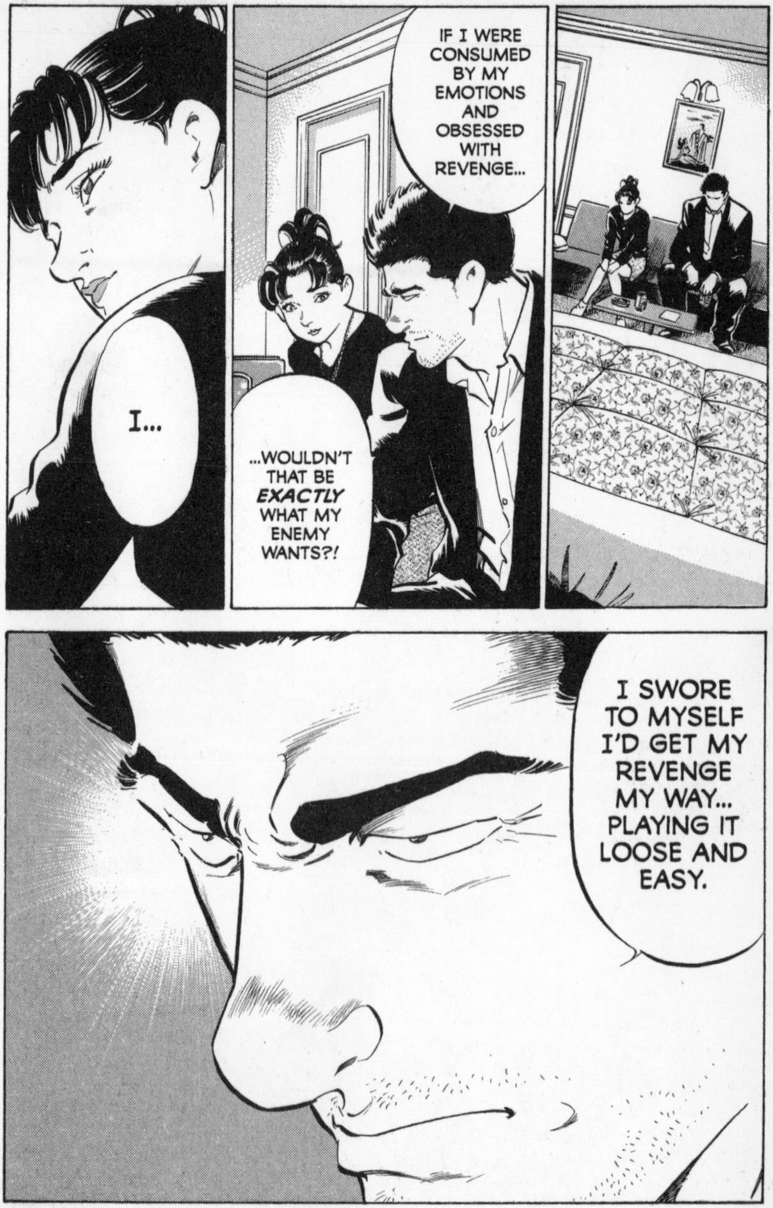
IF I WERE CONSUMED BY MY EMOTIONS AND OBSESSED WITH REVENGE...
...WOULDN'T THAT BE *EXACTLY* WHAT MY ENEMY WANTS?!
I...
I SWORE TO MYSELF I'D GET MY REVENGE MY WAY... PLAYING IT LOOSE AND EASY.

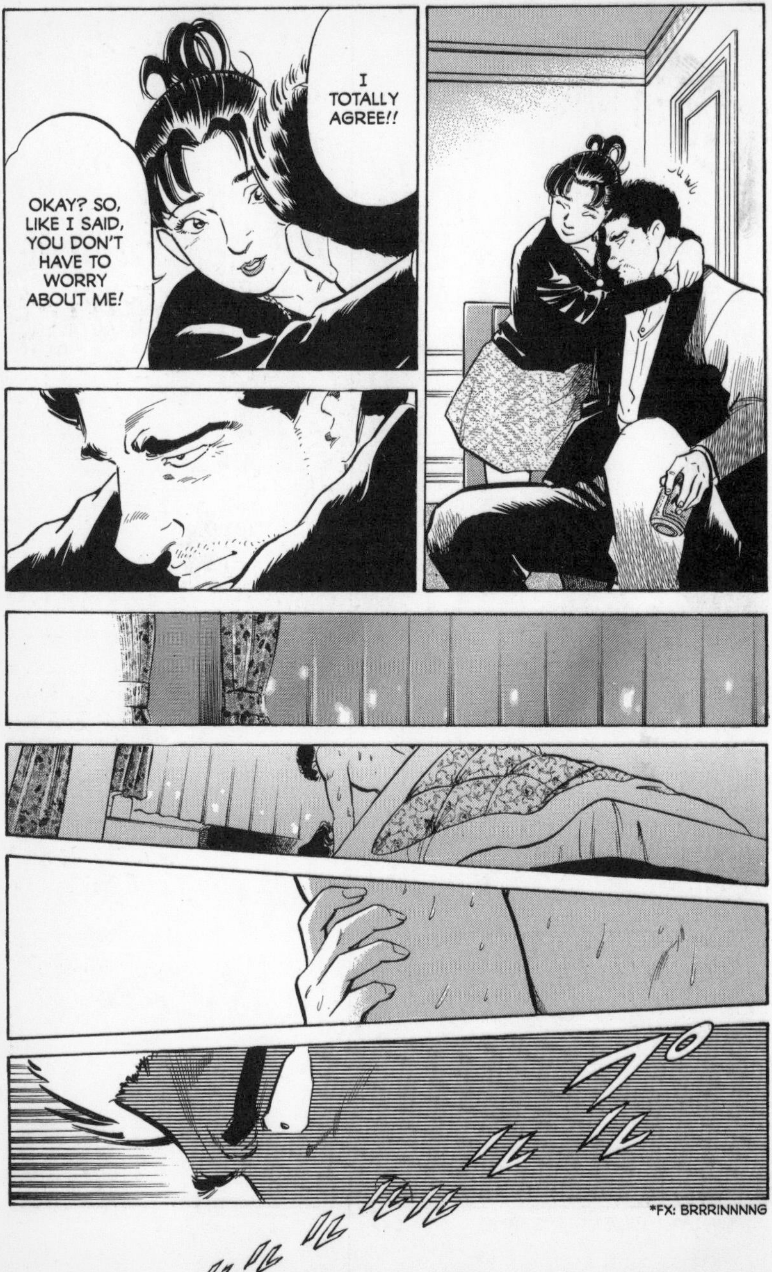
I TOTALLY AGREE!!
OKAY? SO, LIKE I SAID, YOU DON'T HAVE TO WORRY ABOUT ME!
*FX: BRRRINNNNG

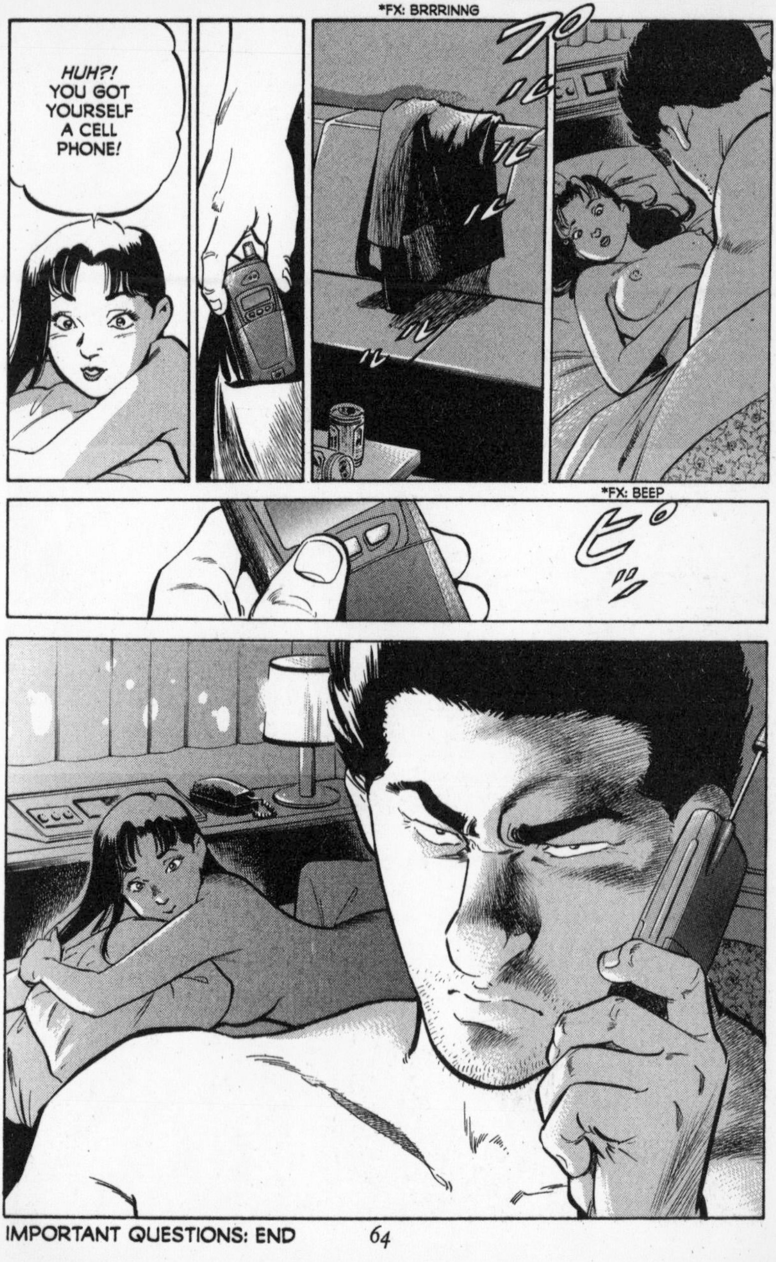
*FX: BRRRINNG
HUH?! YOU GOT YOURSELF A CELL PHONE!
*FX: BEEP

IMPORTANT QUESTIONS: END

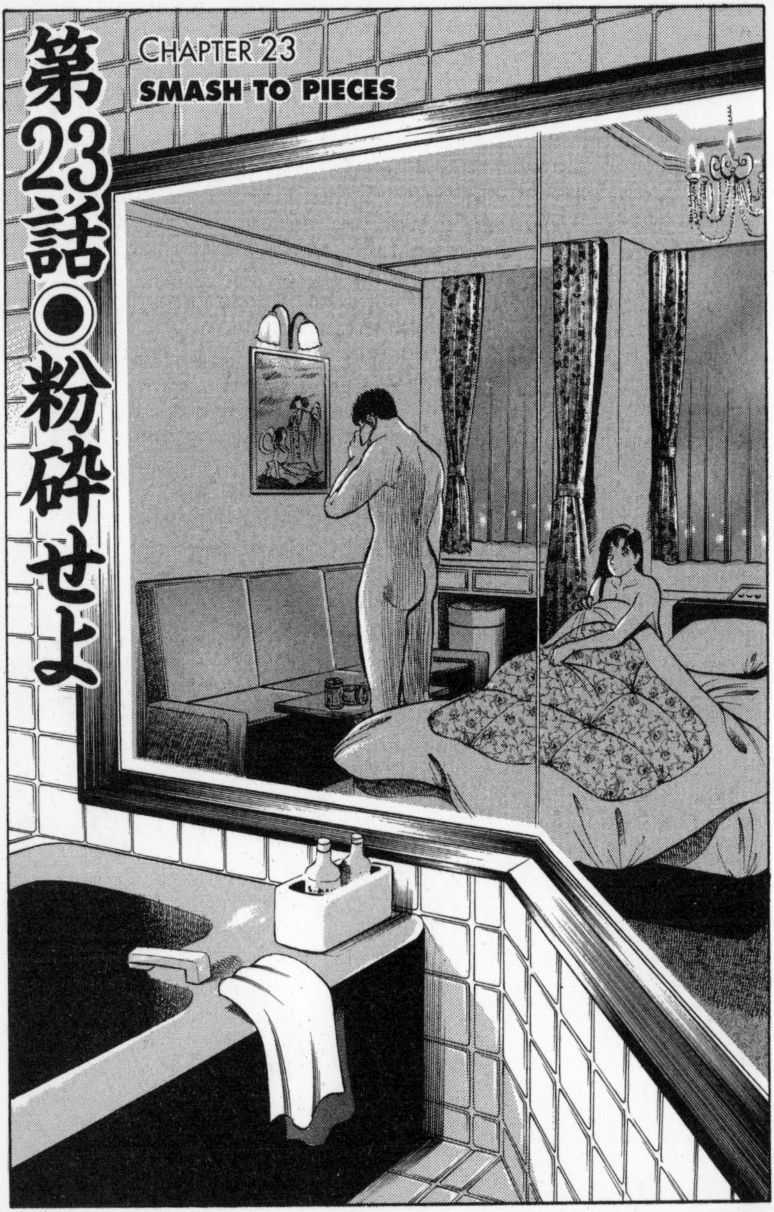

第23話◉粉砕せよ
CHAPTER 23
SMASH TO PIECES

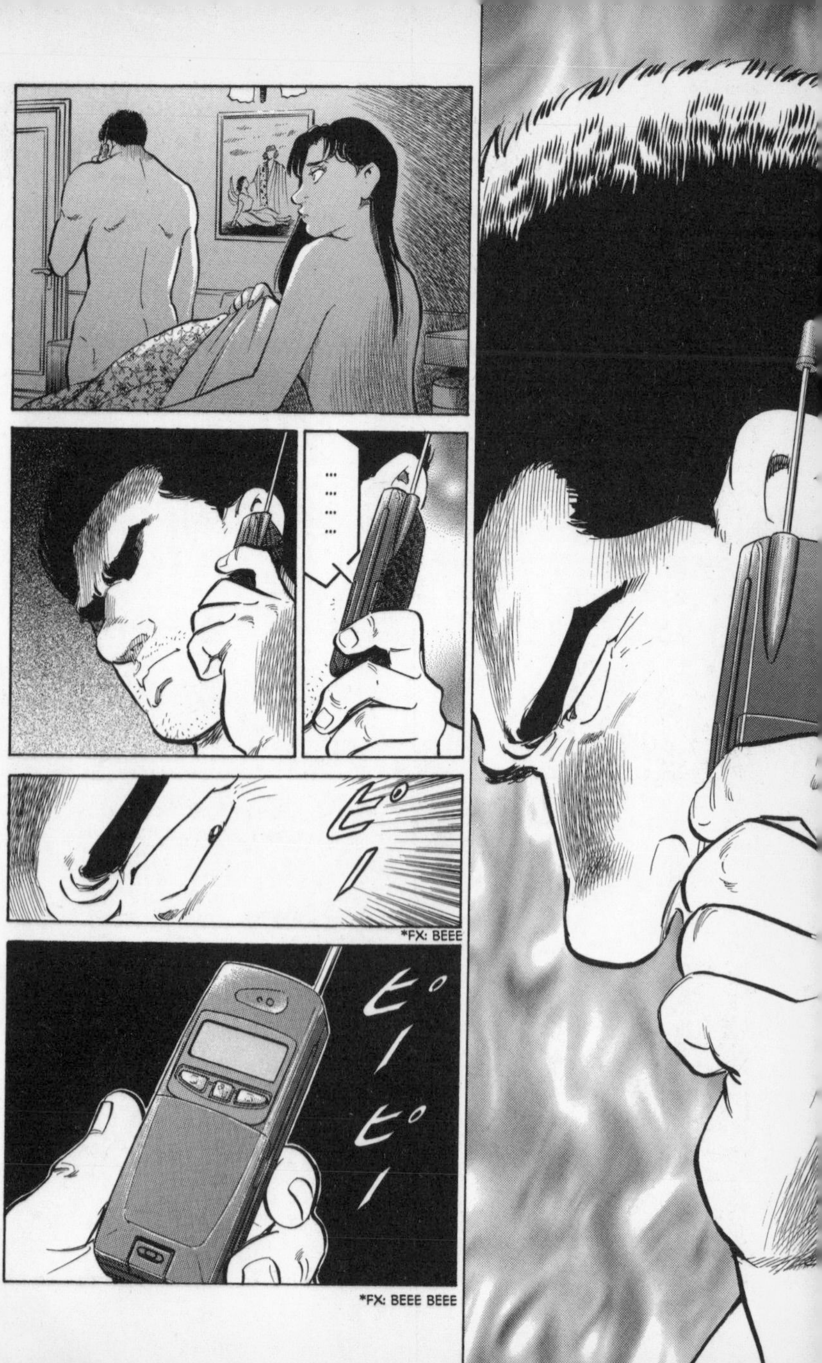
....
ピー
*FX: BEEE
ピーピー
*FX: BEEE BEEE

*FX: CLACK

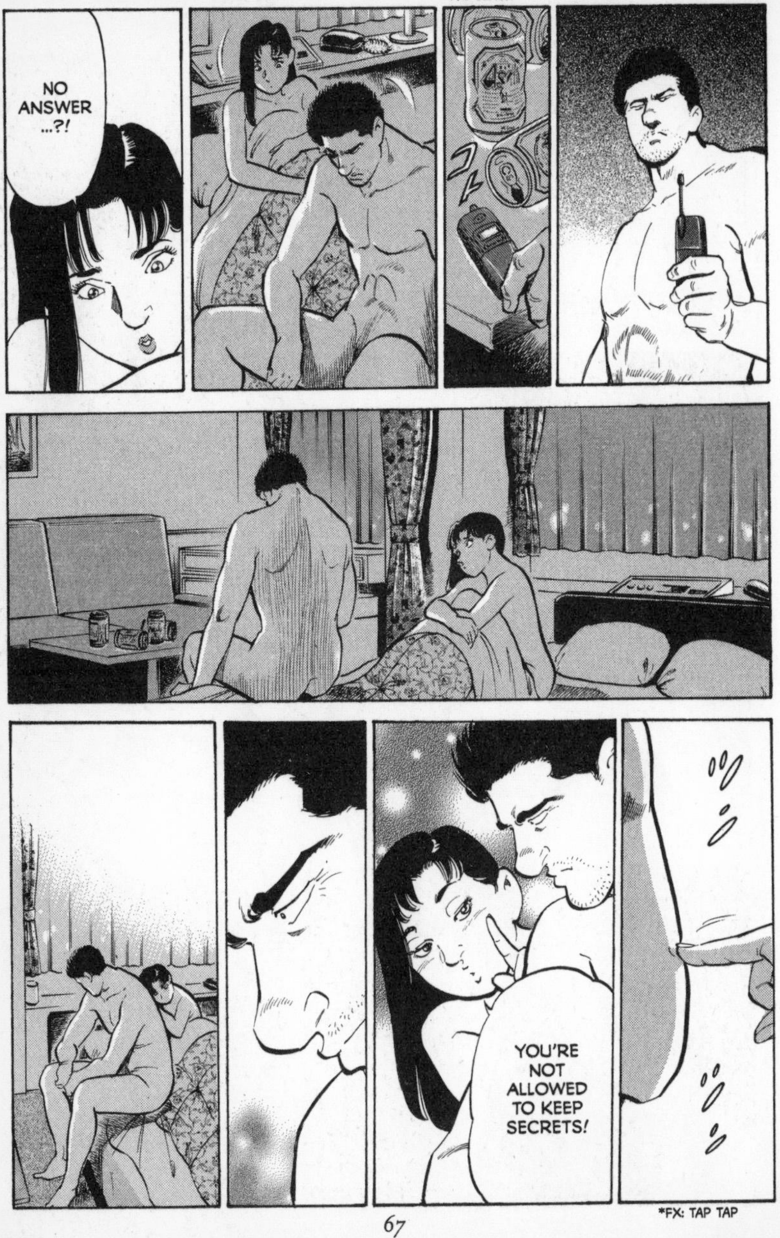
NO ANSWER ...?!
YOU'RE NOT ALLOWED TO KEEP SECRETS!

*FX: TAP TAP

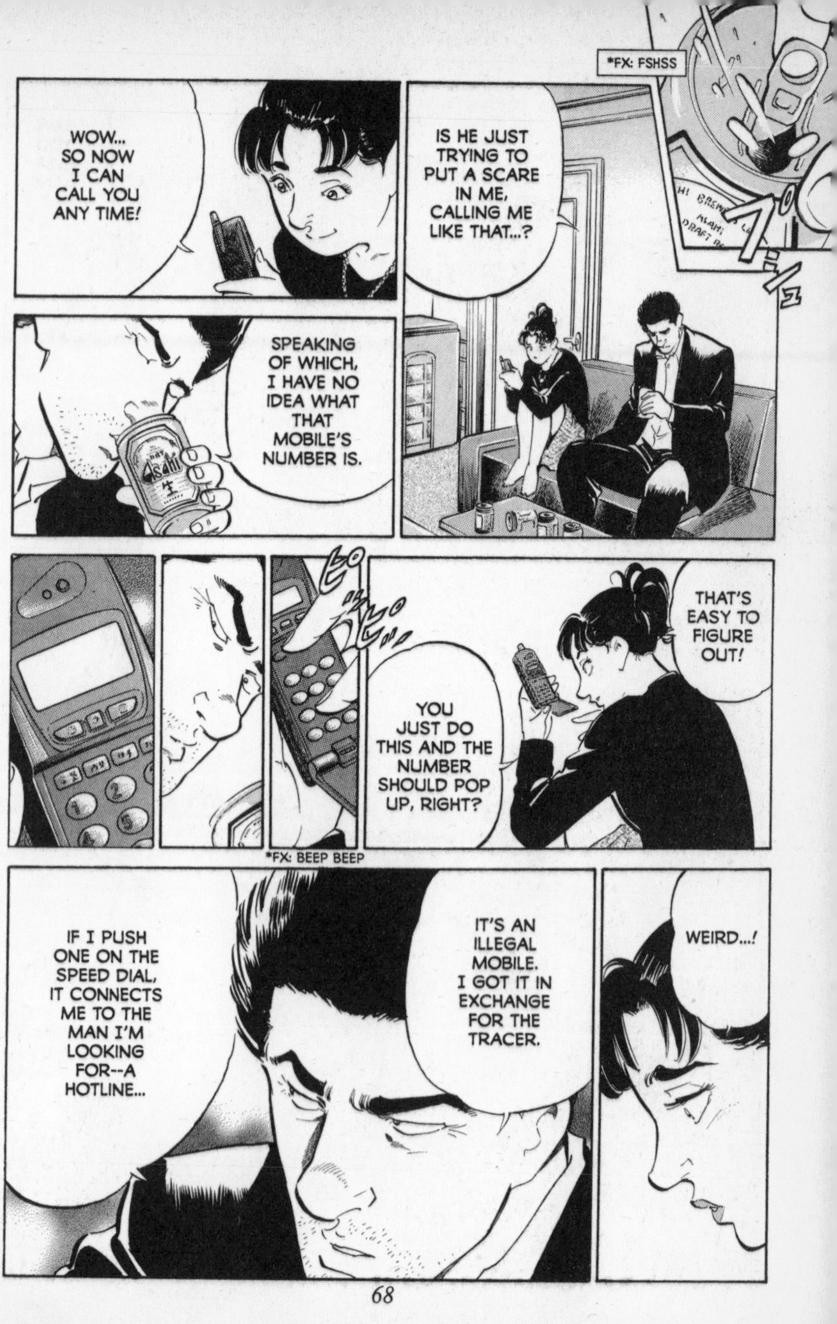
*FX: FSHSS
IS HE JUST TRYING TO PUT A SCARE IN ME, CALLING ME LIKE THAT...?
WOW... SO NOW I CAN CALL YOU ANY TIME!
SPEAKING OF WHICH, I HAVE NO IDEA WHAT THAT MOBILE'S NUMBER IS.
THAT'S EASY TO FIGURE OUT!
YOU JUST DO THIS AND THE NUMBER SHOULD POP UP, RIGHT?
*FX: BEEP BEEP
WEIRD...!
IT'S AN ILLEGAL MOBILE. I GOT IT IN EXCHANGE FOR THE TRACER.
IF I PUSH ONE ON THE SPEED DIAL, IT CONNECTS ME TO THE MAN I'M LOOKING FOR--A HOTLINE...

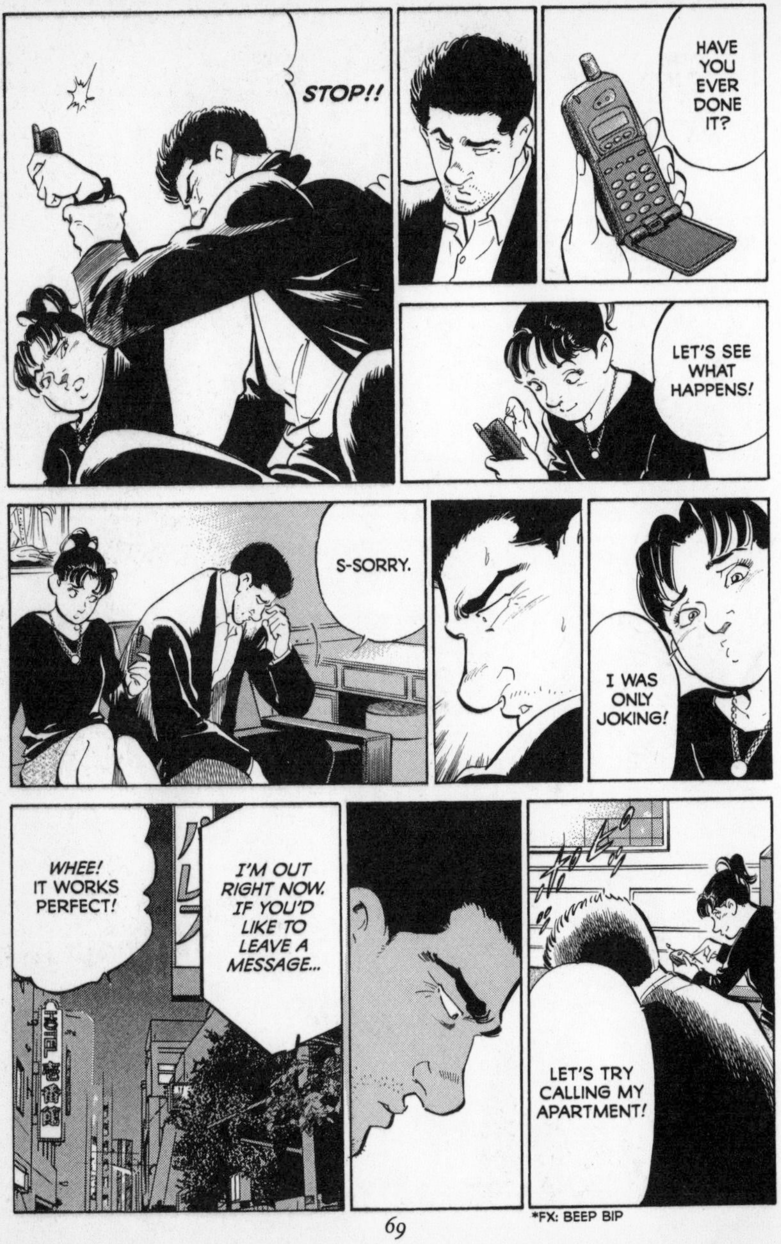
HAVE YOU EVER DONE IT?
LET'S SEE WHAT HAPPENS!
STOP!!
I WAS ONLY JOKING!
S-SORRY.
LET'S TRY CALLING MY APARTMENT!
I'M OUT RIGHT NOW. IF YOU'D LIKE TO LEAVE A MESSAGE...
WHEE! IT WORKS PERFECT!
HOTEL

*FX: BEEP BIP

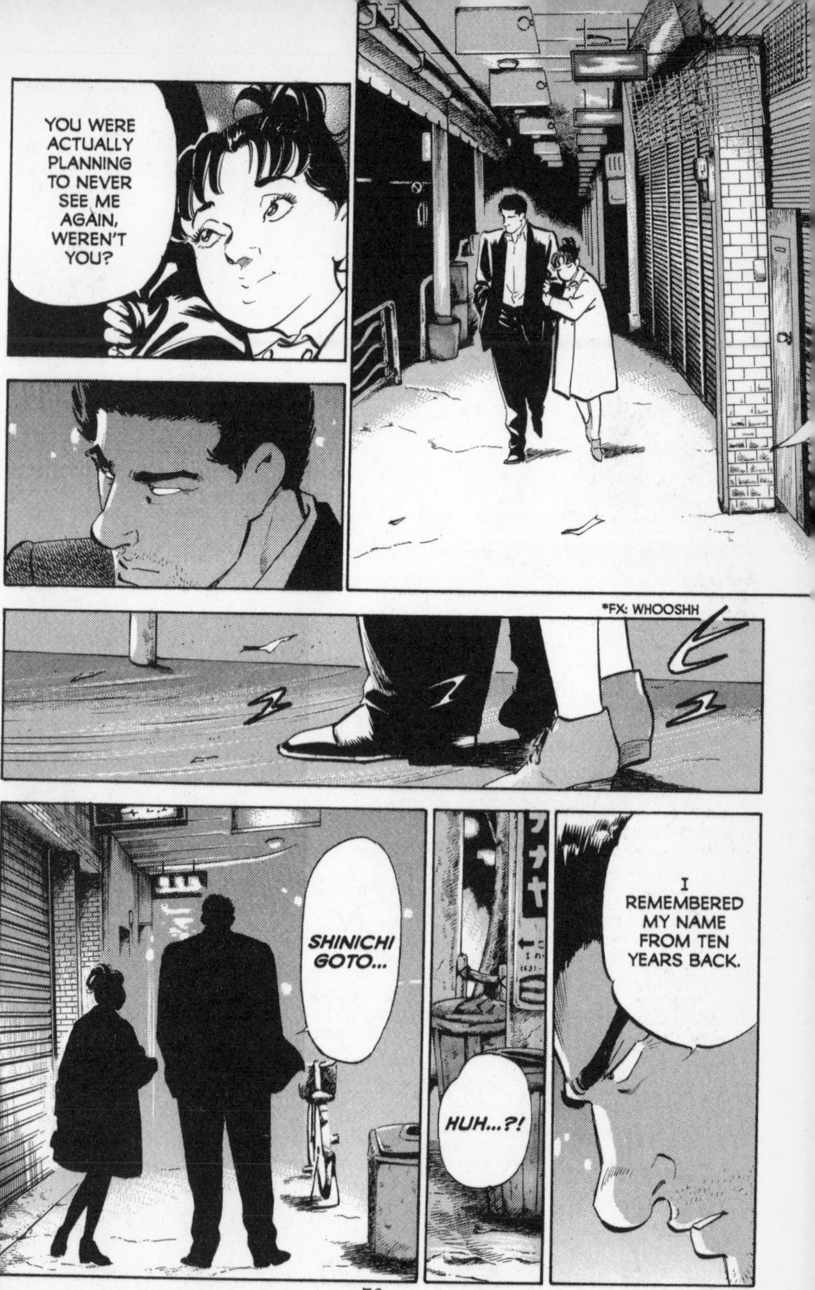
YOU WERE ACTUALLY PLANNING TO NEVER SEE ME AGAIN, WEREN'T YOU?
*FX: WHOOSHH
I REMEMBERED MY NAME FROM TEN YEARS BACK.
HUH...?!
SHINICHI GOTO...

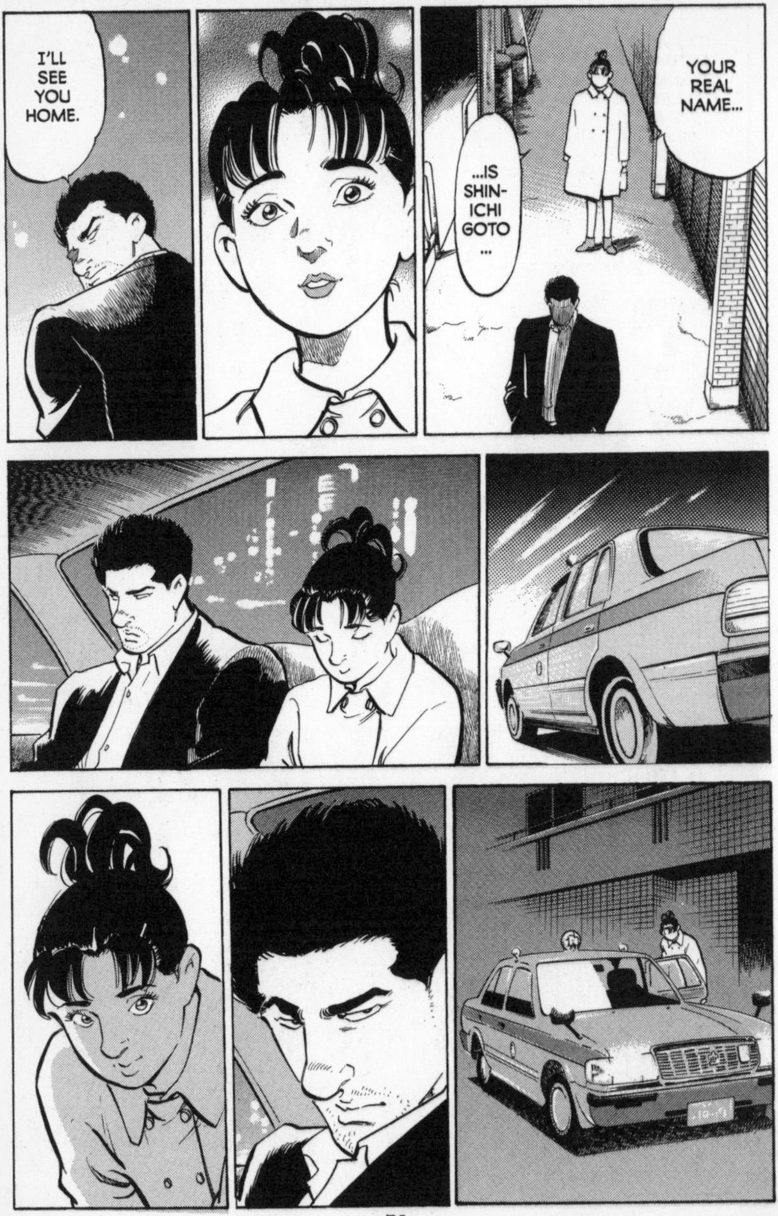
YOUR REAL NAME...
...IS SHIN-ICHI GOTO ...
I'LL SEE YOU HOME.

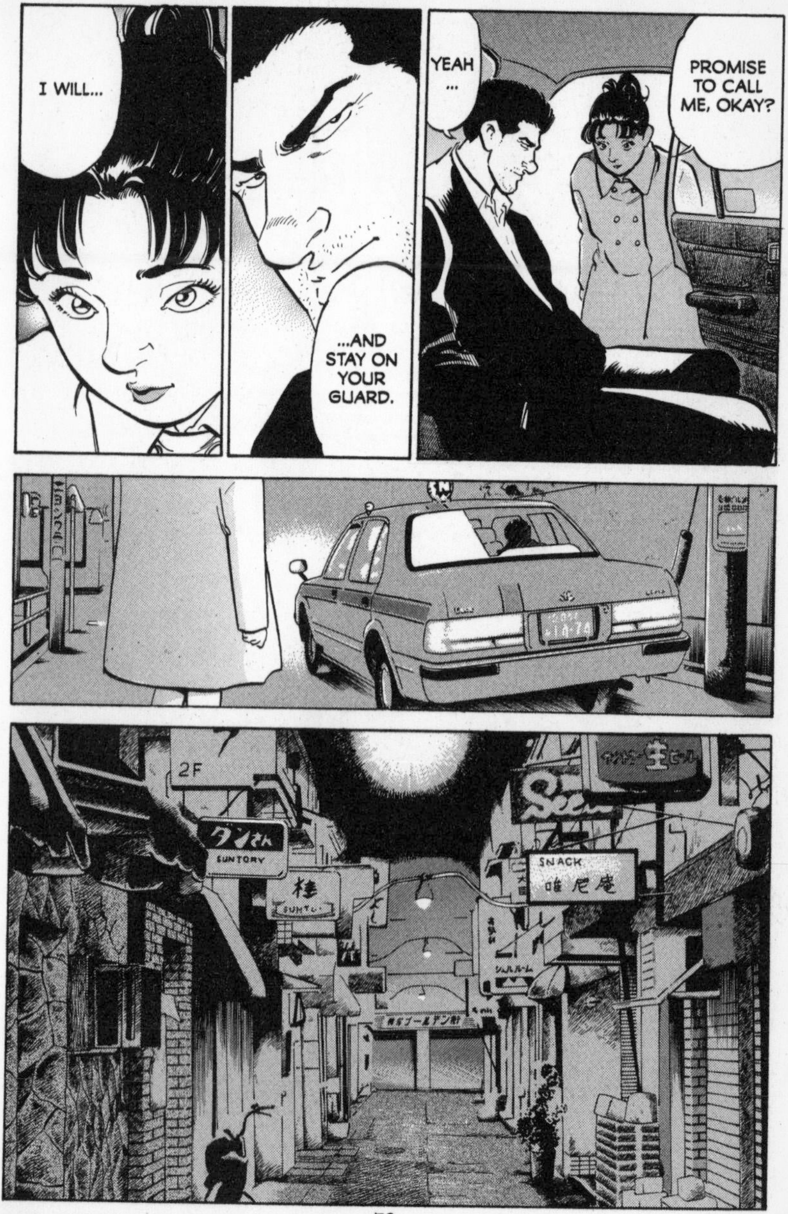
PROMISE TO CALL ME, OKAY?
YEAH ...
...AND STAY ON YOUR GUARD.
I WILL...
2F
SUNTORY
SNACK
唯尼庵

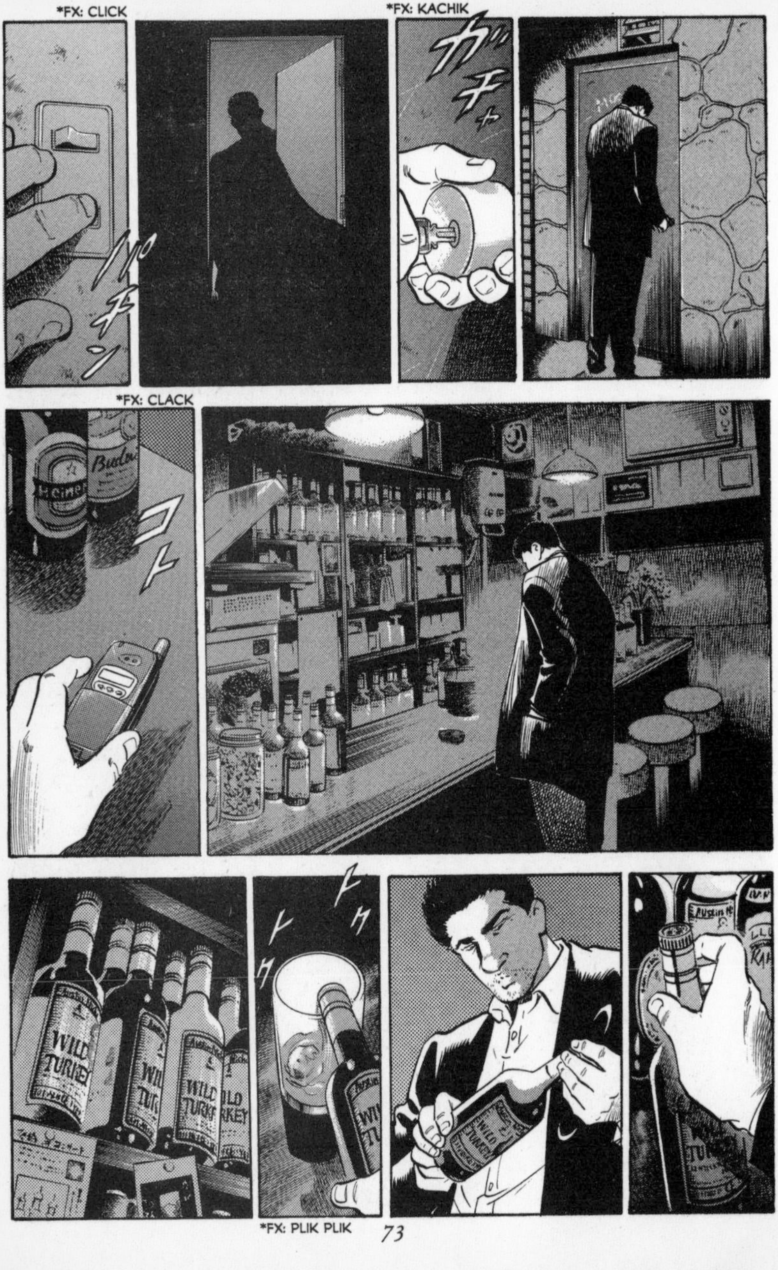
*FX: KACHIK
*FX: CLICK
*FX: CLACK
*FX: PLIK PLIK

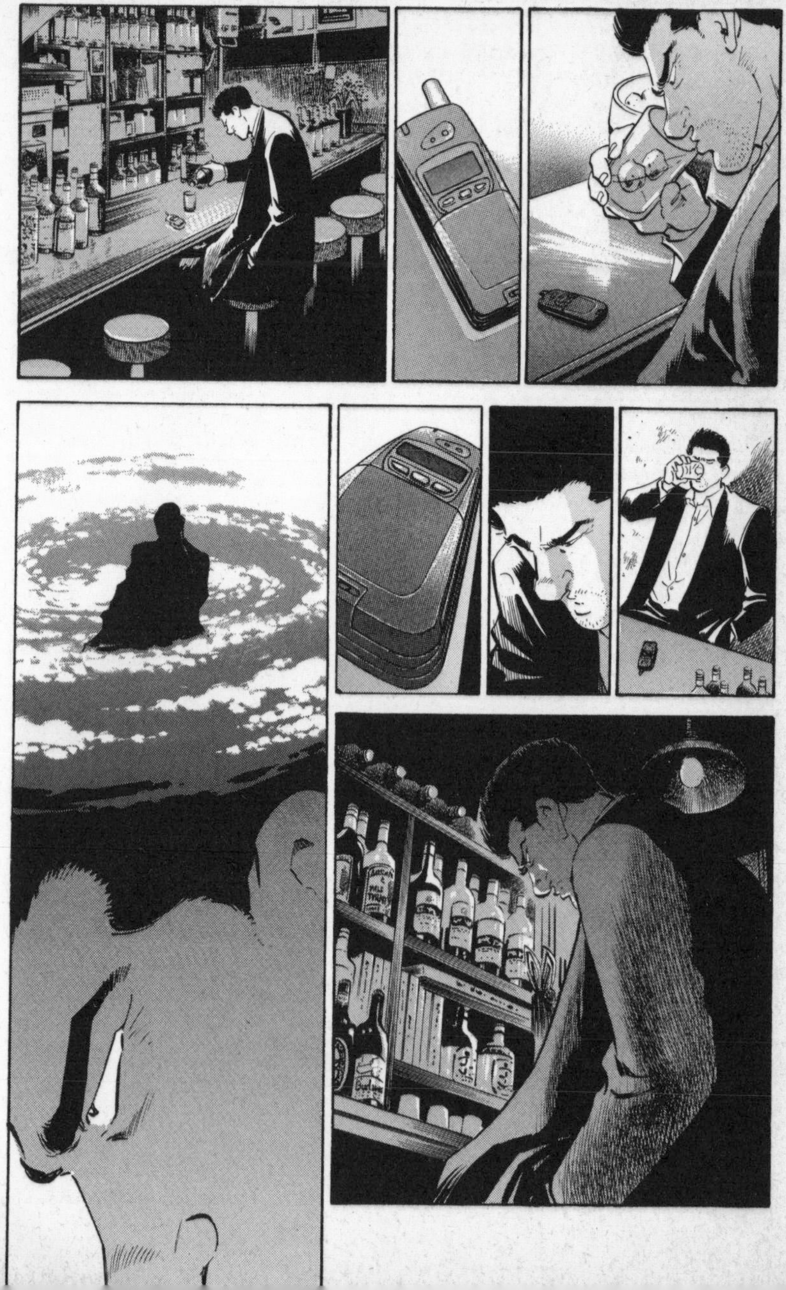

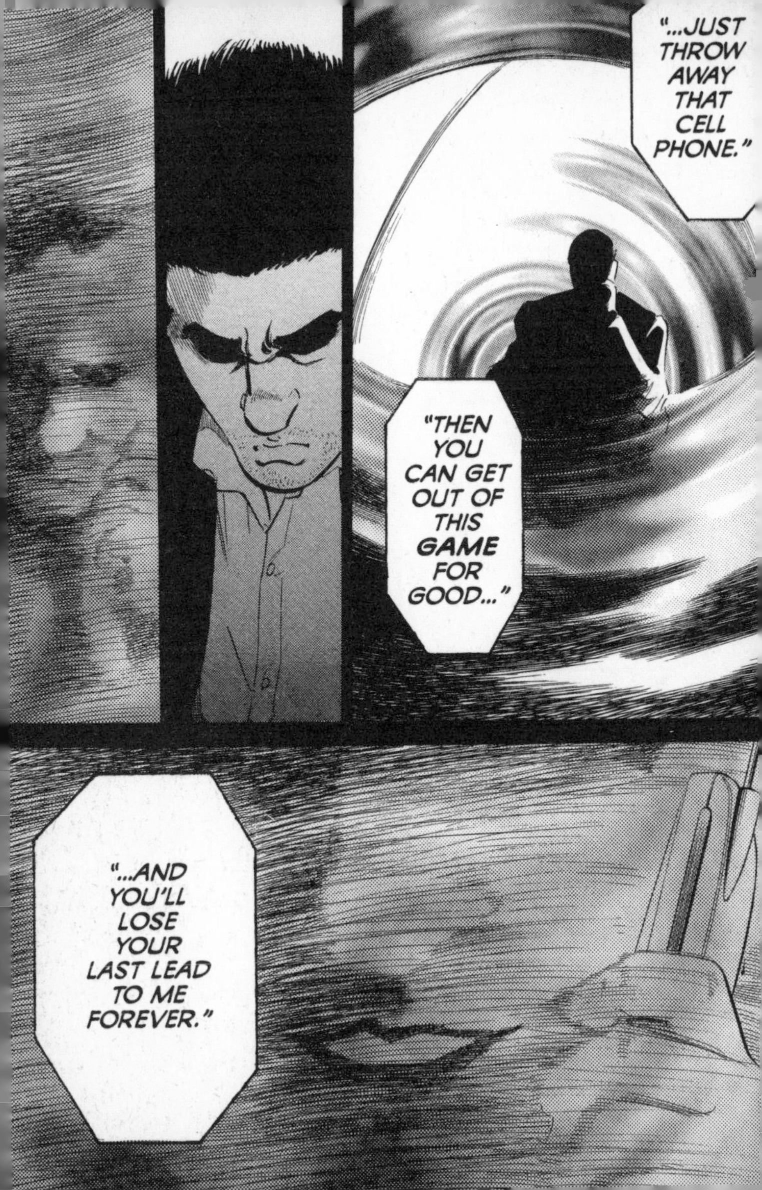
"...JUST THROW AWAY THAT CELL PHONE."
"THEN YOU CAN GET OUT OF THIS GAME FOR GOOD..."
"...AND YOU'LL LOSE YOUR LAST LEAD TO ME FOREVER."

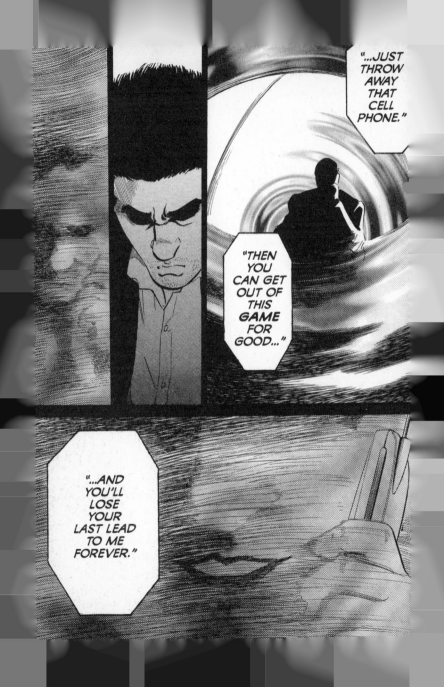

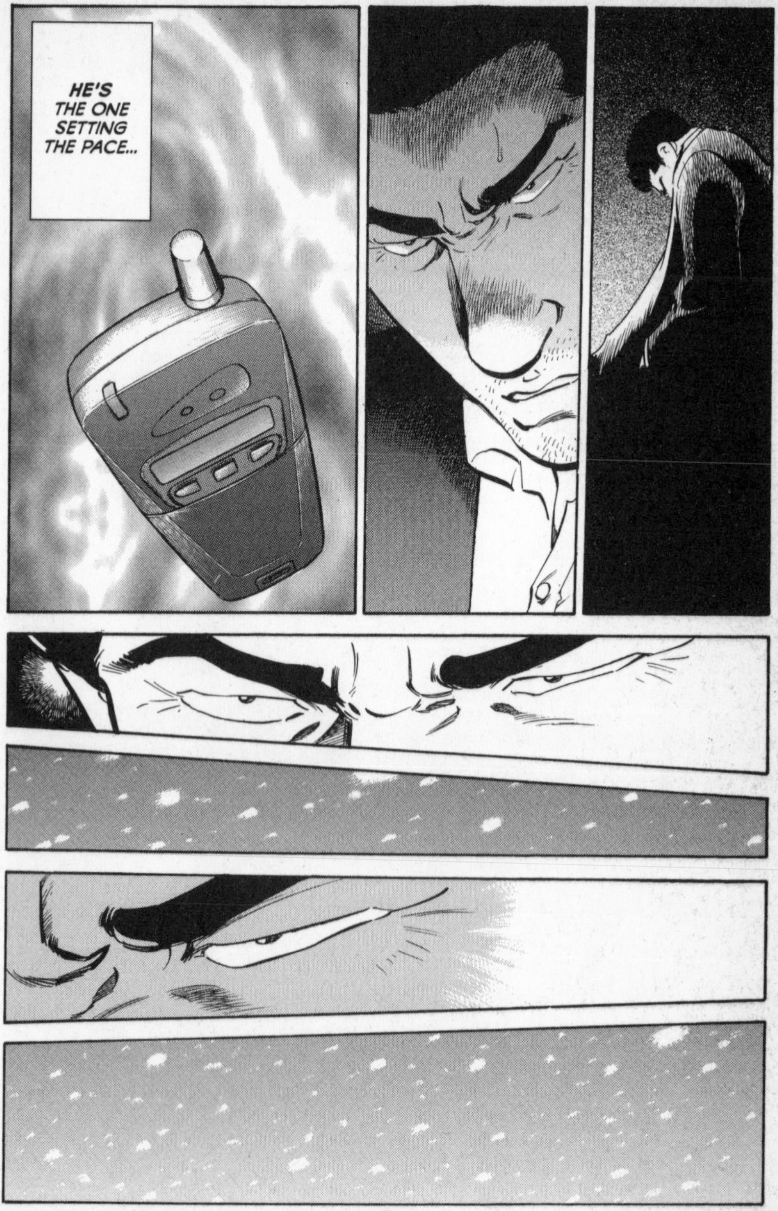
HE'S THE ONE SETTING THE PACE...

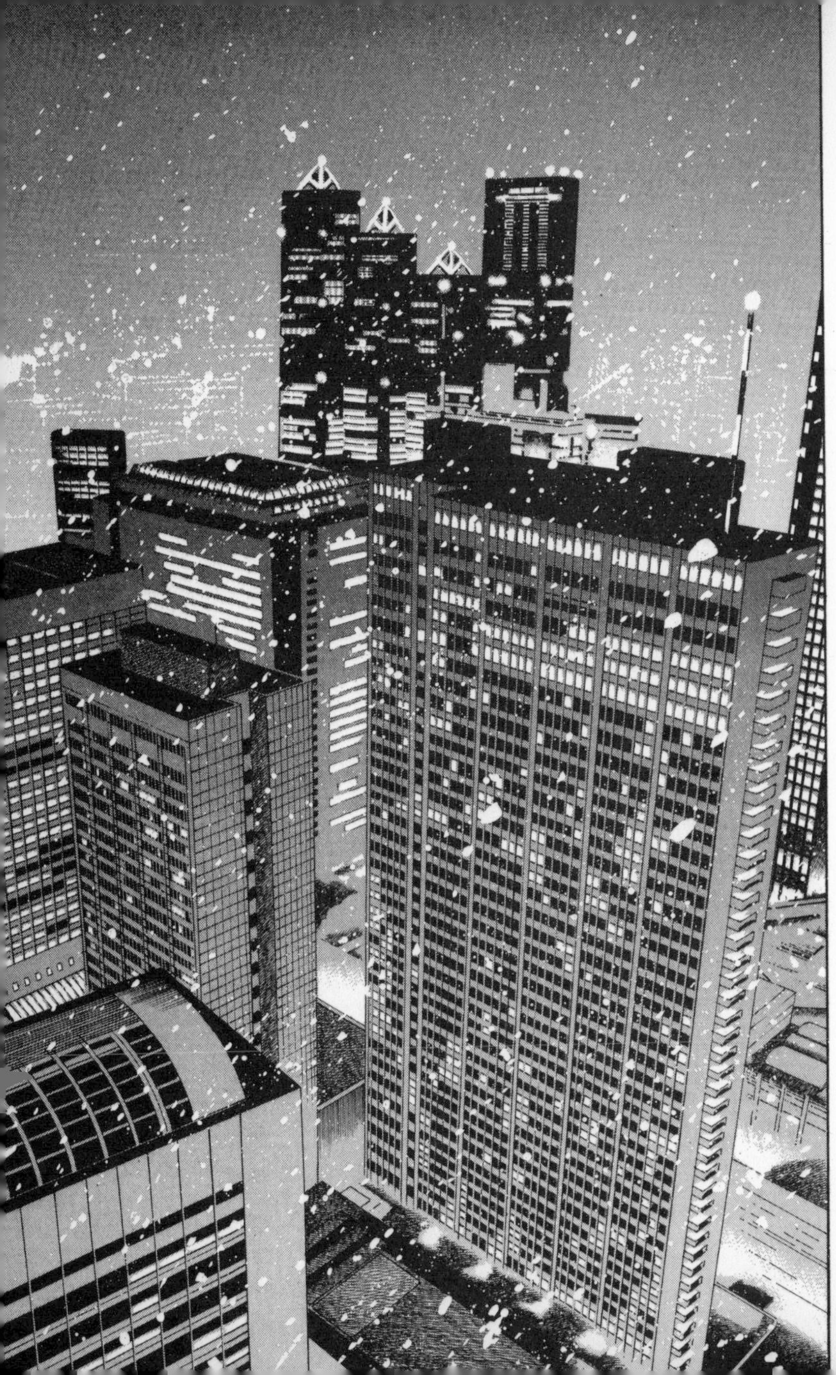

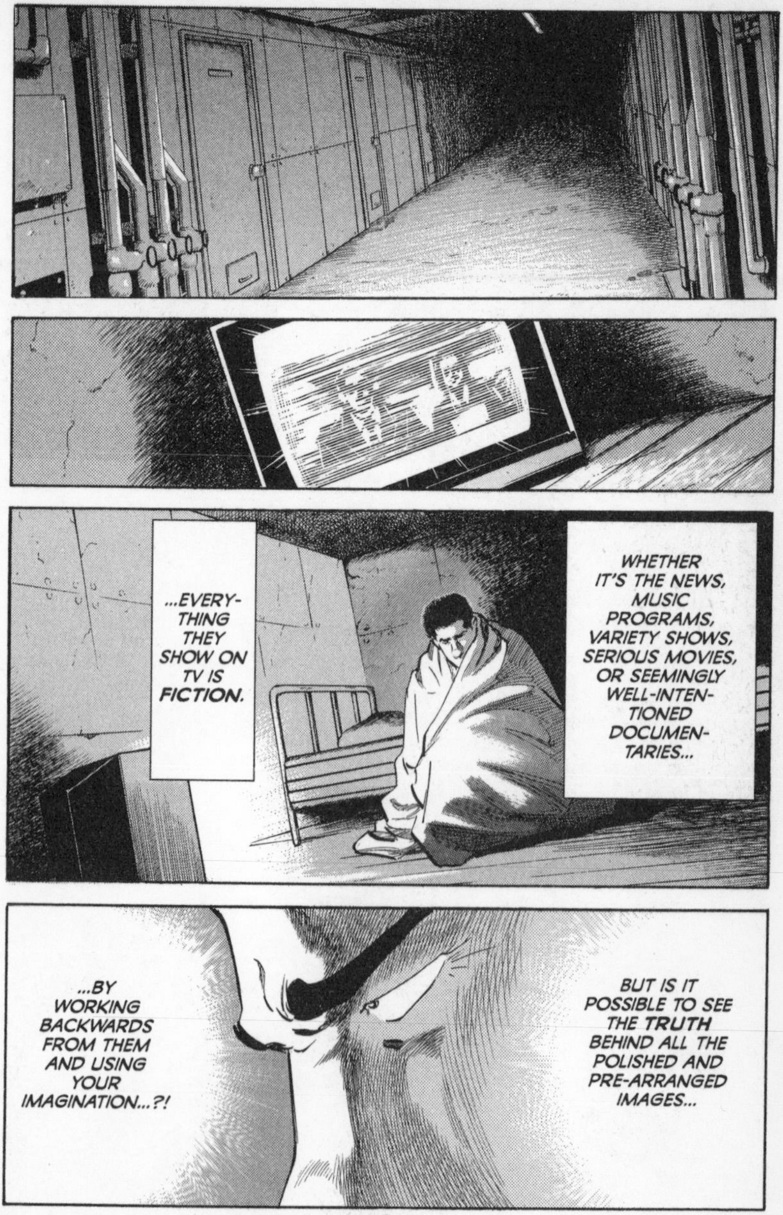
WHETHER IT'S THE NEWS, MUSIC PROGRAMS, VARIETY SHOWS, SERIOUS MOVIES, OR SEEMINGLY WELL-INTENTIONED DOCUMENTARIES...
...EVERYTHING THEY SHOW ON TV IS **FICTION.**
BUT IS IT POSSIBLE TO SEE THE **TRUTH** BEHIND ALL THE POLISHED AND PRE-ARRANGED IMAGES...
...BY WORKING BACKWARDS FROM THEM AND USING YOUR IMAGINATION...?!

DURING THAT BIZARRE, SEEMINGLY ENDLESS LOCK-UP...

...THE THING THAT SAVED MY SANITY WAS DEVOTING MYSELF TO DOING THAT.

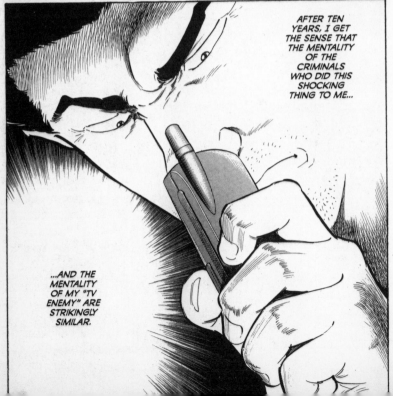

AFTER TEN YEARS, I GET THE SENSE THAT THE MENTALITY OF THE CRIMINALS WHO DID THIS SHOCKING THING TO ME...

...AND THE MENTALITY OF MY "TV ENEMY" ARE STRIKINGLY SIMILAR.

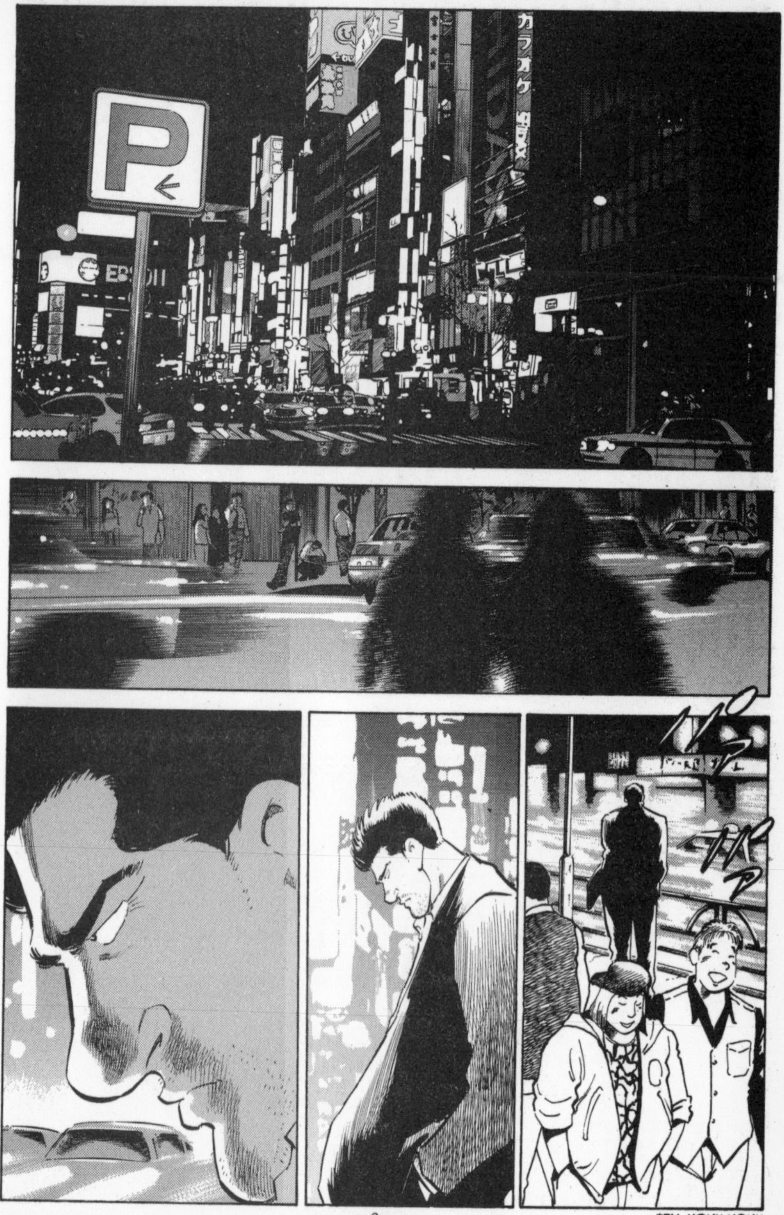

*FX: HONK HONK

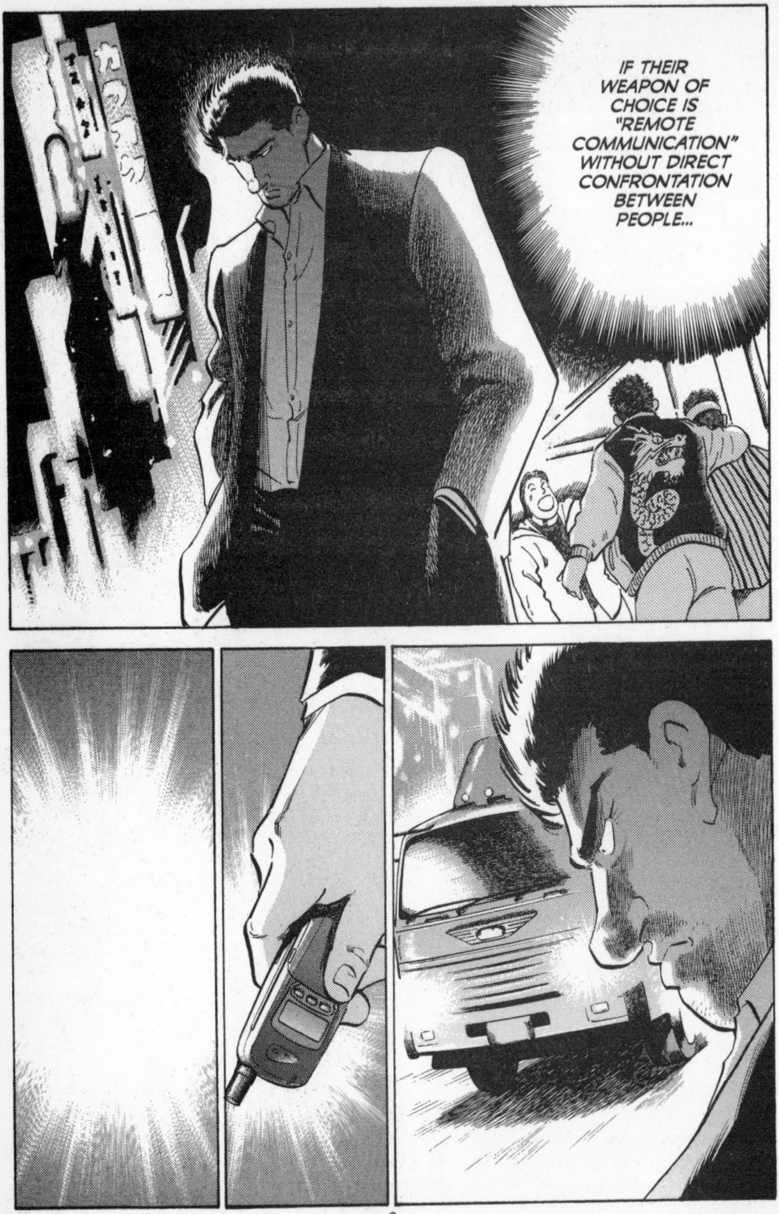
IF THEIR WEAPON OF CHOICE IS "REMOTE COMMUNICATION" WITHOUT DIRECT CONFRONTATION BETWEEN PEOPLE...

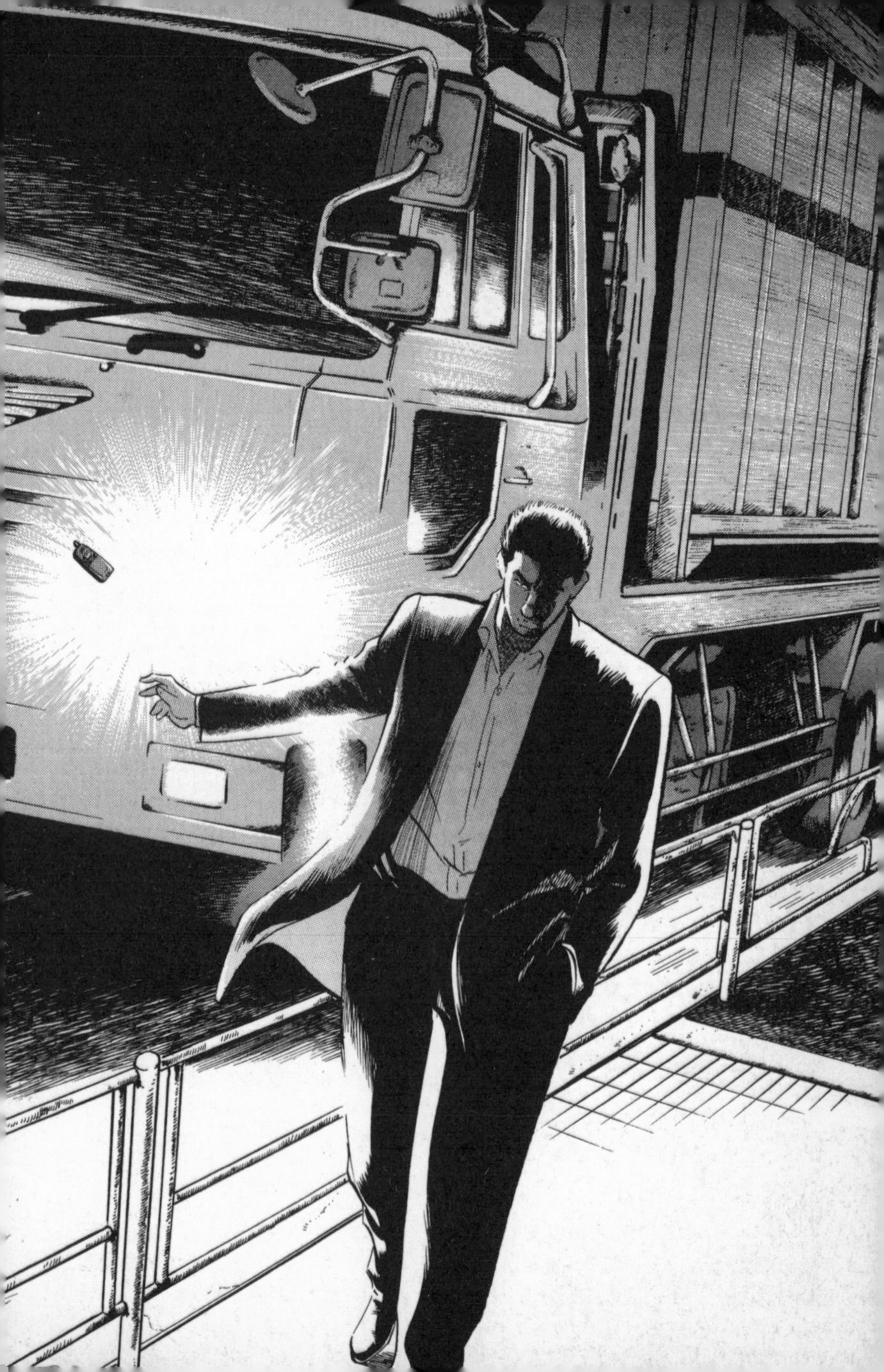

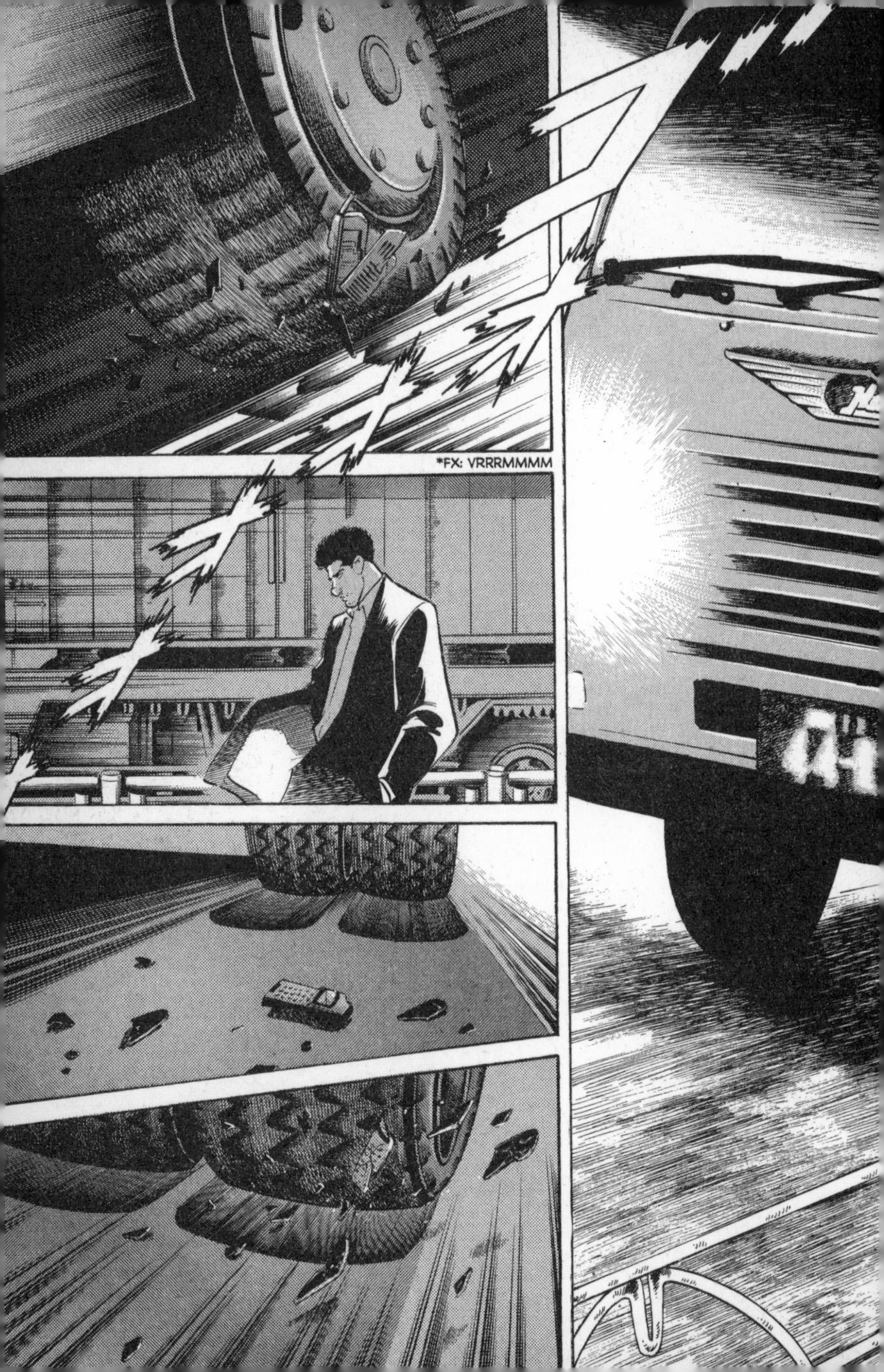
*FX: VRRRMMMM

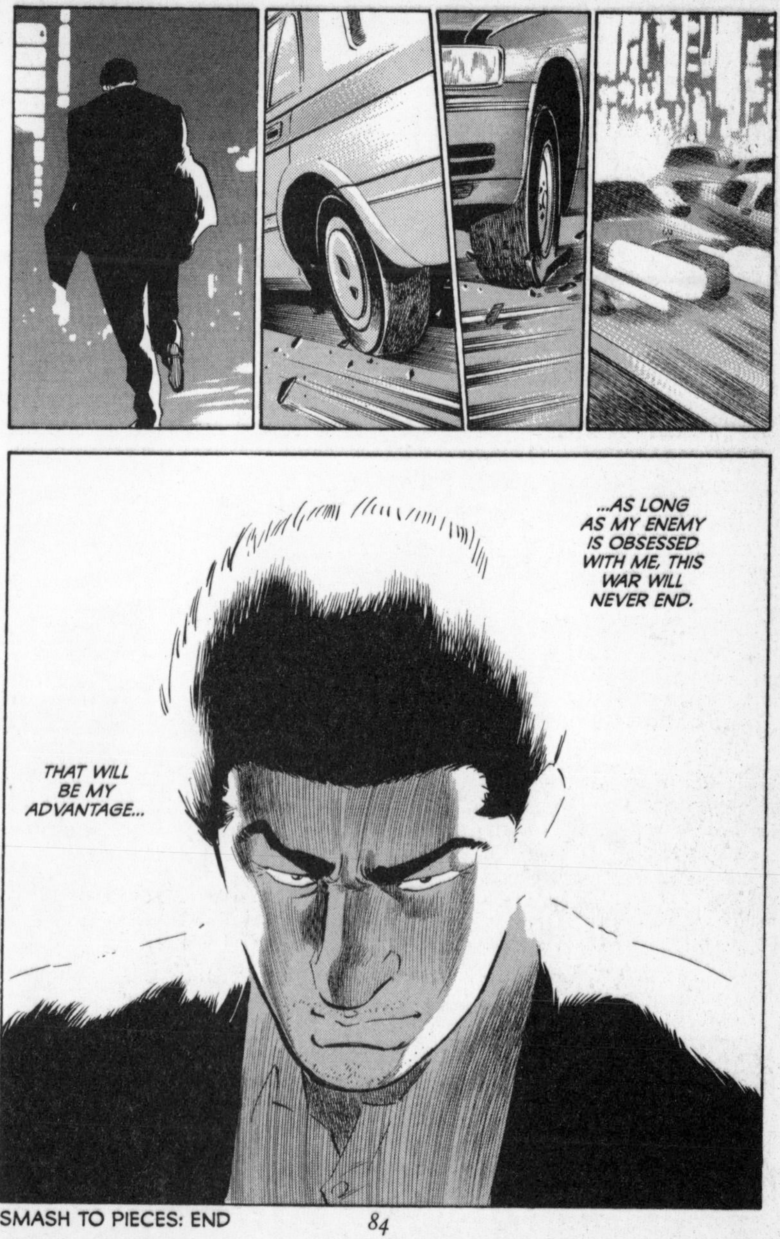
THAT WILL BE MY ADVANTAGE...
...AS LONG AS MY ENEMY IS OBSESSED WITH ME, THIS WAR WILL NEVER END.

SMASH TO PIECES: END

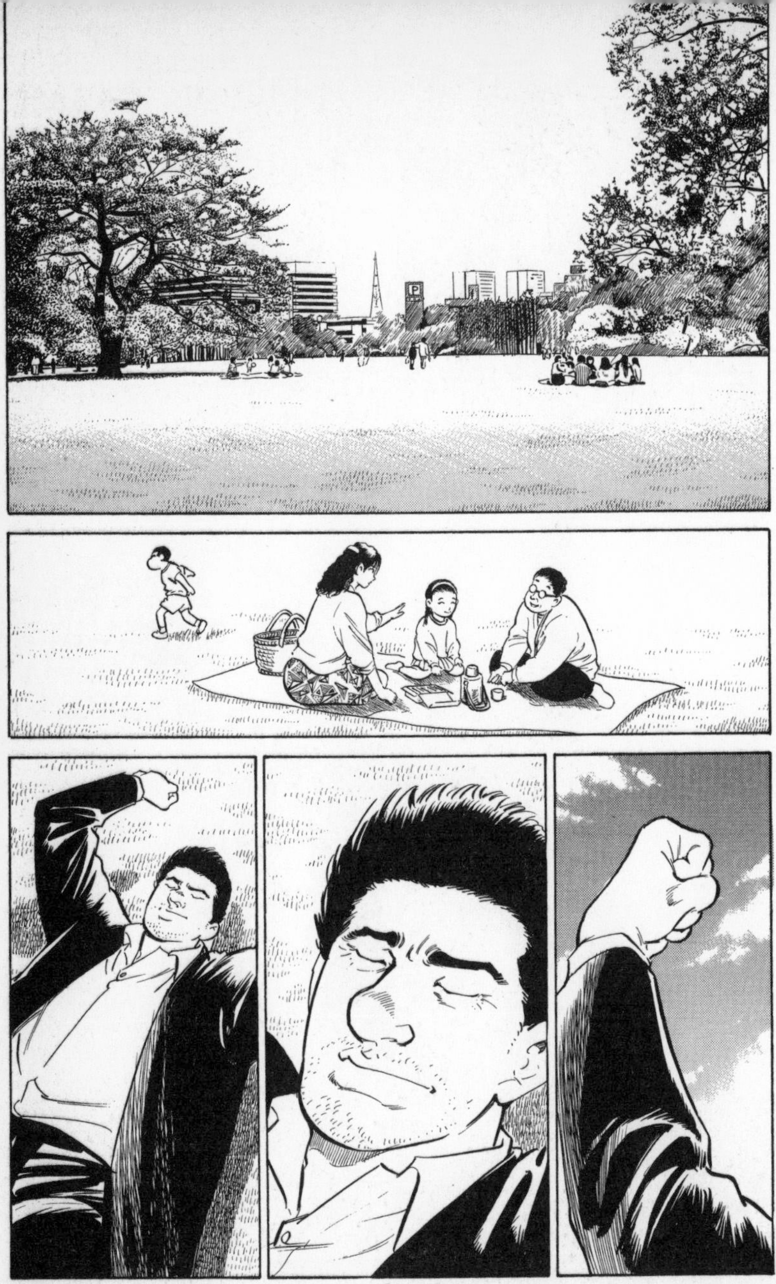

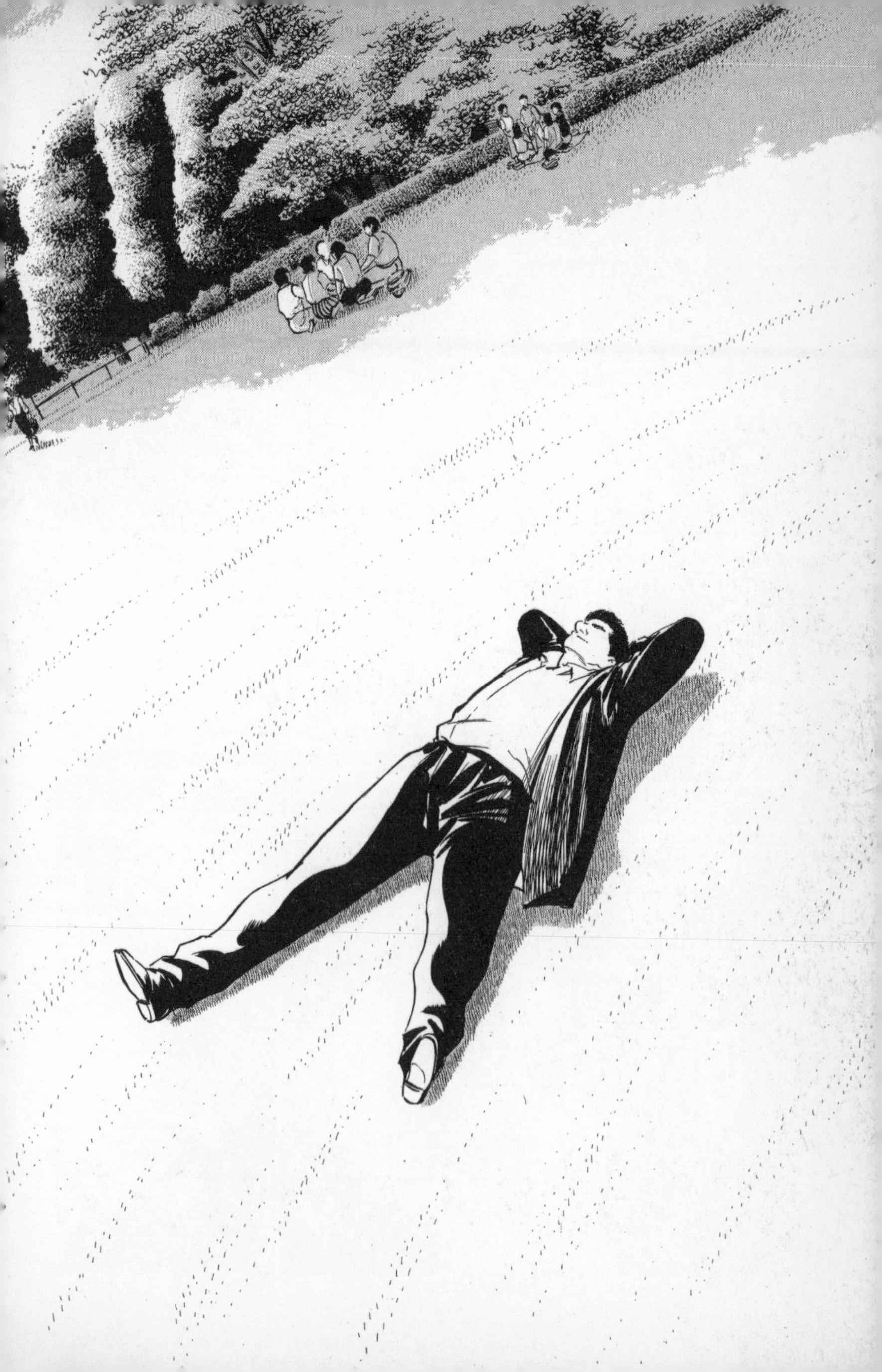

CHAPTER 24
SPARRING

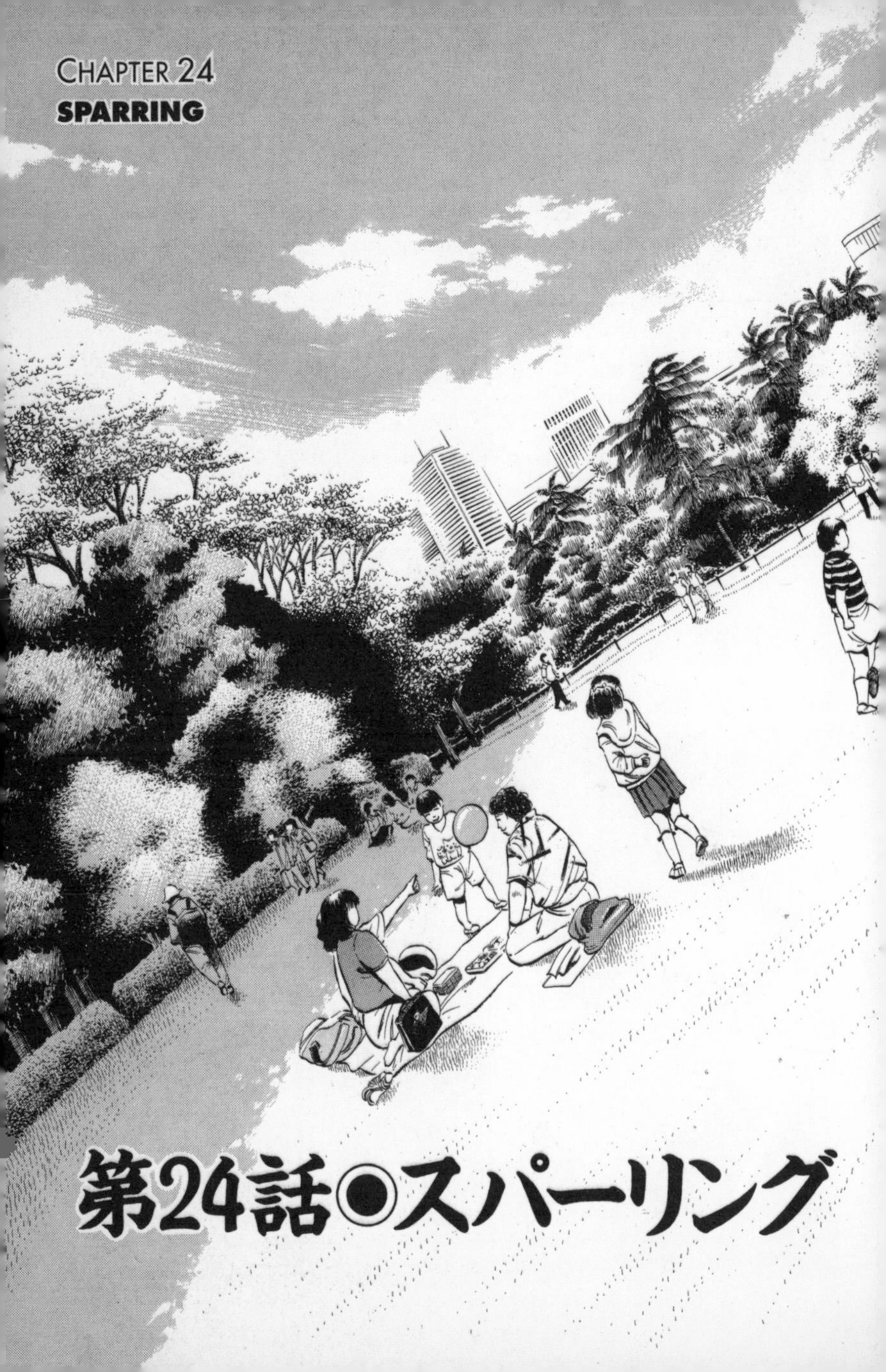

第24話◎スパーリング

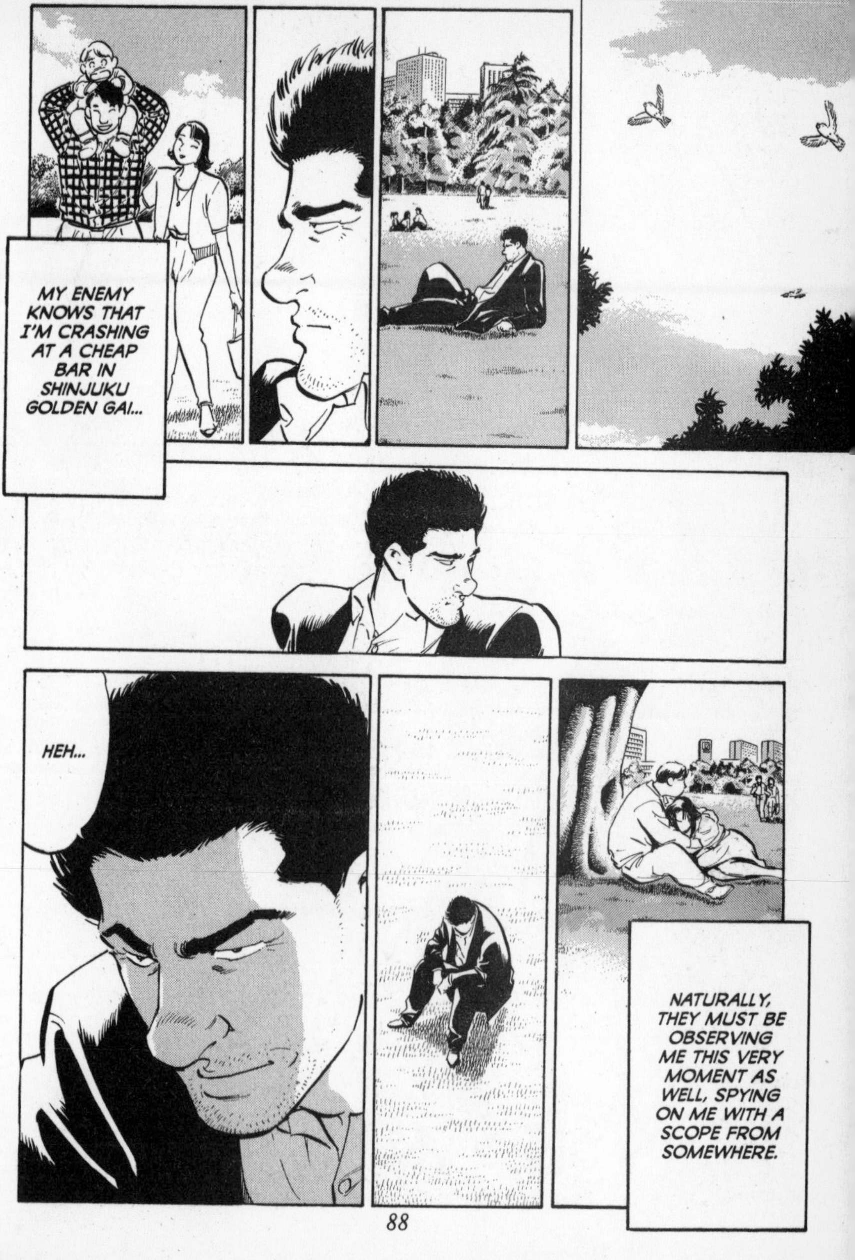
MY ENEMY KNOWS THAT I'M CRASHING AT A CHEAP BAR IN SHINJUKU GOLDEN GAI...
NATURALLY, THEY MUST BE OBSERVING ME THIS VERY MOMENT AS WELL, SPYING ON ME WITH A SCOPE FROM SOMEWHERE.
HEH...

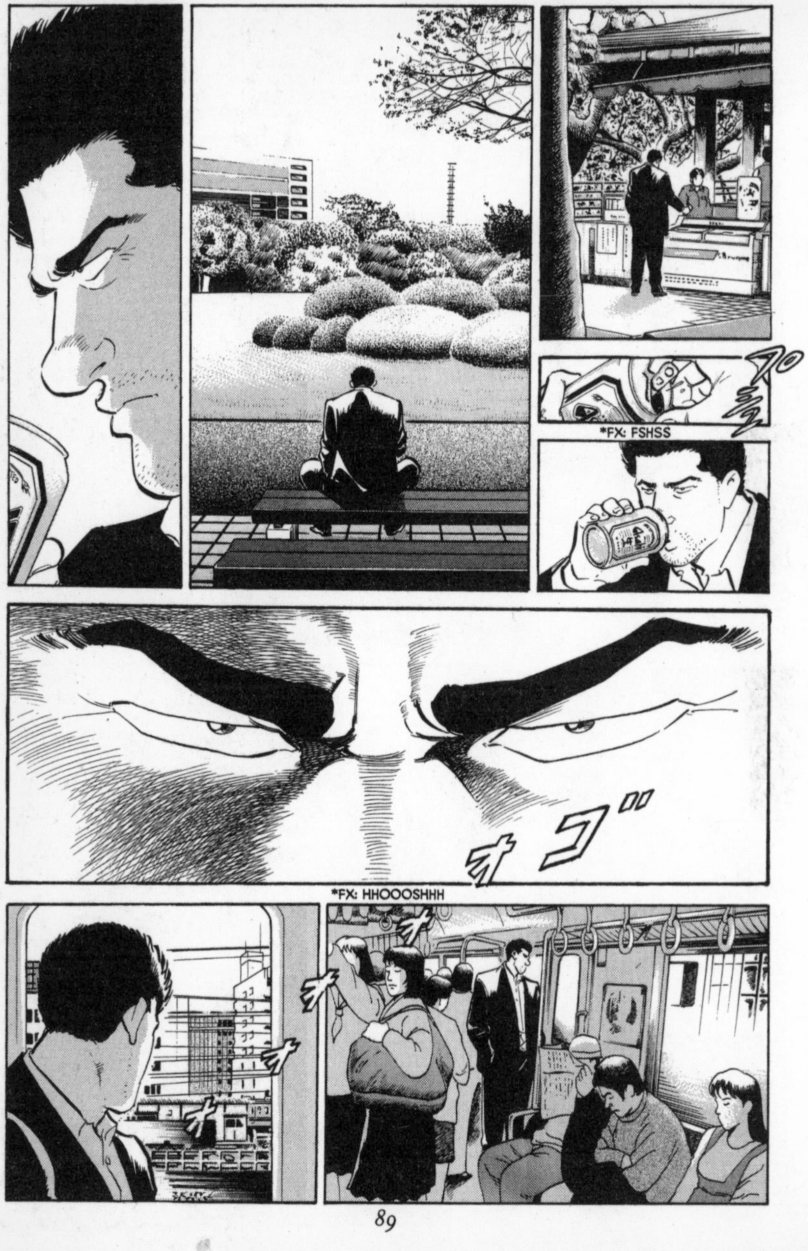
*FX: FSHSS
*FX: HHOOOSHHH

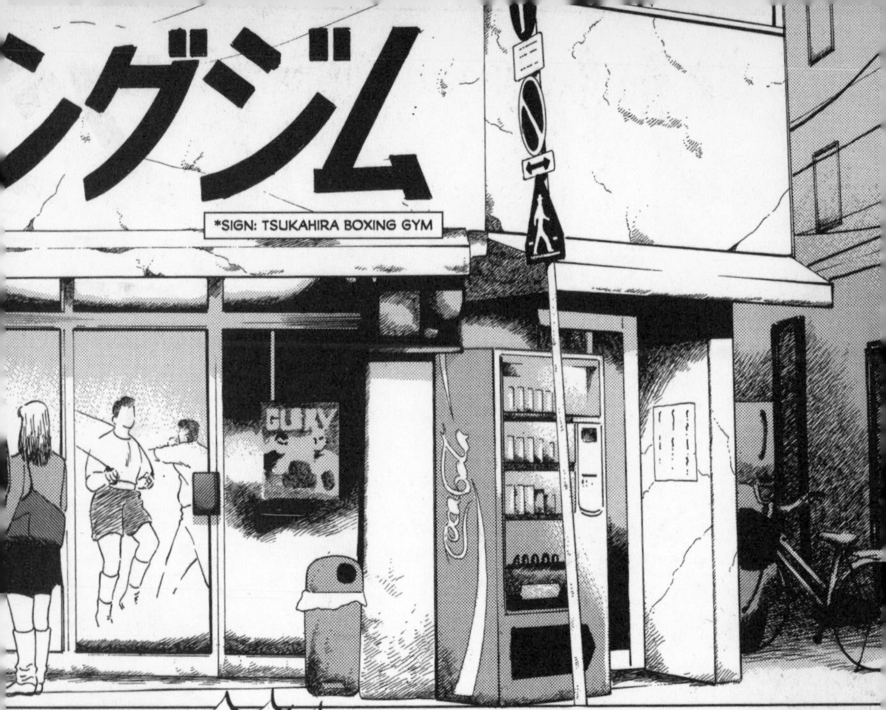
ングジム
*SIGN: TSUKAHIRA BOXING GYM

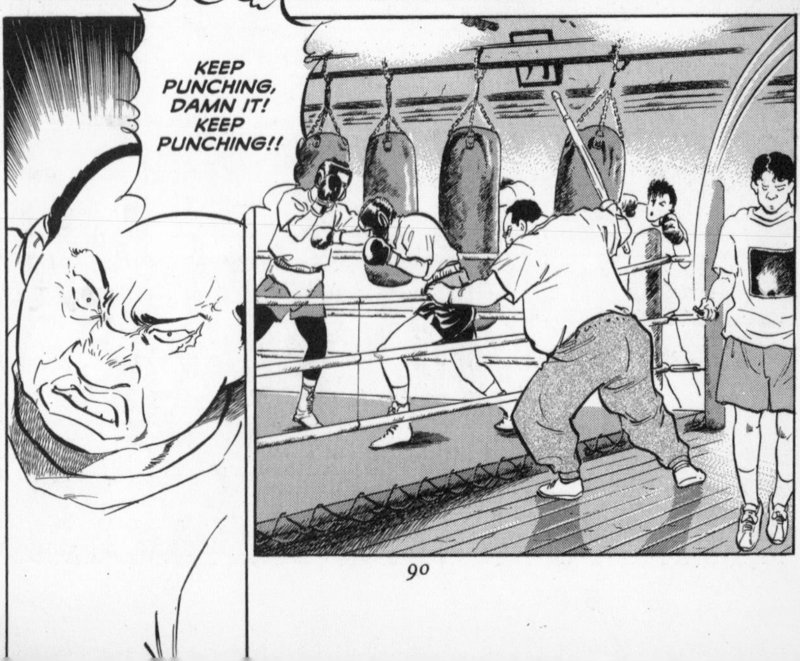
KEEP PUNCHING, DAMN IT! KEEP PUNCHING!!

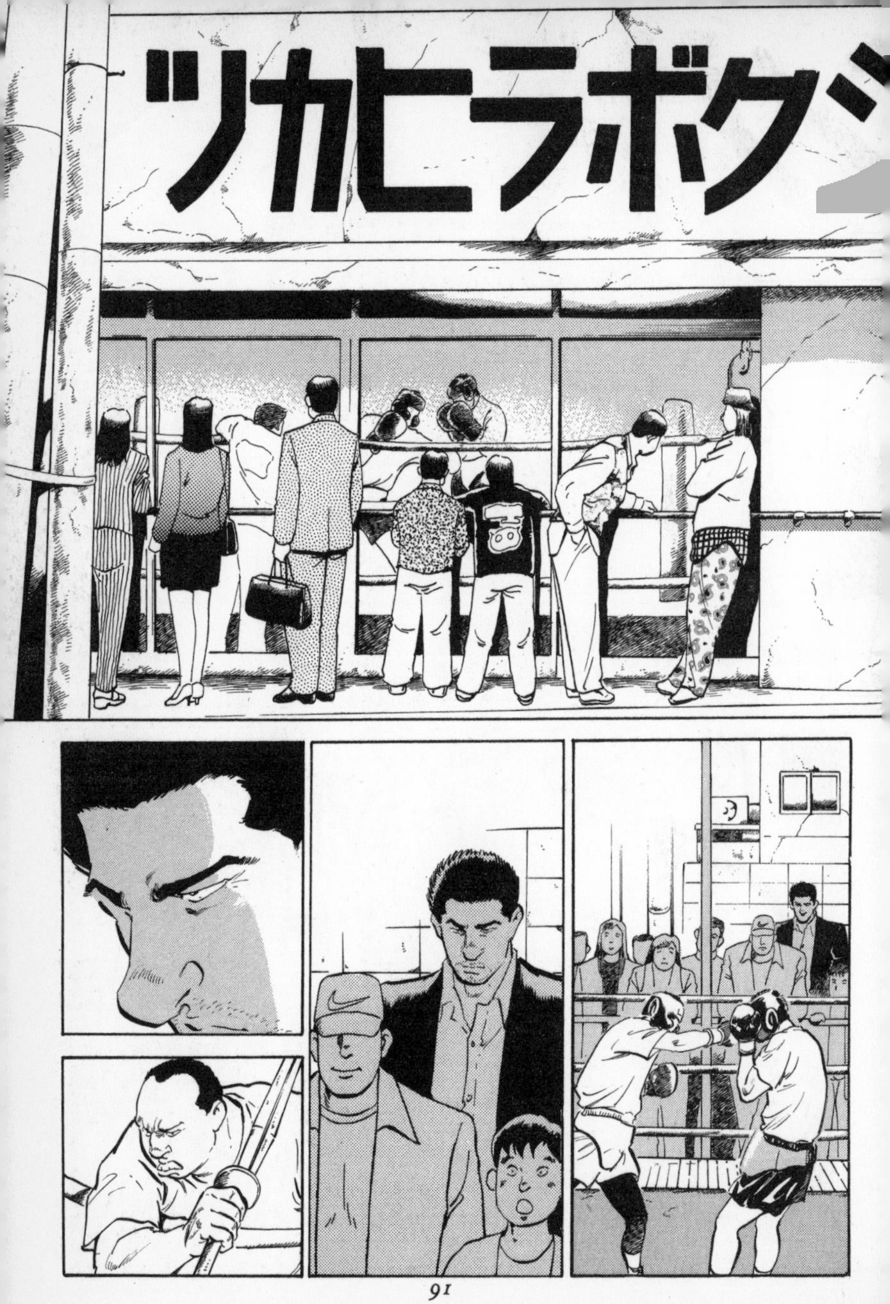
ツカヒラボク

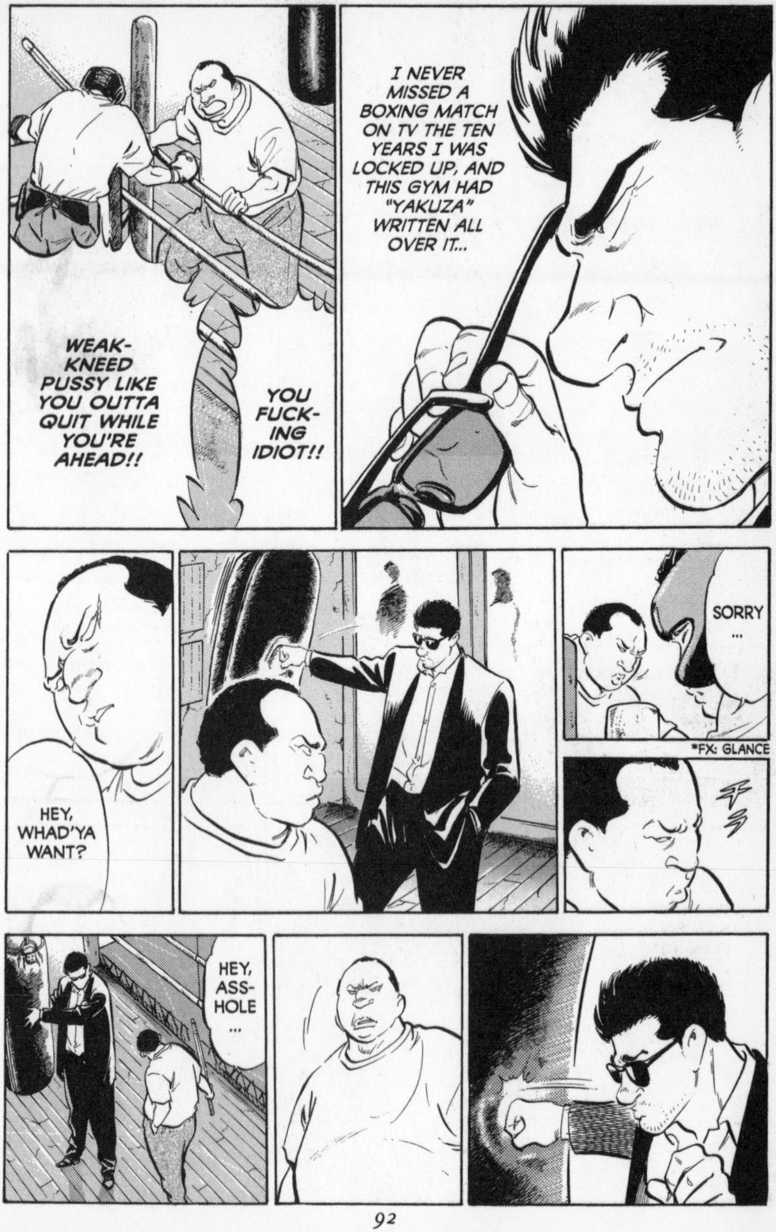
I NEVER MISSED A BOXING MATCH ON TV THE TEN YEARS I WAS LOCKED UP, AND THIS GYM HAD "YAKUZA" WRITTEN ALL OVER IT...
YOU FUCK-ING IDIOT!!
WEAK-KNEED PUSSY LIKE YOU OUTTA QUIT WHILE YOU'RE AHEAD!!
SORRY ...
*FX: GLANCE
チラ
HEY, WHAD'YA WANT?
HEY, ASS-HOLE ...

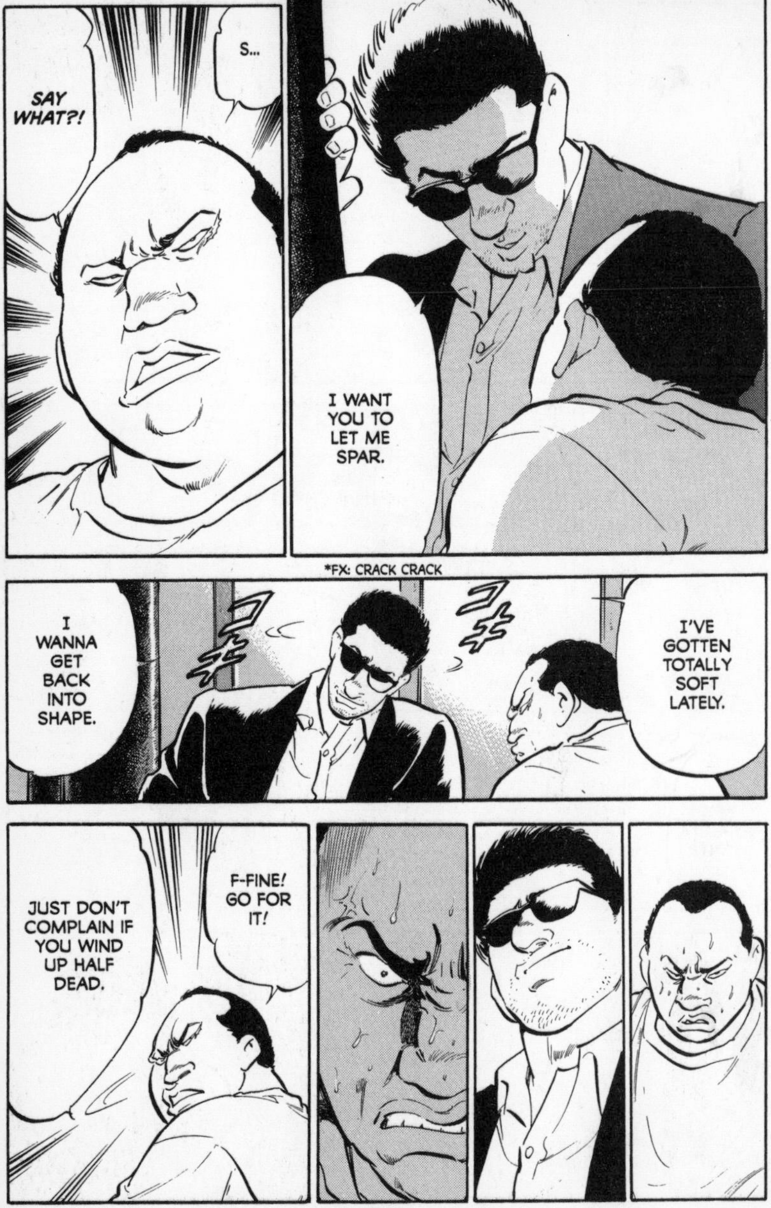
I WANT YOU TO LET ME SPAR.
S...
SAY WHAT?!
*FX: CRACK CRACK
I'VE GOTTEN TOTALLY SOFT LATELY.
I WANNA GET BACK INTO SHAPE.
F-FINE! GO FOR IT!
JUST DON'T COMPLAIN IF YOU WIND UP HALF DEAD.

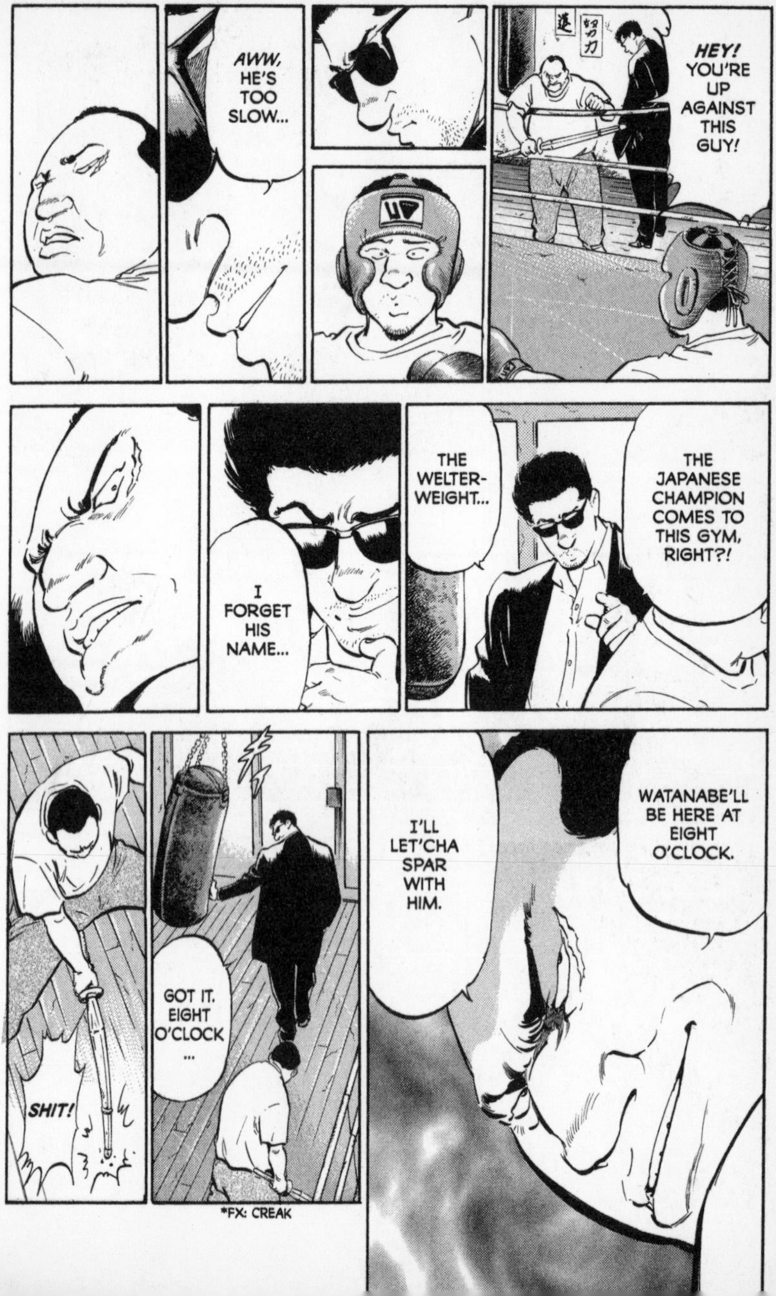
HEY! YOU'RE UP AGAINST THIS GUY!
AWW, HE'S TOO SLOW...
THE JAPANESE CHAMPION COMES TO THIS GYM, RIGHT?!
THE WELTER-WEIGHT...
I FORGET HIS NAME...
WATANABE'LL BE HERE AT EIGHT O'CLOCK.
I'LL LET'CHA SPAR WITH HIM.
GOT IT. EIGHT O'CLOCK ...
SHIT!
*FX: CREAK

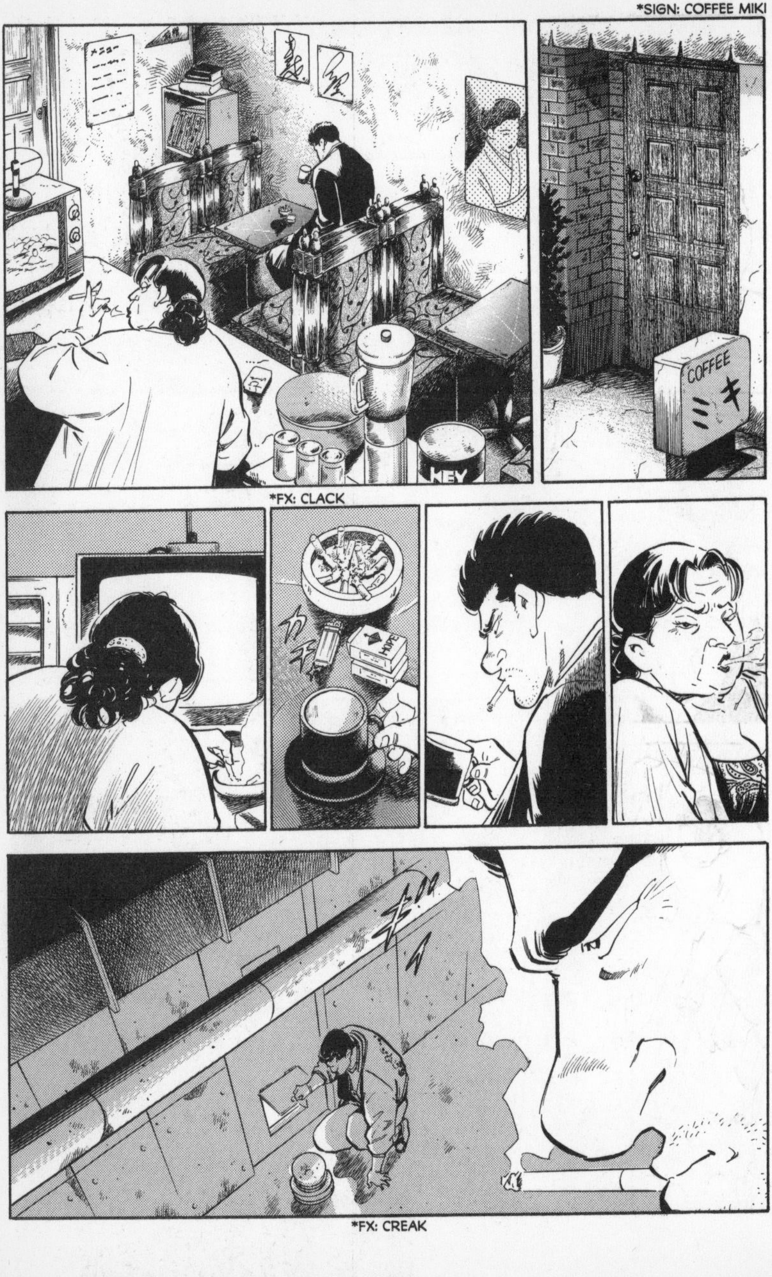
*SIGN: COFFEE MIKI
COFFEE
ミキ
KEY
*FX: CLACK
HOPE
*FX: CREAK

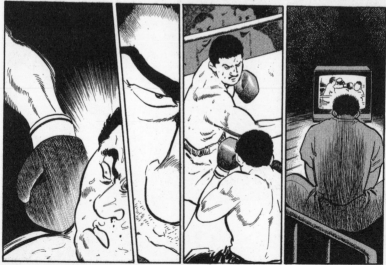

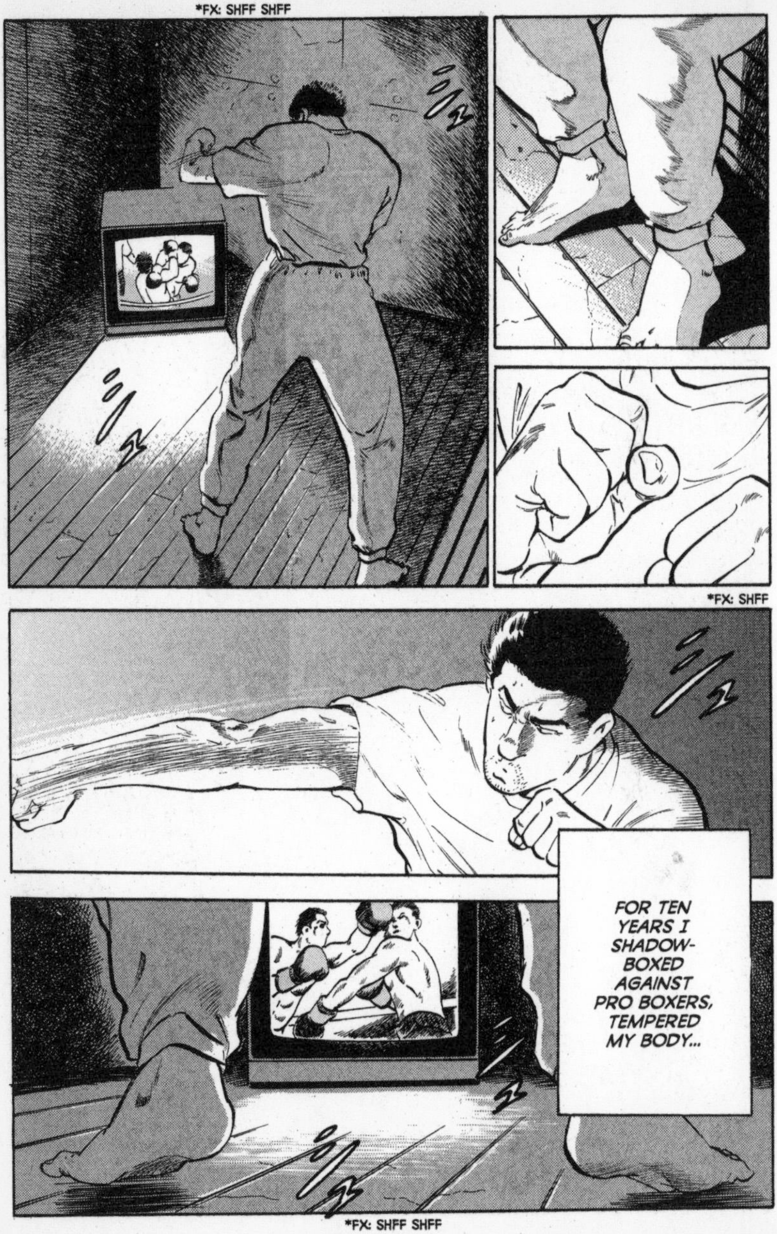
*FX: SHFF SHFF
*FX: SHFF
FOR TEN YEARS I SHADOW-BOXED AGAINST PRO BOXERS, TEMPERED MY BODY...
*FX: SHFF SHFF

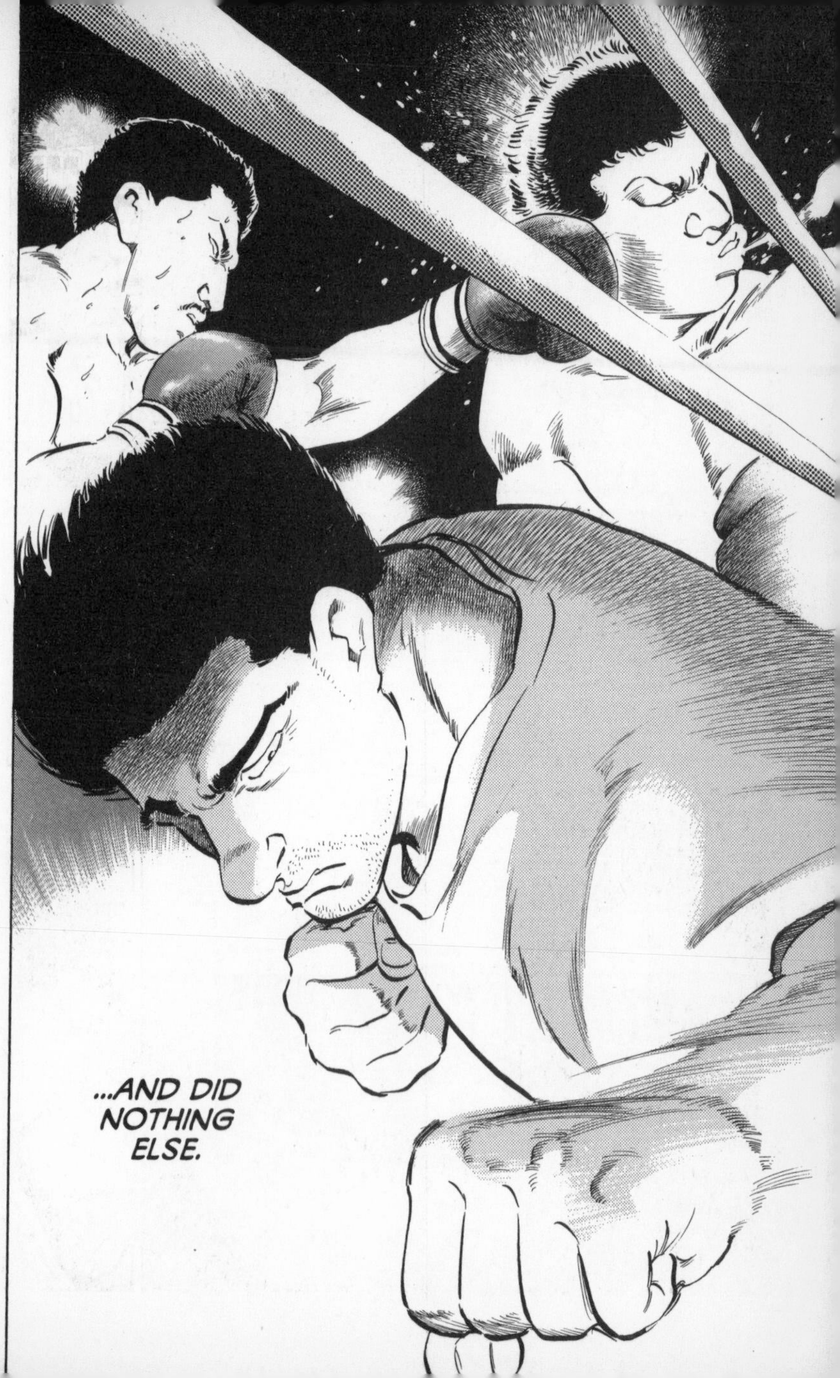
...AND DID NOTHING ELSE.

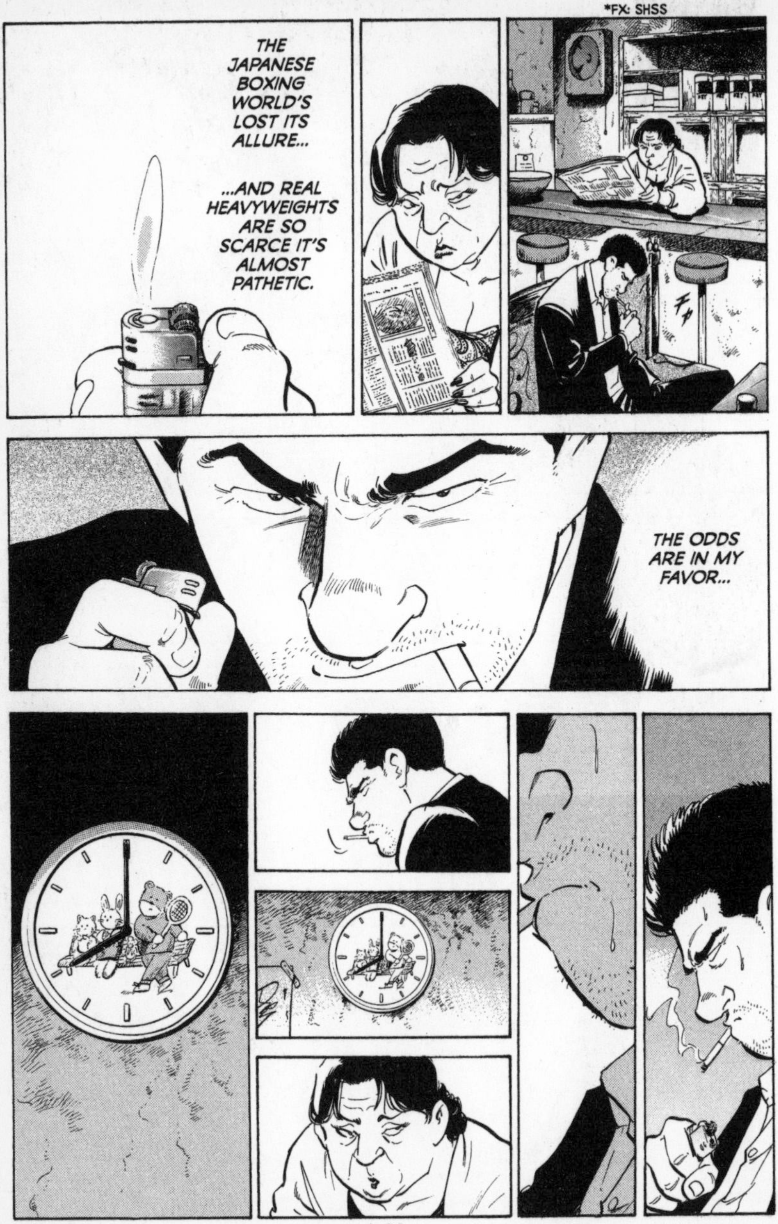
*FX: SHSS
THE JAPANESE BOXING WORLD'S LOST ITS ALLURE...
...AND REAL HEAVYWEIGHTS ARE SO SCARCE IT'S ALMOST PATHETIC.
THE ODDS ARE IN MY FAVOR...

*SIGN: TSUKAHIRA BOXING GYM

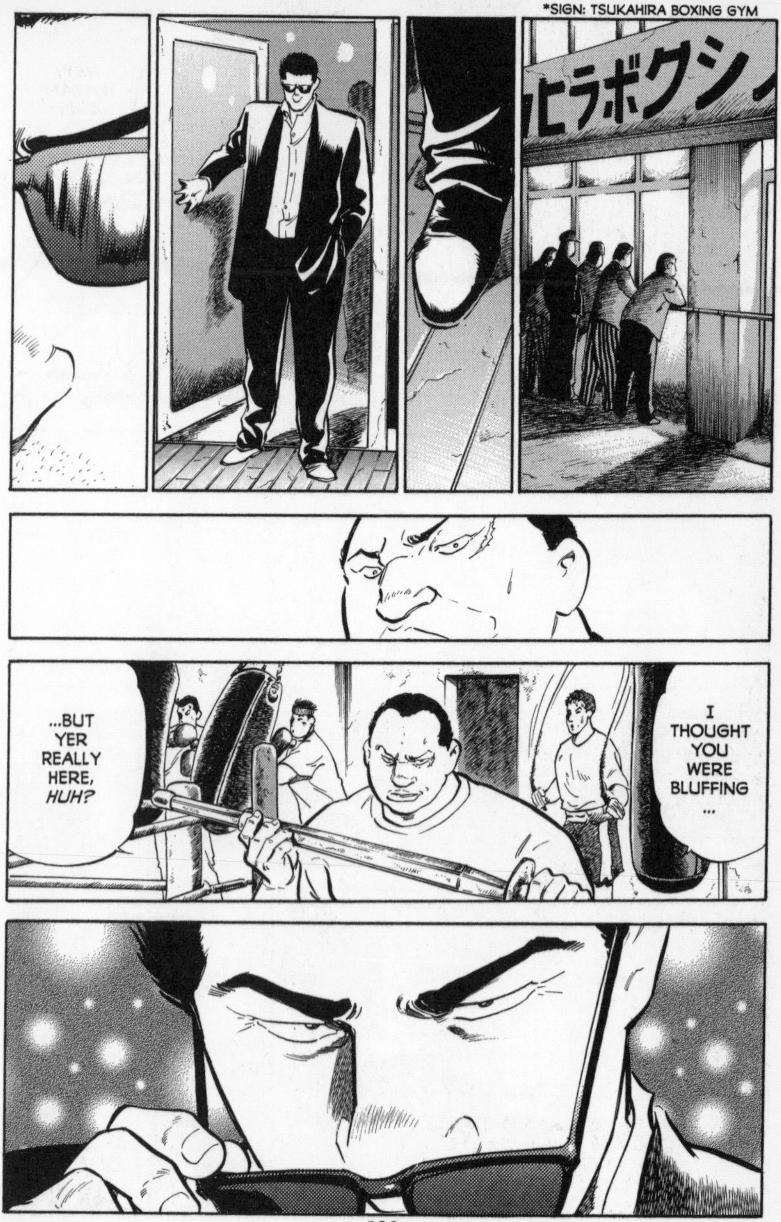
ヒラボクシ
I THOUGHT YOU WERE BLUFFING ...
...BUT YER REALLY HERE, *HUH?*

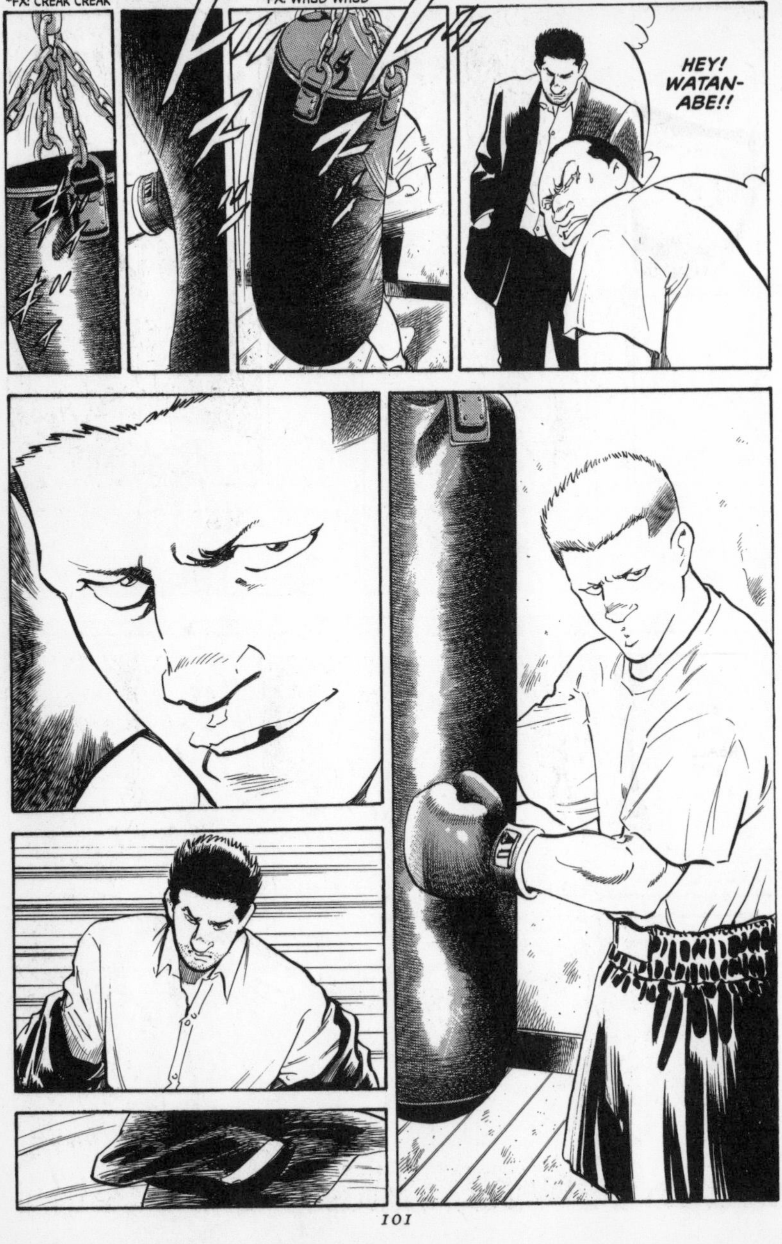
HEY! WATAN-ABE!!
*FX: WHUD WHUD
*FX: CREAK CREAK

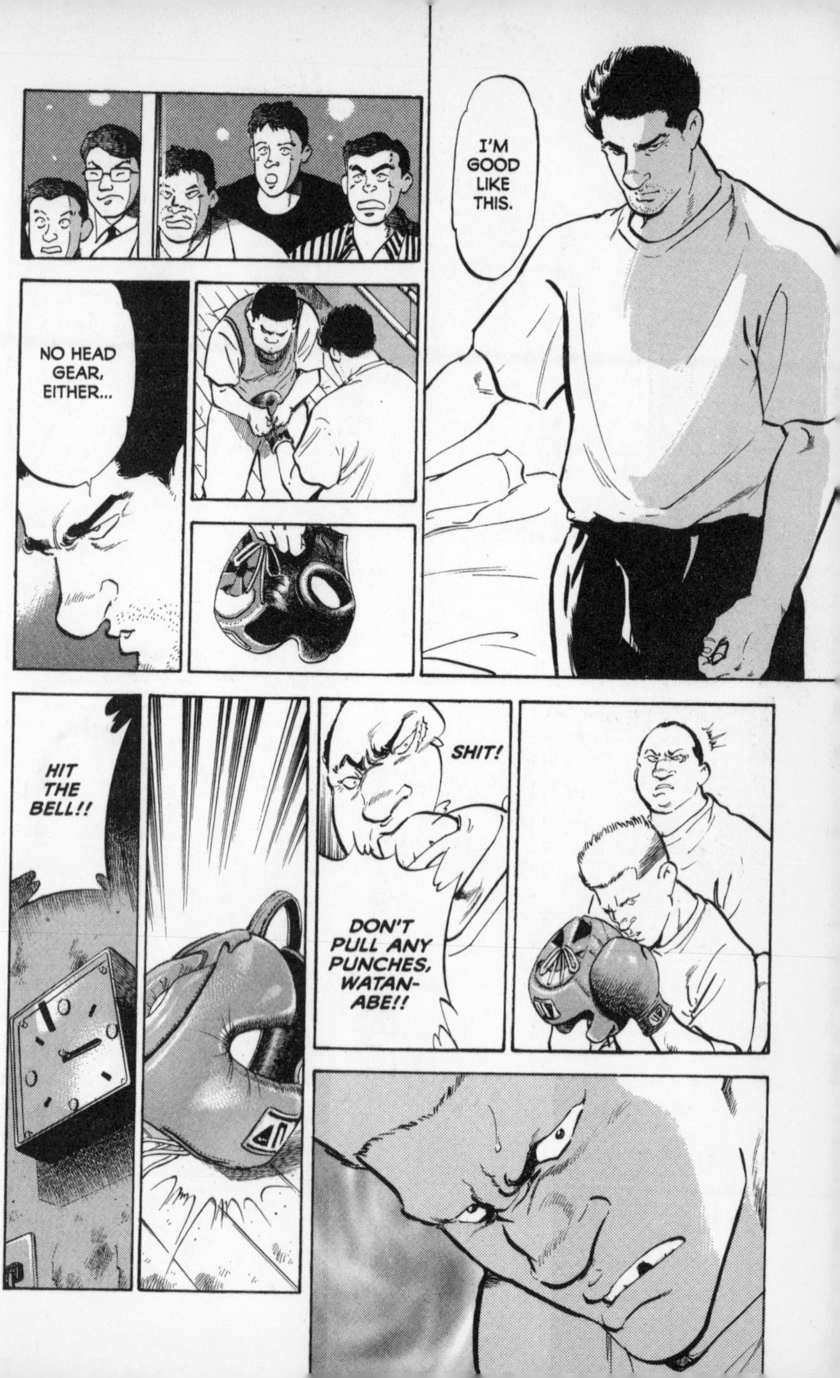
I'M GOOD LIKE THIS.
NO HEAD GEAR, EITHER...
SHIT!
DON'T PULL ANY PUNCHES, WATAN-ABE!!
HIT THE BELL!!

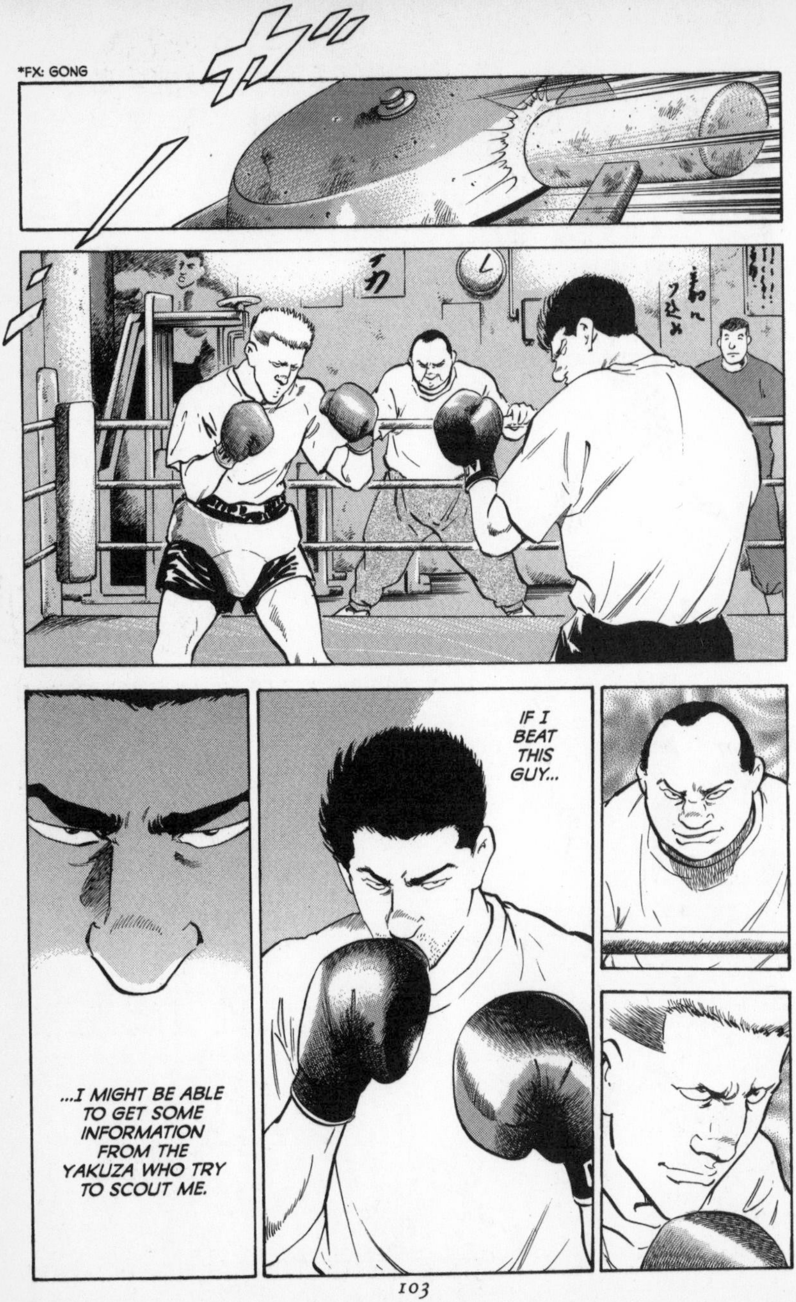
*FX: GONG
IF I BEAT THIS GUY...
...I MIGHT BE ABLE TO GET SOME INFORMATION FROM THE YAKUZA WHO TRY TO SCOUT ME.

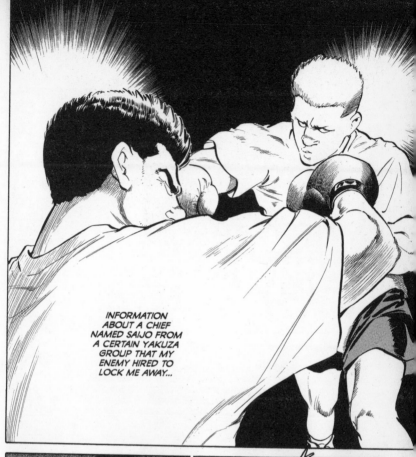

INFORMATION ABOUT A CHIEF NAMED SAIJO FROM A CERTAIN YAKUZA GROUP THAT MY ENEMY HIRED TO LOCK ME AWAY...

SPARRING: END

104

*FX: RRAAAHH!!

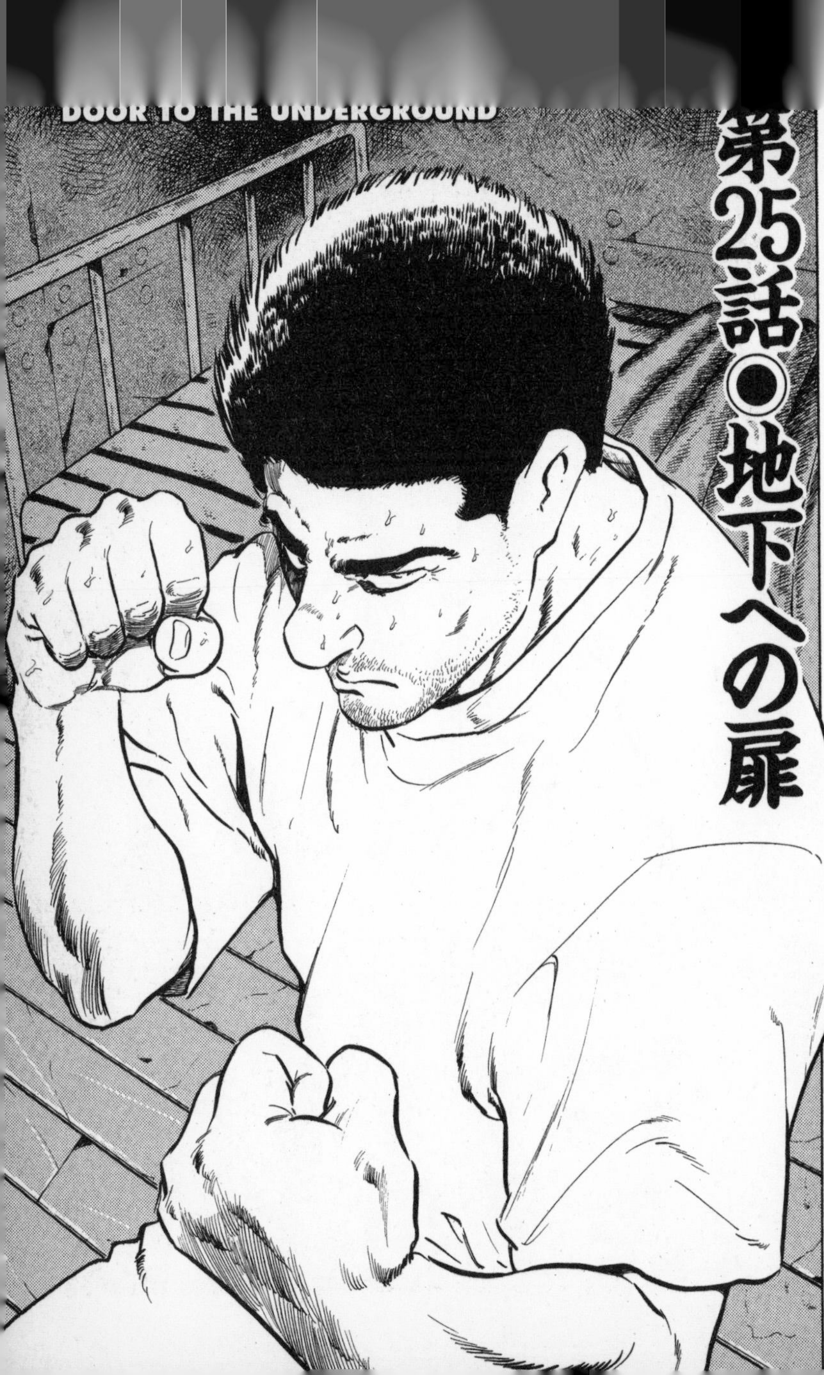
DOOR TO THE UNDERGROUND
第25話●地下への扉

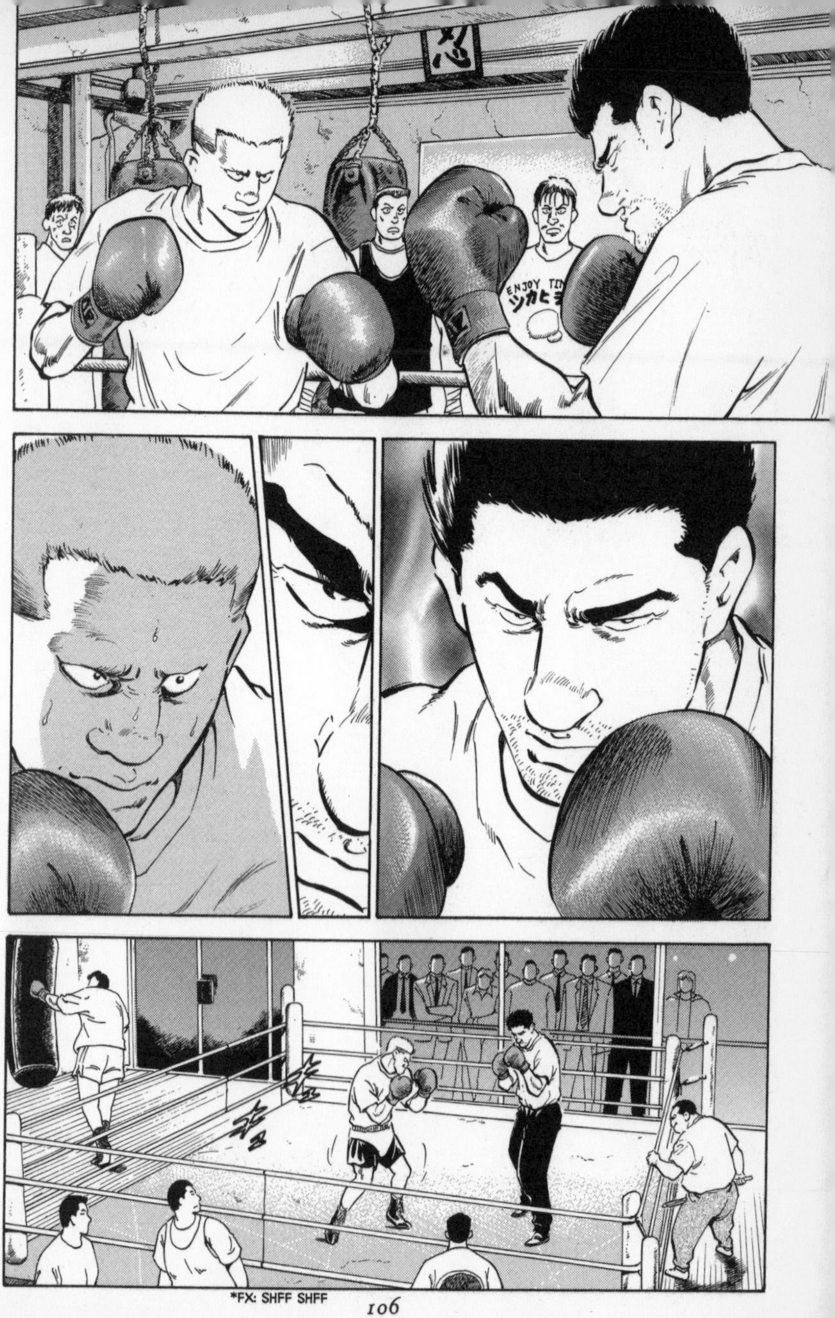

*FX: SHFF SHFF

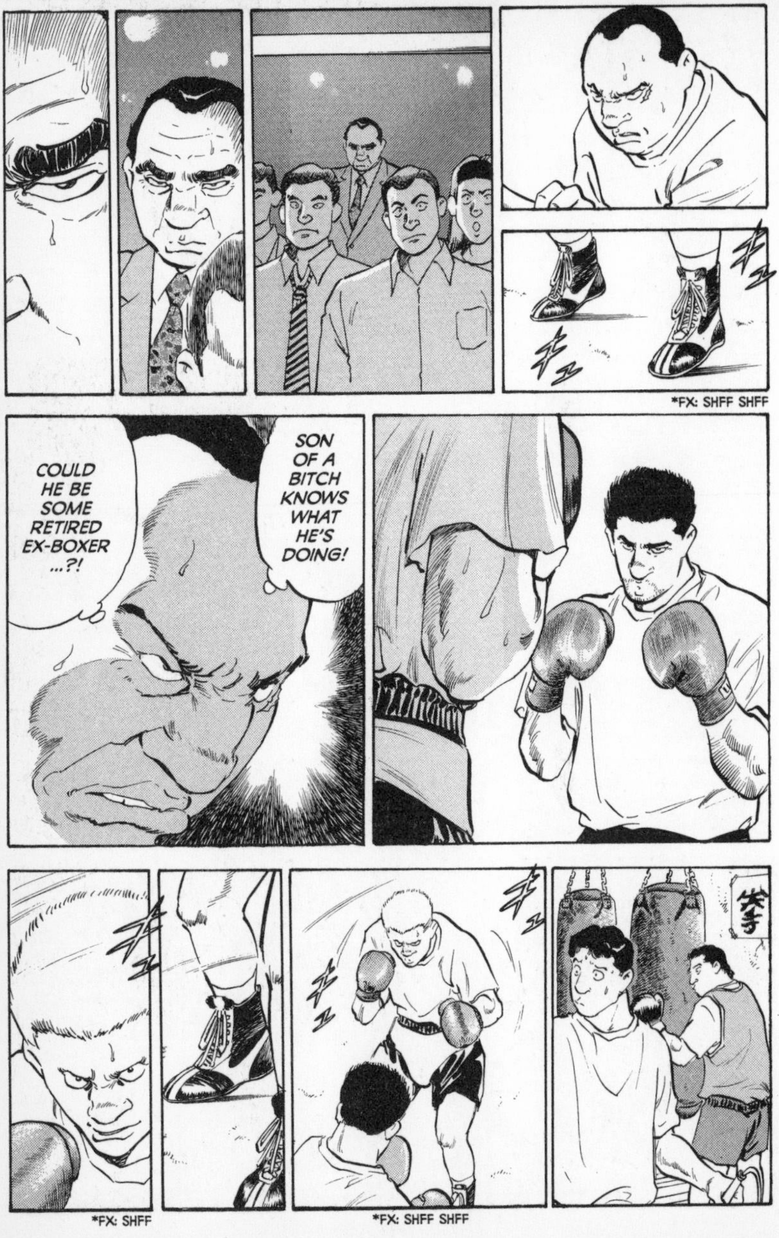
SON OF A BITCH KNOWS WHAT HE'S DOING!
COULD HE BE SOME RETIRED EX-BOXER ...?!
*FX: SHFF SHFF

*FX: SHFF

*FX: SHFF SHFF

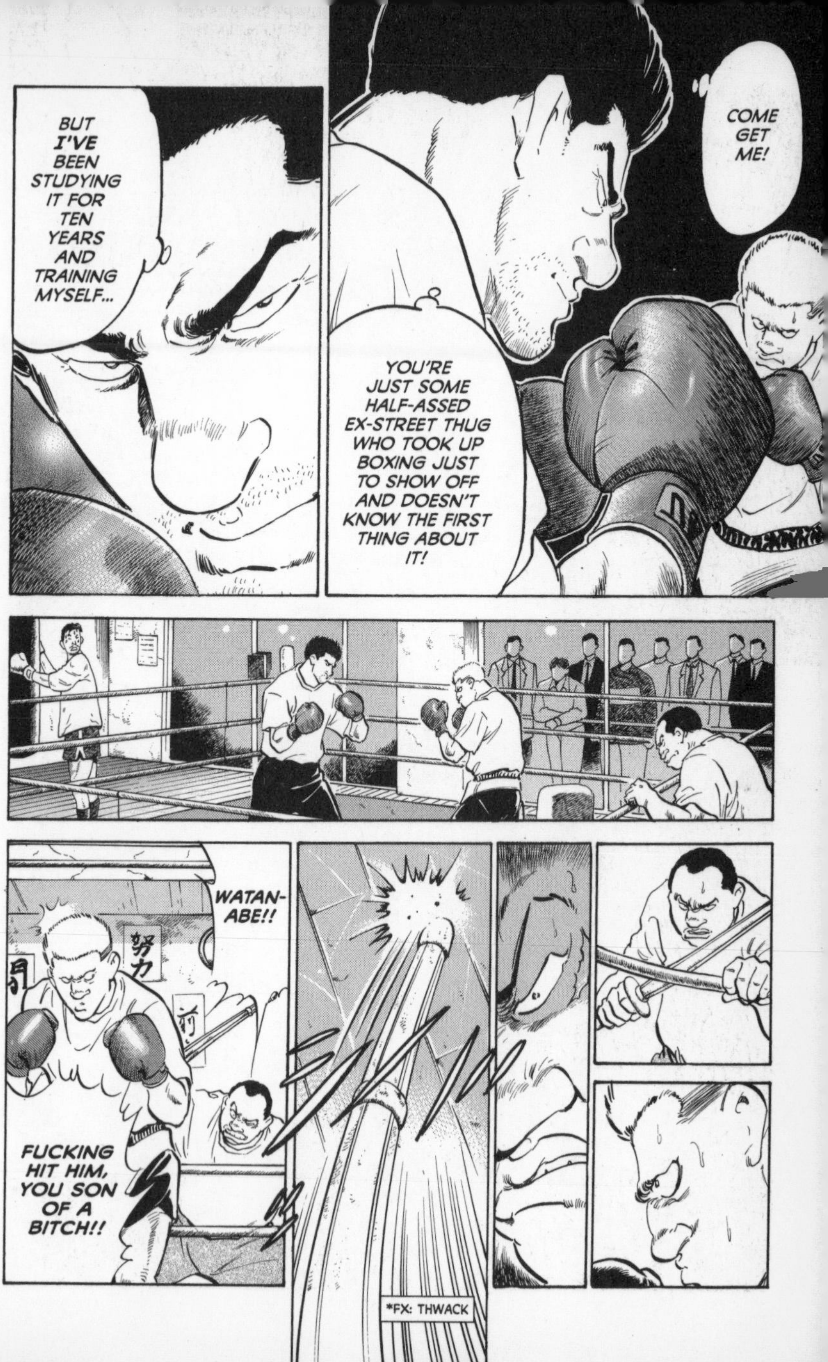
COME GET ME!
YOU'RE JUST SOME HALF-ASSED EX-STREET THUG WHO TOOK UP BOXING JUST TO SHOW OFF AND DOESN'T KNOW THE FIRST THING ABOUT IT!
BUT I'VE BEEN STUDYING IT FOR TEN YEARS AND TRAINING MYSELF...
*FX: THWACK
WATAN-ABE!!
FUCKING HIT HIM, YOU SON OF A BITCH!!

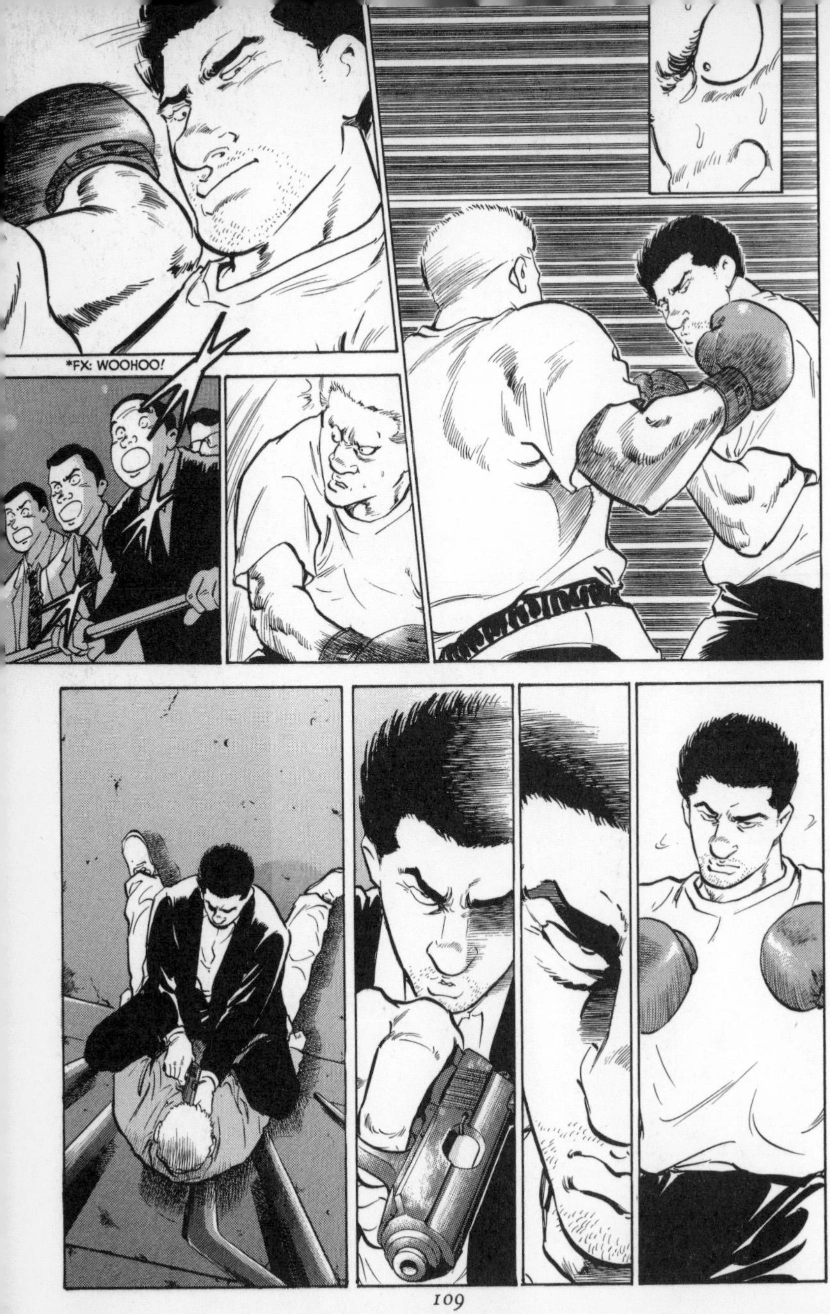
*FX: WOOHOO!

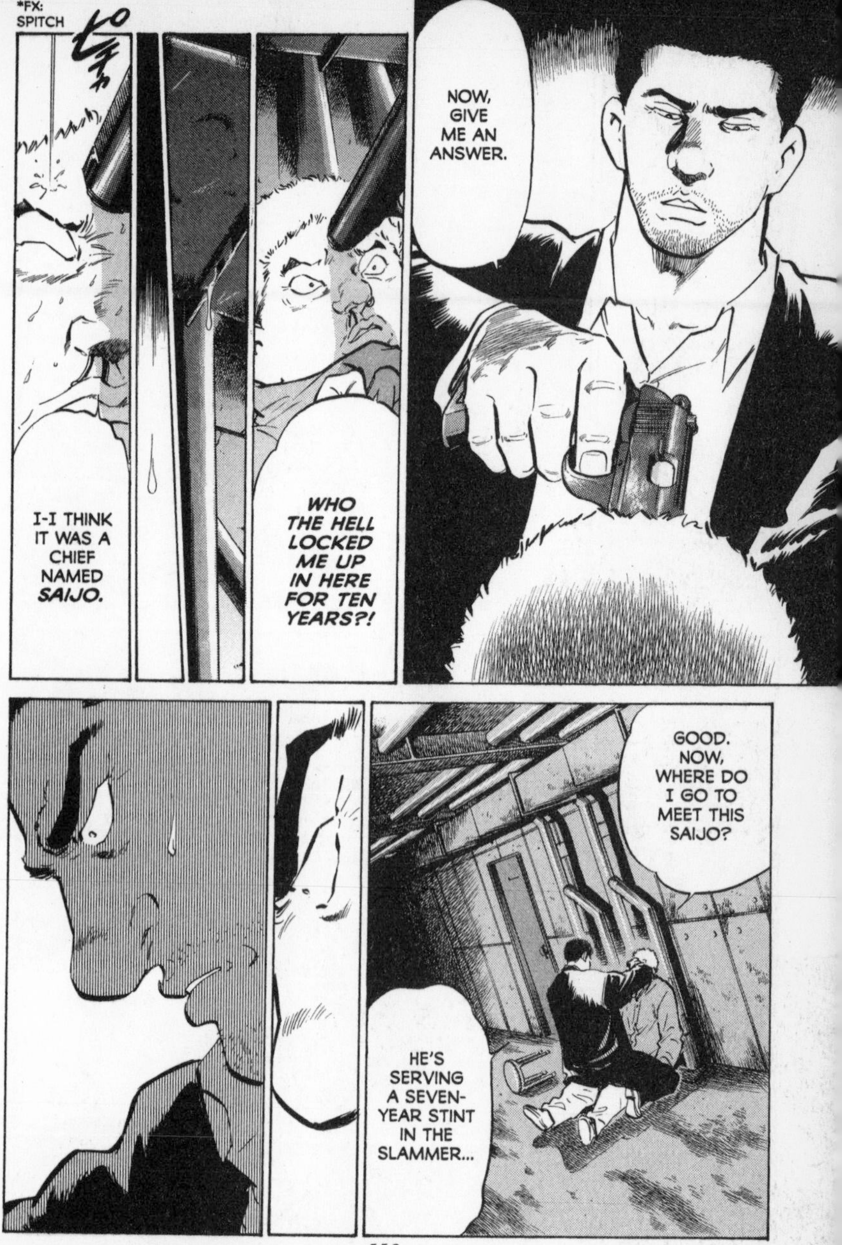
NOW, GIVE ME AN ANSWER.
WHO THE HELL LOCKED ME UP IN HERE FOR TEN YEARS?!
*FX: SPITCH
I-I THINK IT WAS A CHIEF NAMED SAIJO.
GOOD. NOW, WHERE DO I GO TO MEET THIS SAIJO?
HE'S SERVING A SEVEN-YEAR STINT IN THE SLAMMER...

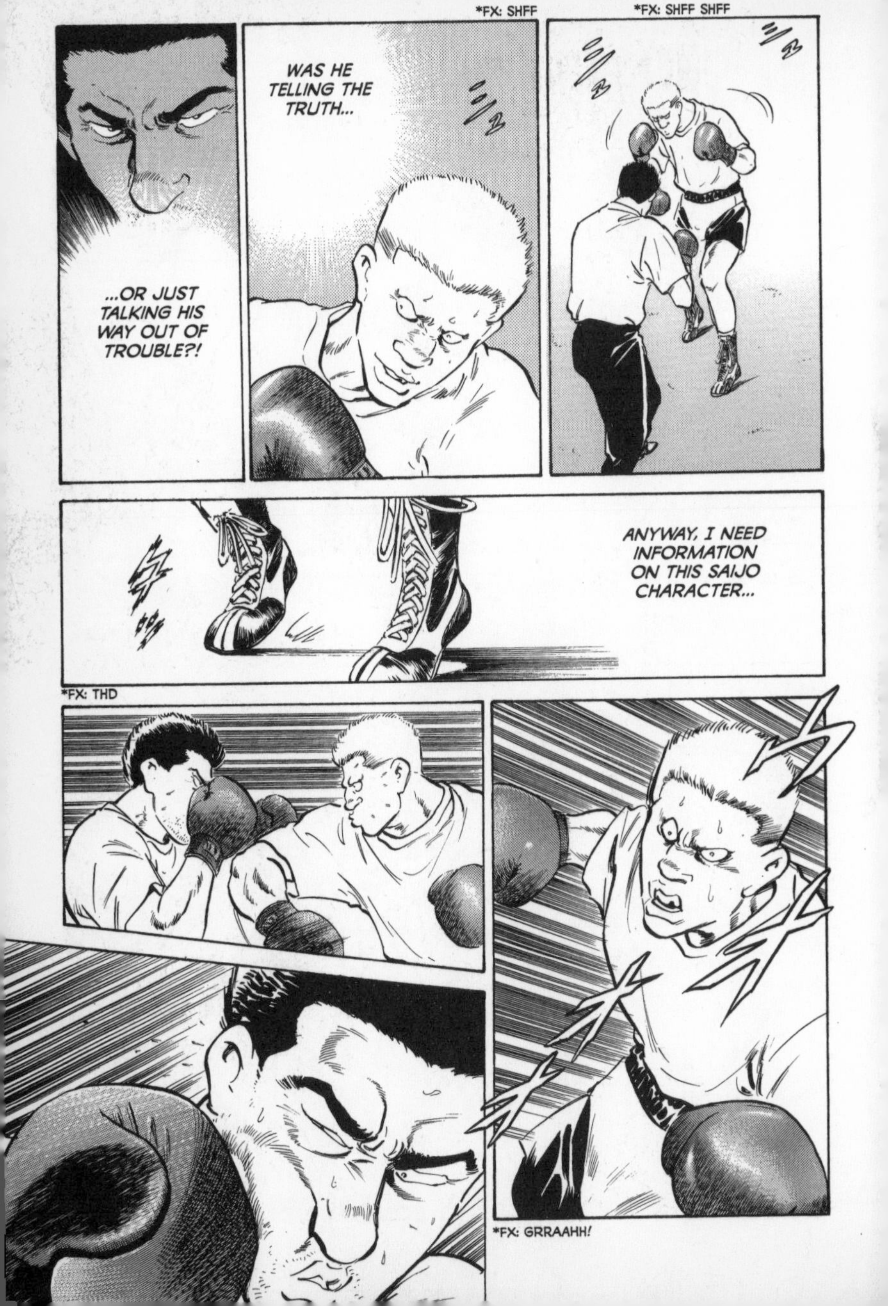
*FX: SHFF SHFF
*FX: SHFF
WAS HE TELLING THE TRUTH...
...OR JUST TALKING HIS WAY OUT OF TROUBLE?!
ANYWAY, I NEED INFORMATION ON THIS SAIJO CHARACTER...
*FX: THD
*FX: GRRAAHH!

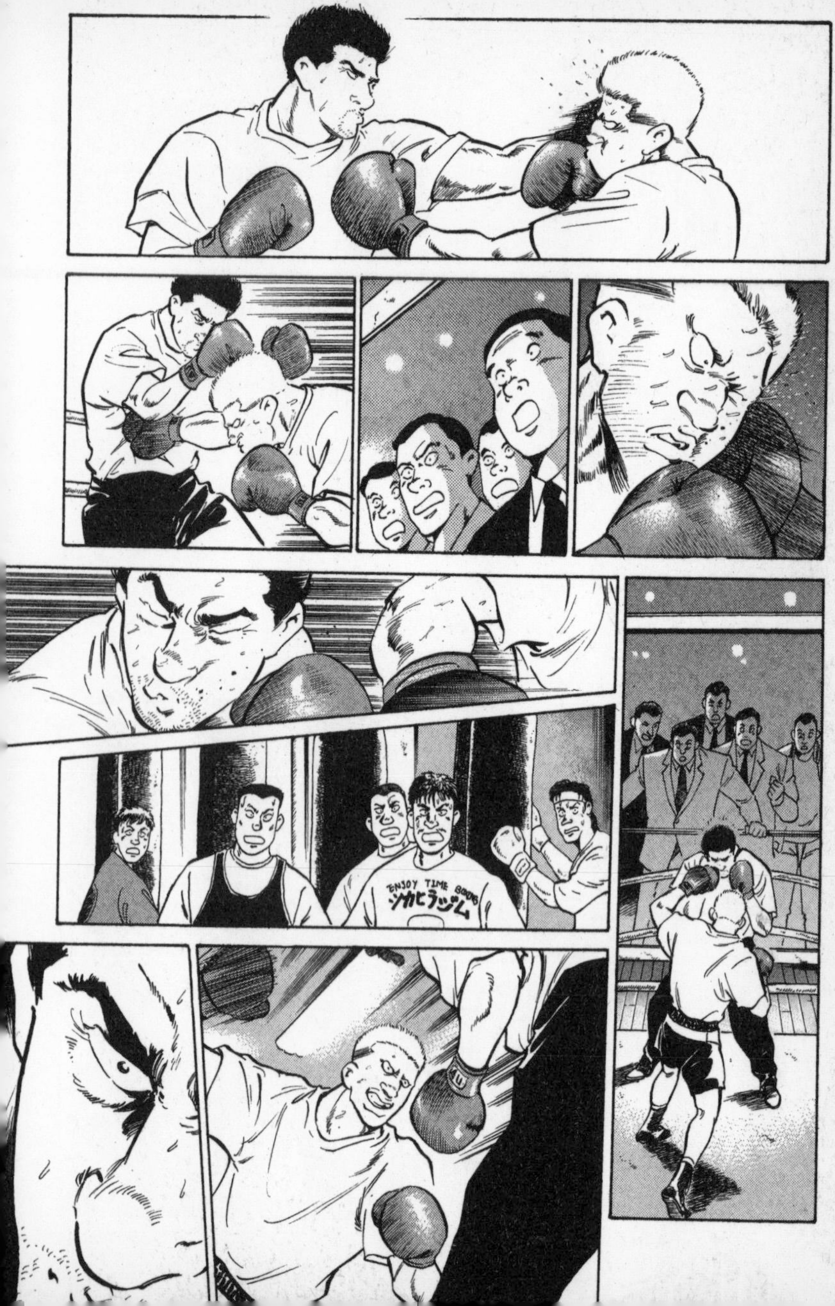
ENJOY TIME BOXING
ツカヒラジム

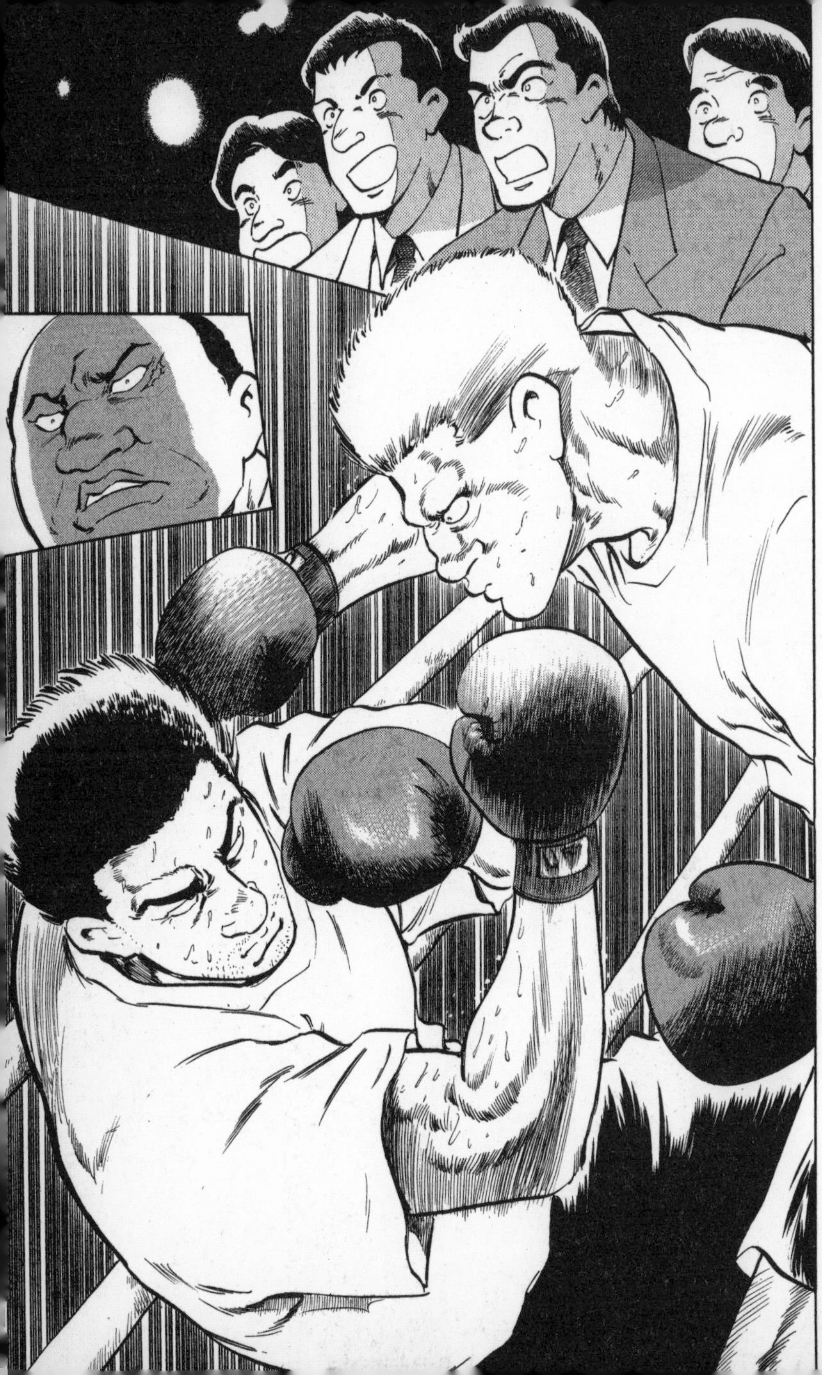

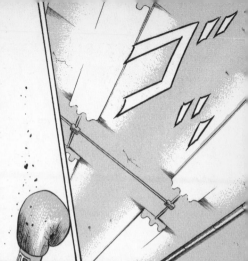

*FX: WHUD

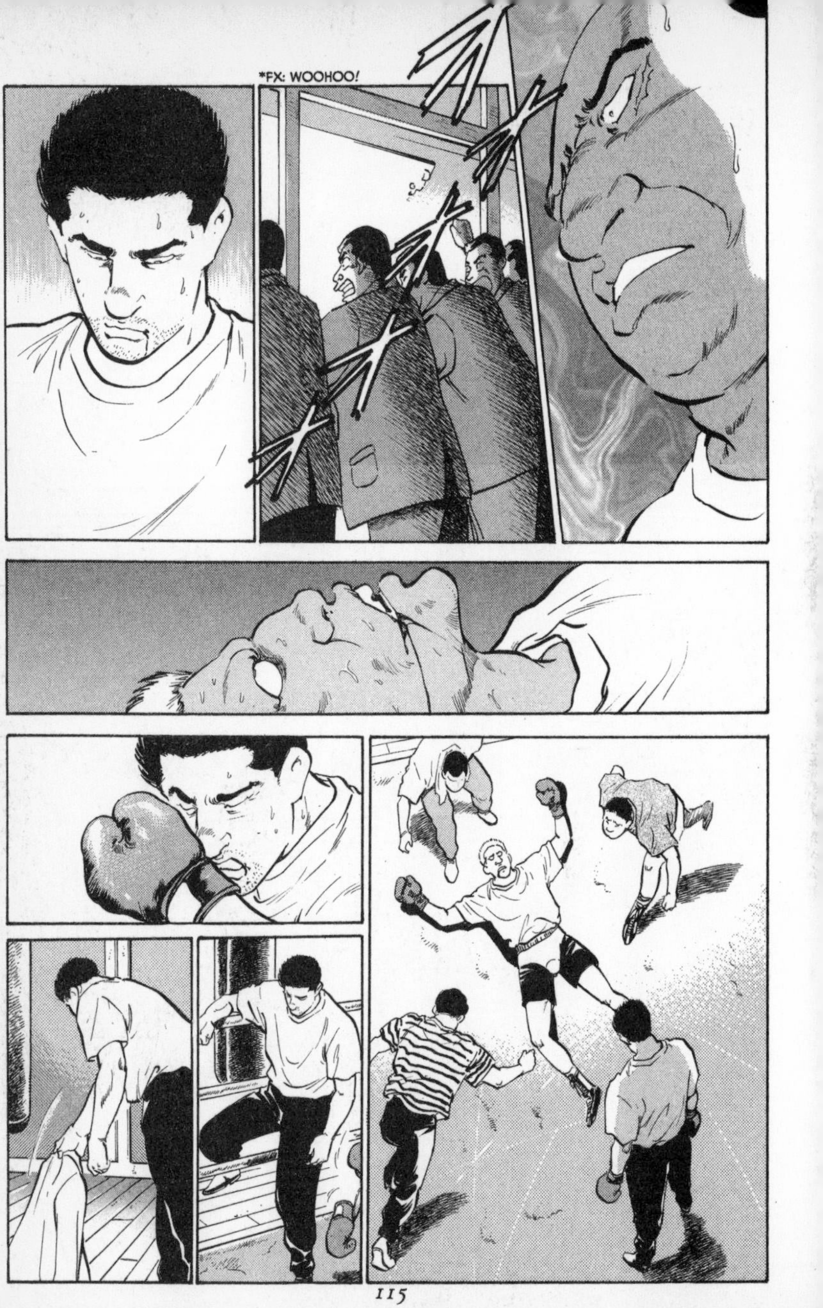
*FX: WOOHOO!

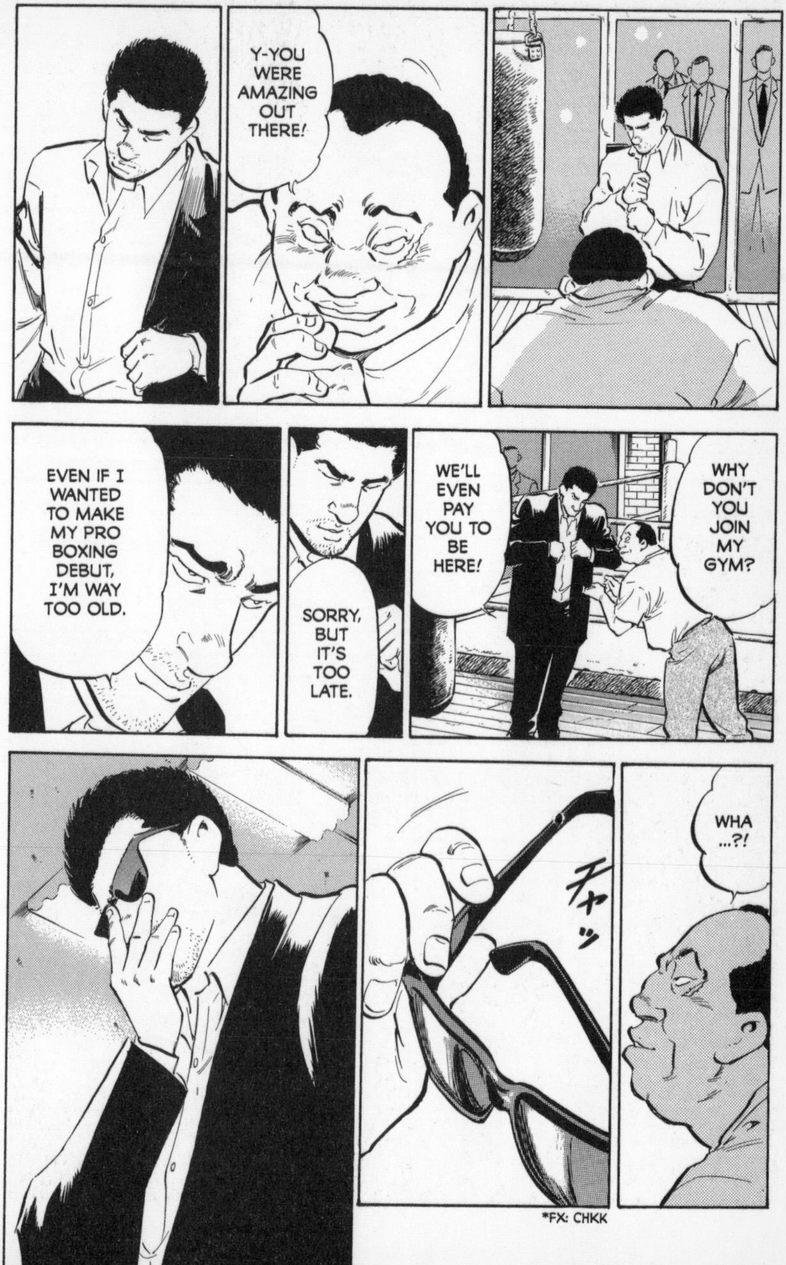
Y-YOU WERE AMAZING OUT THERE!
WHY DON'T YOU JOIN MY GYM?
WE'LL EVEN PAY YOU TO BE HERE!
SORRY, BUT IT'S TOO LATE.
EVEN IF I WANTED TO MAKE MY PRO BOXING DEBUT, I'M WAY TOO OLD.
WHA ...?!
チャッ
*FX: CHKK

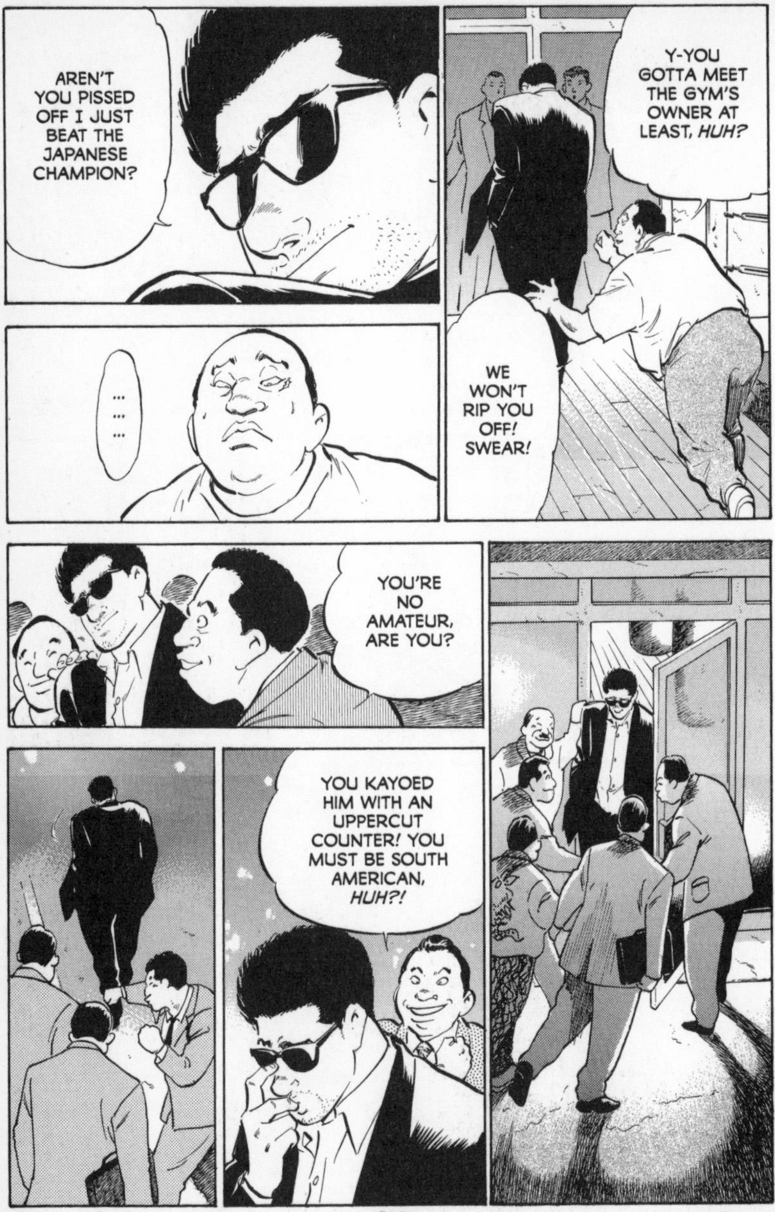
Y-YOU GOTTA MEET THE GYM'S OWNER AT LEAST, *HUH?*
WE WON'T RIP YOU OFF! SWEAR!
AREN'T YOU PISSED OFF I JUST BEAT THE JAPANESE CHAMPION?
......
YOU'RE NO AMATEUR, ARE YOU?
YOU KAYOED HIM WITH AN UPPERCUT COUNTER! YOU MUST BE SOUTH AMERICAN, *HUH?!*

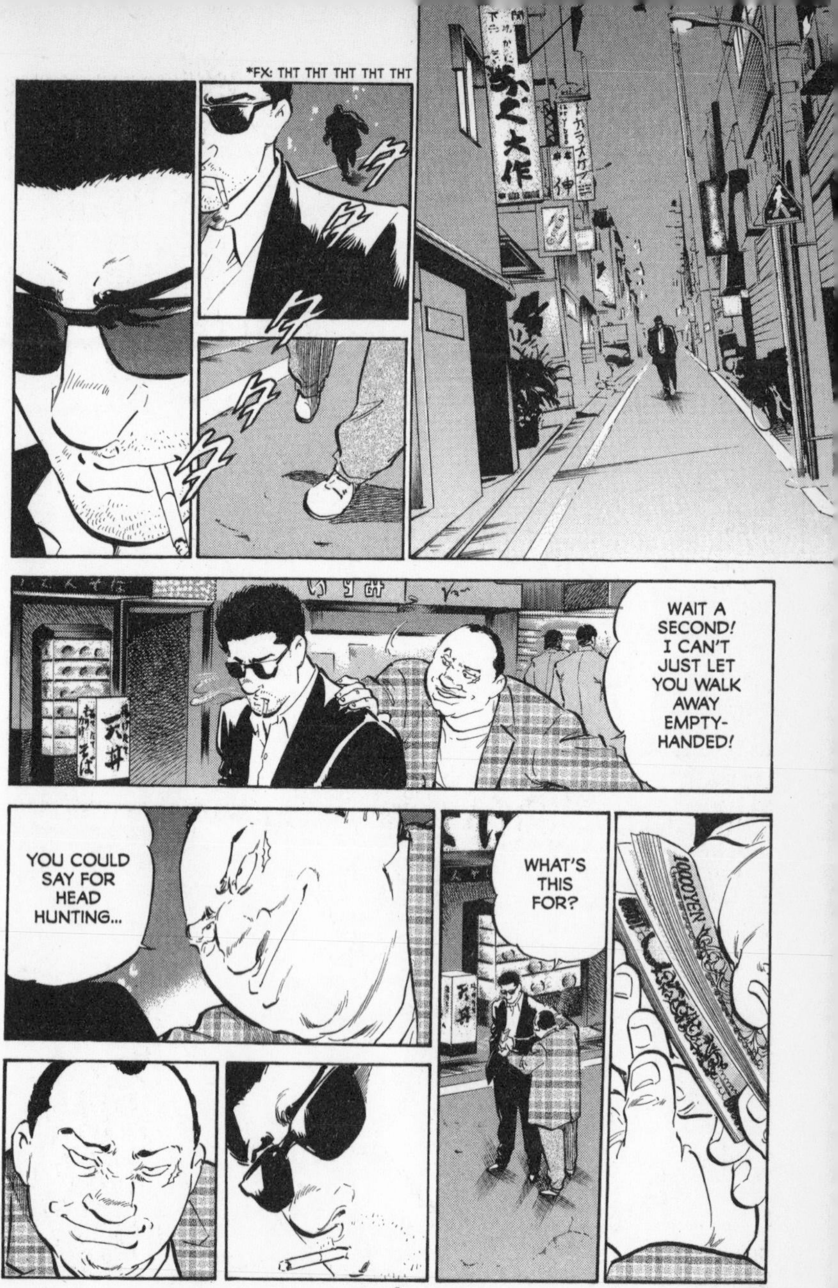
*FX: THT THT THT THT THT
WAIT A SECOND! I CAN'T JUST LET YOU WALK AWAY EMPTY-HANDED!
WHAT'S THIS FOR?
YOU COULD SAY FOR HEAD HUNTING...

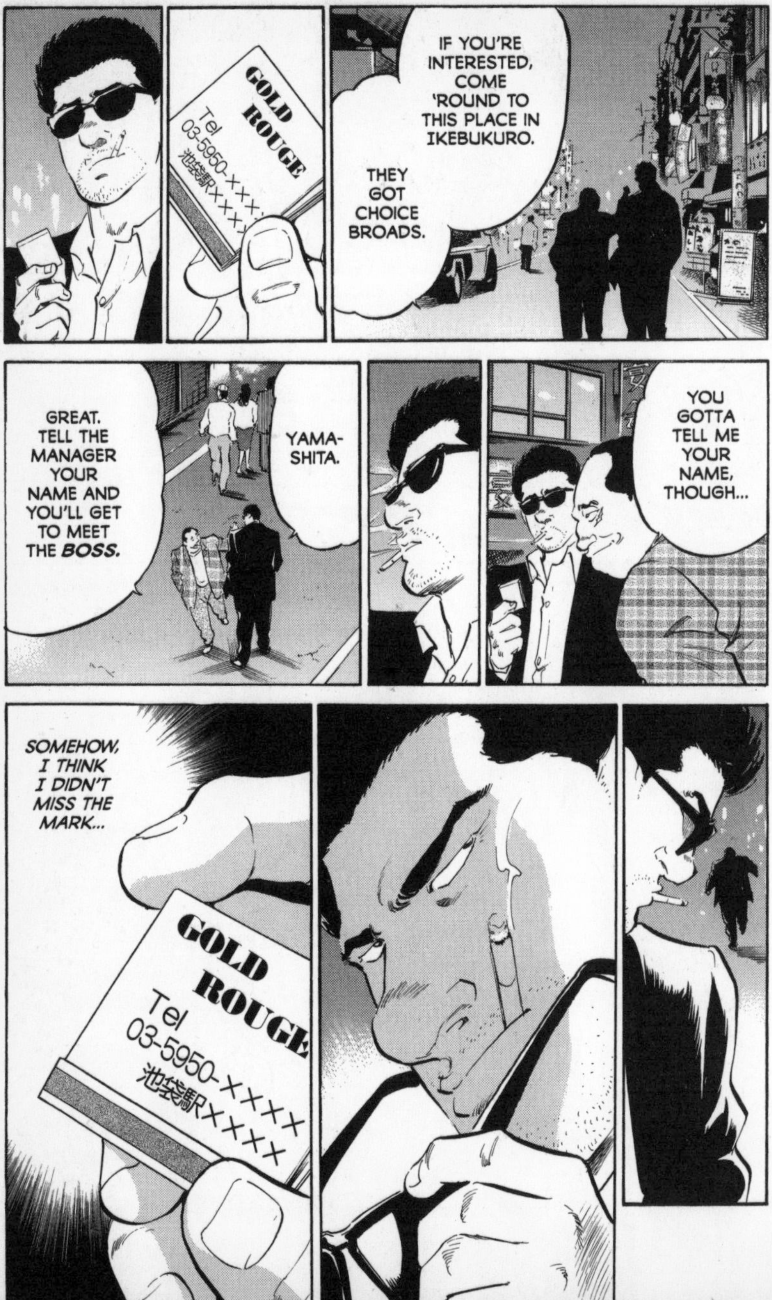
IF YOU'RE INTERESTED, COME 'ROUND TO THIS PLACE IN IKEBUKURO.
THEY GOT CHOICE BROADS.
GOLD ROUGE
Tel 03-5950-××××
池袋駅××××
YOU GOTTA TELL ME YOUR NAME, THOUGH...
YAMA-SHITA.
GREAT. TELL THE MANAGER YOUR NAME AND YOU'LL GET TO MEET THE ***BOSS.***
GOLD ROUGE
Tel 03-5950-××××
池袋駅××××
SOMEHOW, I THINK I DIDN'T MISS THE MARK...

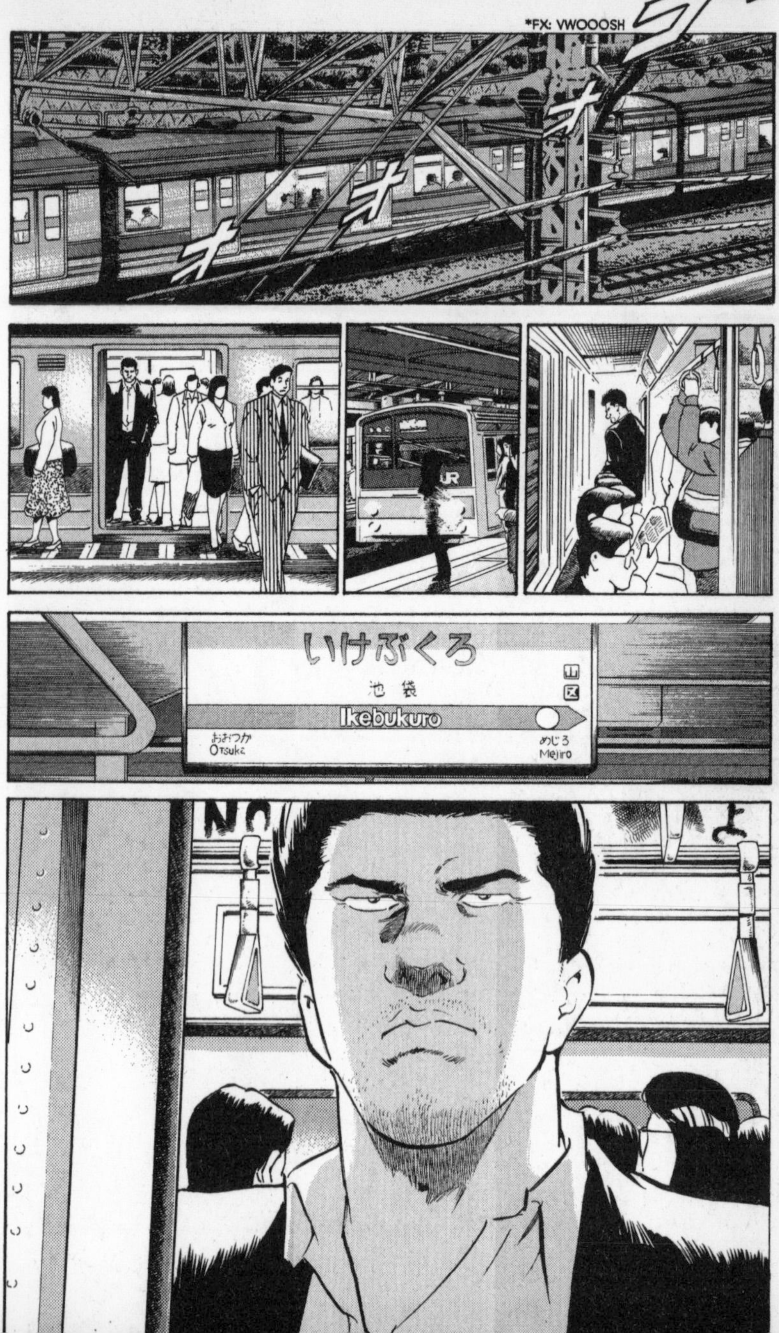
*FX: VWOOOSH
いけぶくろ
池袋
Ikebukuro
おおつか
Otsuka
めじろ
Mejiro

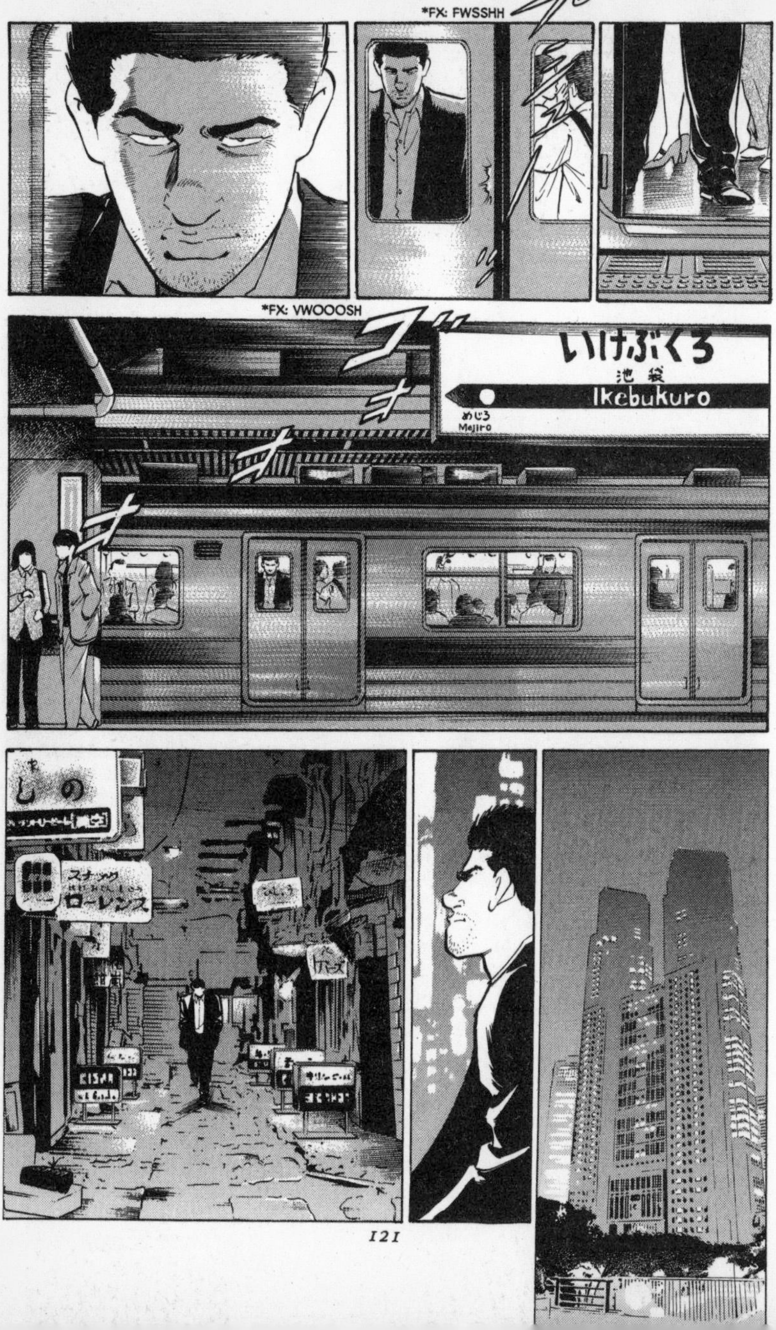
*FX: FWSSHH
*FX: VWOOOSH
いけぶくろ
池袋
Ikebukuro
めじろ
Mejiro
しの
スナック
ローレンス

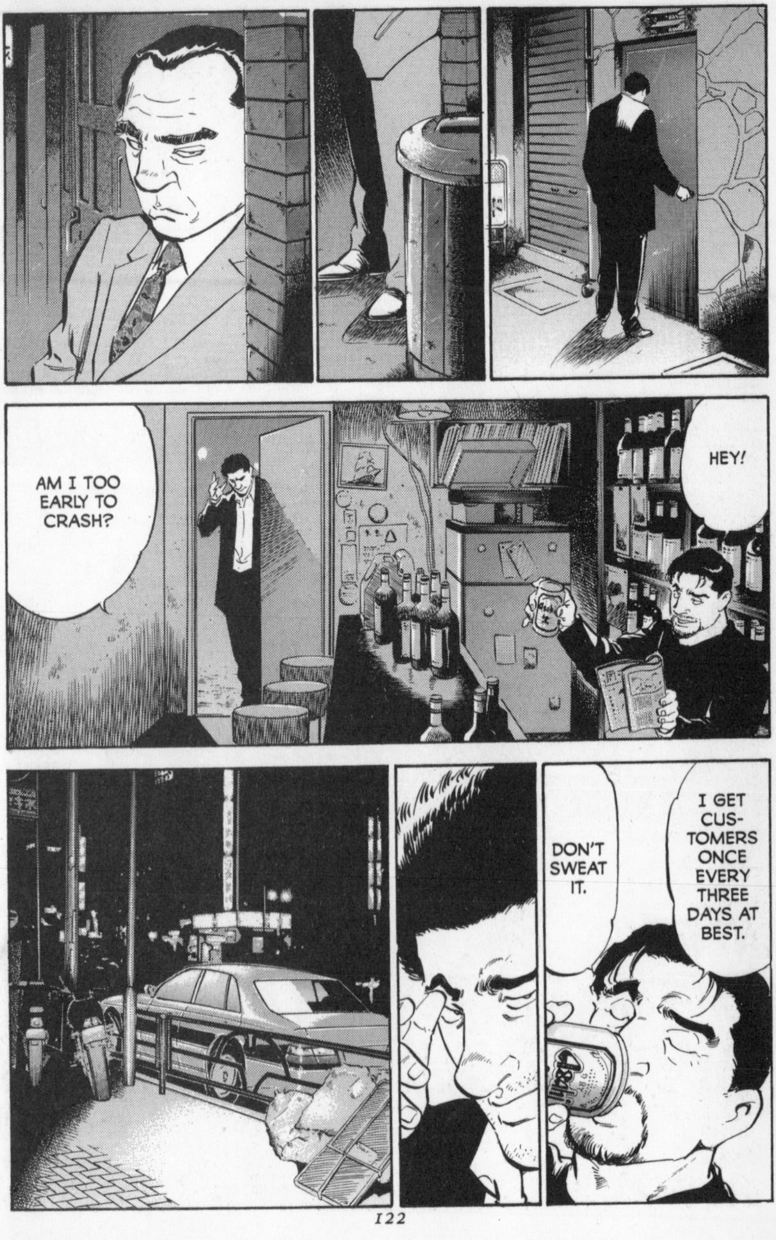
AM I TOO EARLY TO CRASH?
HEY!
DON'T SWEAT IT.
I GET CUS-TOMERS ONCE EVERY THREE DAYS AT BEST.

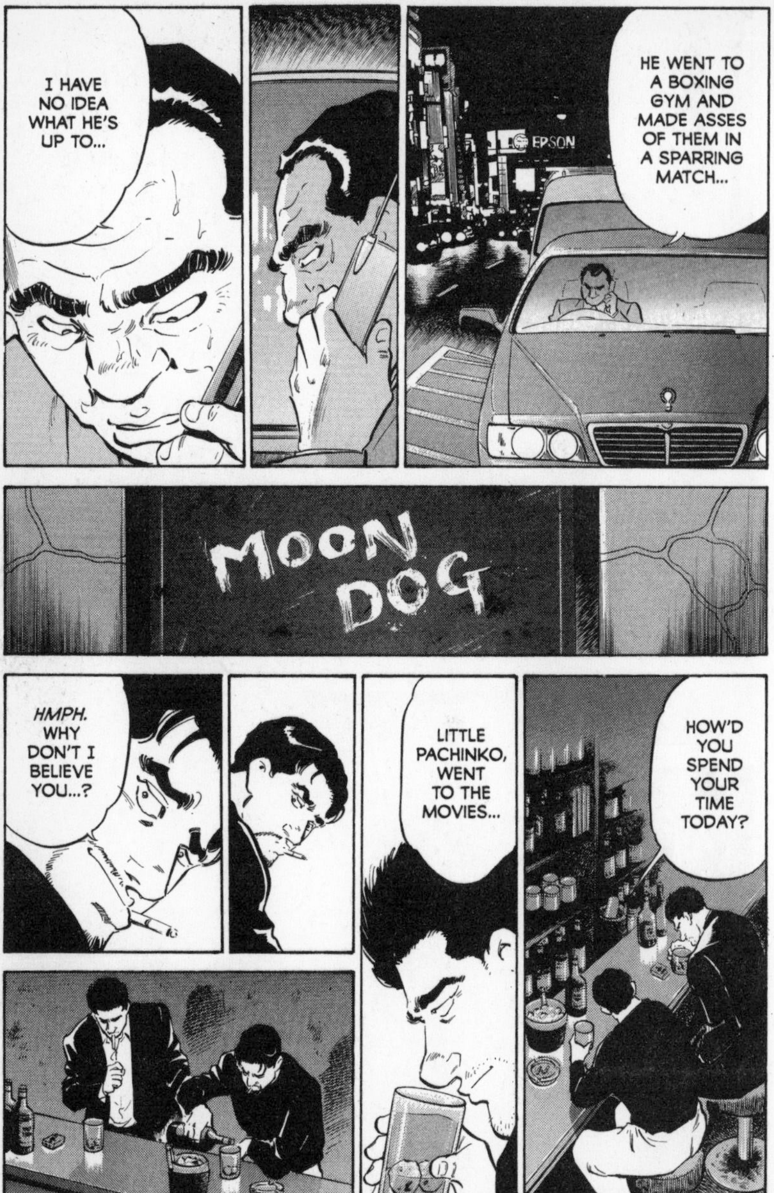
HE WENT TO A BOXING GYM AND MADE ASSES OF THEM IN A SPARRING MATCH...
EPSON
I HAVE NO IDEA WHAT HE'S UP TO...
MOON DOG
HOW'D YOU SPEND YOUR TIME TODAY?
LITTLE PACHINKO, WENT TO THE MOVIES...
HMPH. WHY DON'T I BELIEVE YOU...?

GOT ANY LEADS?

SO WE DON'T KNOW WHY, BUT SOME MAN OUT THERE HATES YOU...

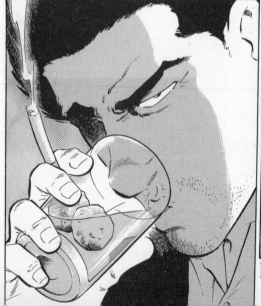

DOOR TO THE UNDERGROUND: END

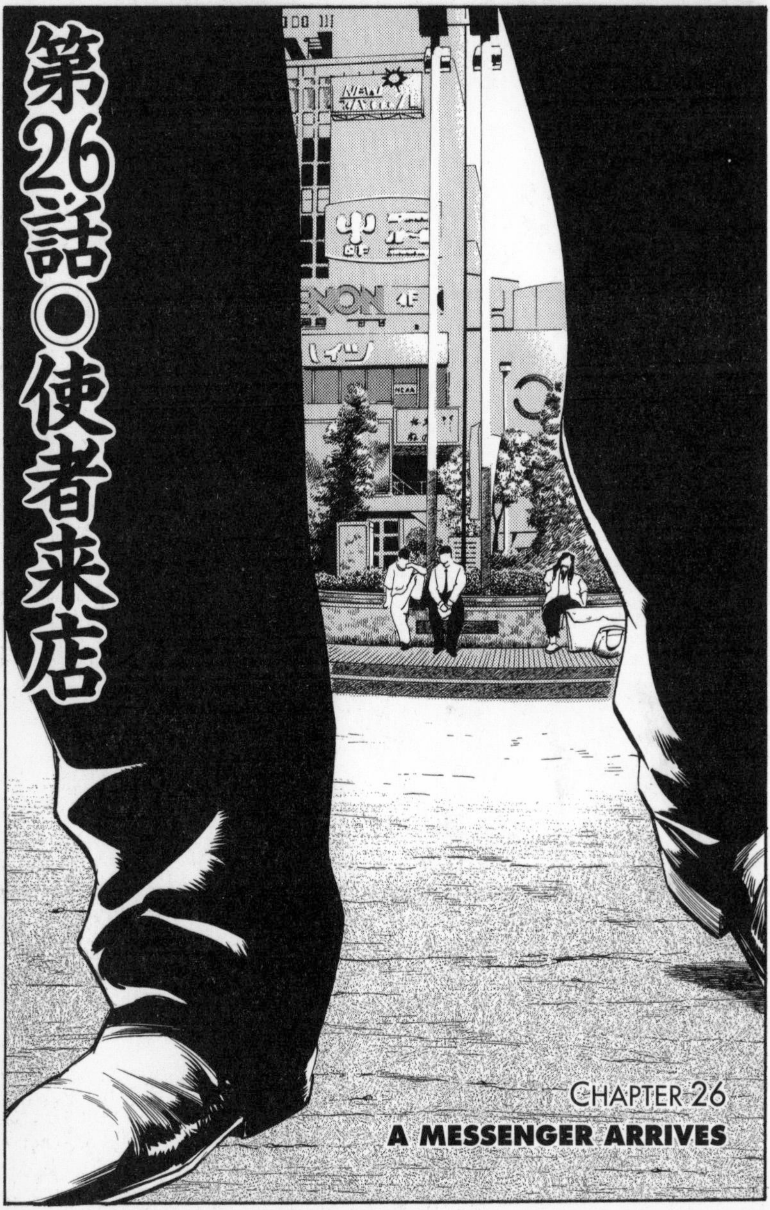
第26話○使者来店
CHAPTER 26
A MESSENGER ARRIVES

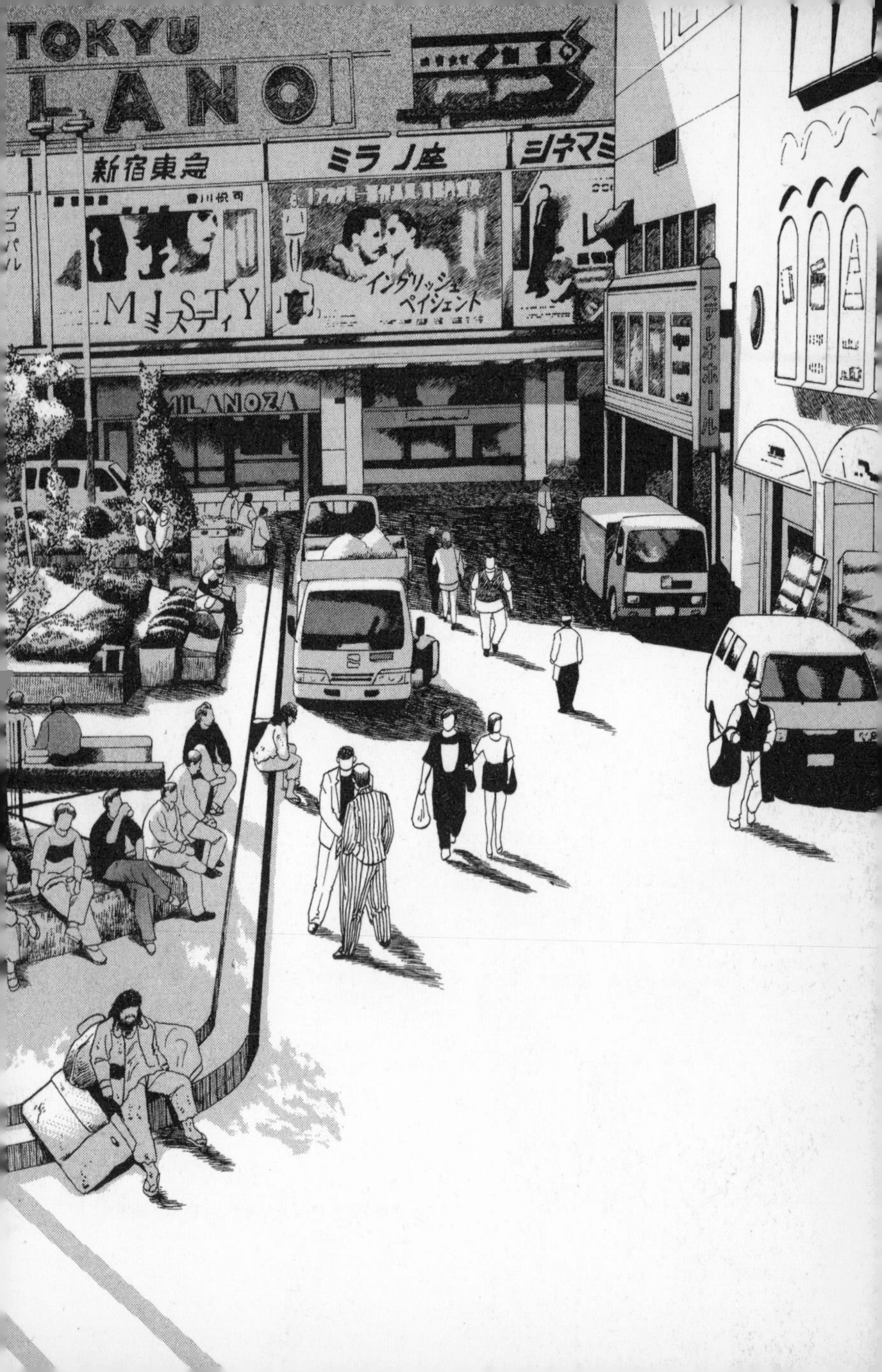
TOKYU
LANO
新宿東急
ミラノ座
シネマミ
MISTY
ミスティ
イングリッシュ
ペイシェント
MILANOZA
ステレオホール

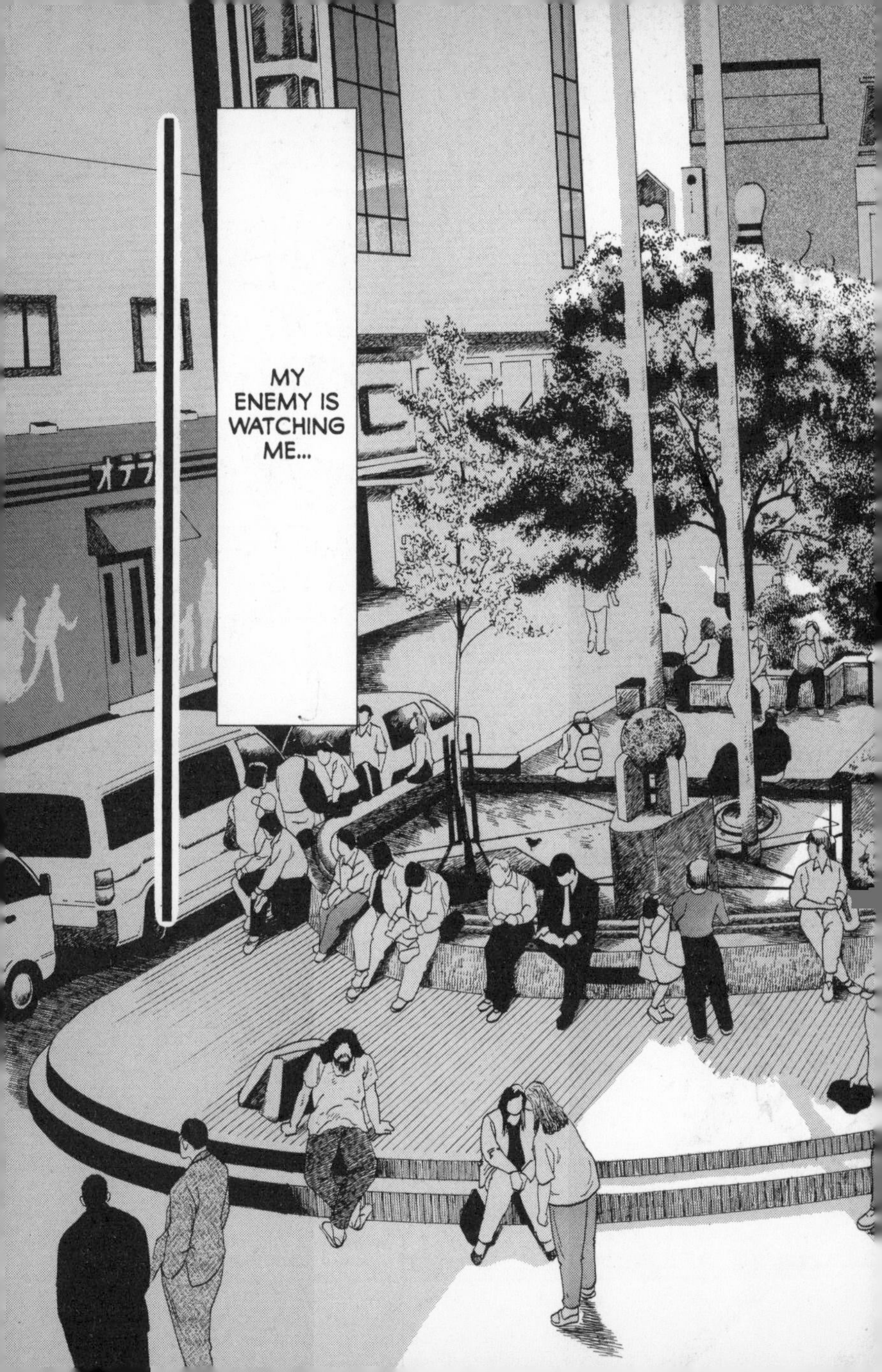
MY ENEMY IS WATCHING ME...

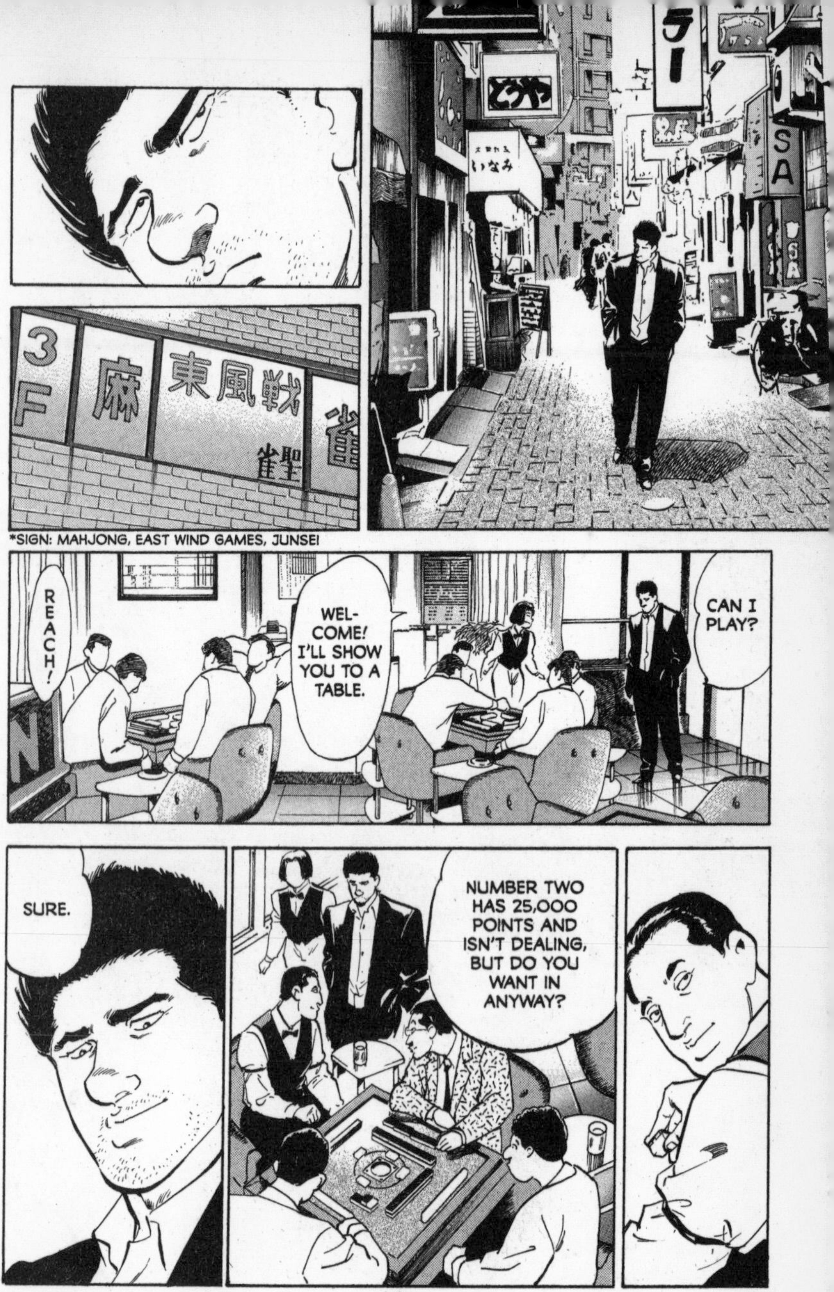
3F
麻
東風戦
雀
雀聖
CAN I PLAY?
WEL-COME! I'LL SHOW YOU TO A TABLE.
REACH!
NUMBER TWO HAS 25,000 POINTS AND ISN'T DEALING, BUT DO YOU WANT IN ANYWAY?
SURE.
*SIGN: MAHJONG, EAST WIND GAMES, JUNSEI

*FX: TAP

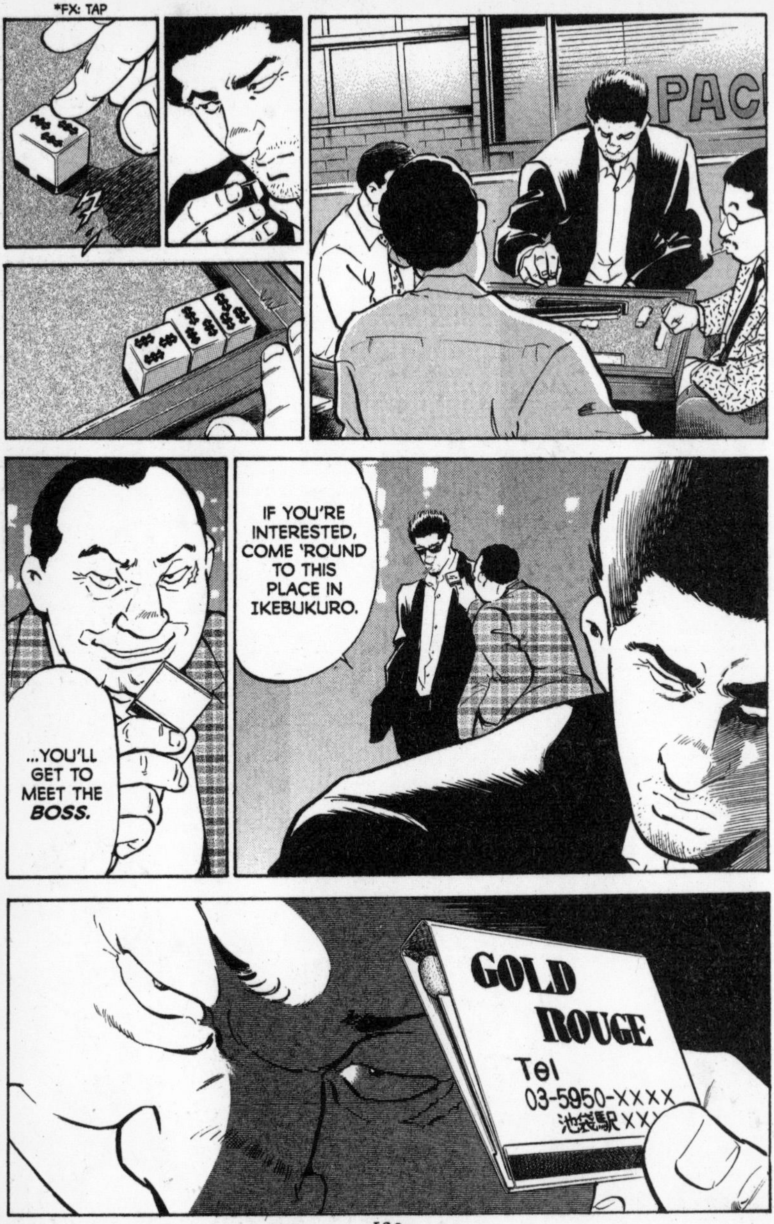
IF YOU'RE INTERESTED, COME 'ROUND TO THIS PLACE IN IKEBUKURO.
...YOU'LL GET TO MEET THE ***BOSS.***
GOLD ROUGE
Tel
03-5950-XXXX
池袋駅XXX

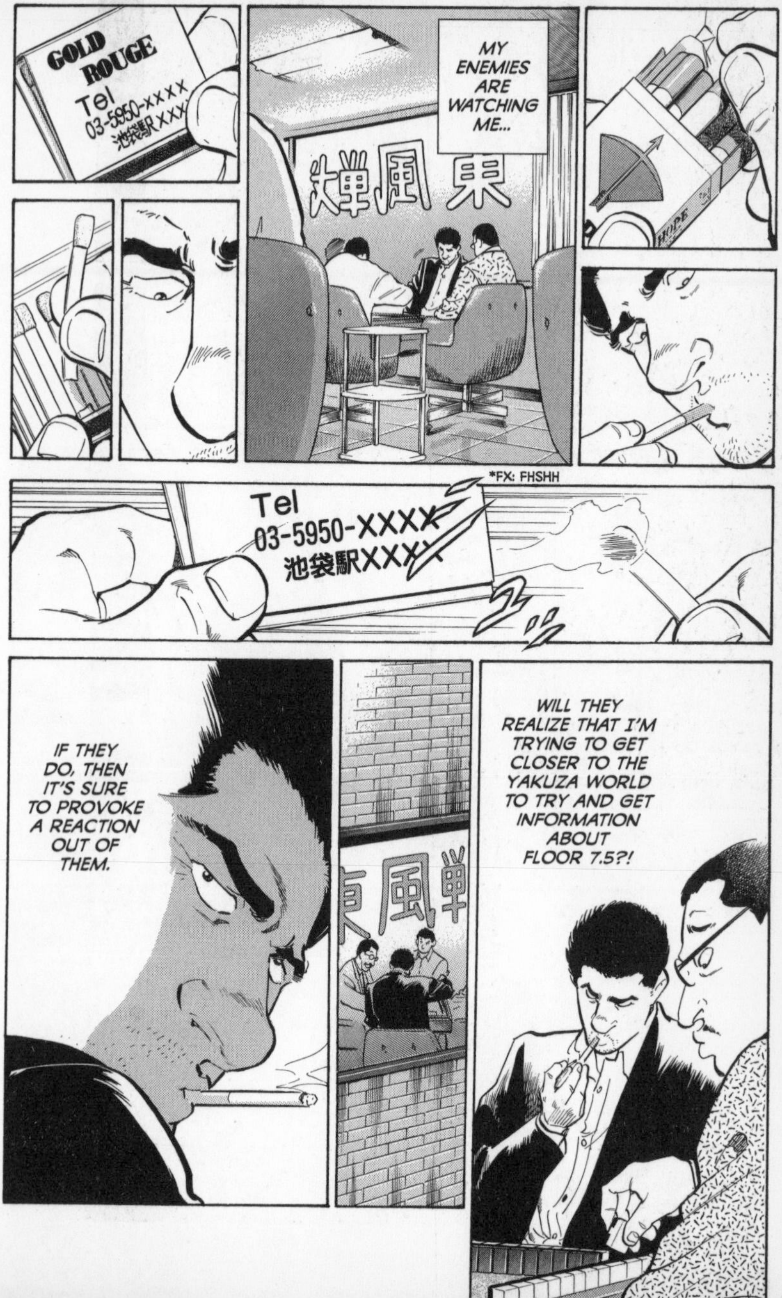
MY ENEMIES ARE WATCHING ME...
GOLD ROUGE
Tel
03-5950-xxxx
*FX: FHSHH
Tel
03-5950-XXXX
池袋駅XXX
WILL THEY REALIZE THAT I'M TRYING TO GET CLOSER TO THE YAKUZA WORLD TO TRY AND GET INFORMATION ABOUT FLOOR 7.5?!
IF THEY DO, THEN IT'S SURE TO PROVOKE A REACTION OUT OF THEM.

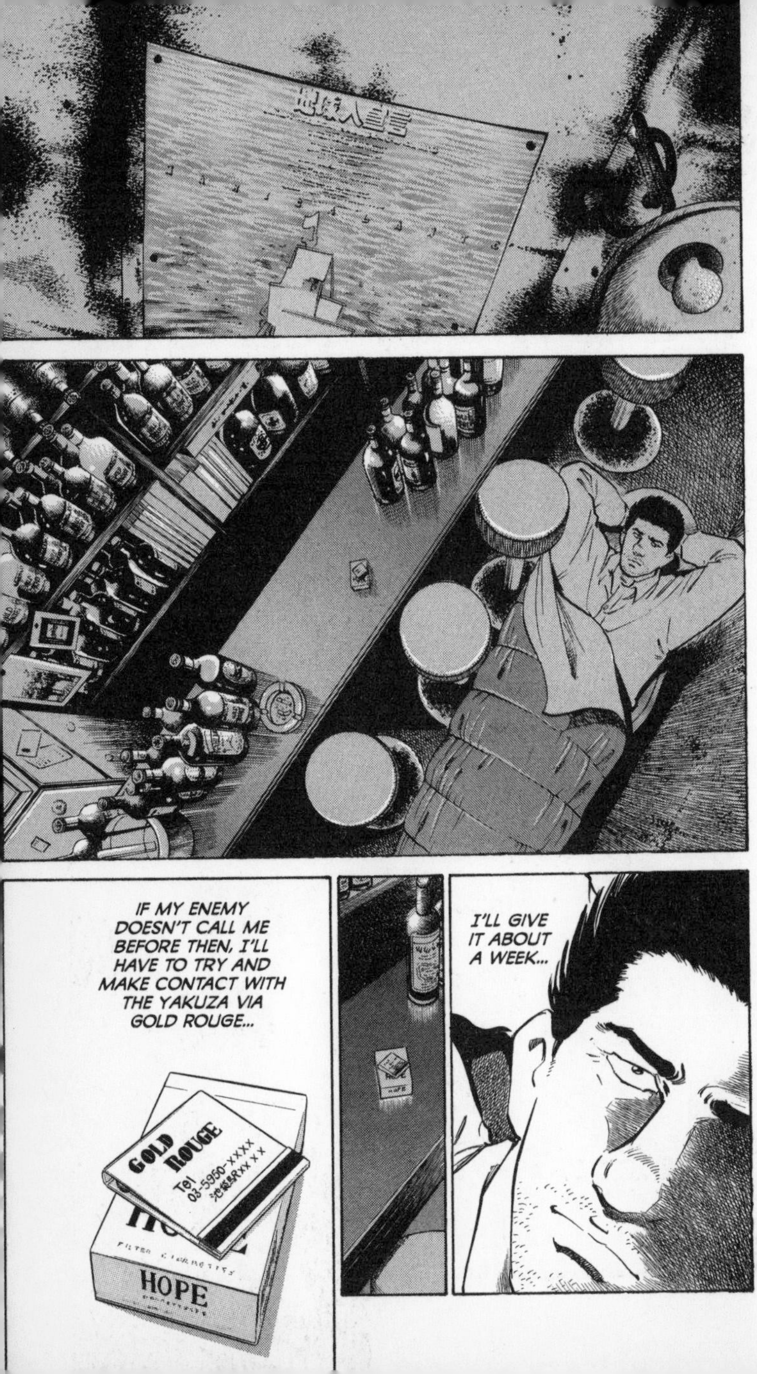
I'LL GIVE IT ABOUT A WEEK...
IF MY ENEMY DOESN'T CALL ME BEFORE THEN, I'LL HAVE TO TRY AND MAKE CONTACT WITH THE YAKUZA VIA GOLD ROUGE...
GOLD ROUGE
Tel 03-5950-XXXX
HOPE

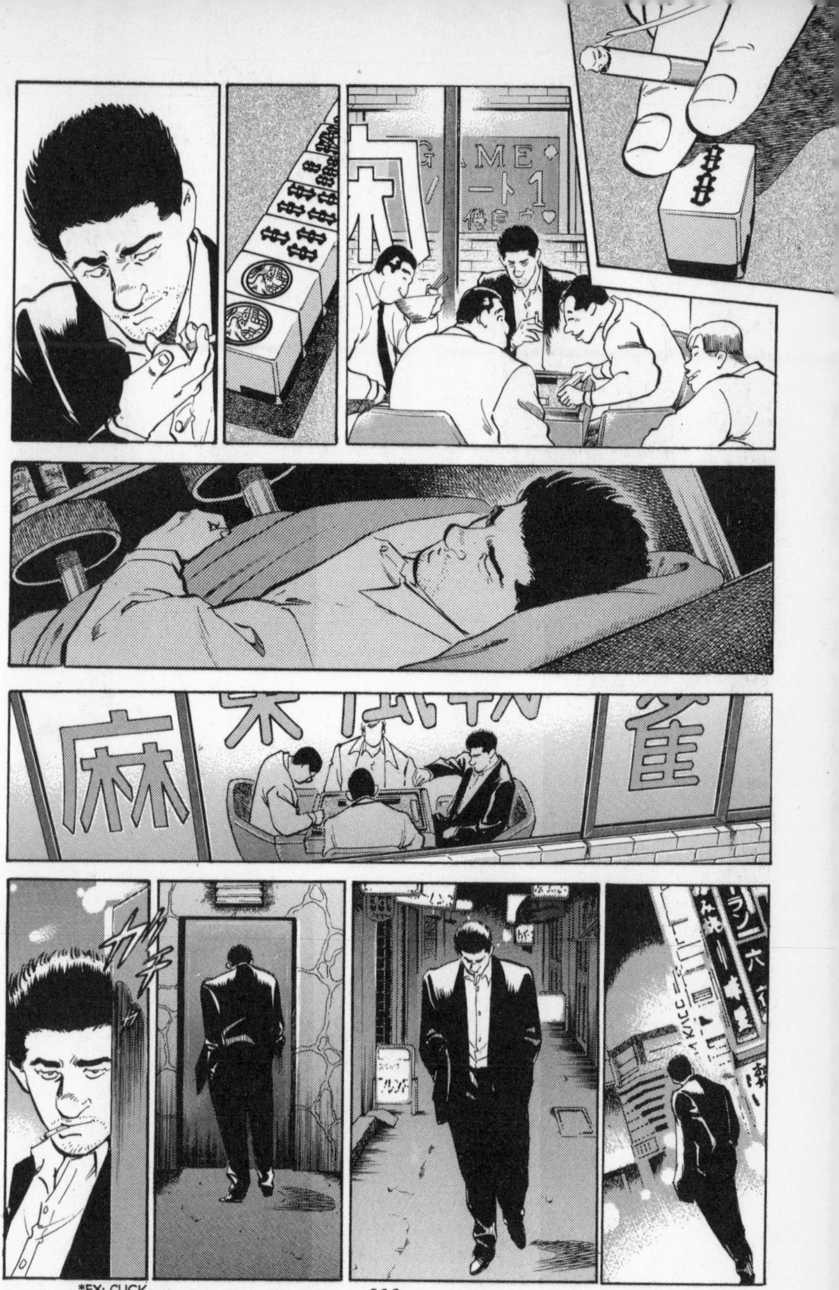
GAME
麻
雀
*FX: CLICK

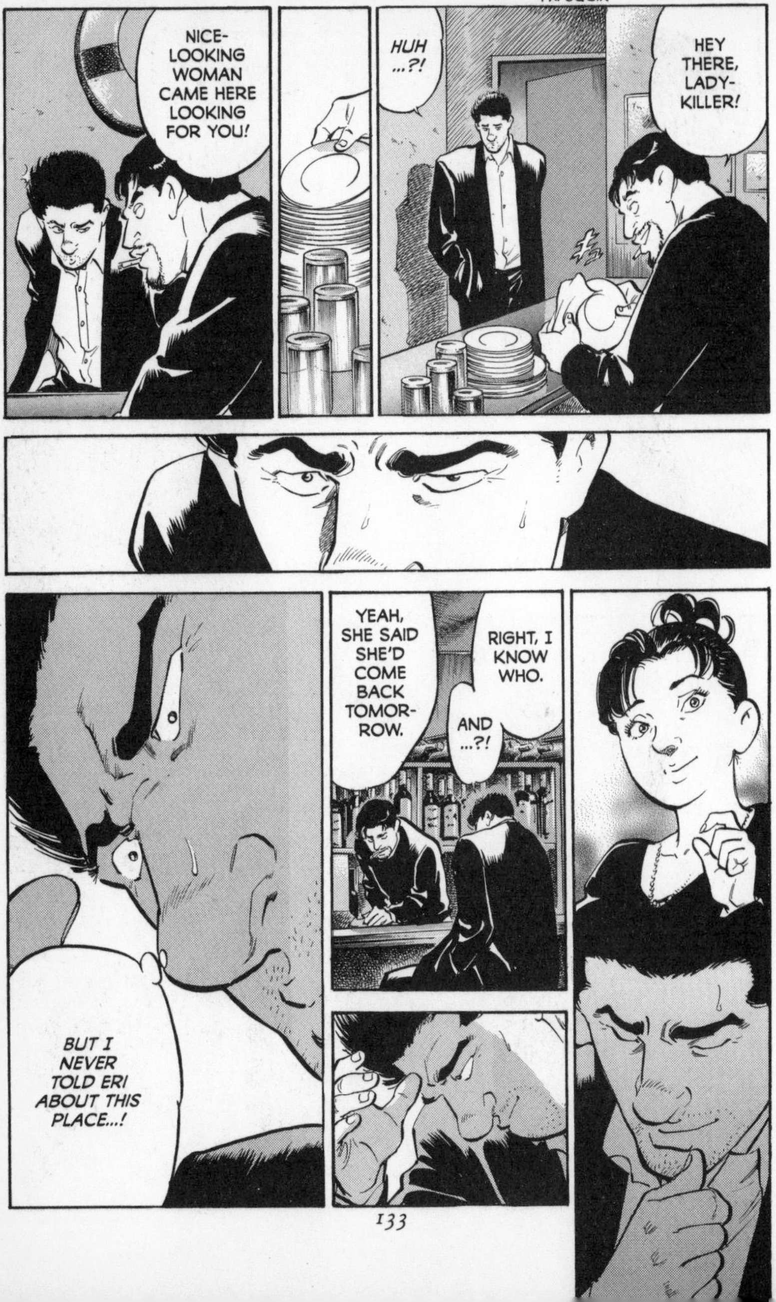
*FX: SQUIK
HEY THERE, LADY-KILLER!
HUH ...?!
NICE-LOOKING WOMAN CAME HERE LOOKING FOR YOU!
RIGHT, I KNOW WHO.
AND ...?!
YEAH, SHE SAID SHE'D COME BACK TOMORROW.
BUT I NEVER TOLD ERI ABOUT THIS PLACE...!

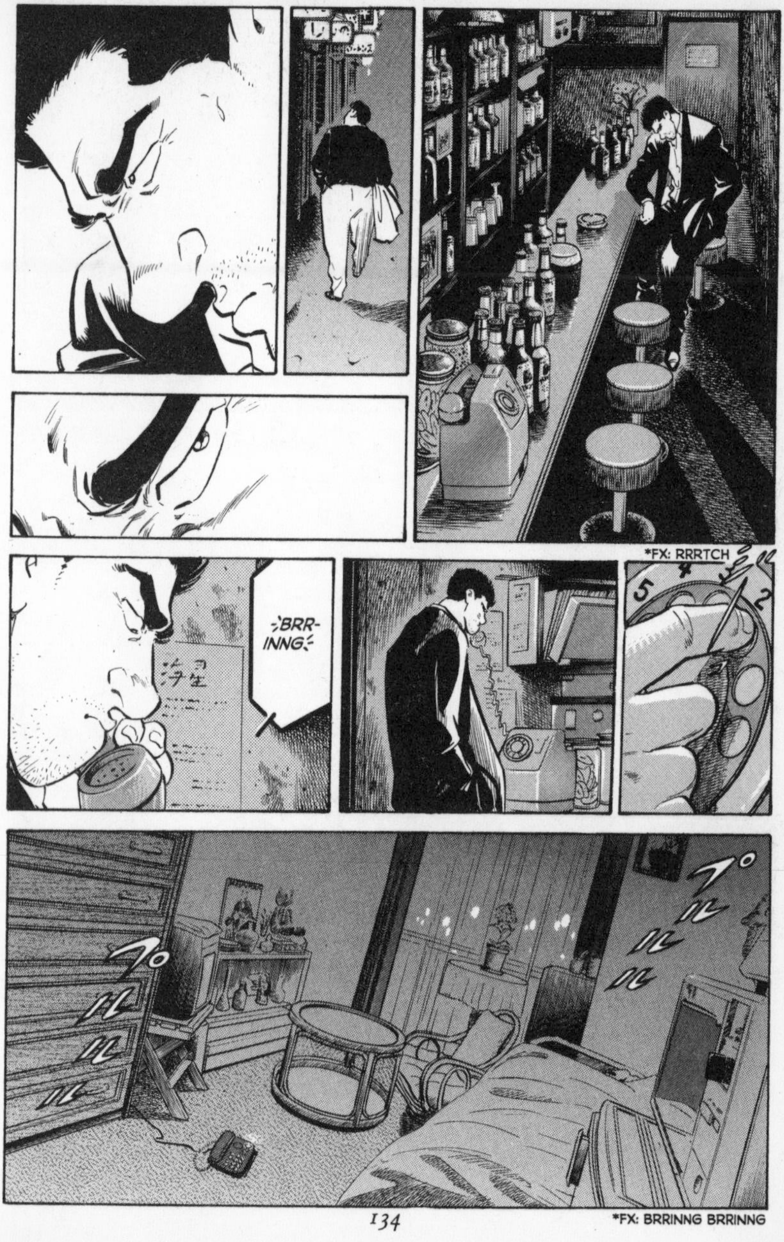
BRR-INNG
*FX: RRRTCH
*FX: BRRINNG BRRINNG

≥CLICK≥

I'M OUT RIGHT NOW. IF YOU'D LIKE TO LEAVE A MESSAGE...

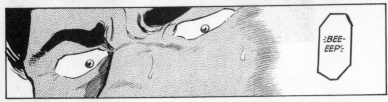

≥BEE-EEP≥

DID YOU COME TO THE BAR BEFORE?

IT'S ME...

DID MY ENEMIES TRY TO THREATEN YOU SOMEHOW...?

*FX: KACHIK

135

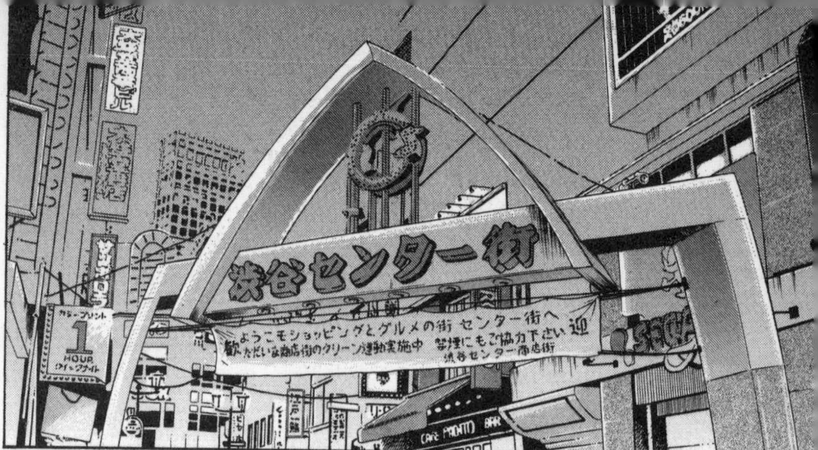
渋谷センター街

*SIGN: SHIBUYA CENTER STREET

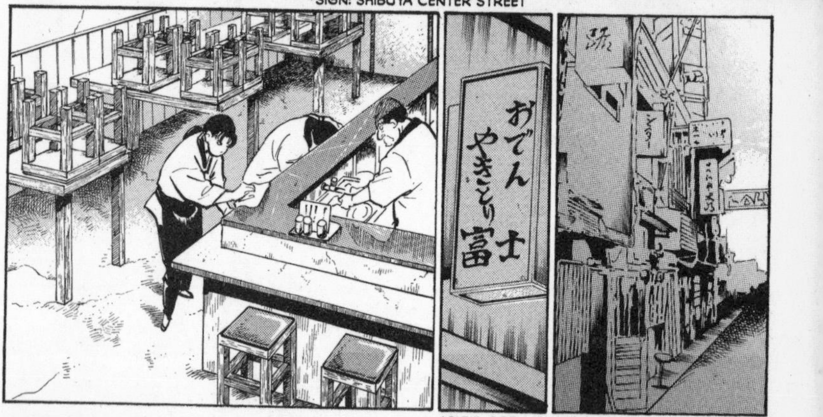
おでん
やきとり
富士

*SIGN: ODEN YAKITORI "FUJI"

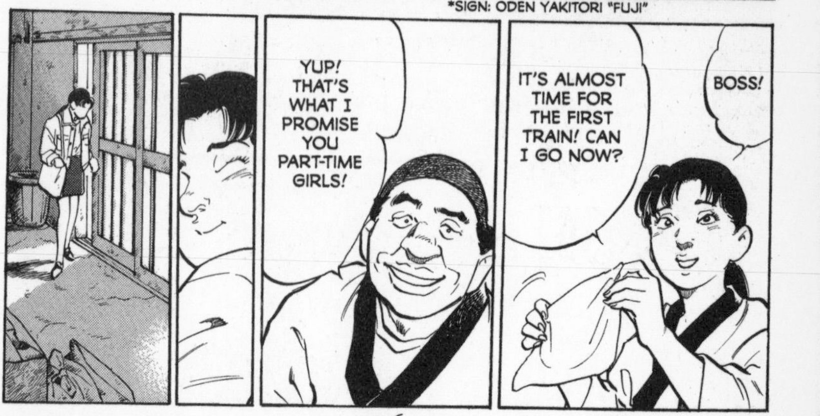
BOSS!
IT'S ALMOST TIME FOR THE FIRST TRAIN! CAN I GO NOW?
YUP! THAT'S WHAT I PROMISE YOU PART-TIME GIRLS!

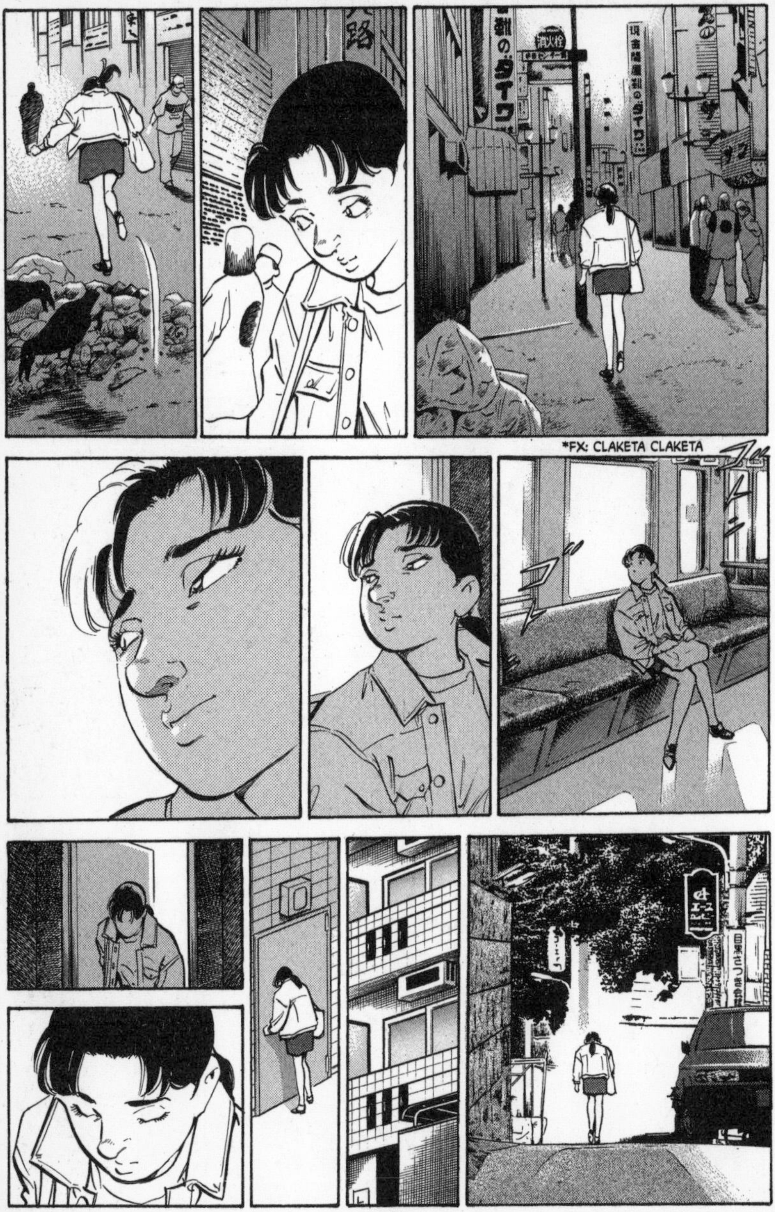
*FX: CLAKETA CLAKETA

*FX: BEEP

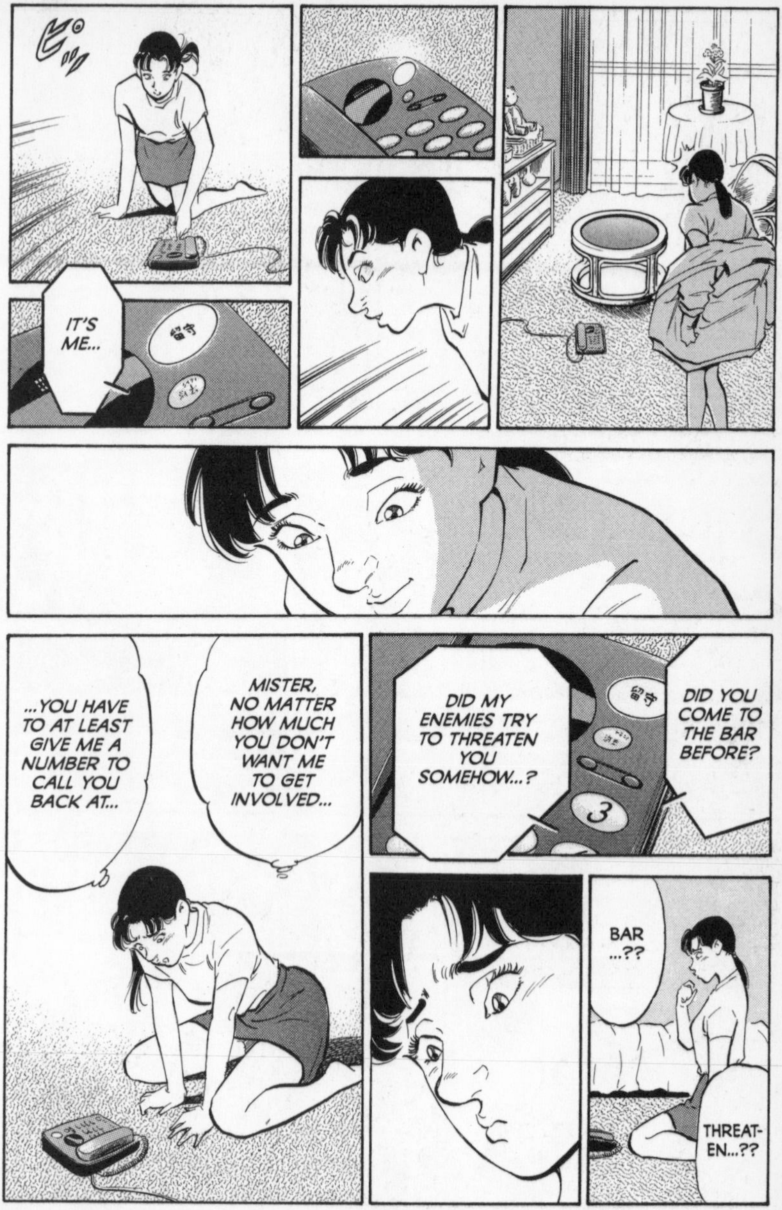
ピッ
IT'S ME...
DID YOU COME TO THE BAR BEFORE?
DID MY ENEMIES TRY TO THREATEN YOU SOMEHOW...?
BAR ...??
THREAT- EN...??
MISTER, NO MATTER HOW MUCH YOU DON'T WANT ME TO GET INVOLVED...
...YOU HAVE TO AT LEAST GIVE ME A NUMBER TO CALL YOU BACK AT...

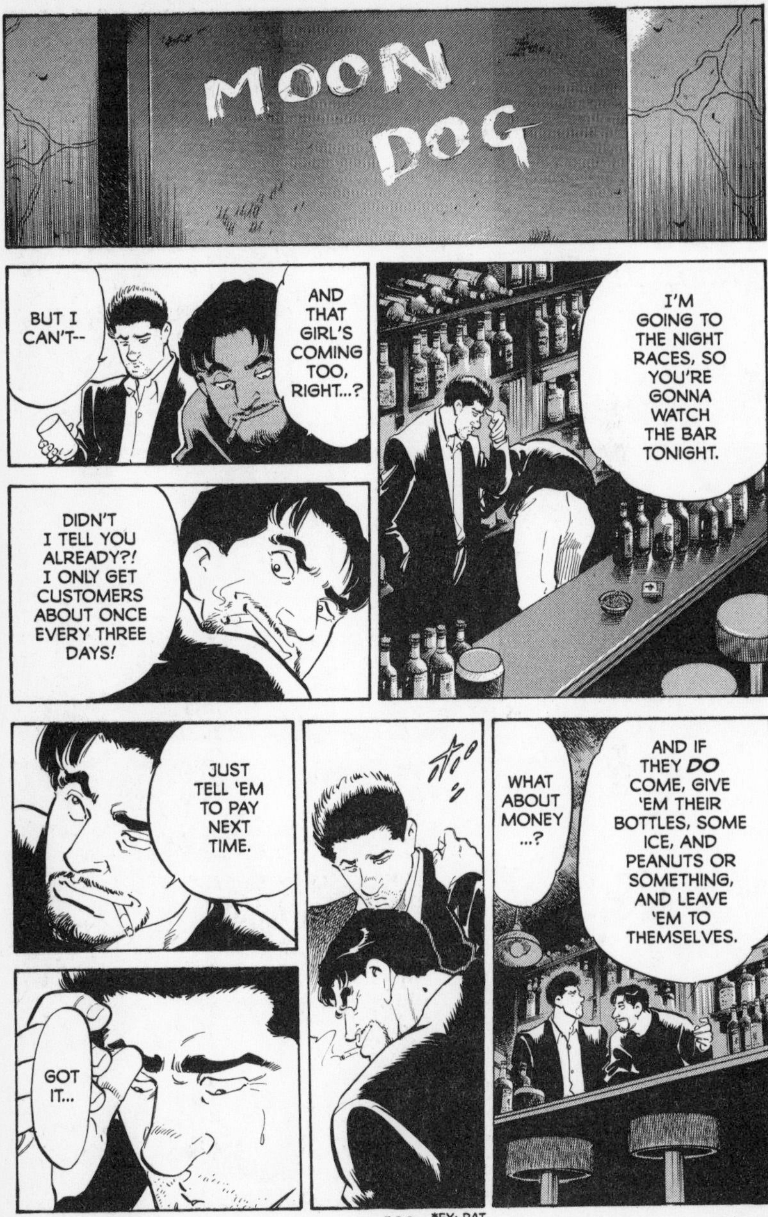
MOON DOG
I'M GOING TO THE NIGHT RACES, SO YOU'RE GONNA WATCH THE BAR TONIGHT.
AND THAT GIRL'S COMING TOO, RIGHT...?
BUT I CAN'T--
DIDN'T I TELL YOU ALREADY?! I ONLY GET CUSTOMERS ABOUT ONCE EVERY THREE DAYS!
AND IF THEY *DO* COME, GIVE 'EM THEIR BOTTLES, SOME ICE, AND PEANUTS OR SOMETHING, AND LEAVE 'EM TO THEMSELVES.
WHAT ABOUT MONEY ...?
JUST TELL 'EM TO PAY NEXT TIME.
GOT IT...

*FX: PAT

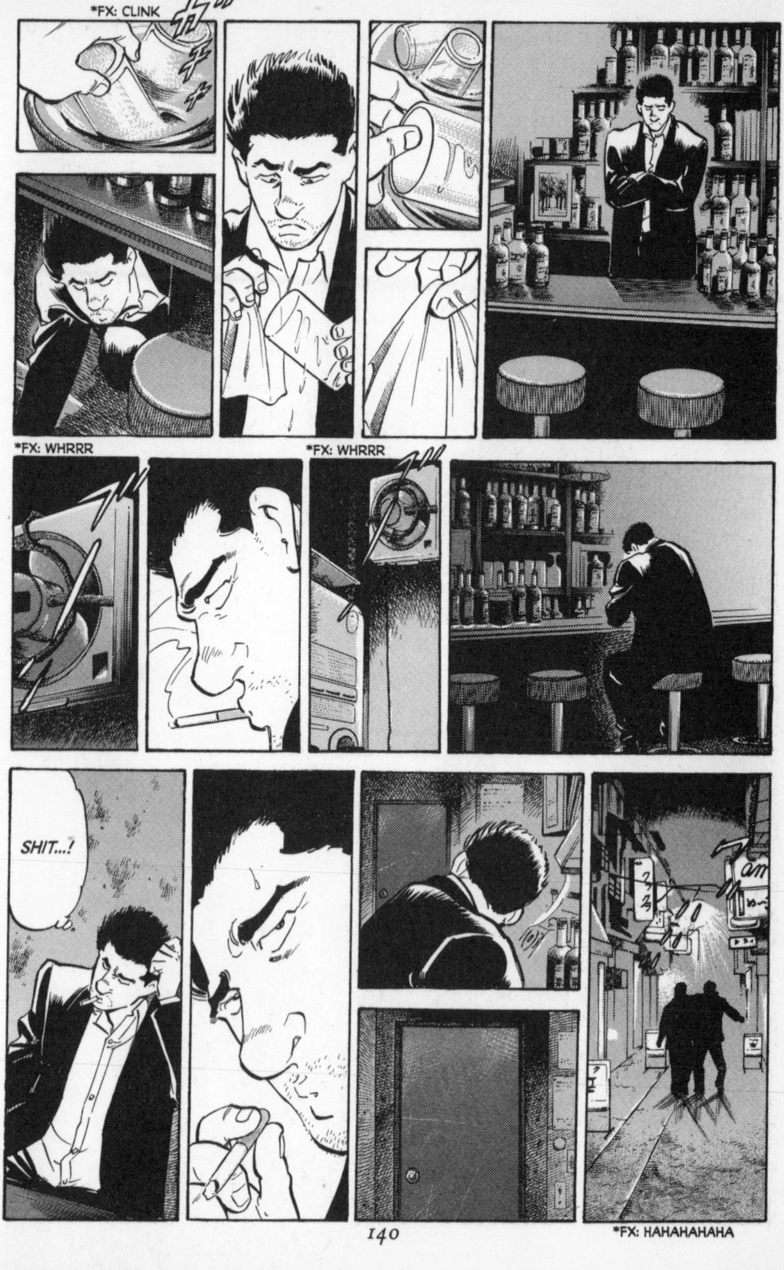
*FX: CLINK
*FX: WHRRR
*FX: WHRRR
*FX: HAHAHAHAHA
SHIT...!

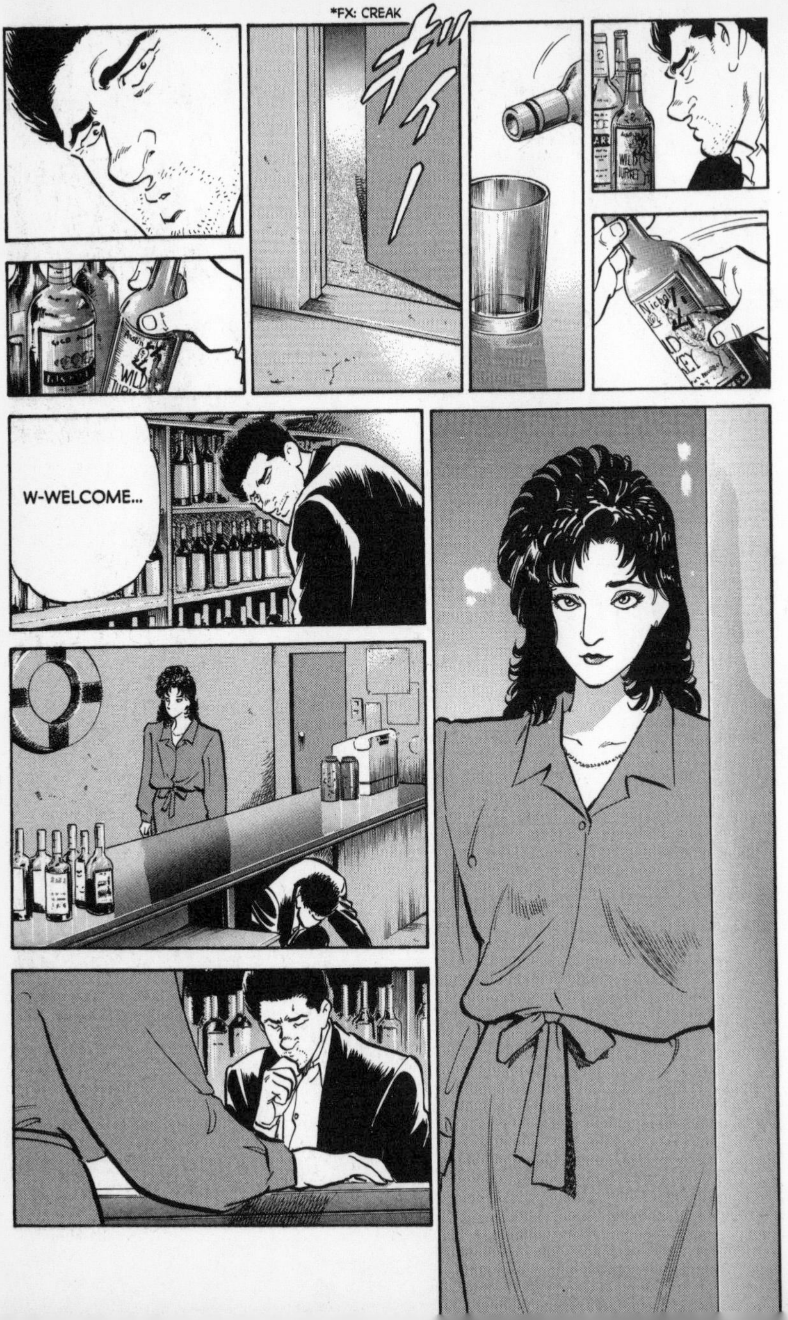
*FX: CREAK
チャイー
W-WELCOME...

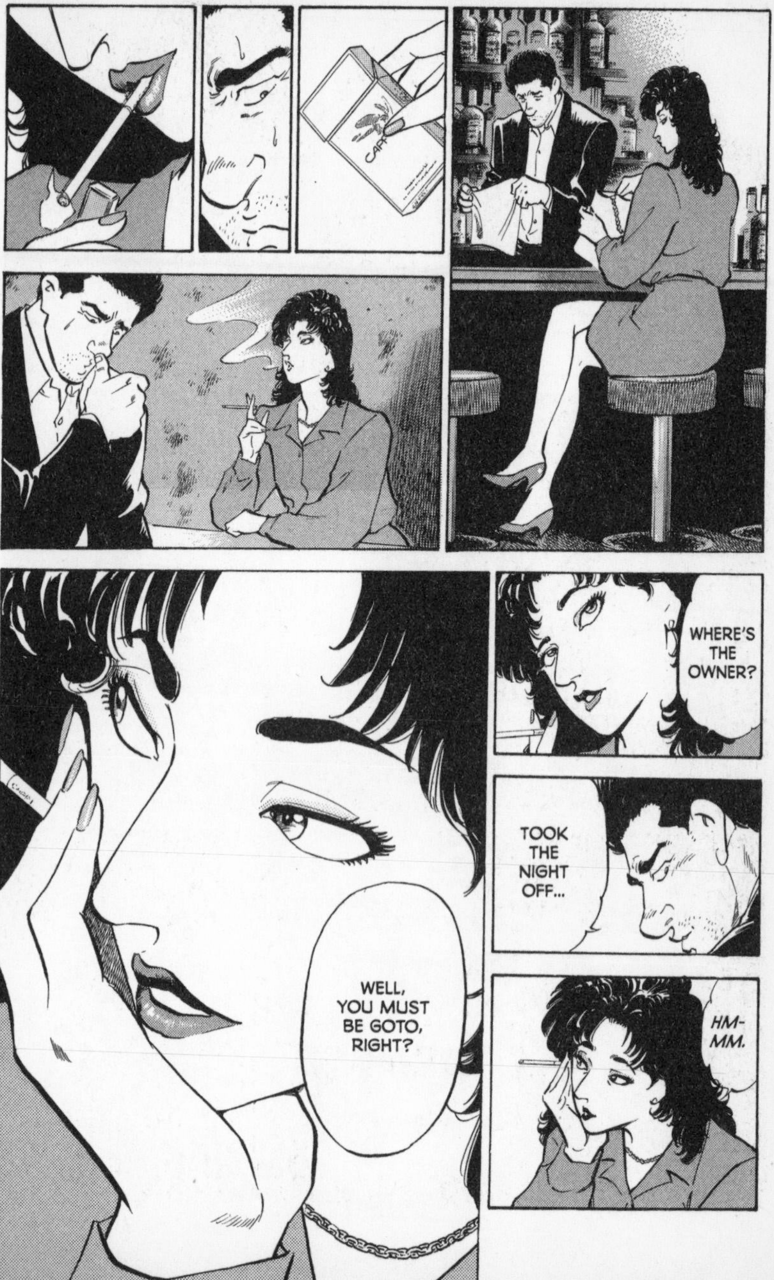
WHERE'S THE OWNER?
TOOK THE NIGHT OFF...
HM-MM.
WELL, YOU MUST BE GOTO, RIGHT?

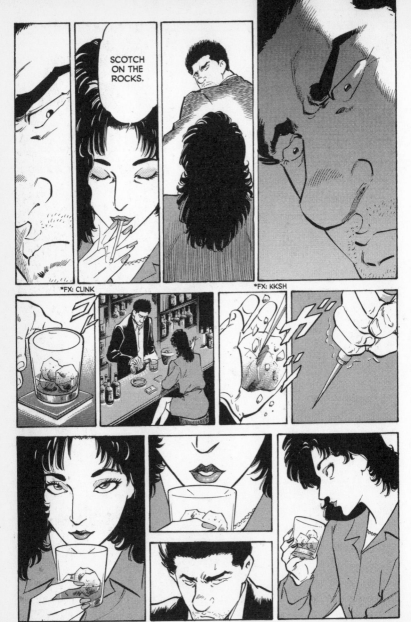

SCOTCH ON THE ROCKS.

*FX: CLINK

*FX: KKSH

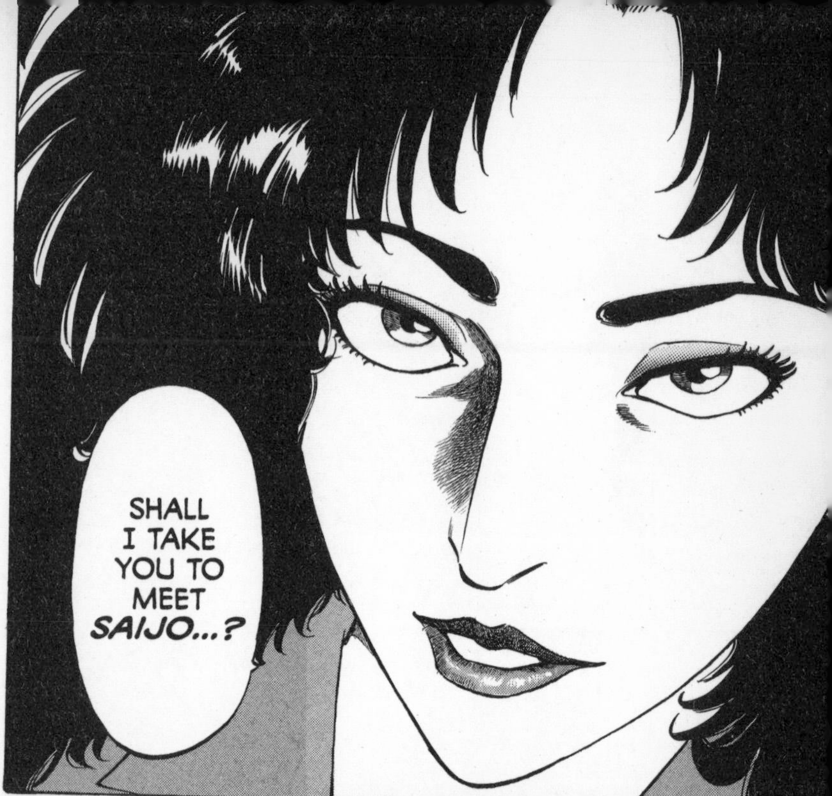
SHALL I TAKE YOU TO MEET *SAIJO...?*

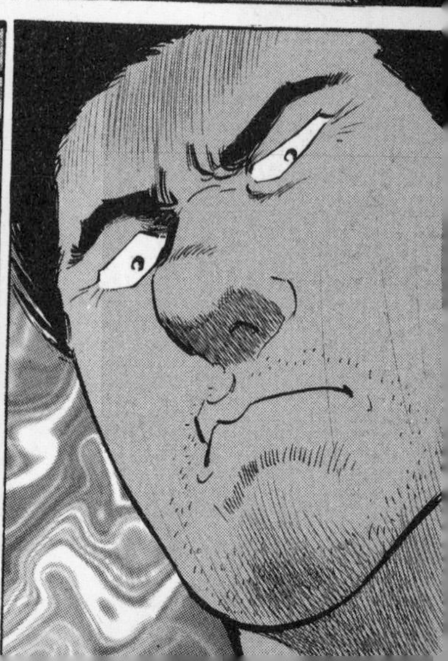

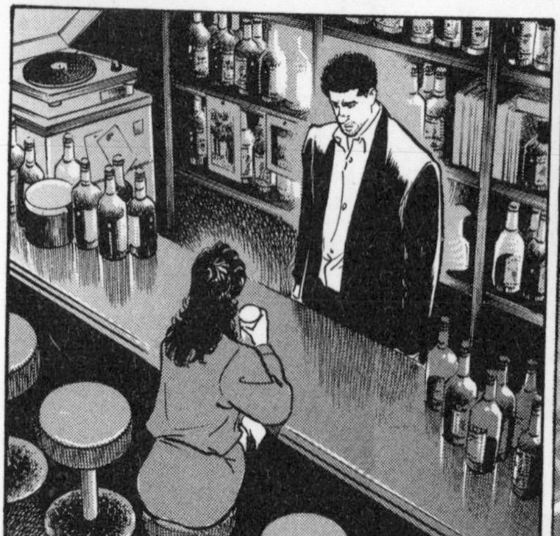

A MESSENGER ARRIVES: END

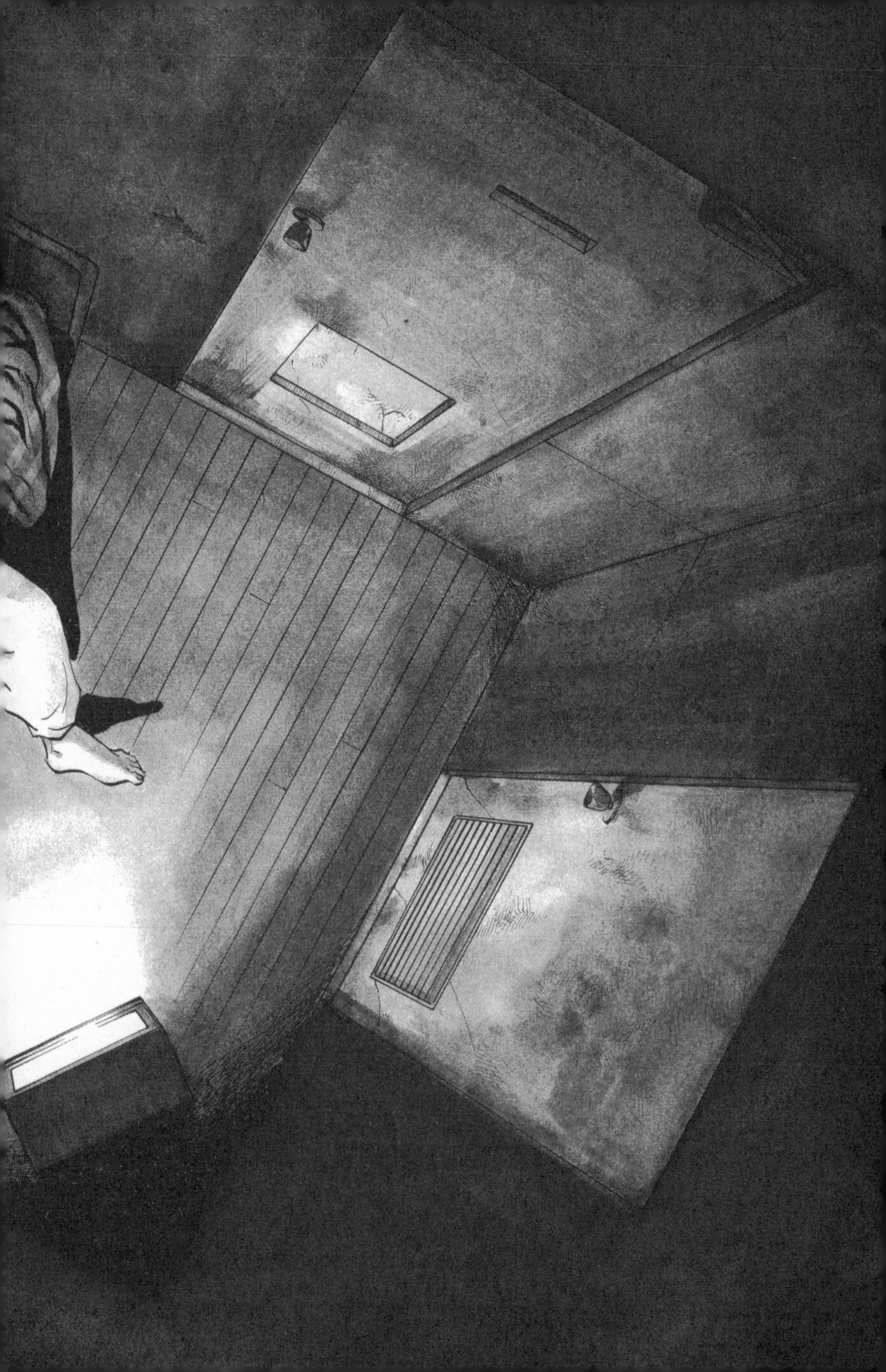

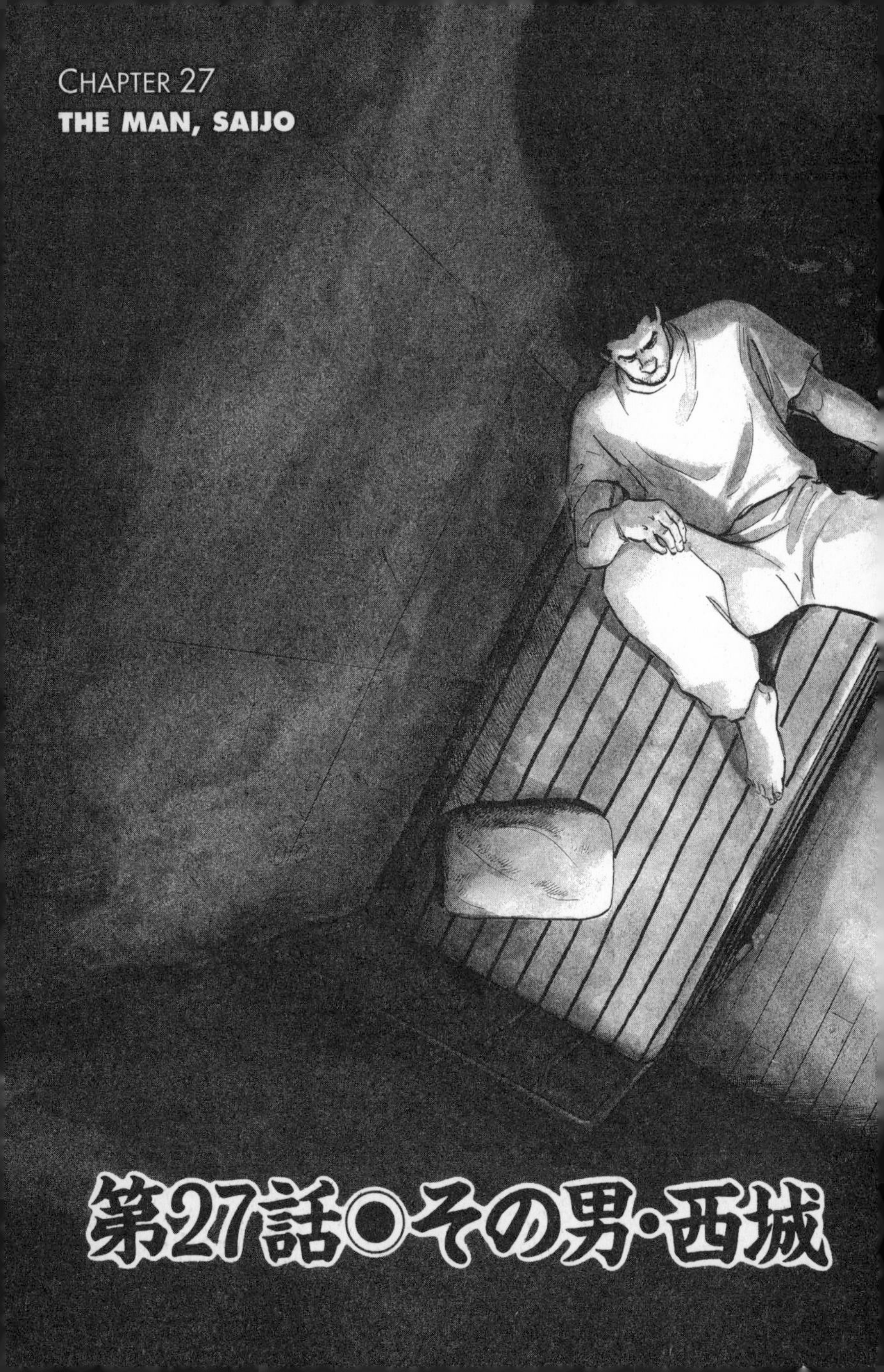
CHAPTER 27
THE MAN, SAIJO
第27話○その男・西城

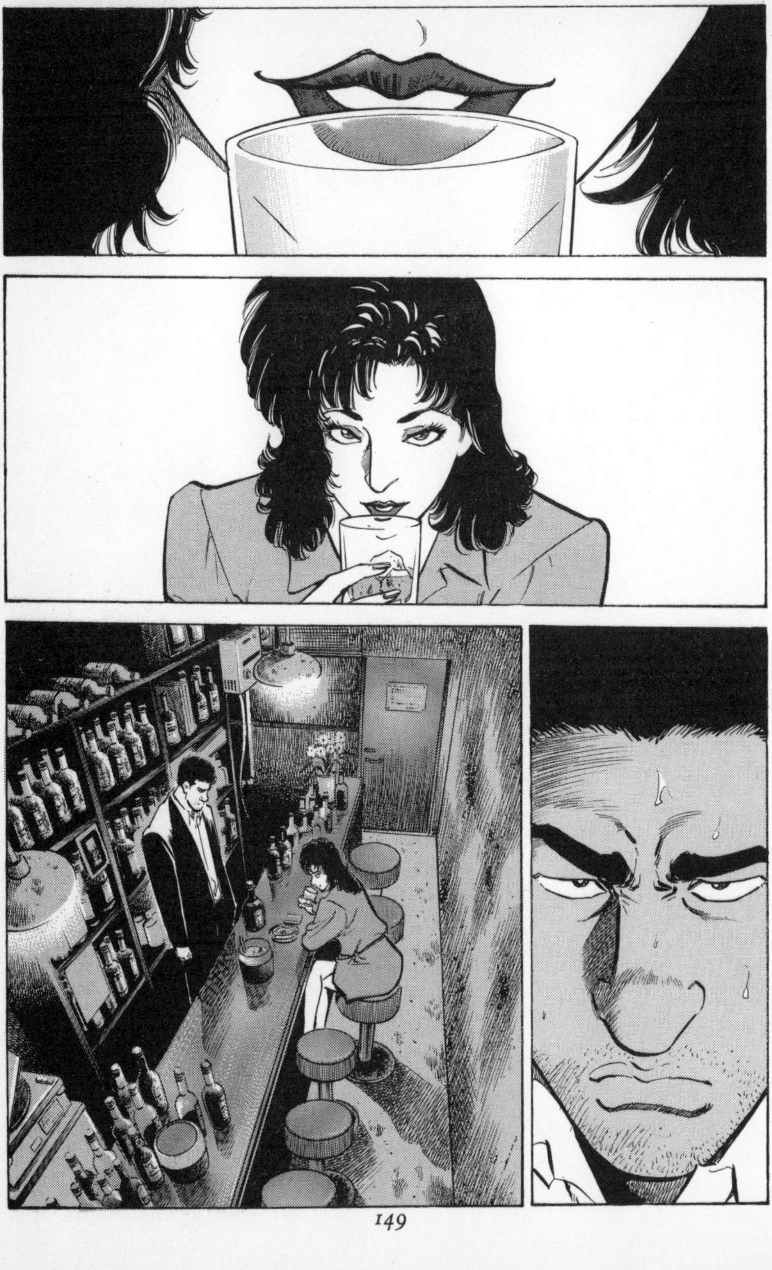

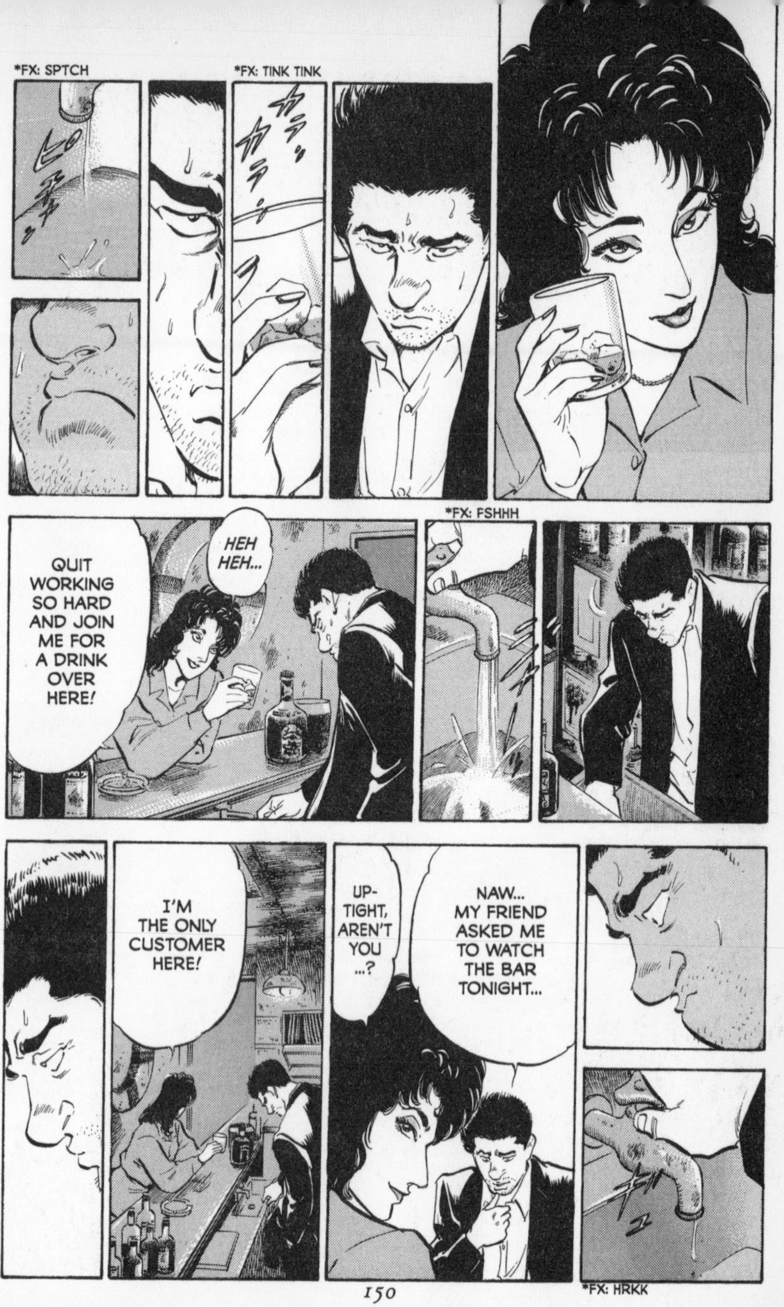
*FX: TINK TINK
*FX: SPTCH
*FX: FSHHH
HEH HEH...
QUIT WORKING SO HARD AND JOIN ME FOR A DRINK OVER HERE!
*FX: HRKK
NAW... MY FRIEND ASKED ME TO WATCH THE BAR TONIGHT...
UP-TIGHT, AREN'T YOU ...?
I'M THE ONLY CUSTOMER HERE!

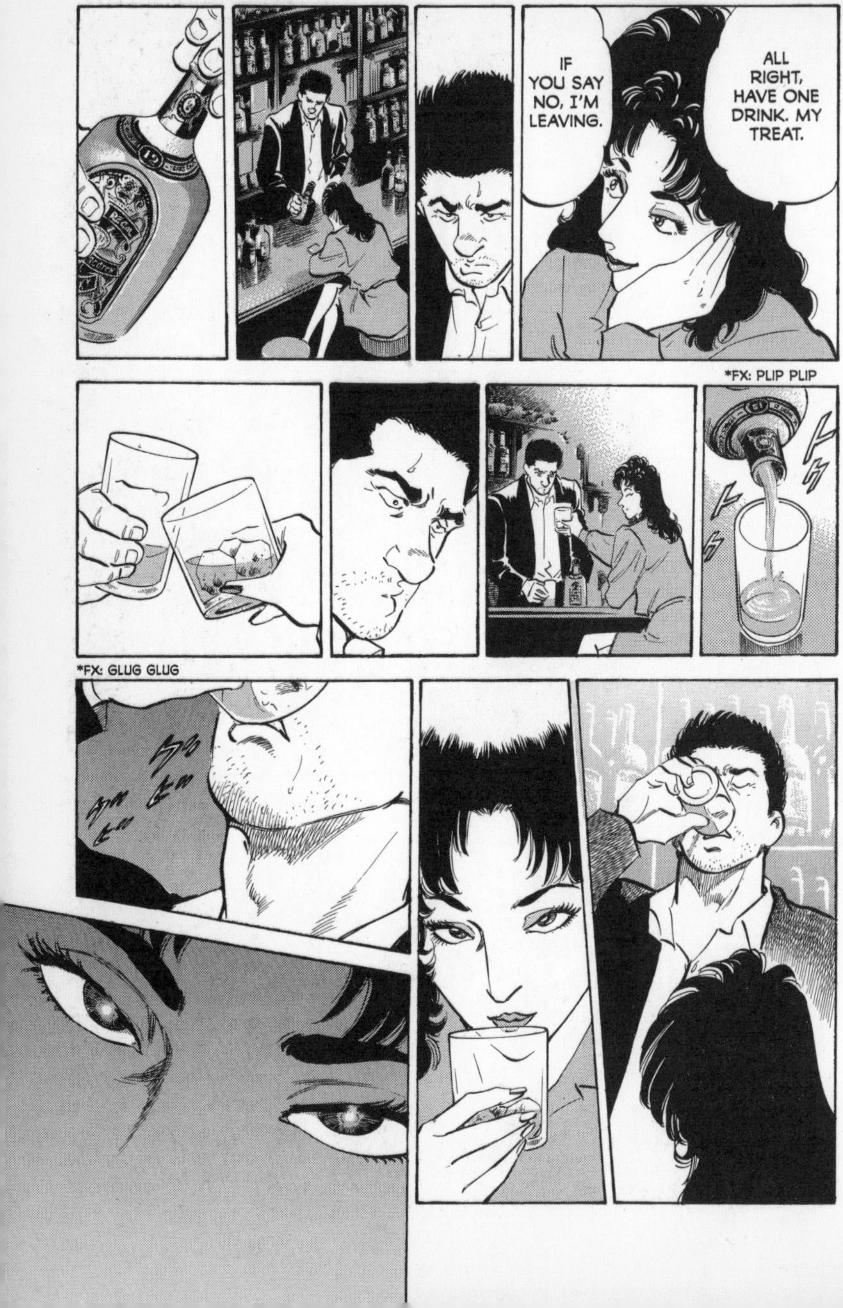
ALL RIGHT, HAVE ONE DRINK. MY TREAT.
IF YOU SAY NO, I'M LEAVING.
*FX: PLIP PLIP
*FX: GLUG GLUG

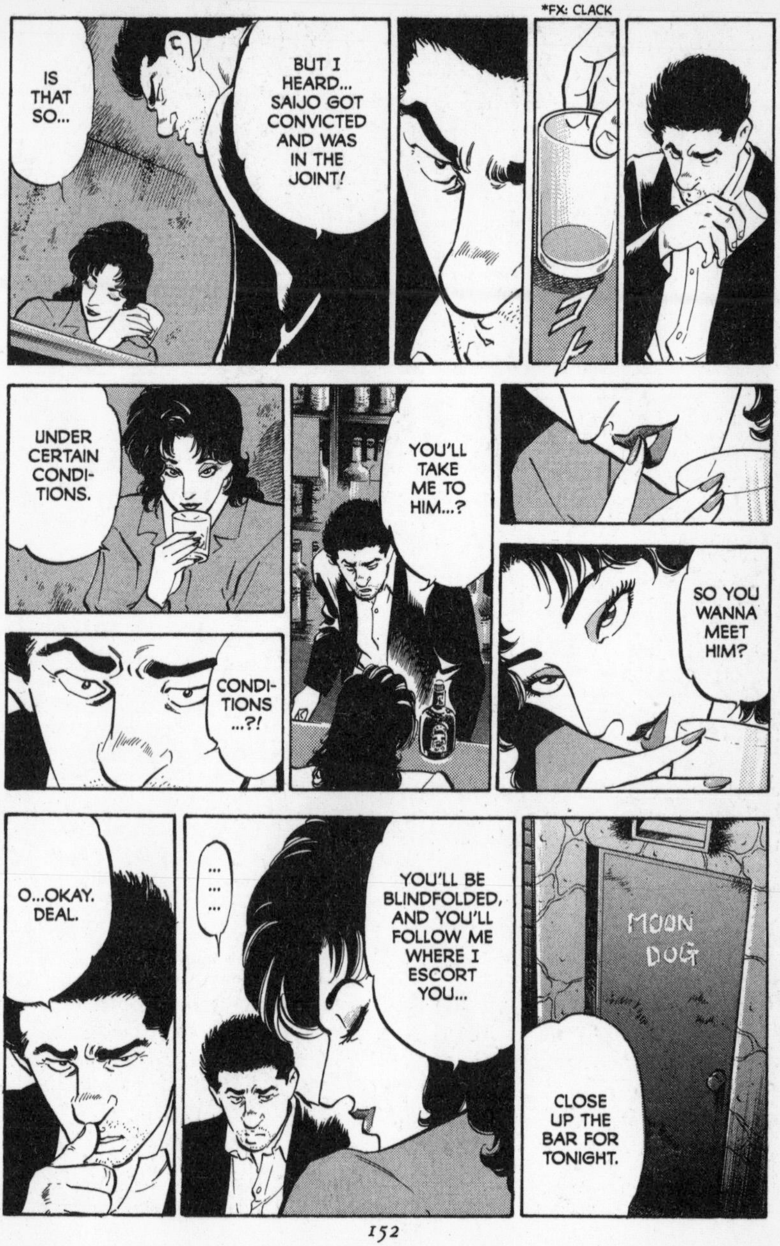
*FX: CLACK
BUT I HEARD... SAIJO GOT CONVICTED AND WAS IN THE JOINT!
IS THAT SO...
SO YOU WANNA MEET HIM?
YOU'LL TAKE ME TO HIM...?
UNDER CERTAIN CONDI-TIONS.
CONDI-TIONS ...?!
MOON DOG
CLOSE UP THE BAR FOR TONIGHT.
YOU'LL BE BLINDFOLDED, AND YOU'LL FOLLOW ME WHERE I ESCORT YOU...
... ...
O...OKAY. DEAL.

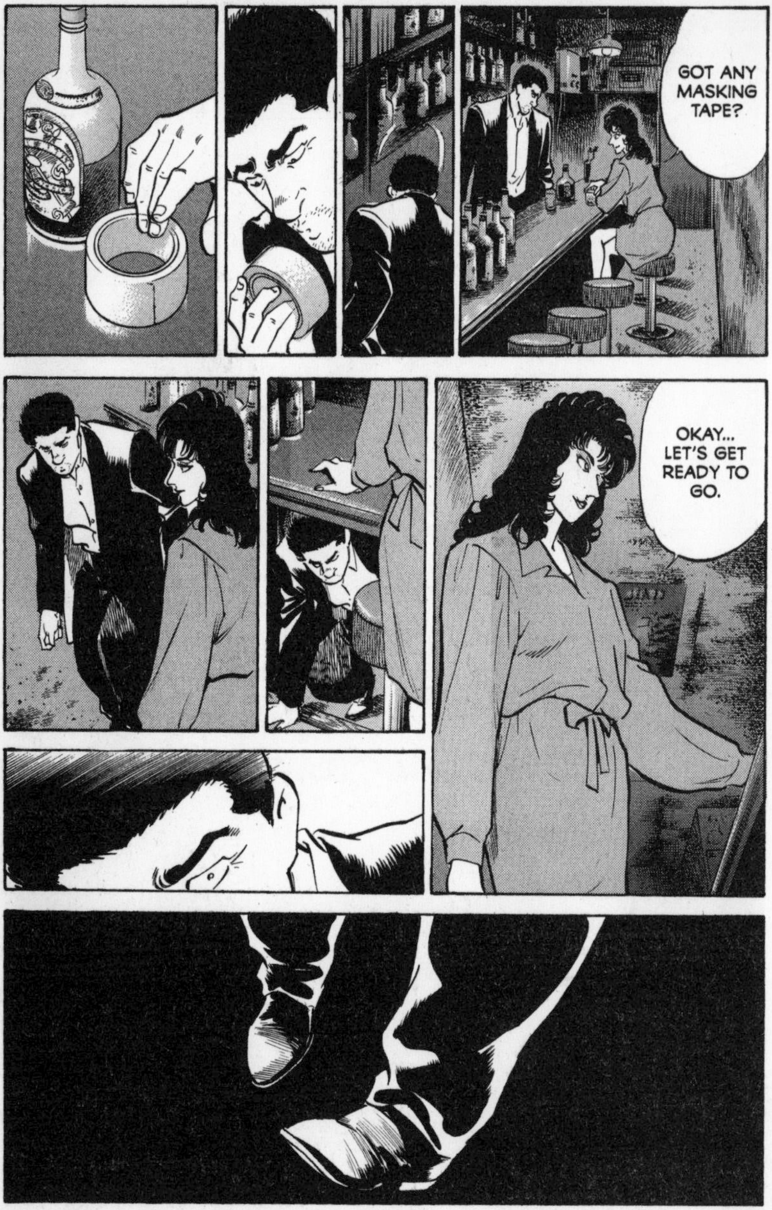
GOT ANY MASKING TAPE?
OKAY... LET'S GET READY TO GO.

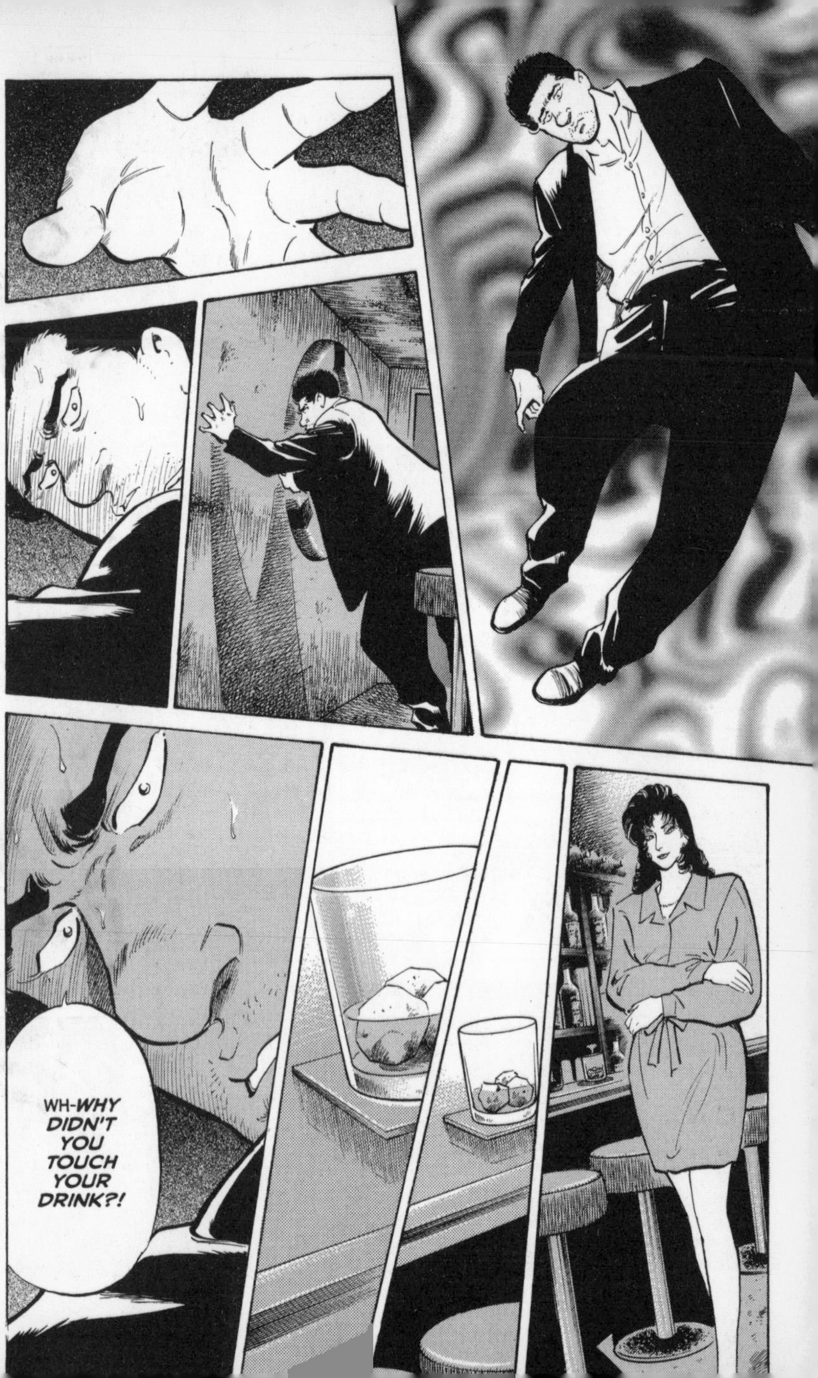
WH-WHY DIDN'T YOU TOUCH YOUR DRINK?!

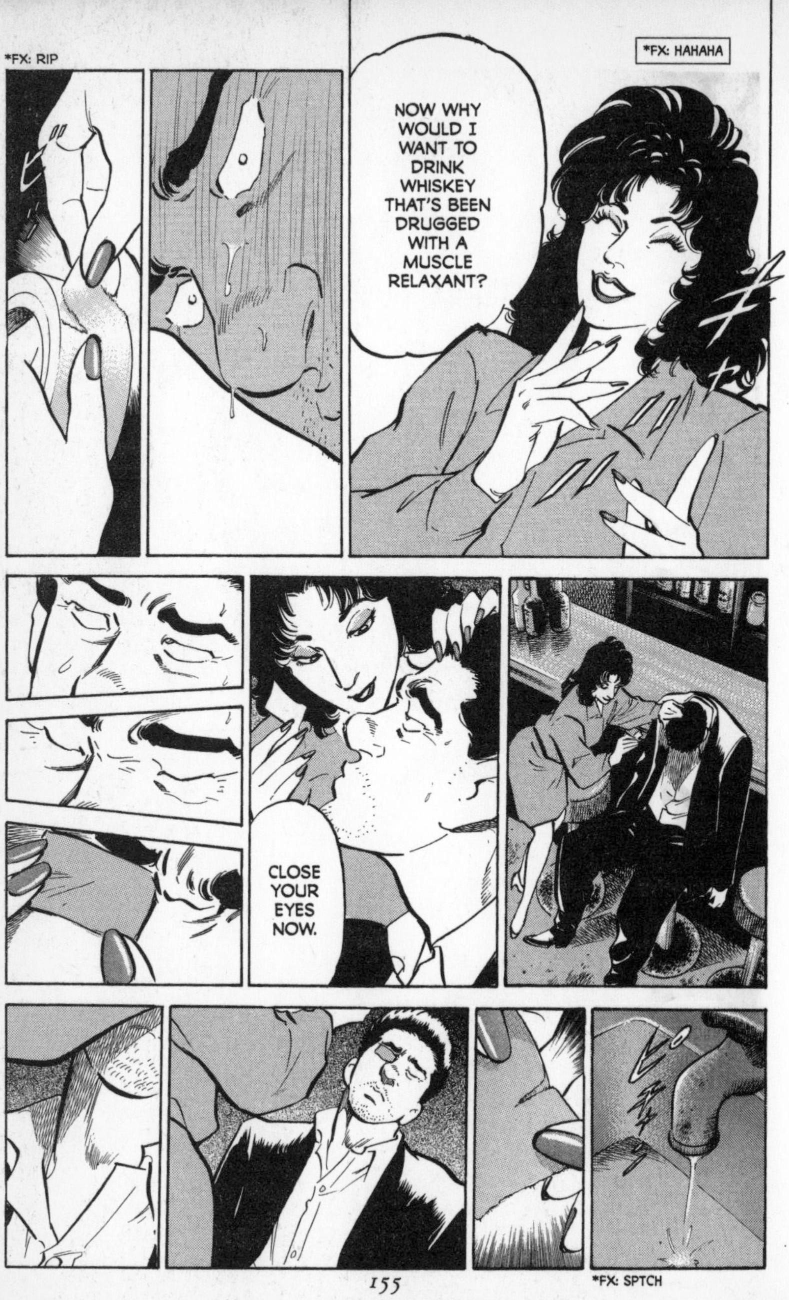
*FX: HAHAHA
NOW WHY WOULD I WANT TO DRINK WHISKEY THAT'S BEEN DRUGGED WITH A MUSCLE RELAXANT?
*FX: RIP
CLOSE YOUR EYES NOW.
*FX: SPTCH

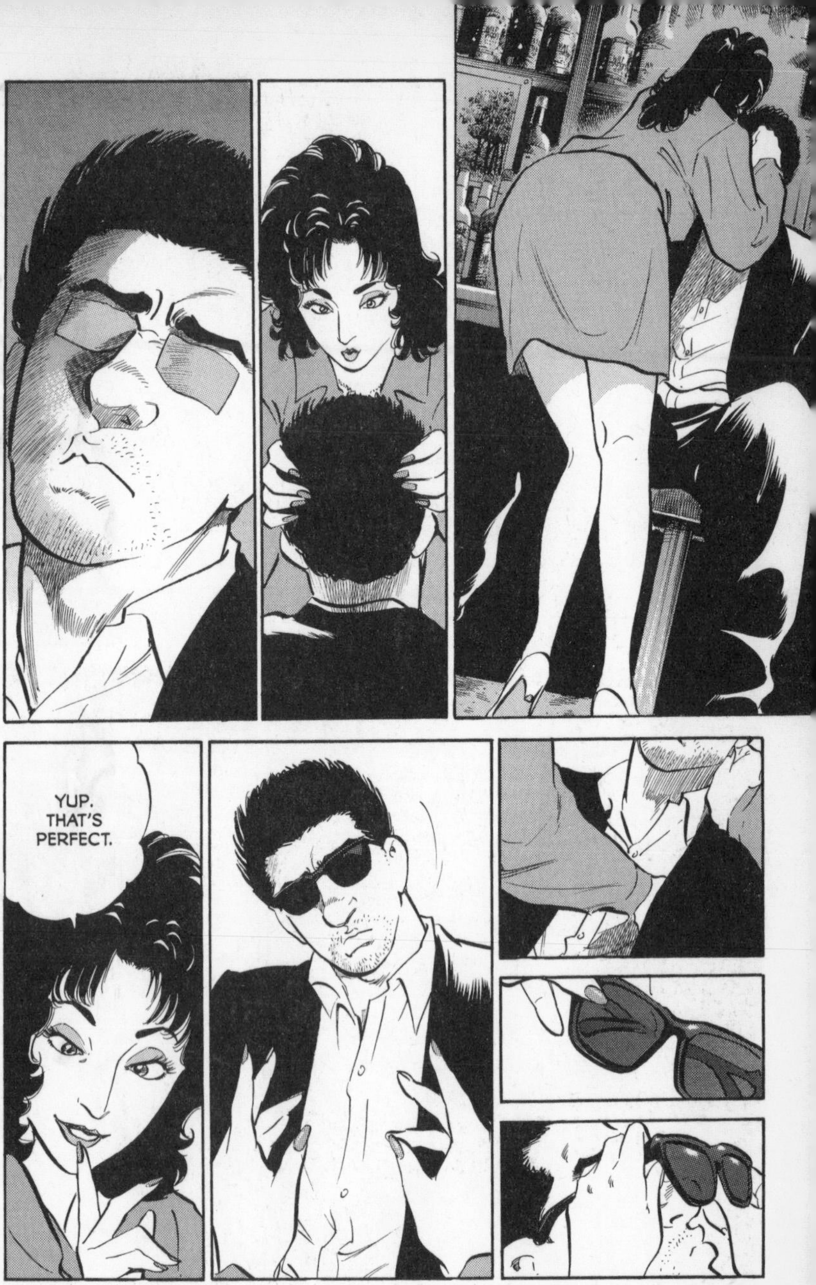
YUP.
THAT'S
PERFECT.

*SIGN: SHINJUKU GOLDEN GAI

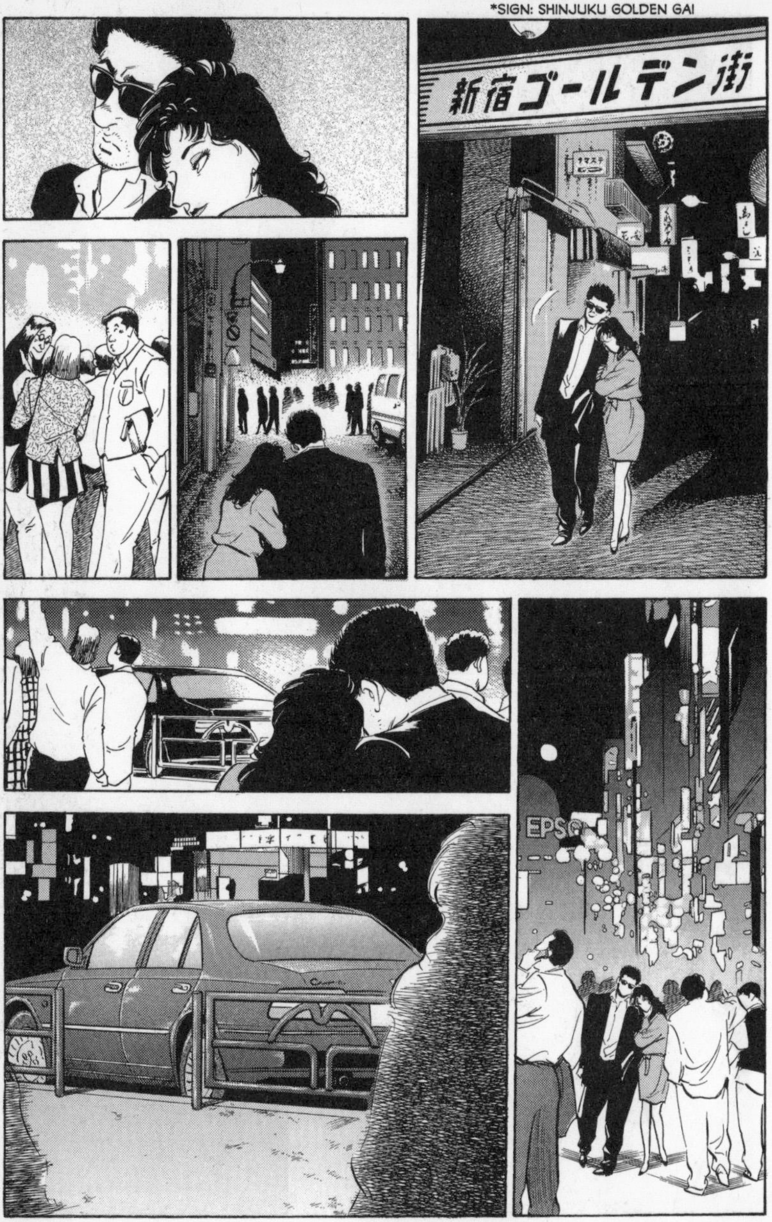
新宿ゴールデン街

*FX: KACHIK

CABBIE, COULD YOU PLEASE TAKE US TO THE PLACE ON THIS MAP?

*FX: BAM

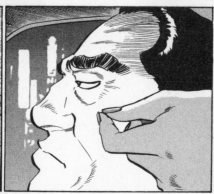

158

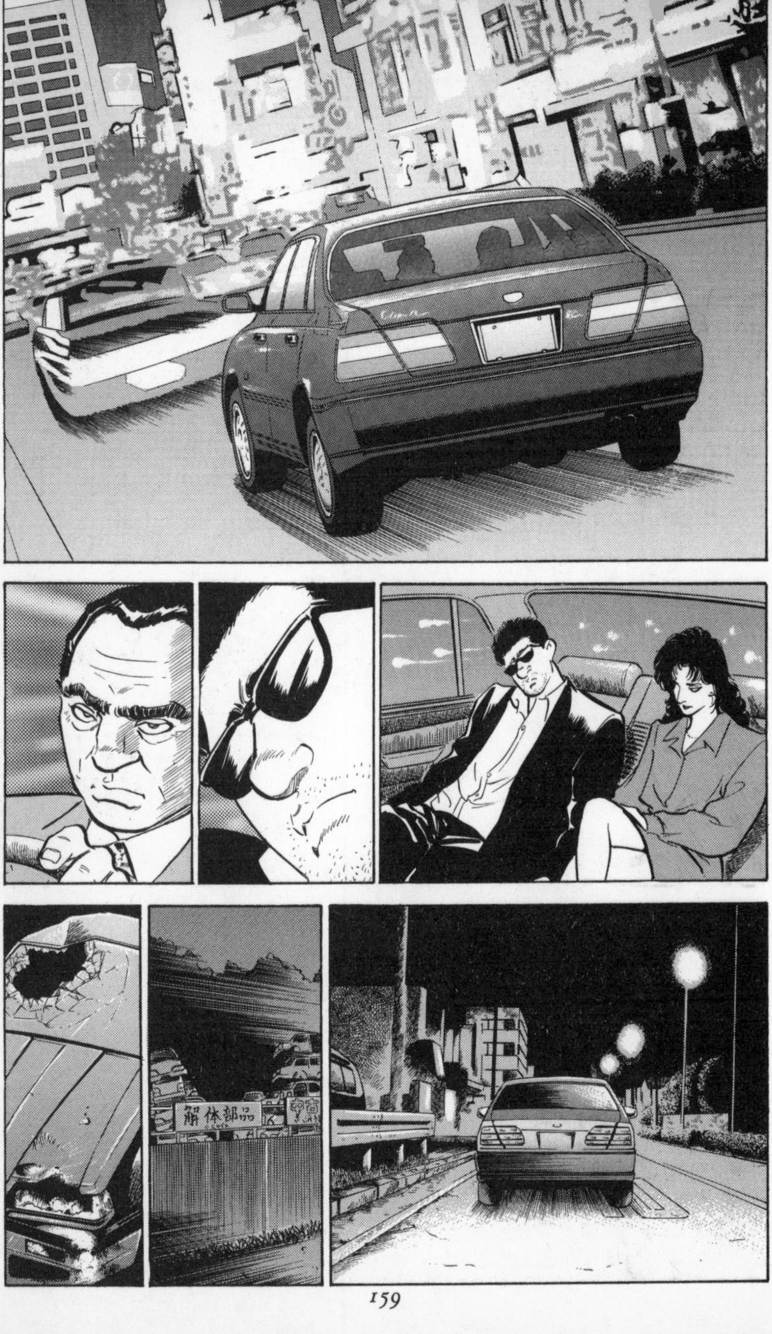
解体部品

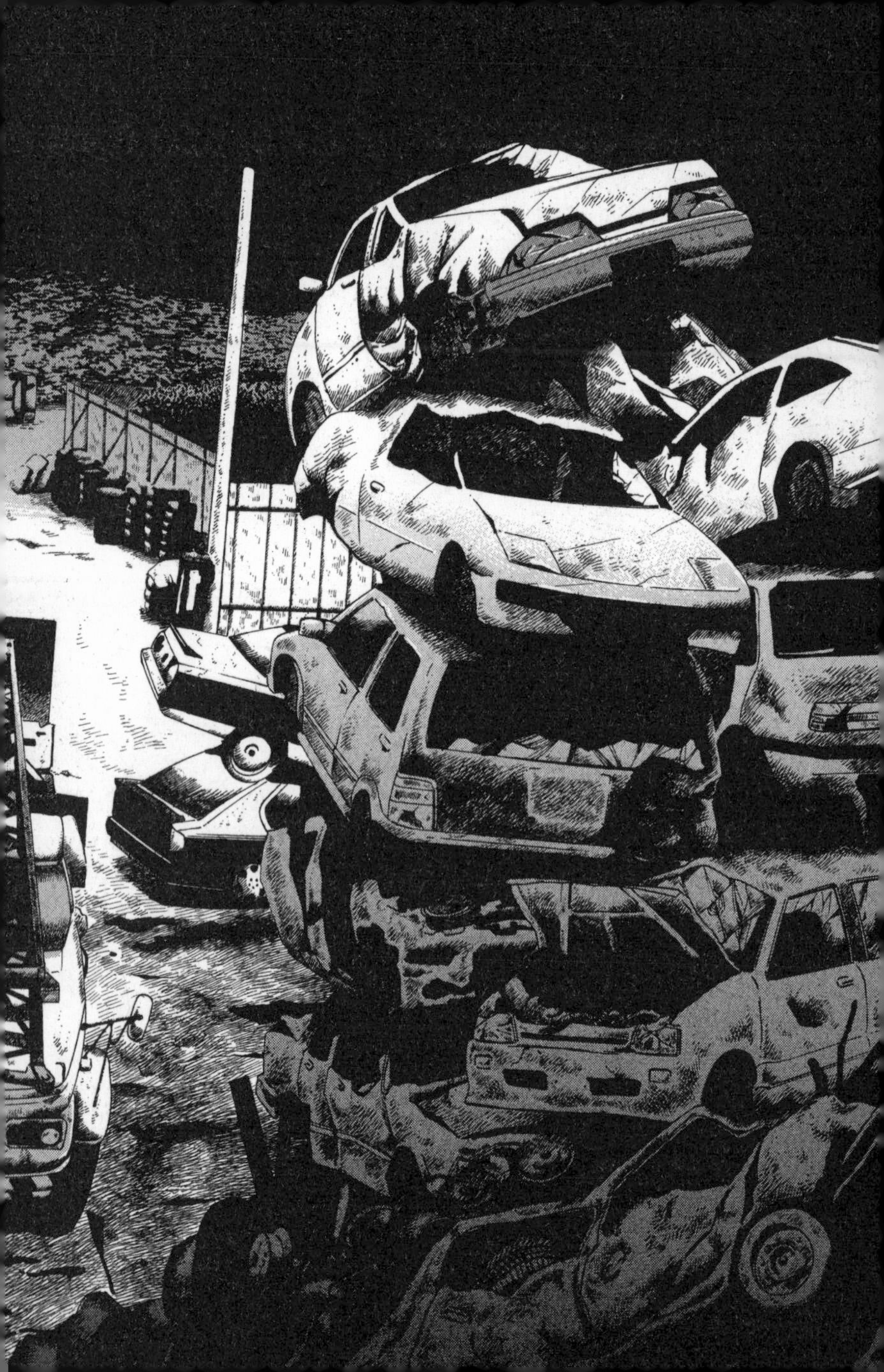

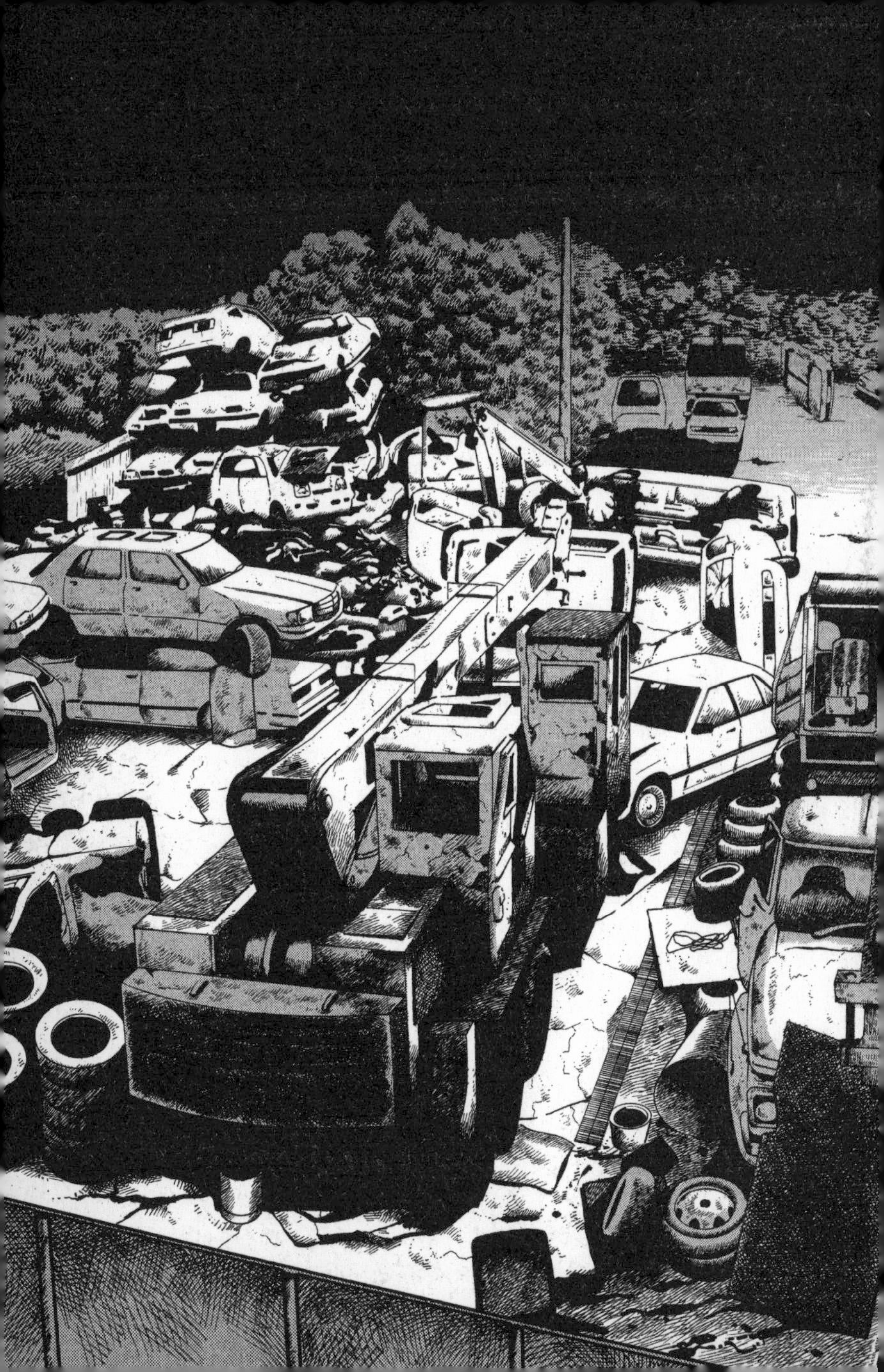

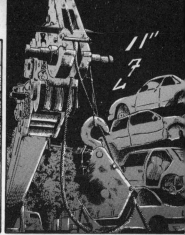

*FX: BAM

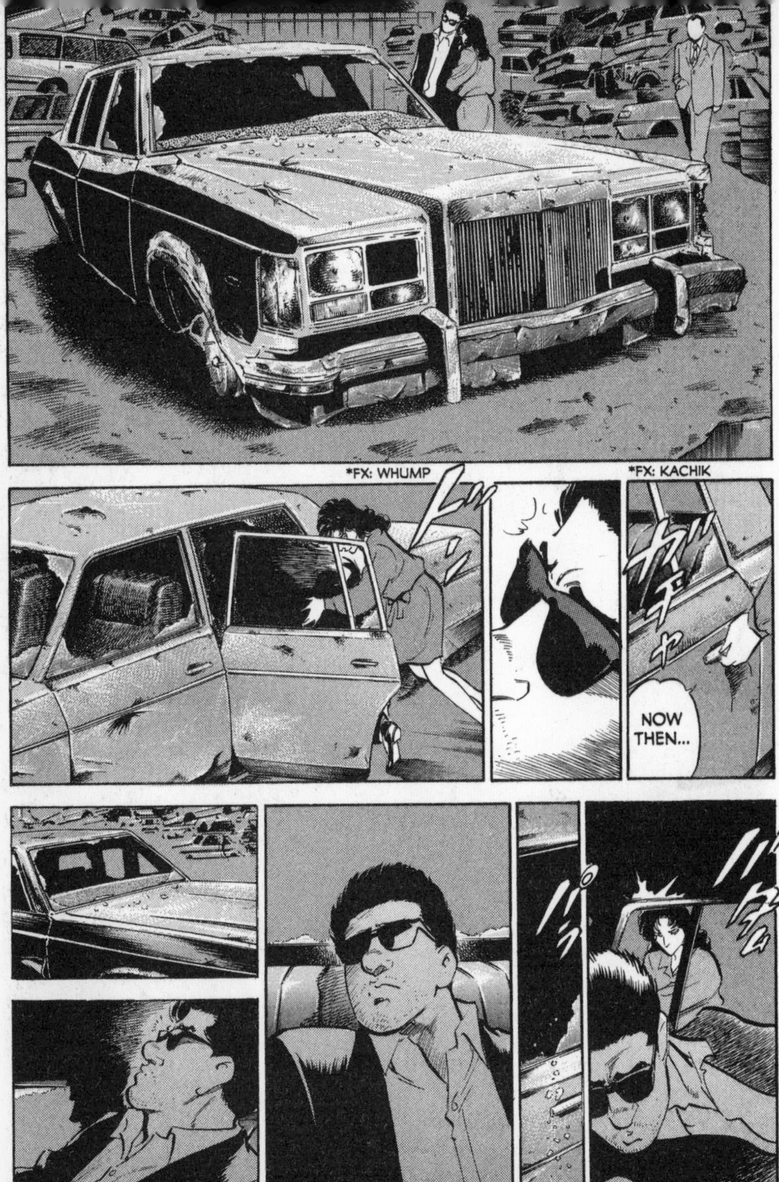
*FX: KACHIK
NOW THEN...
*FX: WHUMP
*FX: BAM
*FX: CLINK

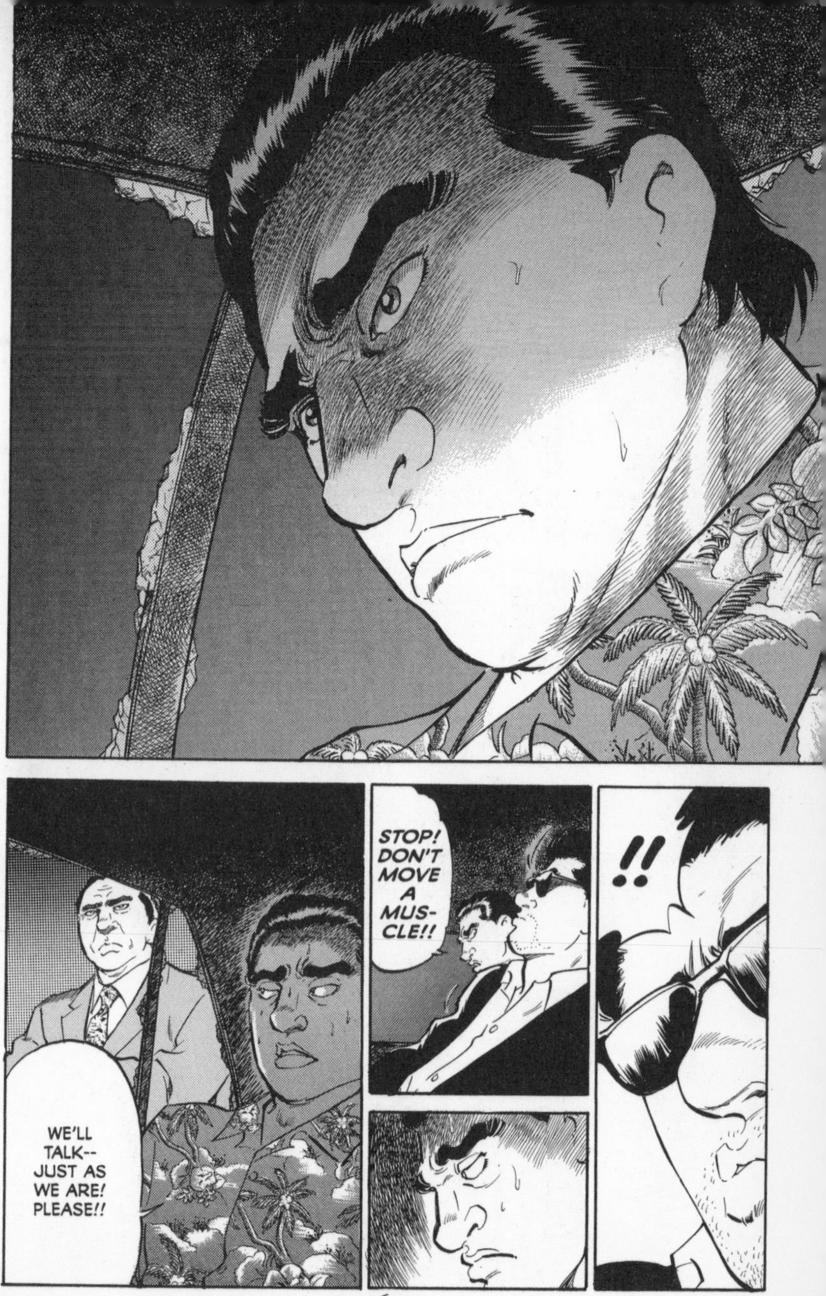
!!
STOP! DON'T MOVE A MUS-CLE!!
WE'LL TALK-- JUST AS WE ARE! PLEASE!!

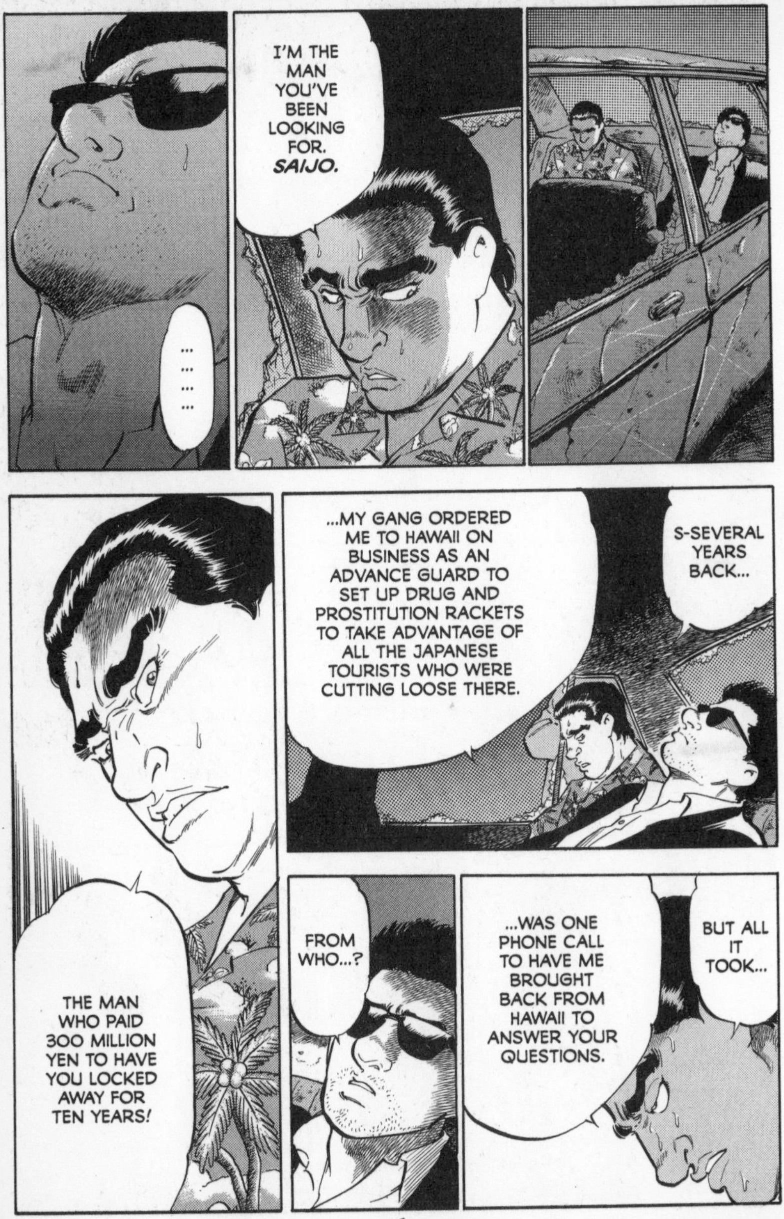
I'M THE MAN YOU'VE BEEN LOOKING FOR. SAIJO.
...
S-SEVERAL YEARS BACK...
...MY GANG ORDERED ME TO HAWAII ON BUSINESS AS AN ADVANCE GUARD TO SET UP DRUG AND PROSTITUTION RACKETS TO TAKE ADVANTAGE OF ALL THE JAPANESE TOURISTS WHO WERE CUTTING LOOSE THERE.
BUT ALL IT TOOK...
...WAS ONE PHONE CALL TO HAVE ME BROUGHT BACK FROM HAWAII TO ANSWER YOUR QUESTIONS.
FROM WHO...?
THE MAN WHO PAID 300 MILLION YEN TO HAVE YOU LOCKED AWAY FOR TEN YEARS!

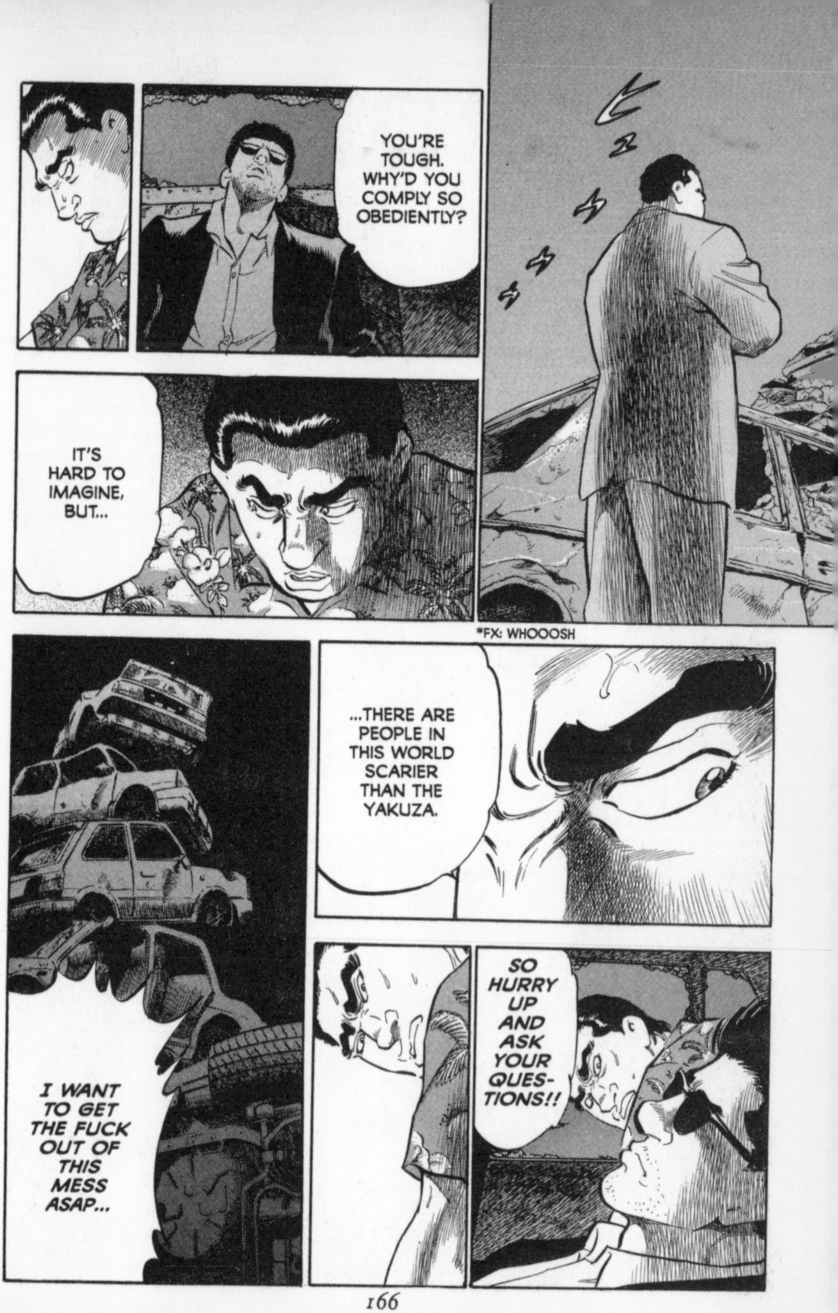
*FX: WHOOOSH
YOU'RE TOUGH. WHY'D YOU COMPLY SO OBEDIENTLY?
IT'S HARD TO IMAGINE, BUT...
...THERE ARE PEOPLE IN THIS WORLD SCARIER THAN THE YAKUZA.
SO HURRY UP AND ASK YOUR QUES-TIONS!!
I WANT TO GET THE FUCK OUT OF THIS MESS ASAP...

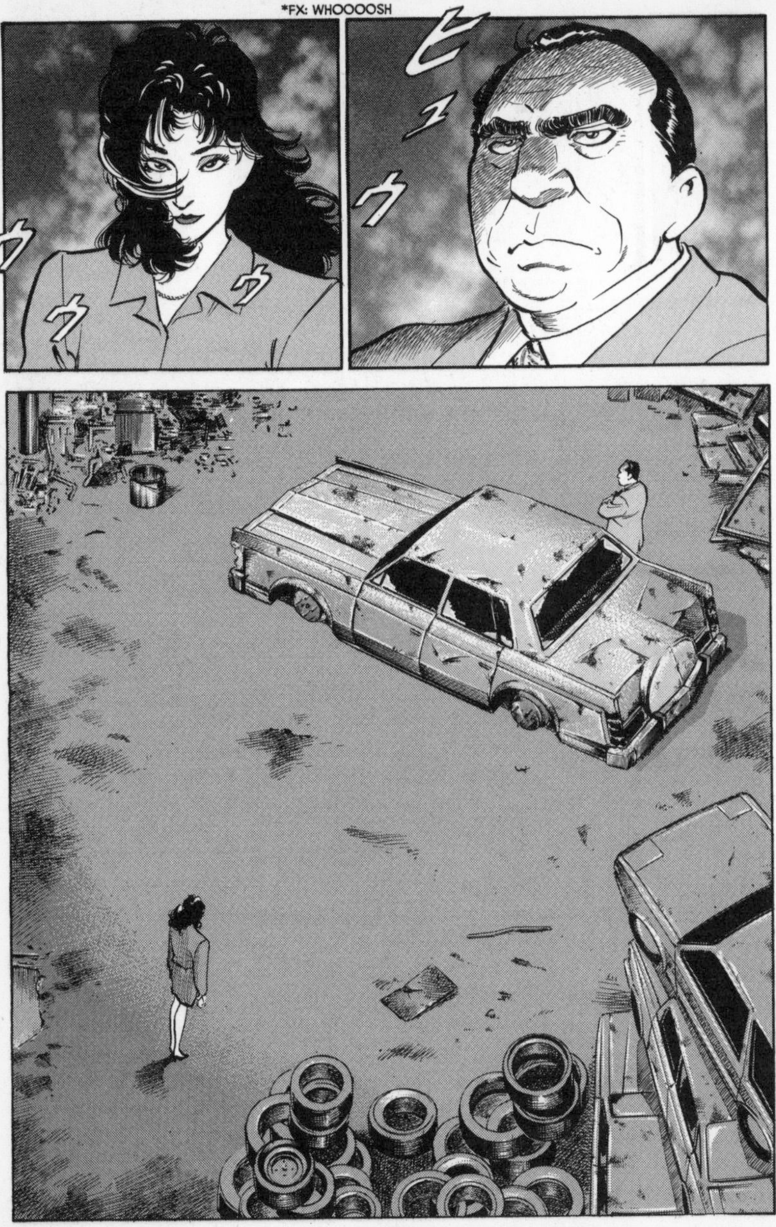
*FX: WHOOOOSH
ヒュウウ
ウウウ

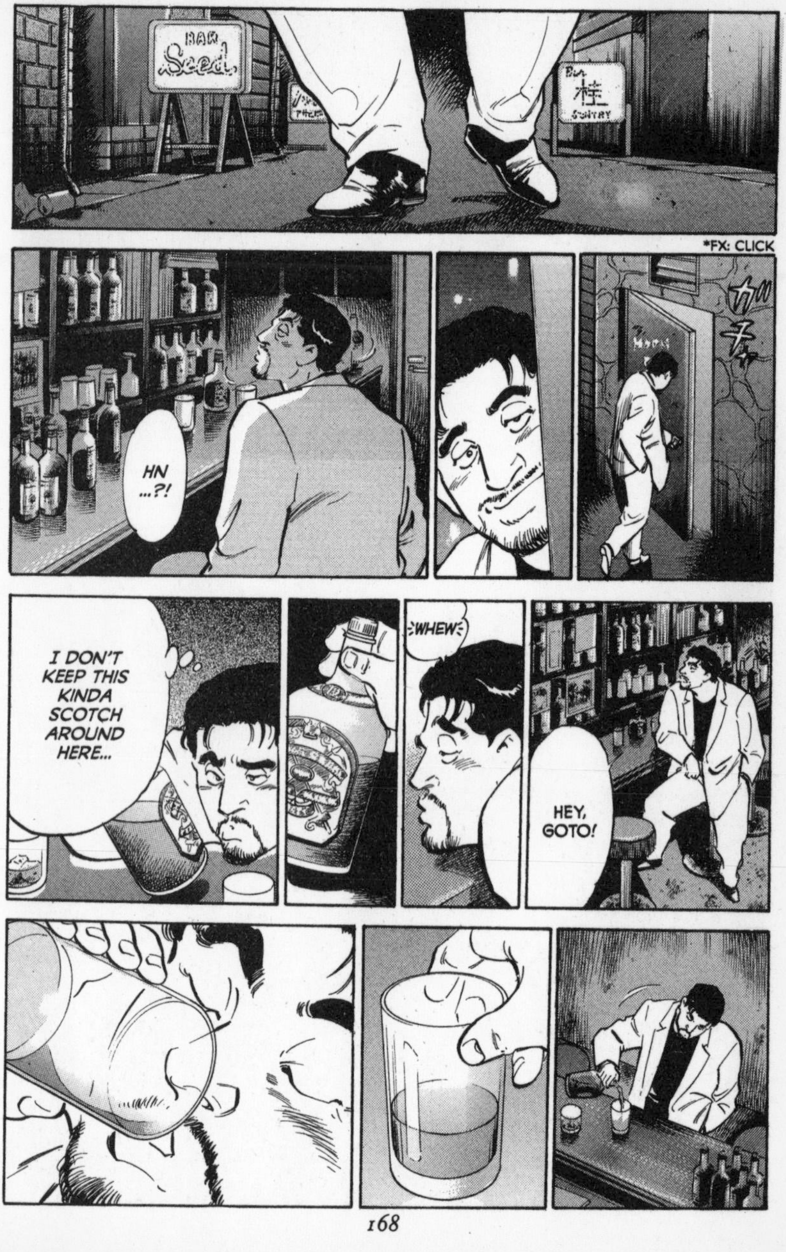
BAR
Seed
*FX: CLICK
カチャ
HN ...?!
HEY, GOTO!
WHEW
I DON'T KEEP THIS KINDA SCOTCH AROUND HERE...

*FX: CREAK

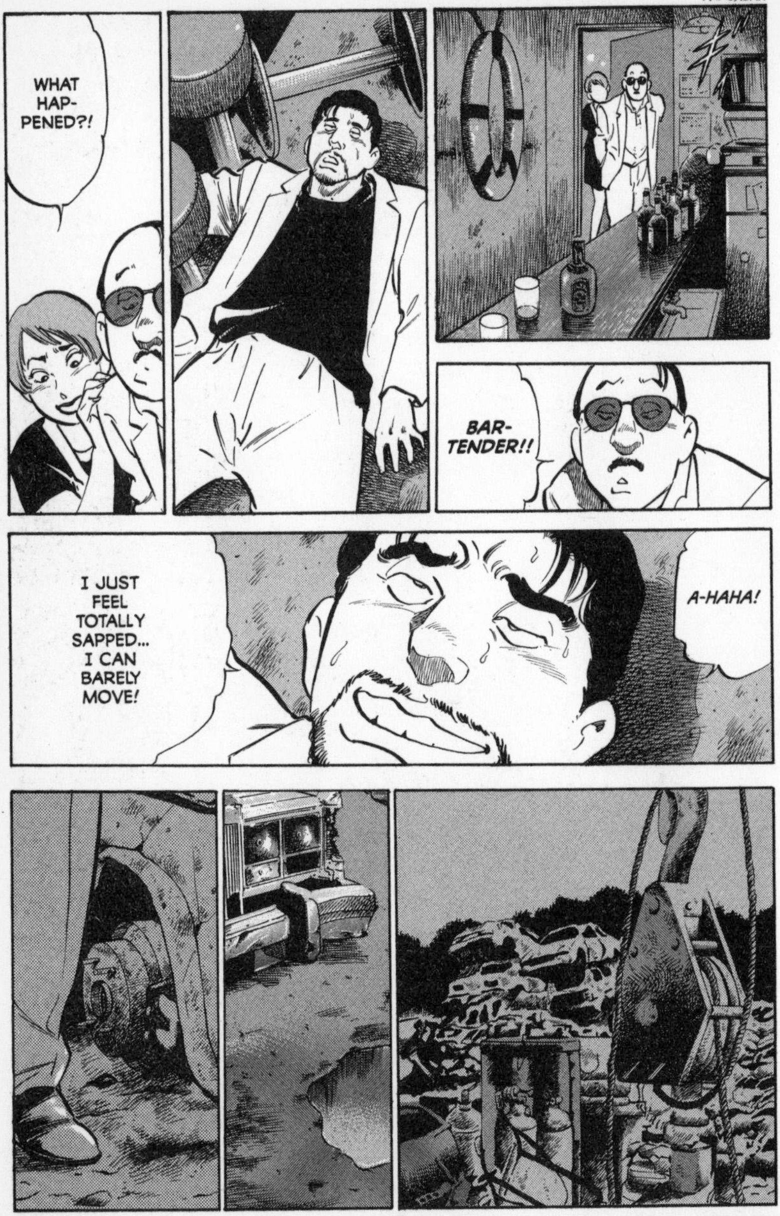
BAR-TENDER!!
WHAT HAP-PENED?!
A-HAHA!
I JUST FEEL TOTALLY SAPPED... I CAN BARELY MOVE!

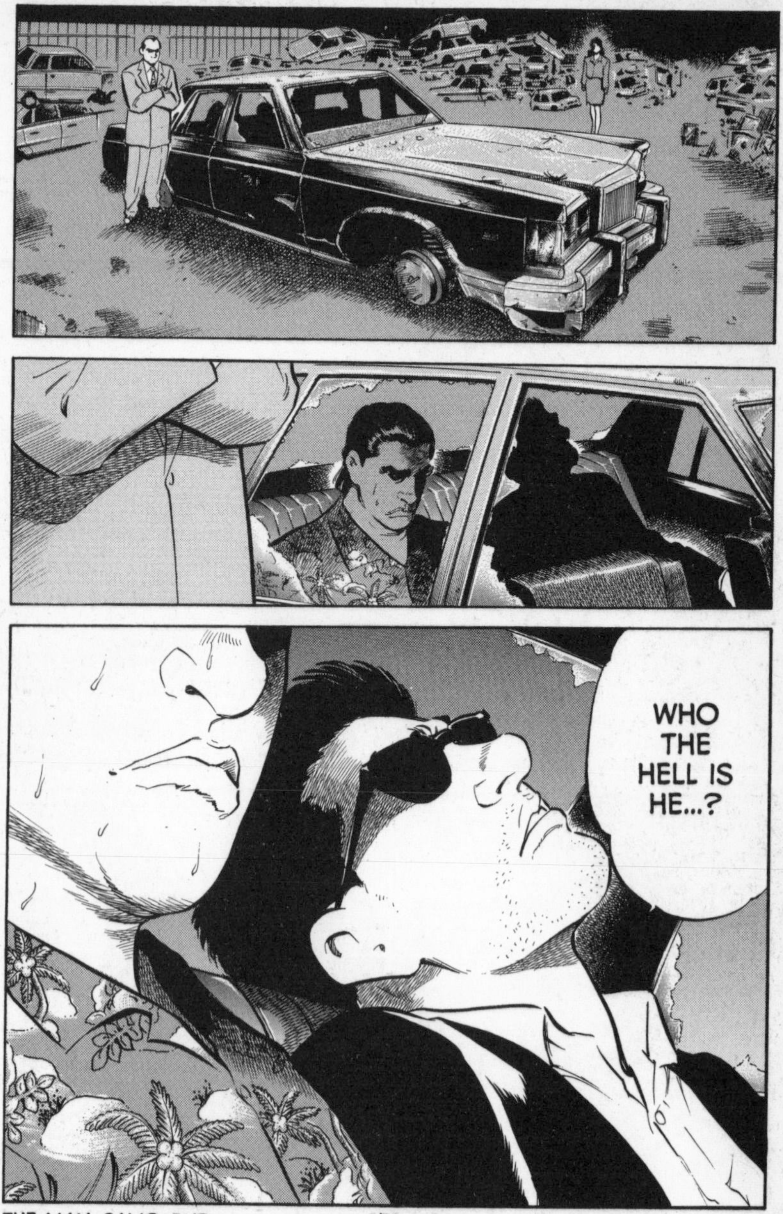
WHO THE HELL IS HE...?

THE MAN, SAIJO: END

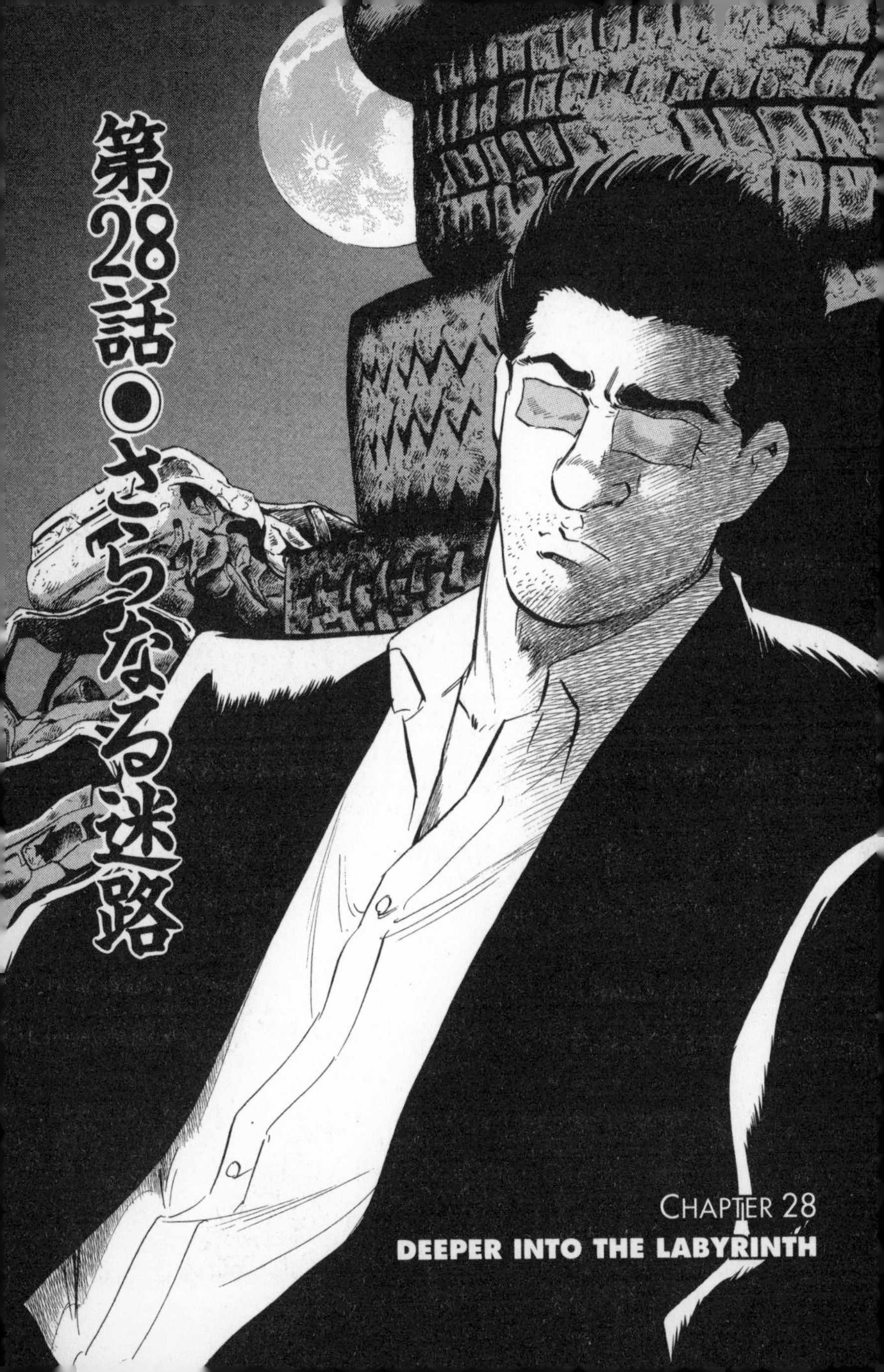
第28話●さらなる迷路
CHAPTER 28
DEEPER INTO THE LABYRINTH

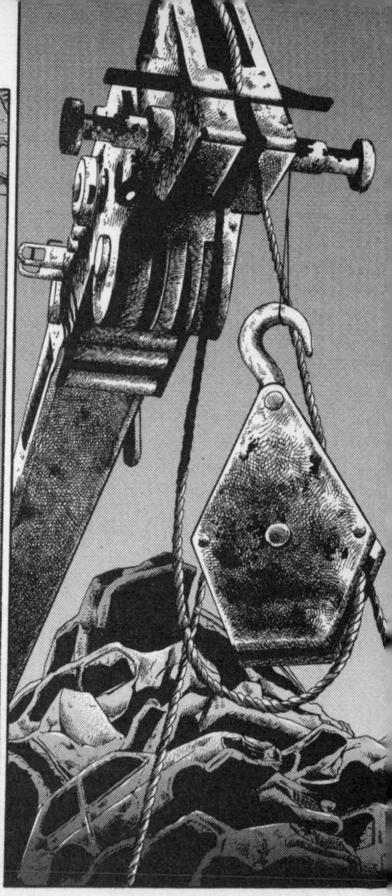

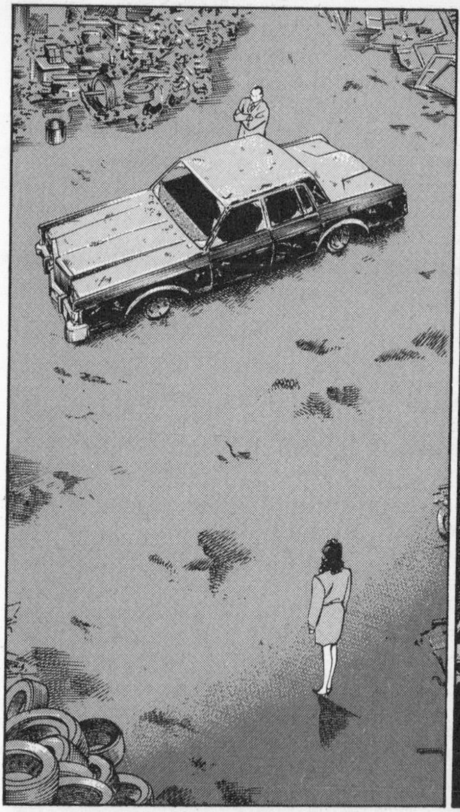

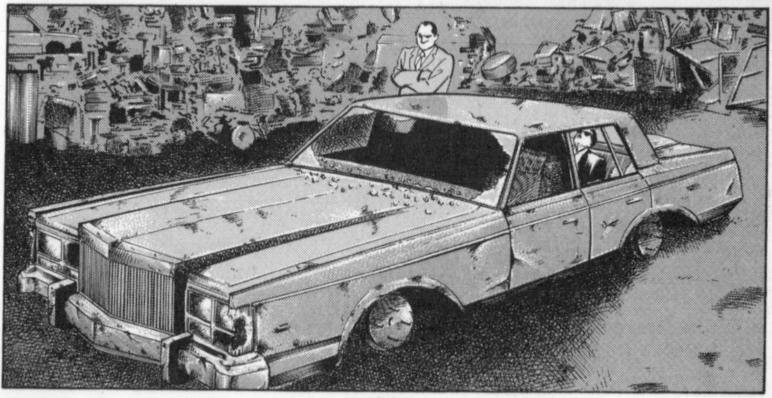

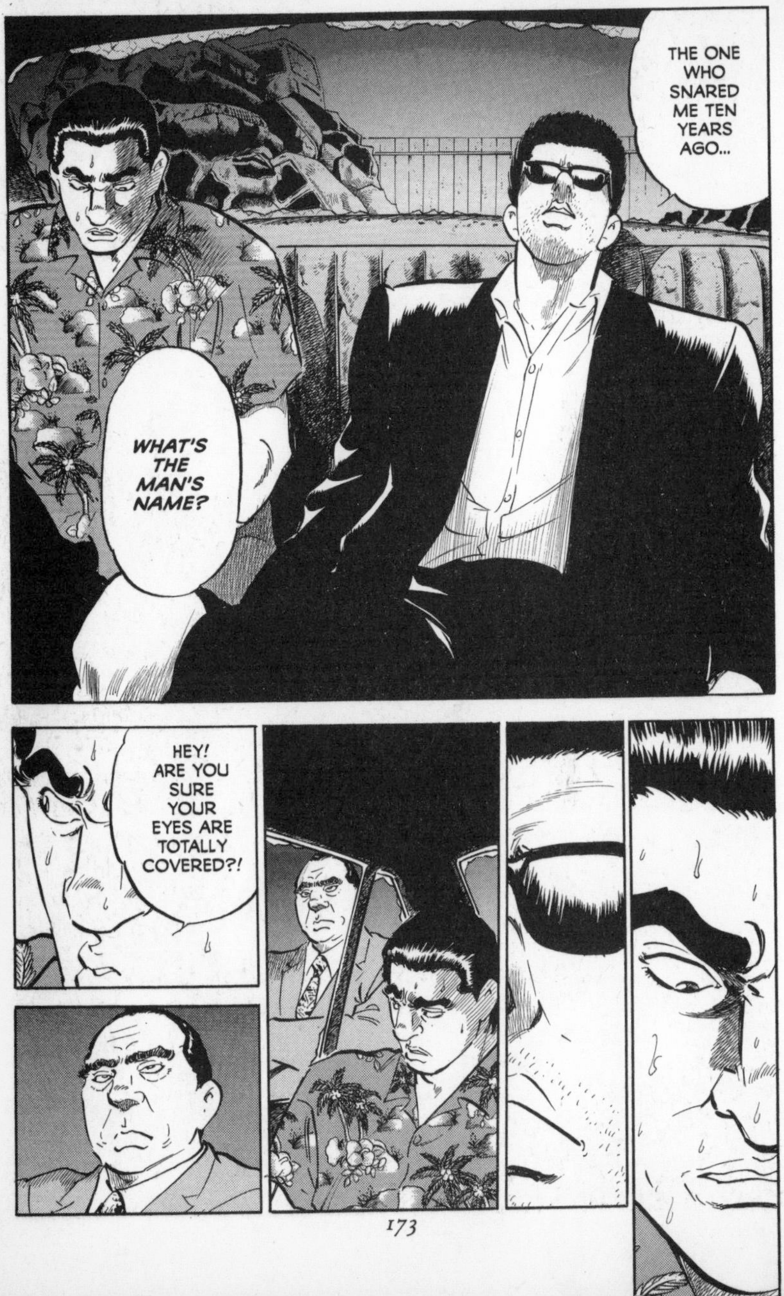
THE ONE WHO SNARED ME TEN YEARS AGO...
WHAT'S THE MAN'S NAME?
HEY! ARE YOU SURE YOUR EYES ARE TOTALLY COVERED?!

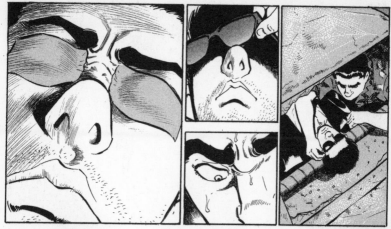

...SAID
HIS
NAME
WAS
DOJIMA.

THE
MAN...

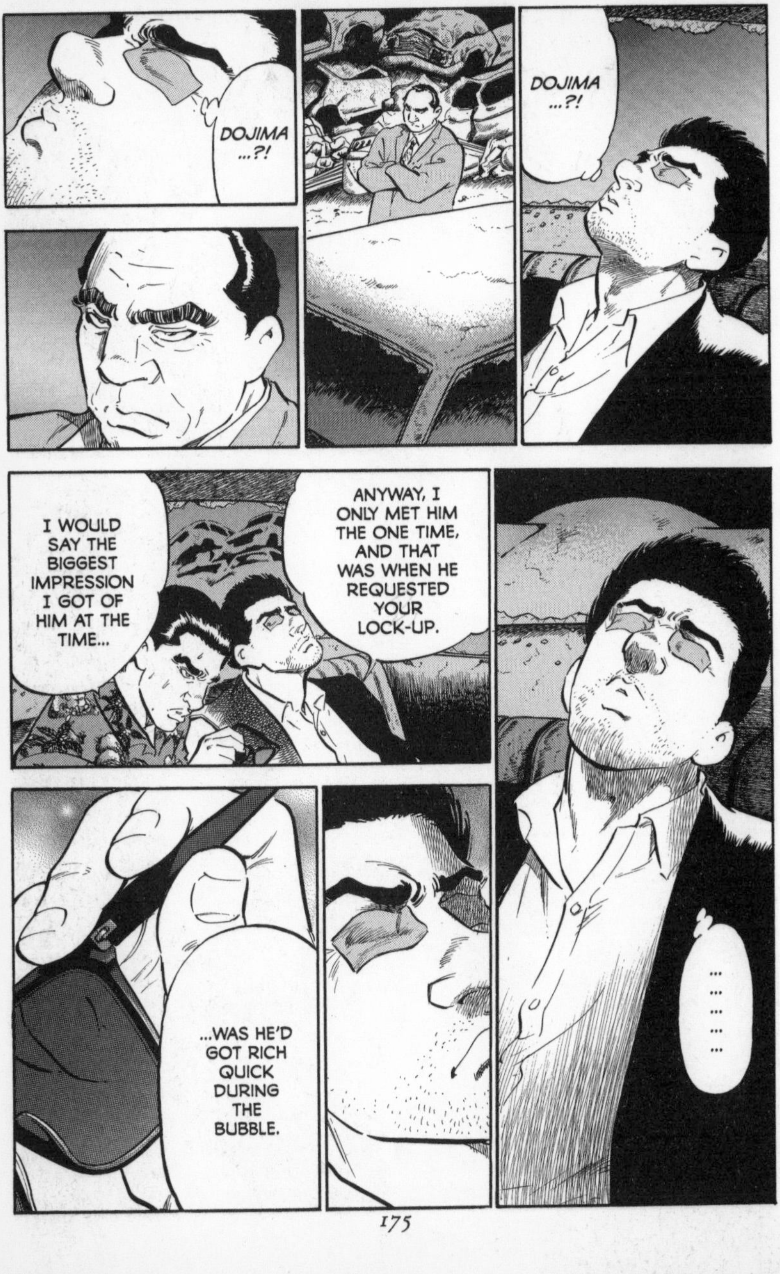
DOJIMA ...?!
DOJIMA ...?!
......
ANYWAY, I ONLY MET HIM THE ONE TIME, AND THAT WAS WHEN HE REQUESTED YOUR LOCK-UP.
I WOULD SAY THE BIGGEST IMPRESSION I GOT OF HIM AT THE TIME...
...WAS HE'D GOT RICH QUICK DURING THE BUBBLE.

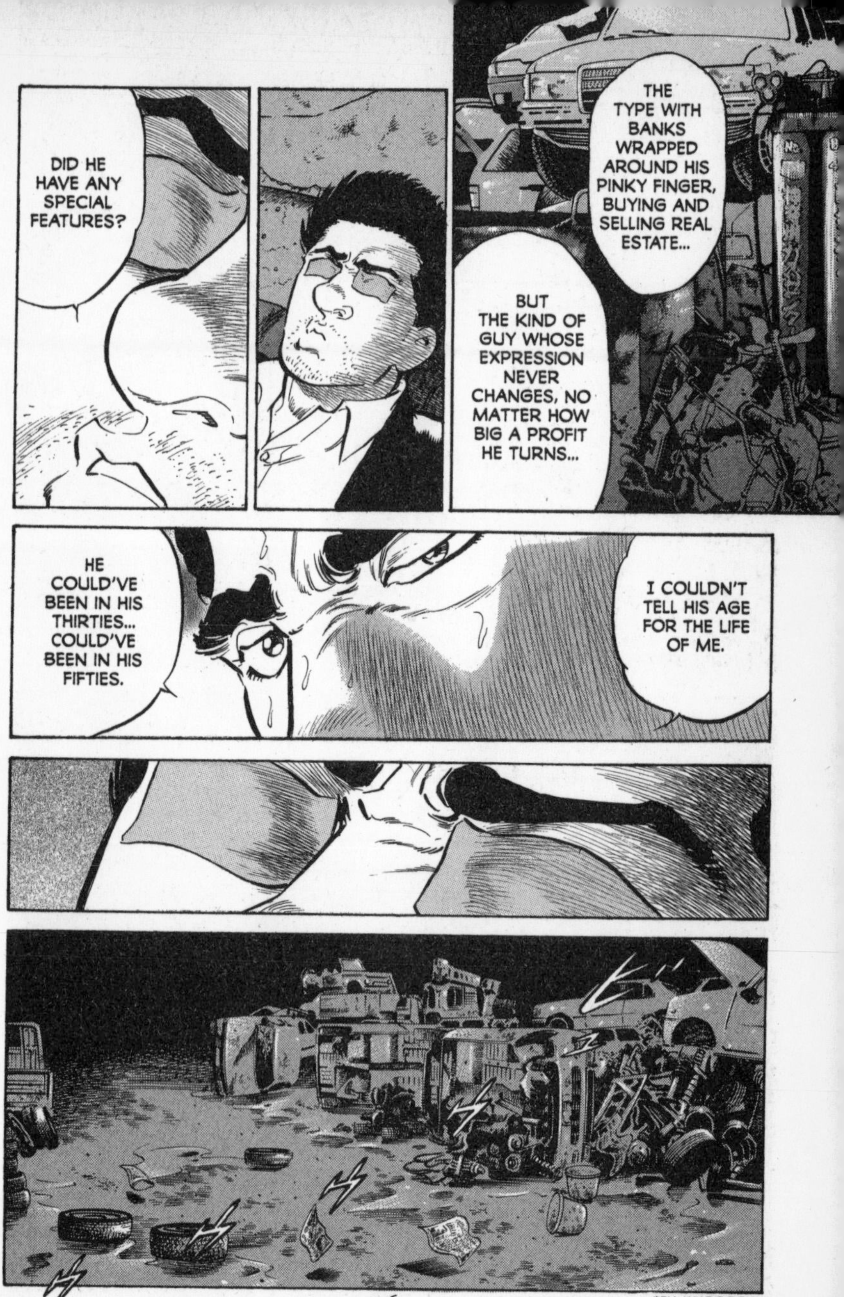
THE TYPE WITH BANKS WRAPPED AROUND HIS PINKY FINGER, BUYING AND SELLING REAL ESTATE...
BUT THE KIND OF GUY WHOSE EXPRESSION NEVER CHANGES, NO MATTER HOW BIG A PROFIT HE TURNS...
DID HE HAVE ANY SPECIAL FEATURES?
I COULDN'T TELL HIS AGE FOR THE LIFE OF ME.
HE COULD'VE BEEN IN HIS THIRTIES... COULD'VE BEEN IN HIS FIFTIES.

*FX: WHOOOOSH

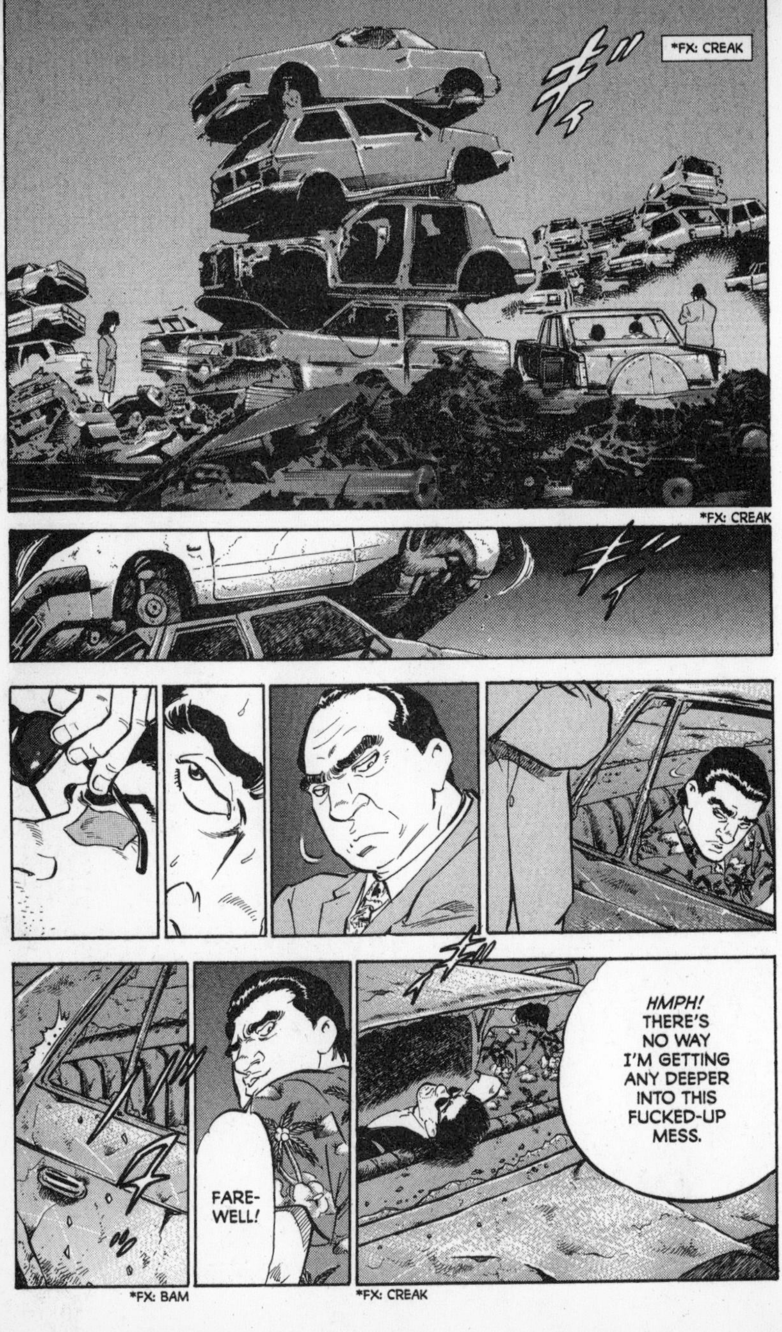
*FX: CREAK
*FX: CREAK
HMPH! THERE'S NO WAY I'M GETTING ANY DEEPER INTO THIS FUCKED-UP MESS.
*FX: CREAK
FARE-WELL!
*FX: BAM

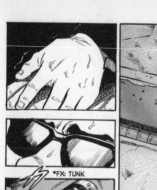

*FX: TUNK

*FX: WHOOOSH

*FX: TUNK TUNK TUNK TUNK

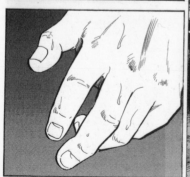

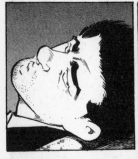

179

*FX: PHEW

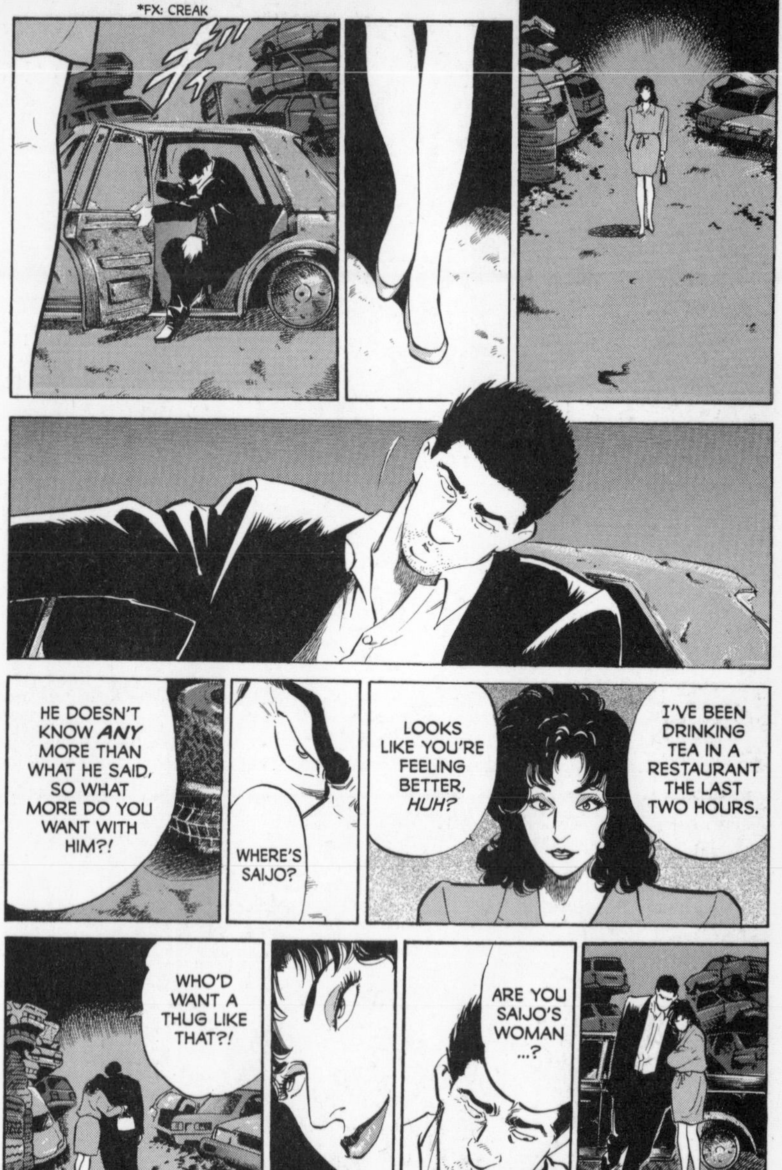
*FX: CREAK
I'VE BEEN DRINKING TEA IN A RESTAURANT THE LAST TWO HOURS.
LOOKS LIKE YOU'RE FEELING BETTER, *HUH?*
WHERE'S SAIJO?
HE DOESN'T KNOW ***ANY*** MORE THAN WHAT HE SAID, SO WHAT MORE DO YOU WANT WITH HIM?!
ARE YOU SAIJO'S WOMAN ...?
WHO'D WANT A THUG LIKE THAT?!

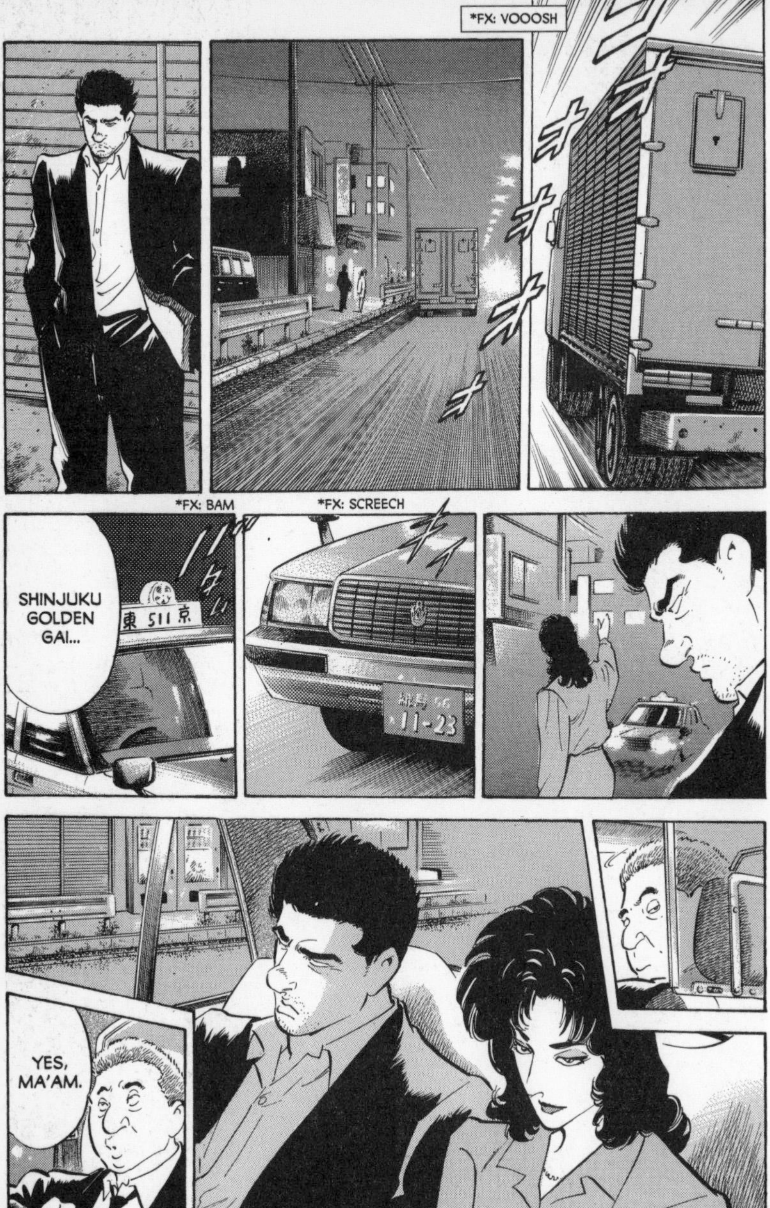
*FX: VOOOSH
*FX: SCREECH
*FX: BAM
SHINJUKU GOLDEN GAI...
YES, MA'AM.

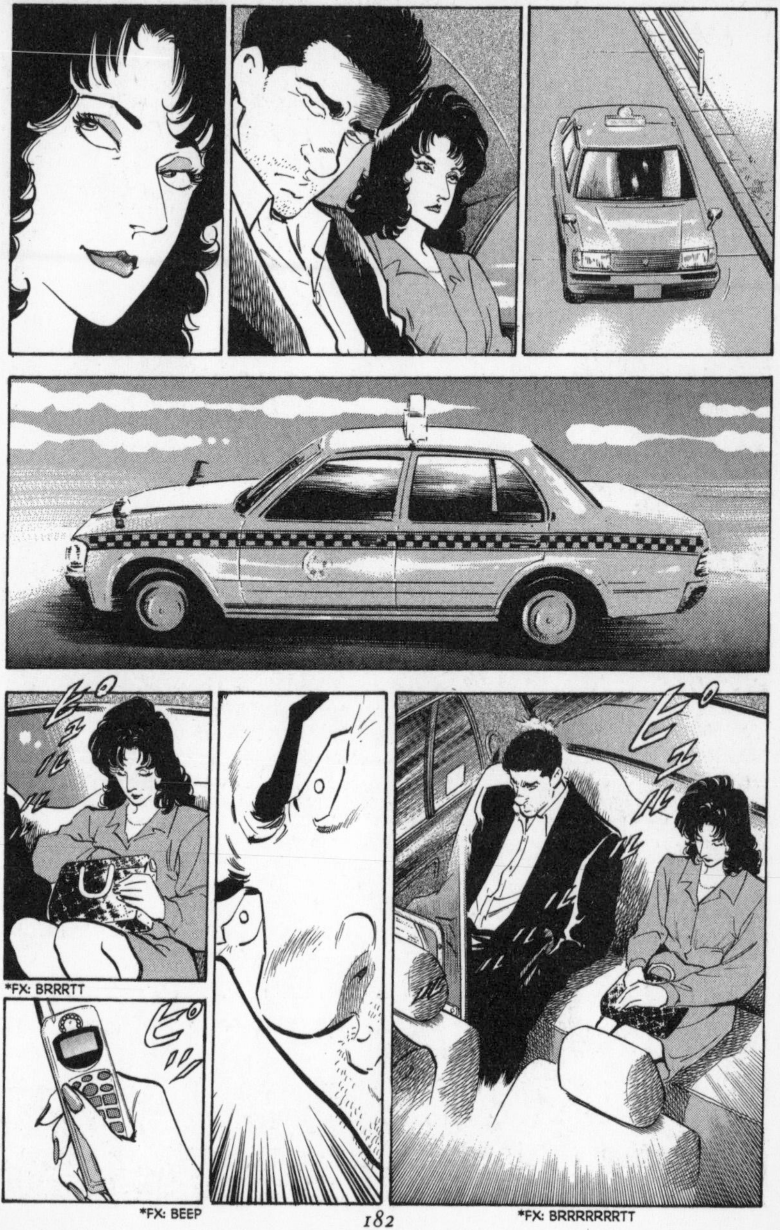
*FX: BRRRRRRRTT
*FX: BRRRTT
*FX: BEEP

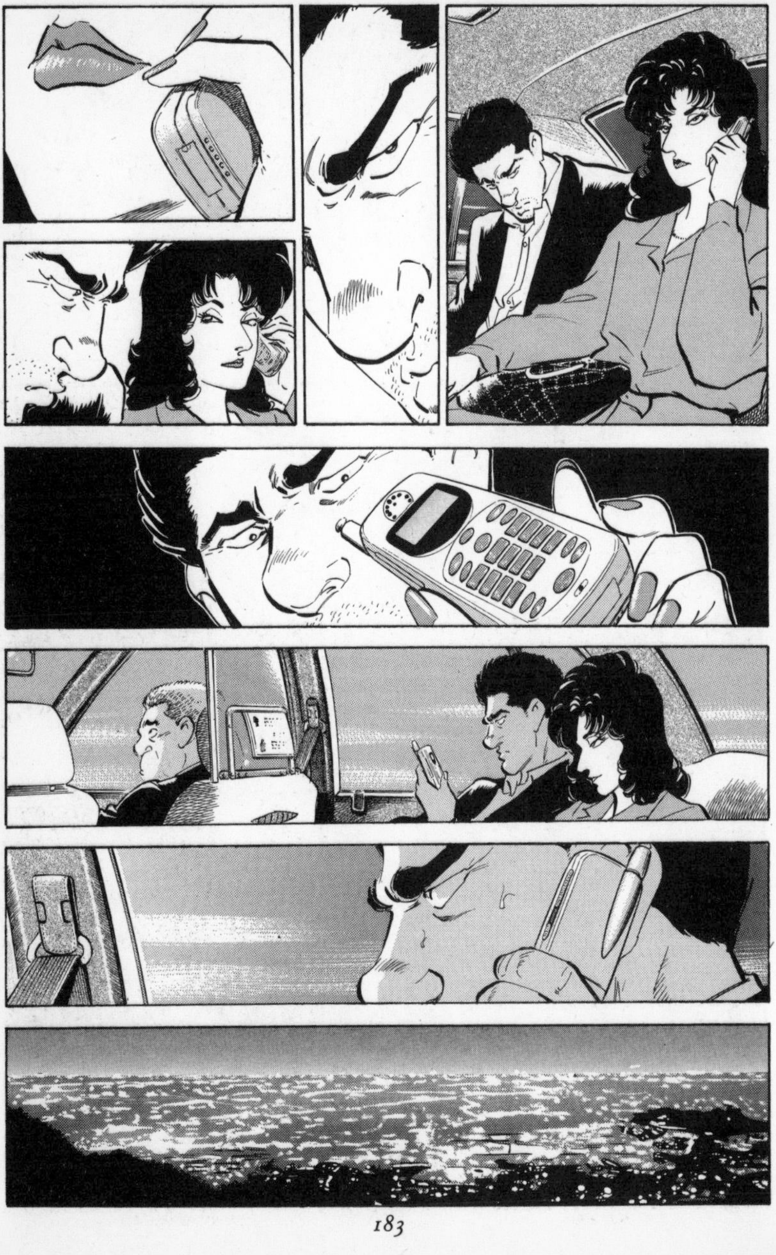

EVENING, MR. GOTO.

...
...
...
...

*FX: VRRRMMM

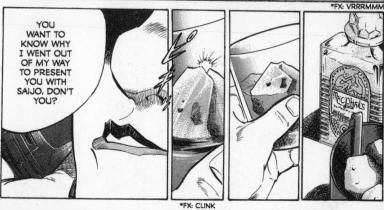

YOU WANT TO KNOW WHY I WENT OUT OF MY WAY TO PRESENT YOU WITH SAIJO, DON'T YOU?

*FX: CLINK

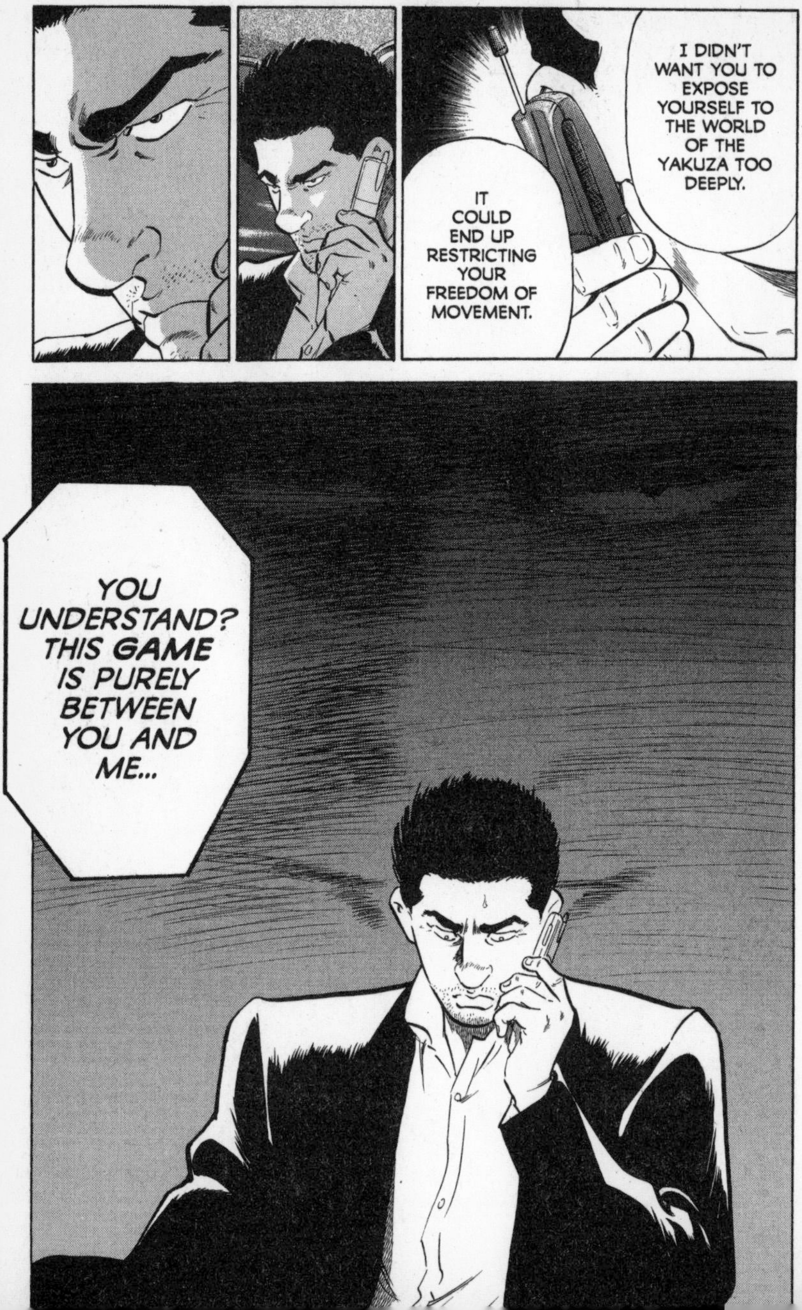
I DIDN'T WANT YOU TO EXPOSE YOURSELF TO THE WORLD OF THE YAKUZA TOO DEEPLY.
IT COULD END UP RESTRICTING YOUR FREEDOM OF MOVEMENT.
YOU UNDERSTAND? THIS GAME IS PURELY BETWEEN YOU AND ME...

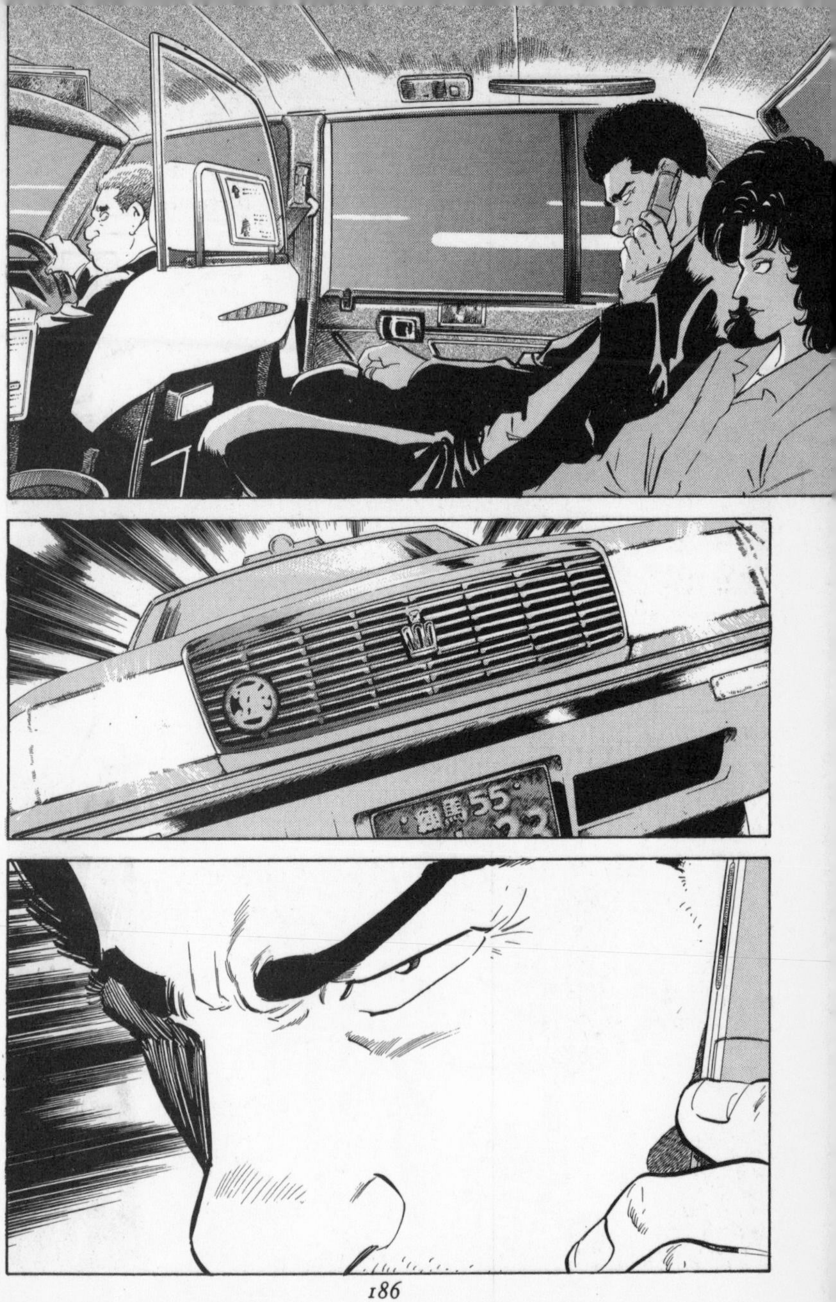
練馬55

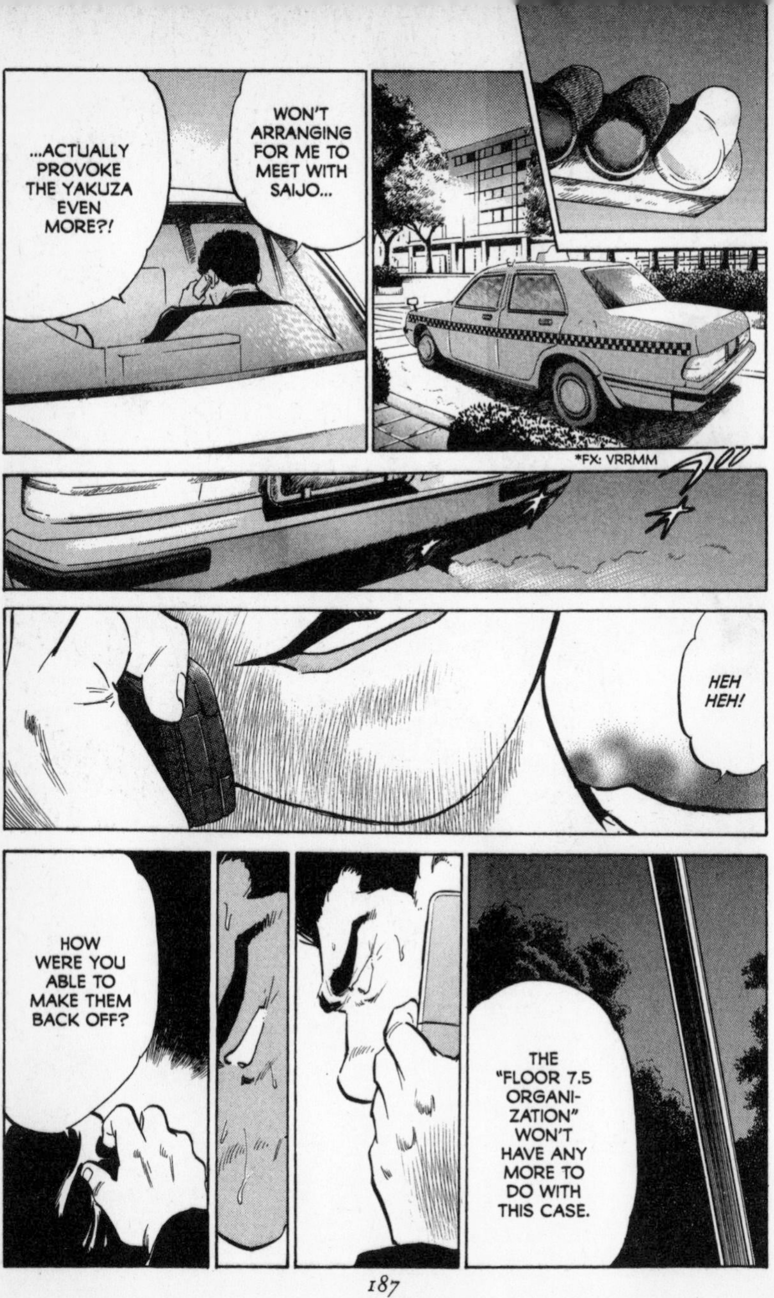
WON'T ARRANGING FOR ME TO MEET WITH SAIJO...
...ACTUALLY PROVOKE THE YAKUZA EVEN MORE?!
*FX: VRRMM
HEH HEH!
THE "FLOOR 7.5 ORGANI-ZATION" WON'T HAVE ANY MORE TO DO WITH THIS CASE.
HOW WERE YOU ABLE TO MAKE THEM BACK OFF?

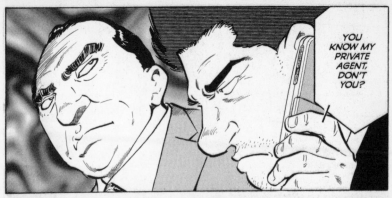

YOU KNOW MY PRIVATE AGENT, DON'T YOU?
HE'S WORKED UNDER A LONG LINE OF HIGH-RANKING GOVERNMENT OFFICIALS. HE'S ONE OF THE BEST THERE IS.
I HEAD-HUNTED HIM JUST BEFORE THE END OF YOUR LOCK-UP.
THE YAKUZA THESE DAYS ARE LIMITED TO ECONOMIC ACTIVITIES VIA CORPORATE ASSOCIATIONS...
MY MAN FOUND OUT EVERY DETAIL OF THE FLOOR 7.5 ORGANIZATION'S TAX DODGING AND THREATENED TO REPORT THEM TO THE REGIONAL TAX BUREAU.

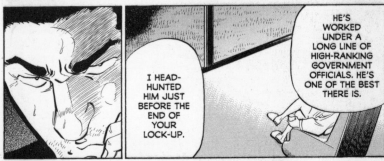

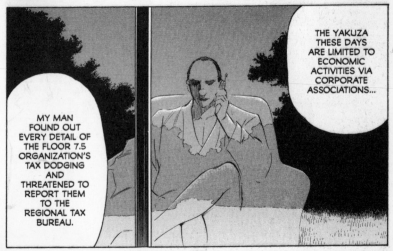

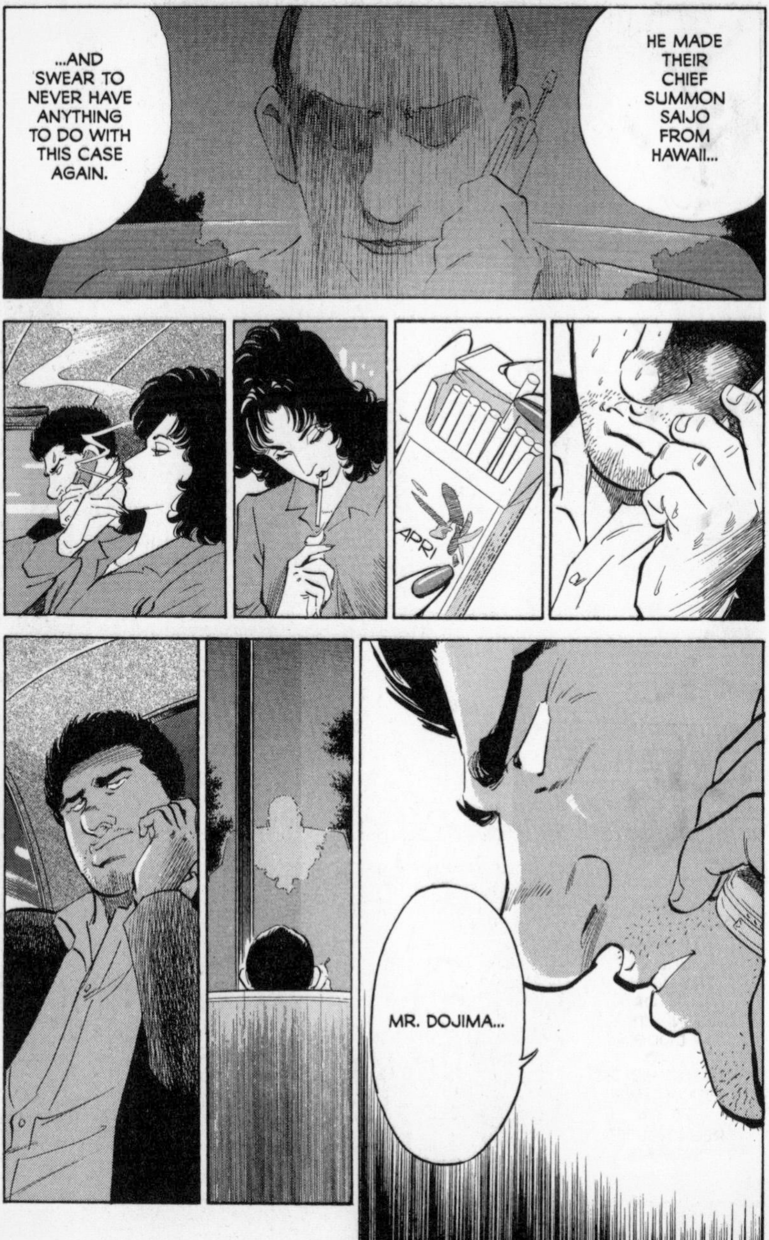
HE MADE THEIR CHIEF SUMMON SAIJO FROM HAWAII...
...AND SWEAR TO NEVER HAVE ANYTHING TO DO WITH THIS CASE AGAIN.
MR. DOJIMA...

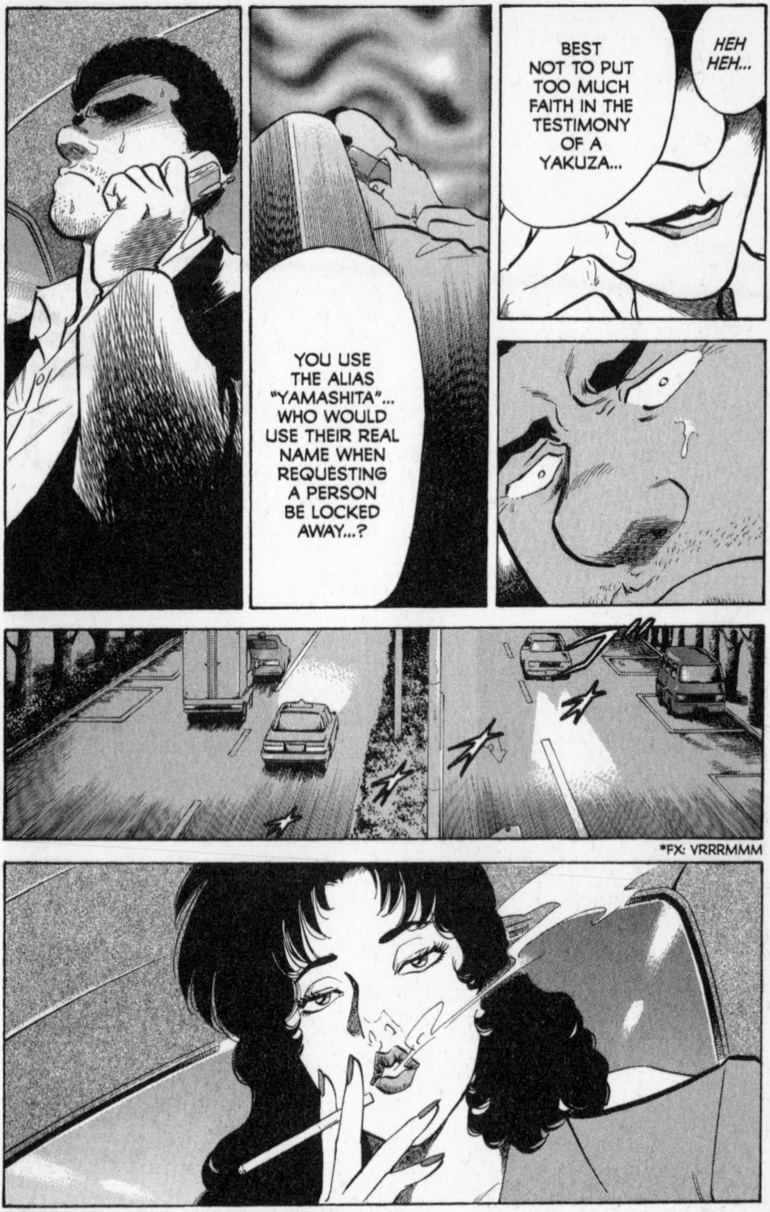
HEH HEH...
BEST NOT TO PUT TOO MUCH FAITH IN THE TESTIMONY OF A YAKUZA...
YOU USE THE ALIAS "YAMASHITA"... WHO WOULD USE THEIR REAL NAME WHEN REQUESTING A PERSON BE LOCKED AWAY...?
*FX: VRRRMMM

DEEPER INTO THE LABYRINTH: END

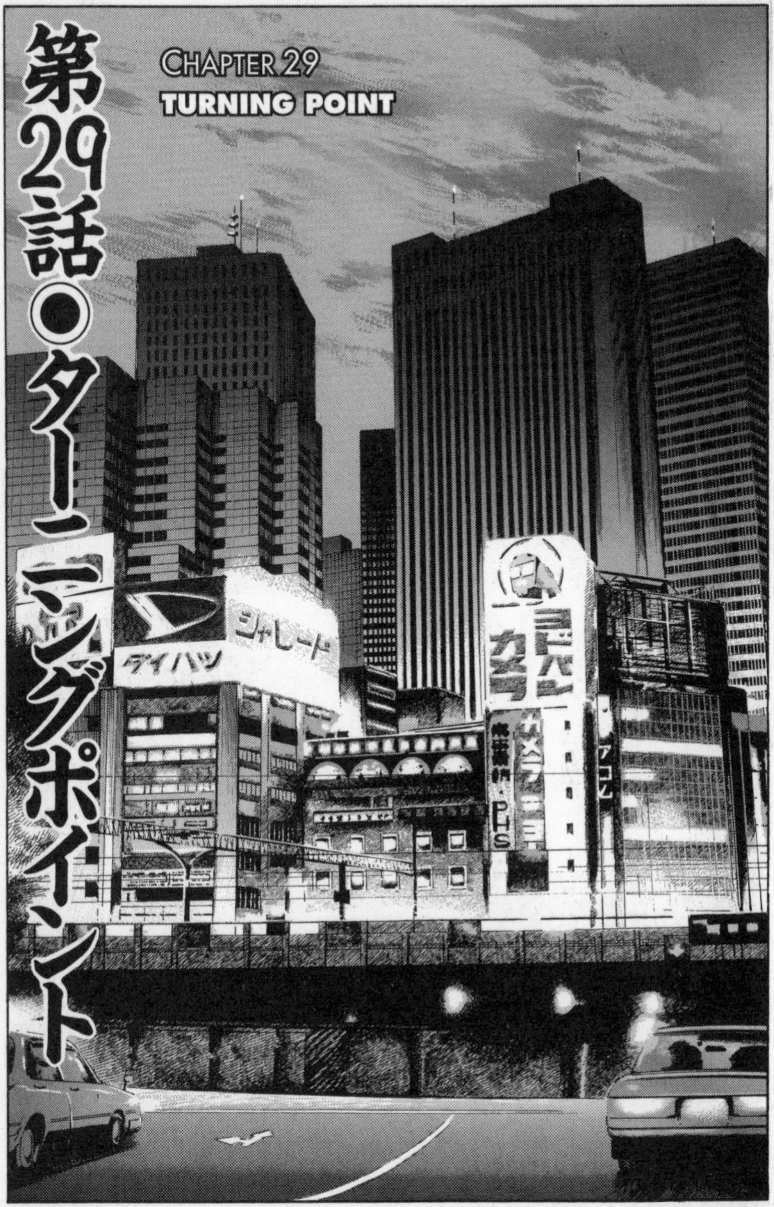
第29話●ターニングポイント
CHAPTER 29
TURNING POINT
ダイハツ
シャレード
ヨドバシカメラ
PHS

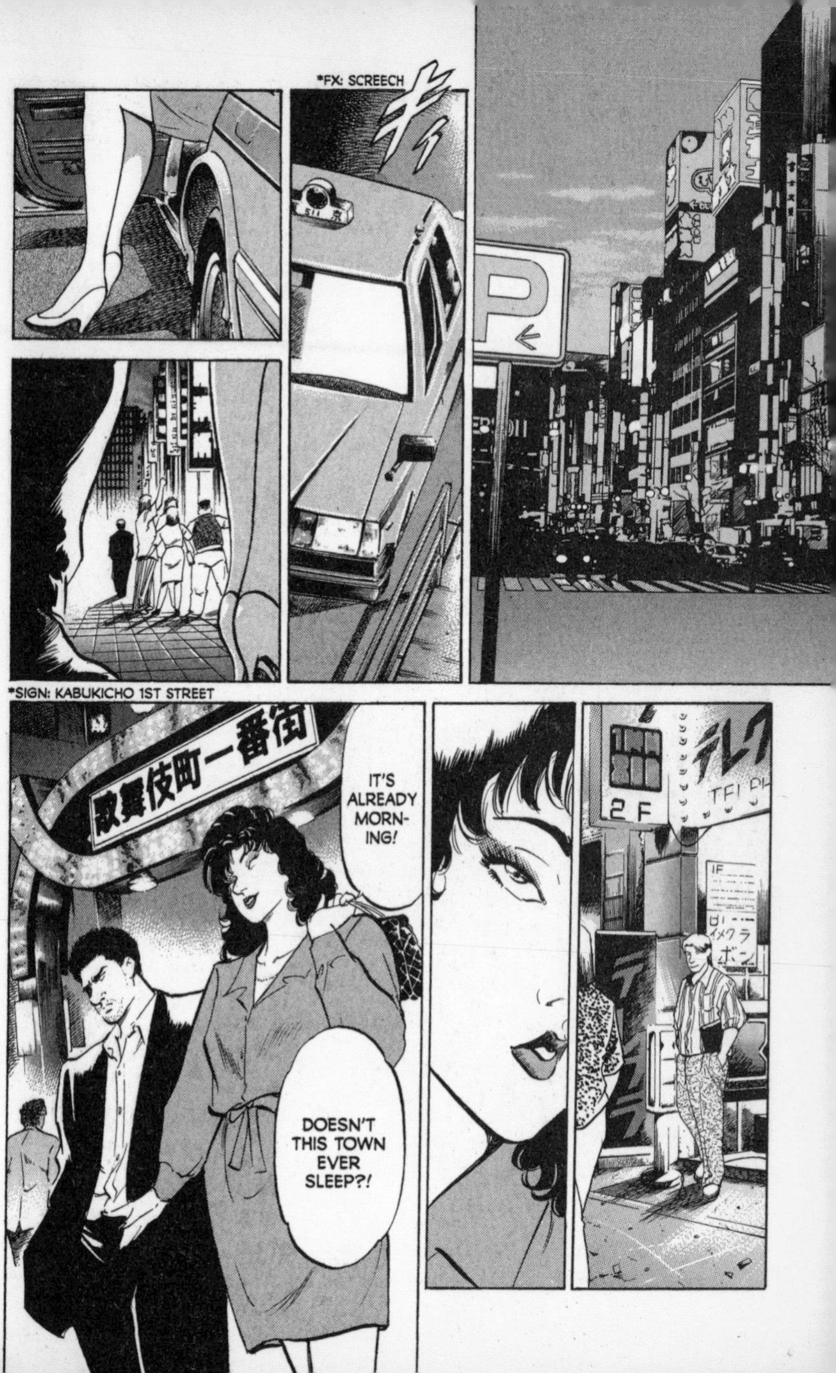
*FX: SCREECH
*SIGN: KABUKICHO 1ST STREET
IT'S ALREADY MORNING!
DOESN'T THIS TOWN EVER SLEEP?!

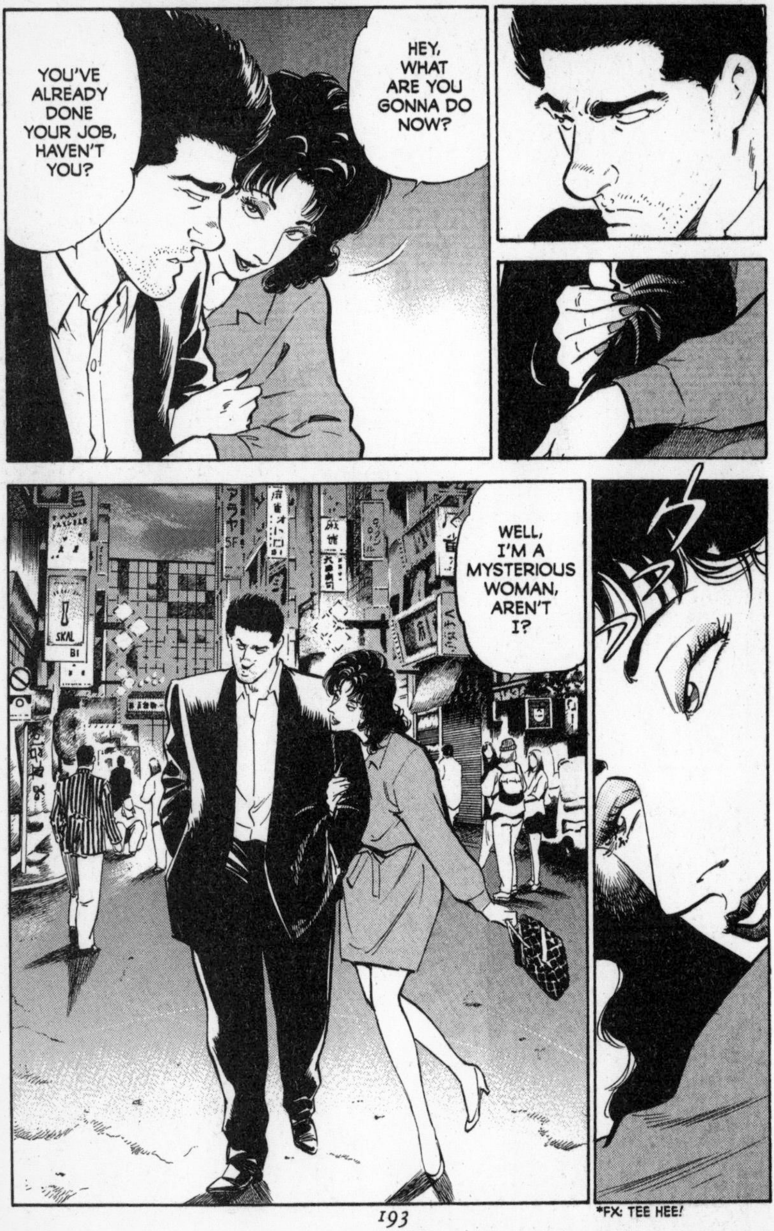
HEY, WHAT ARE YOU GONNA DO NOW?
YOU'VE ALREADY DONE YOUR JOB, HAVEN'T YOU?
WELL, I'M A MYSTERIOUS WOMAN, AREN'T I?
*FX: TEE HEE!

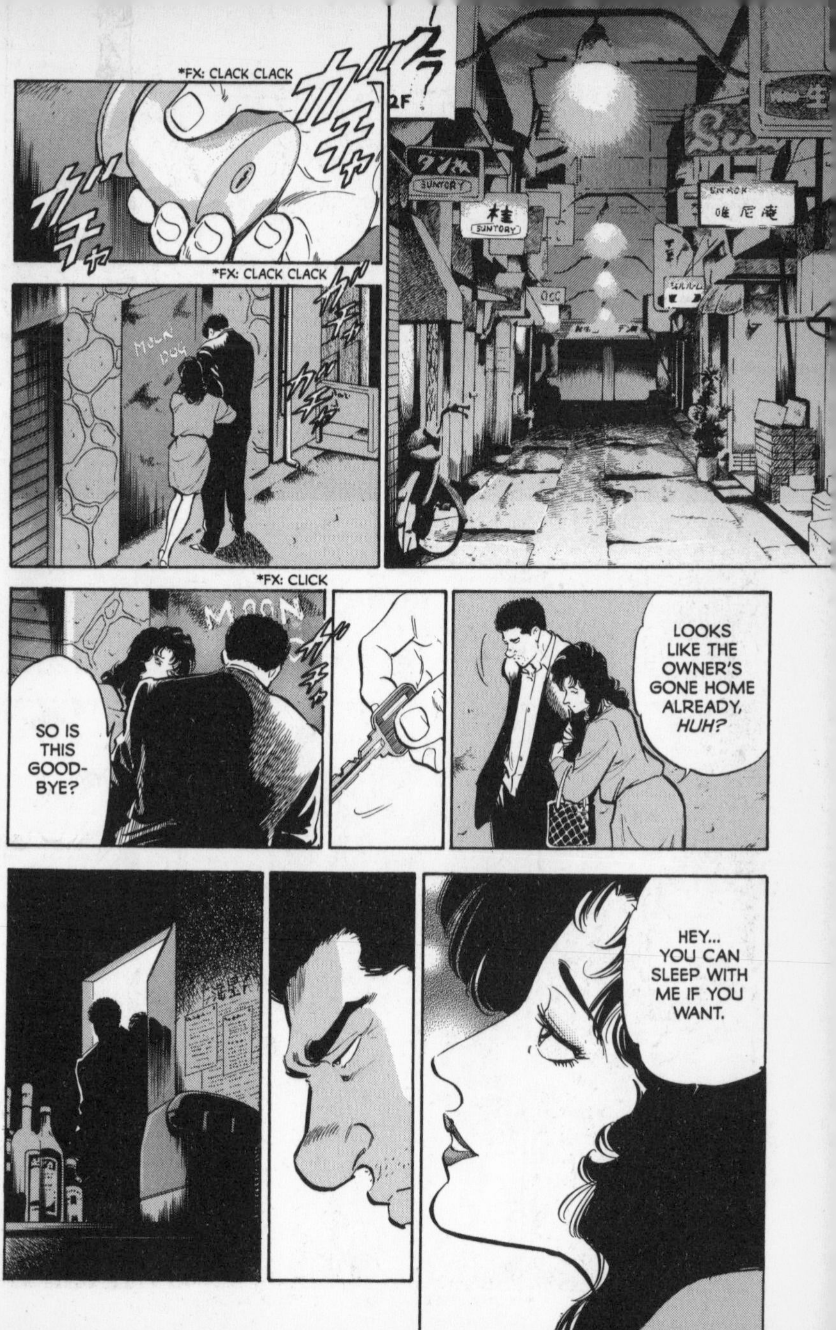
2F
SUNTORY
桂
SUNTORY
SNACK
唯尼庵
*FX: CLACK CLACK
*FX: CLACK CLACK
MOON DOG
LOOKS LIKE THE OWNER'S GONE HOME ALREADY, *HUH?*
*FX: CLICK
SO IS THIS GOOD-BYE?
HEY... YOU CAN SLEEP WITH ME IF YOU WANT.

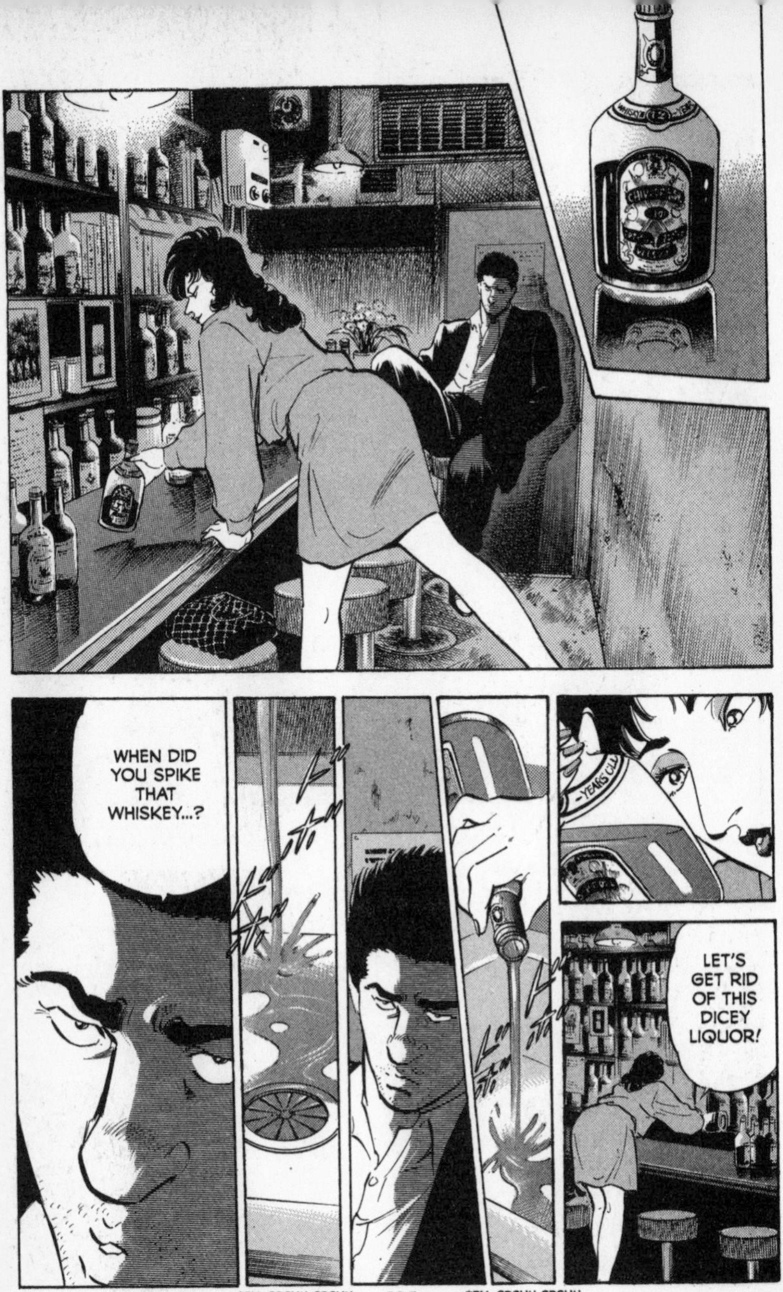
LET'S GET RID OF THIS DICEY LIQUOR!
WHEN DID YOU SPIKE THAT WHISKEY...?

*FX: SPSHH SPSHH *FX: SPSHH SPSHH

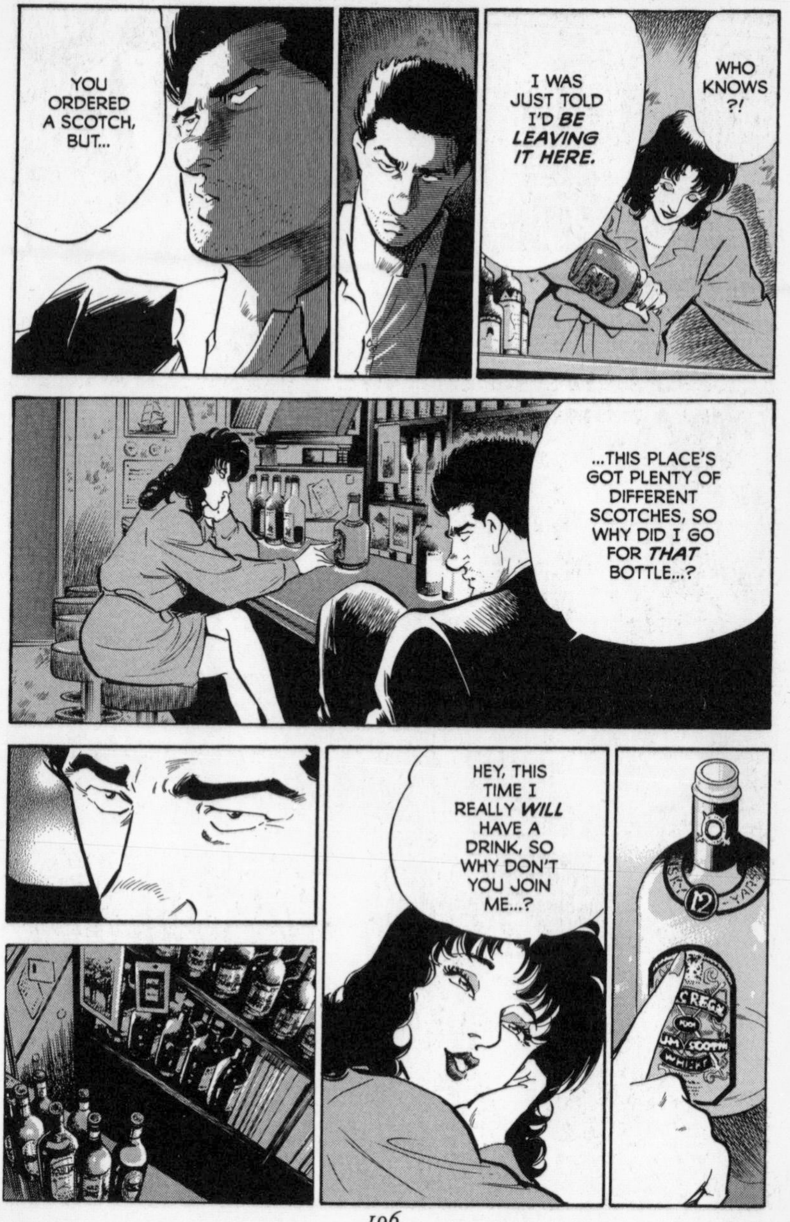
YOU ORDERED A SCOTCH, BUT...
I WAS JUST TOLD I'D BE LEAVING IT HERE.
WHO KNOWS ?!
...THIS PLACE'S GOT PLENTY OF DIFFERENT SCOTCHES, SO WHY DID I GO FOR THAT BOTTLE...?
HEY, THIS TIME I REALLY WILL HAVE A DRINK, SO WHY DON'T YOU JOIN ME...?
12

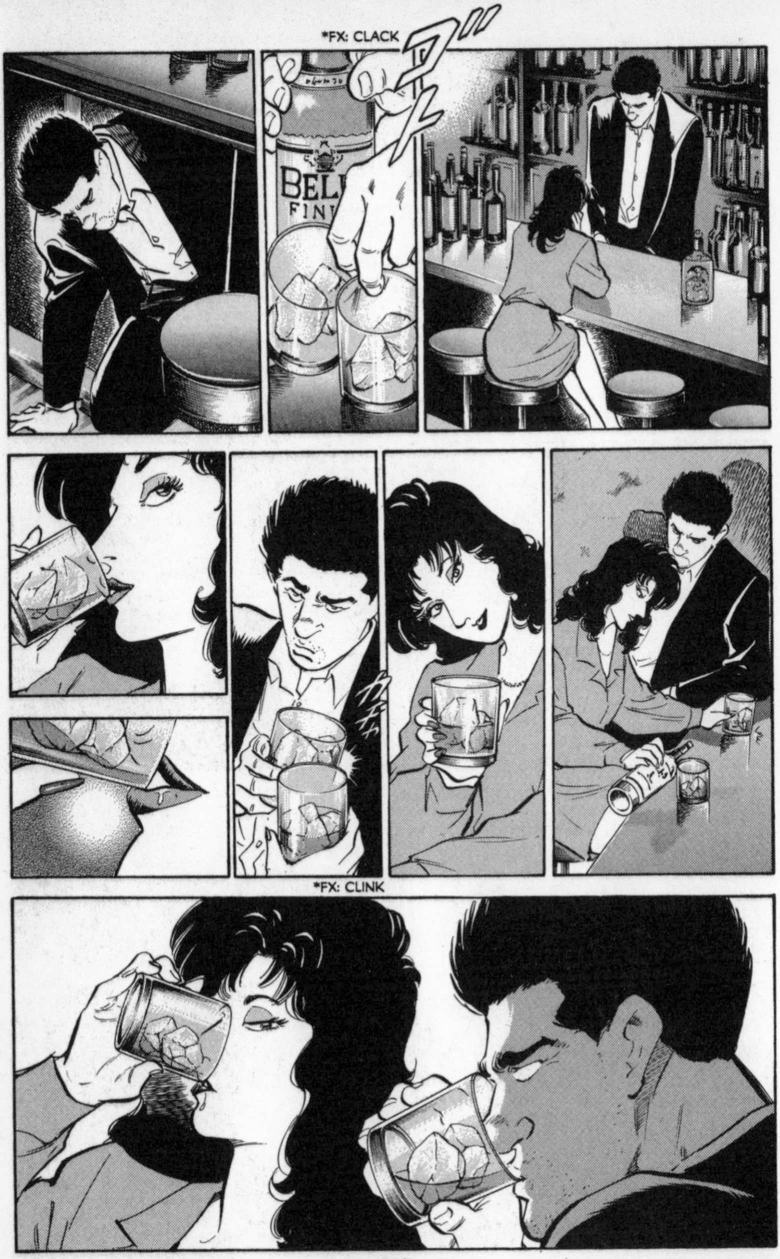
*FX: CLACK
*FX: CLINK

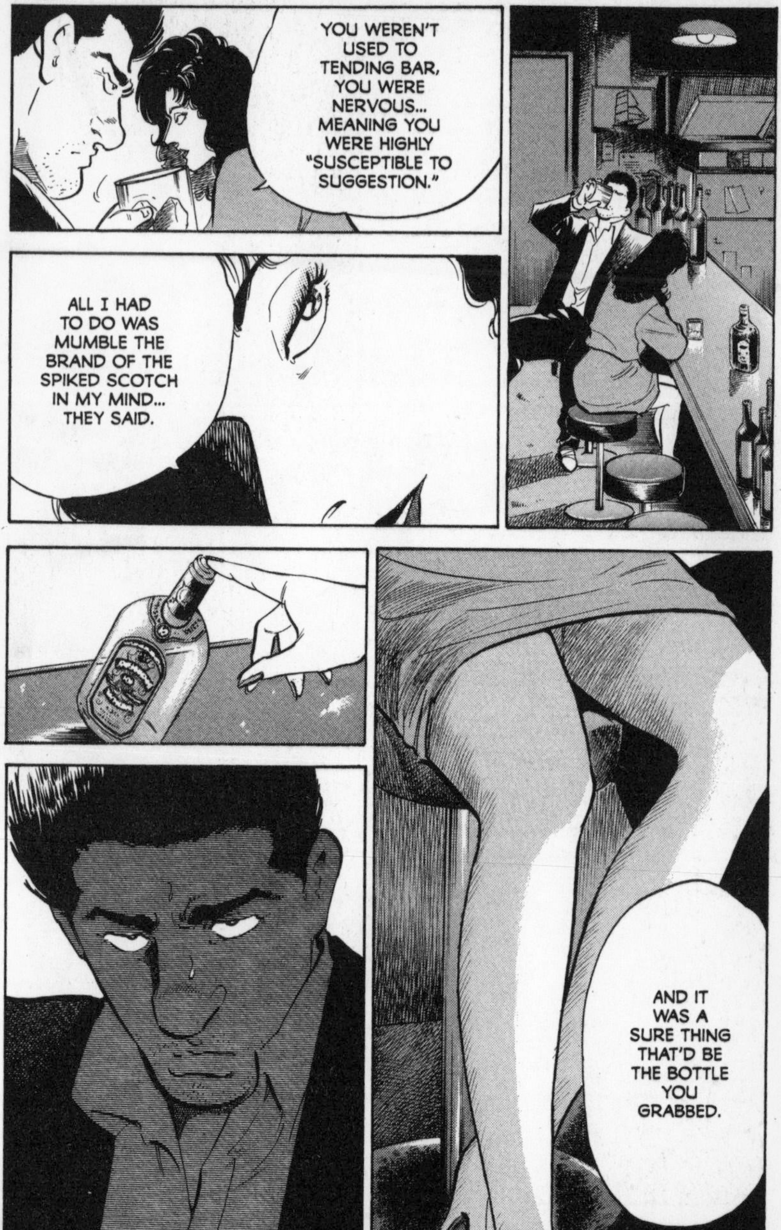
YOU WEREN'T USED TO TENDING BAR, YOU WERE NERVOUS... MEANING YOU WERE HIGHLY "SUSCEPTIBLE TO SUGGESTION."
ALL I HAD TO DO WAS MUMBLE THE BRAND OF THE SPIKED SCOTCH IN MY MIND... THEY SAID.
AND IT WAS A SURE THING THAT'D BE THE BOTTLE YOU GRABBED.

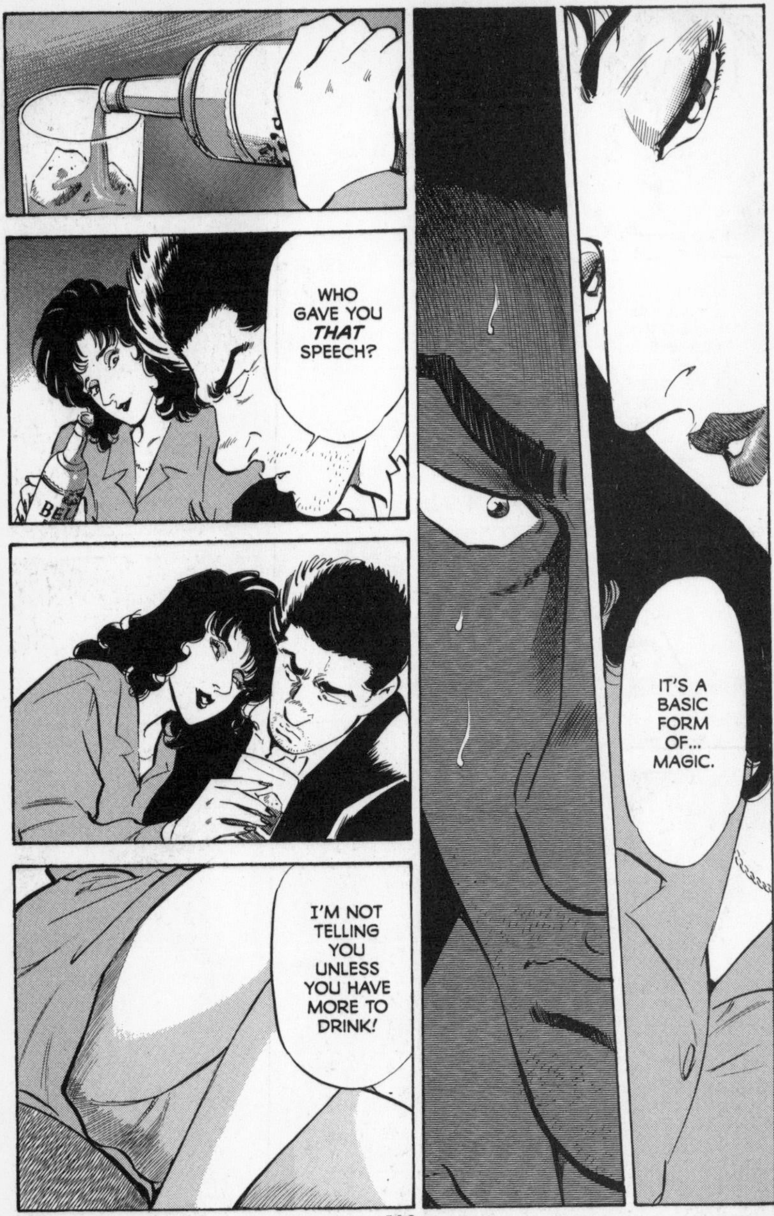
WHO GAVE YOU *THAT* SPEECH?
I'M NOT TELLING YOU UNLESS YOU HAVE MORE TO DRINK!
IT'S A BASIC FORM OF... MAGIC.

*FX: GULP

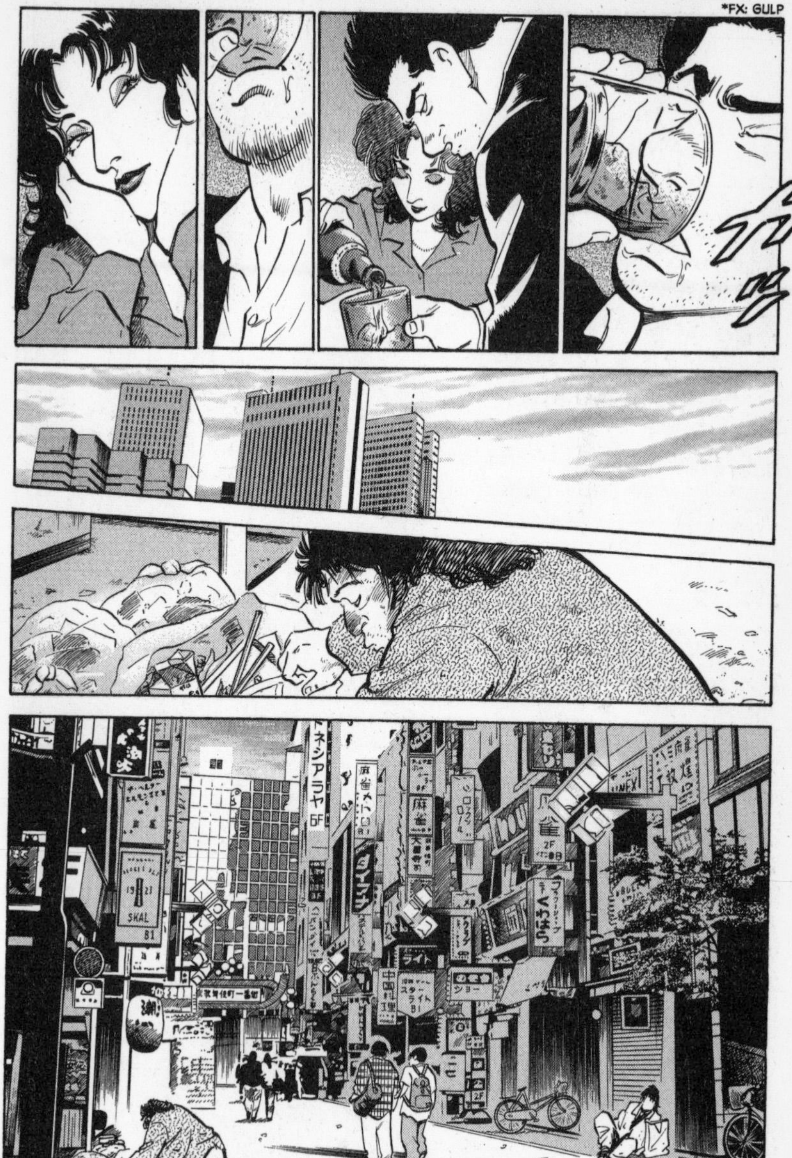

ネシアアラヤ 6F
麻雀
SKAL
B1
くわはら
ライト
スターライト B1
ショー

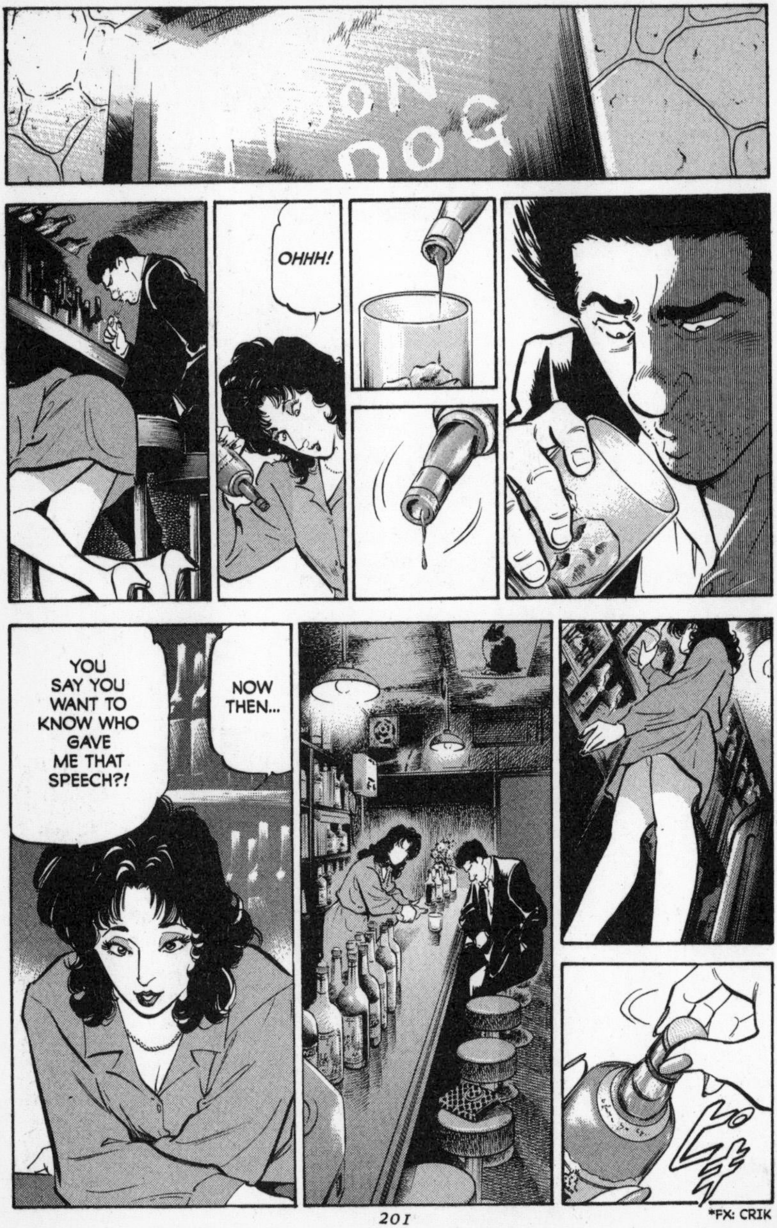
OHHH!
NOW THEN...
YOU SAY YOU WANT TO KNOW WHO GAVE ME THAT SPEECH?!

*FX: CRIK

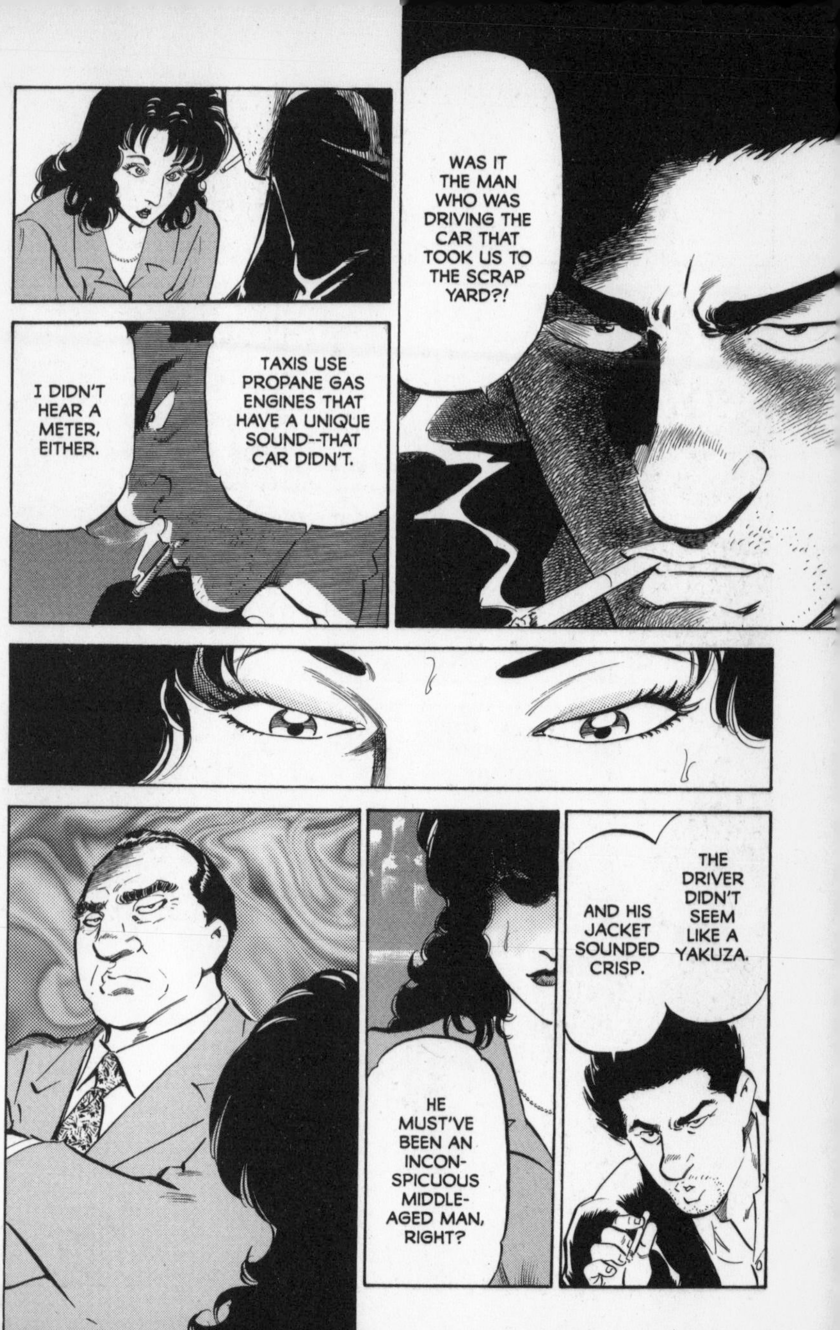
WAS IT THE MAN WHO WAS DRIVING THE CAR THAT TOOK US TO THE SCRAP YARD?!
TAXIS USE PROPANE GAS ENGINES THAT HAVE A UNIQUE SOUND--THAT CAR DIDN'T.
I DIDN'T HEAR A METER, EITHER.
THE DRIVER DIDN'T SEEM LIKE A YAKUZA.
AND HIS JACKET SOUNDED CRISP.
HE MUST'VE BEEN AN INCON-SPICUOUS MIDDLE-AGED MAN, RIGHT?

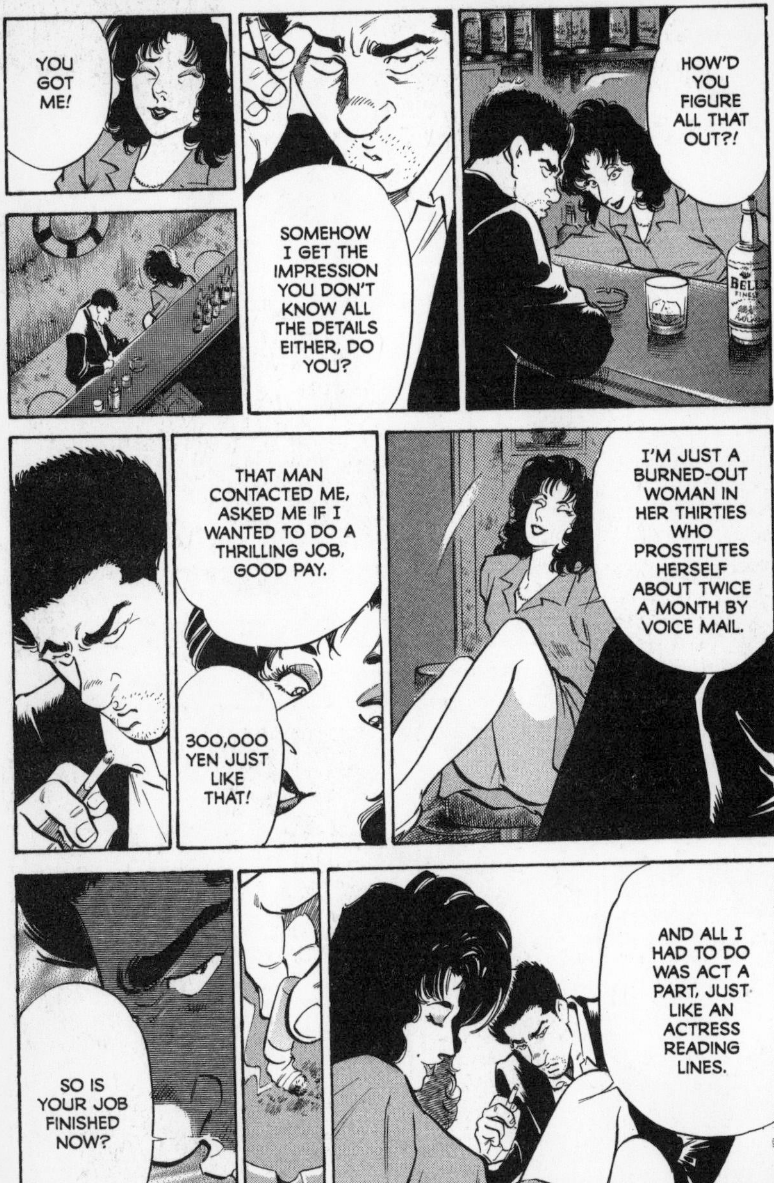
HOW'D YOU FIGURE ALL THAT OUT?!
SOMEHOW I GET THE IMPRESSION YOU DON'T KNOW ALL THE DETAILS EITHER, DO YOU?
YOU GOT ME!
I'M JUST A BURNED-OUT WOMAN IN HER THIRTIES WHO PROSTITUTES HERSELF ABOUT TWICE A MONTH BY VOICE MAIL.
THAT MAN CONTACTED ME, ASKED ME IF I WANTED TO DO A THRILLING JOB, GOOD PAY.
300,000 YEN JUST LIKE THAT!
AND ALL I HAD TO DO WAS ACT A PART, JUST LIKE AN ACTRESS READING LINES.
SO IS YOUR JOB FINISHED NOW?

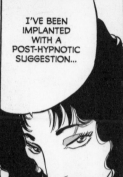

HYP-NOTIC...?!

I'VE BEEN IMPLANTED WITH A POST-HYPNOTIC SUGGESTION...

TEE HEE HEE...

SO THAT IF WE HAVE SEX AND YOU MAKE ME COME...

...I CAN GIVE YOU A VERY IMPORTANT HINT IN THIS *GAME!*

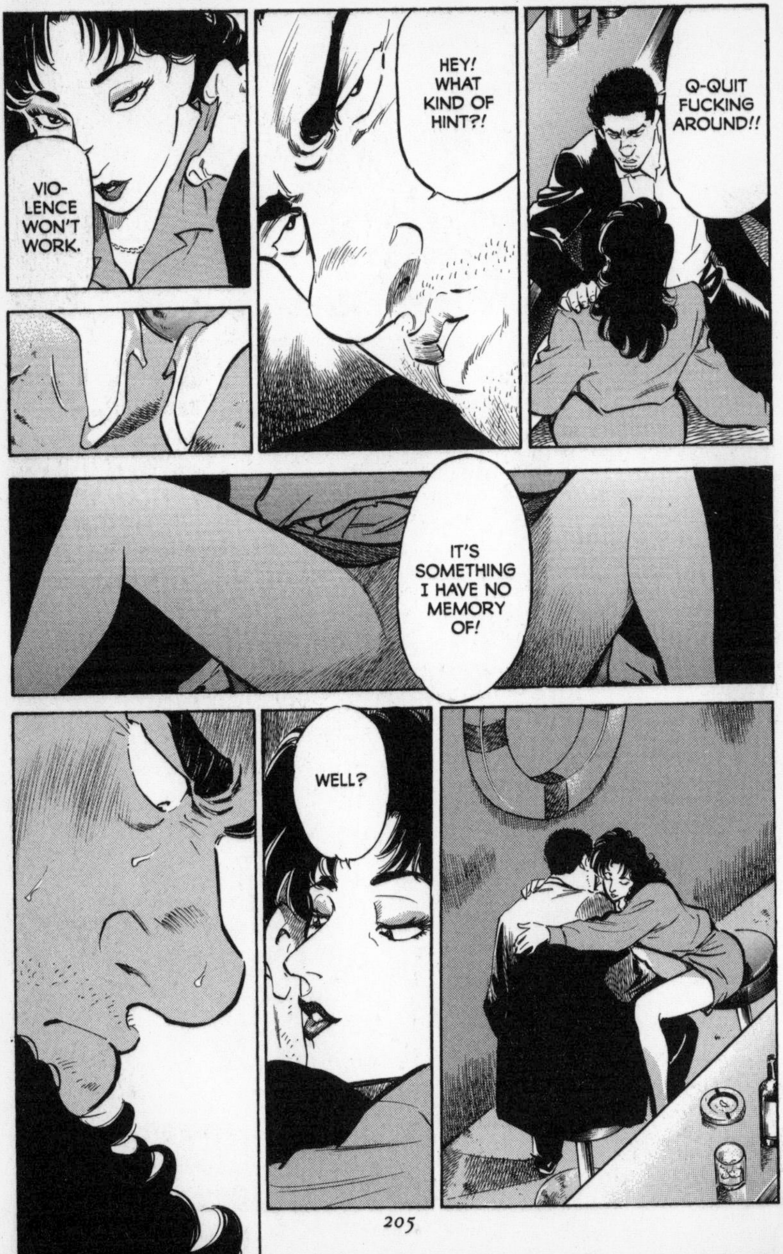
Q-QUIT FUCKING AROUND!!
HEY! WHAT KIND OF HINT?!
VIO-LENCE WON'T WORK.
IT'S SOMETHING I HAVE NO MEMORY OF!
WELL?

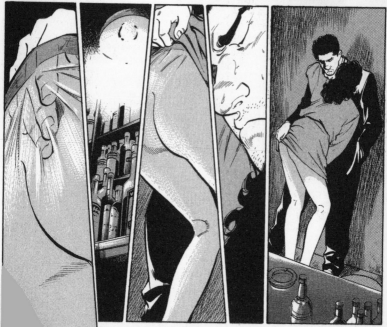

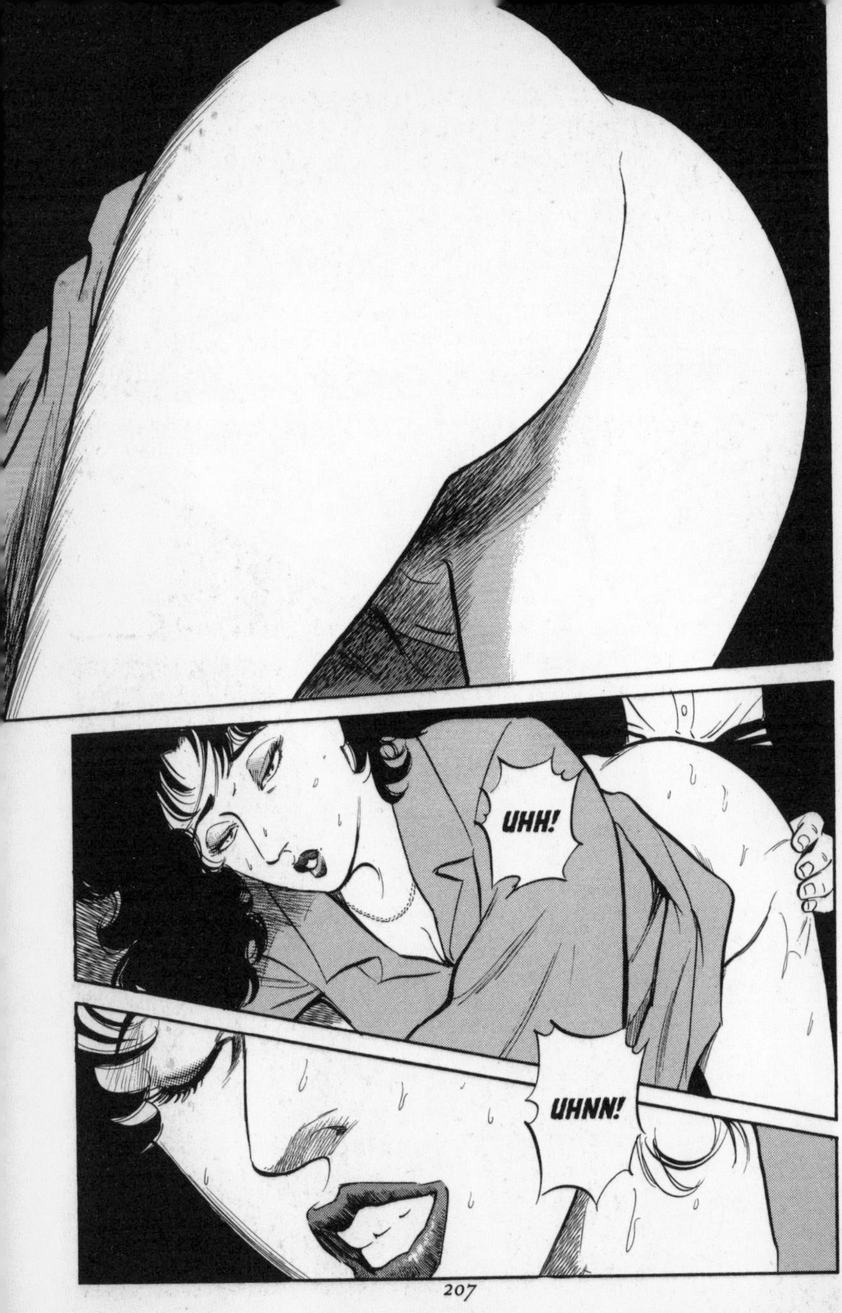
UHH!
UHNN!

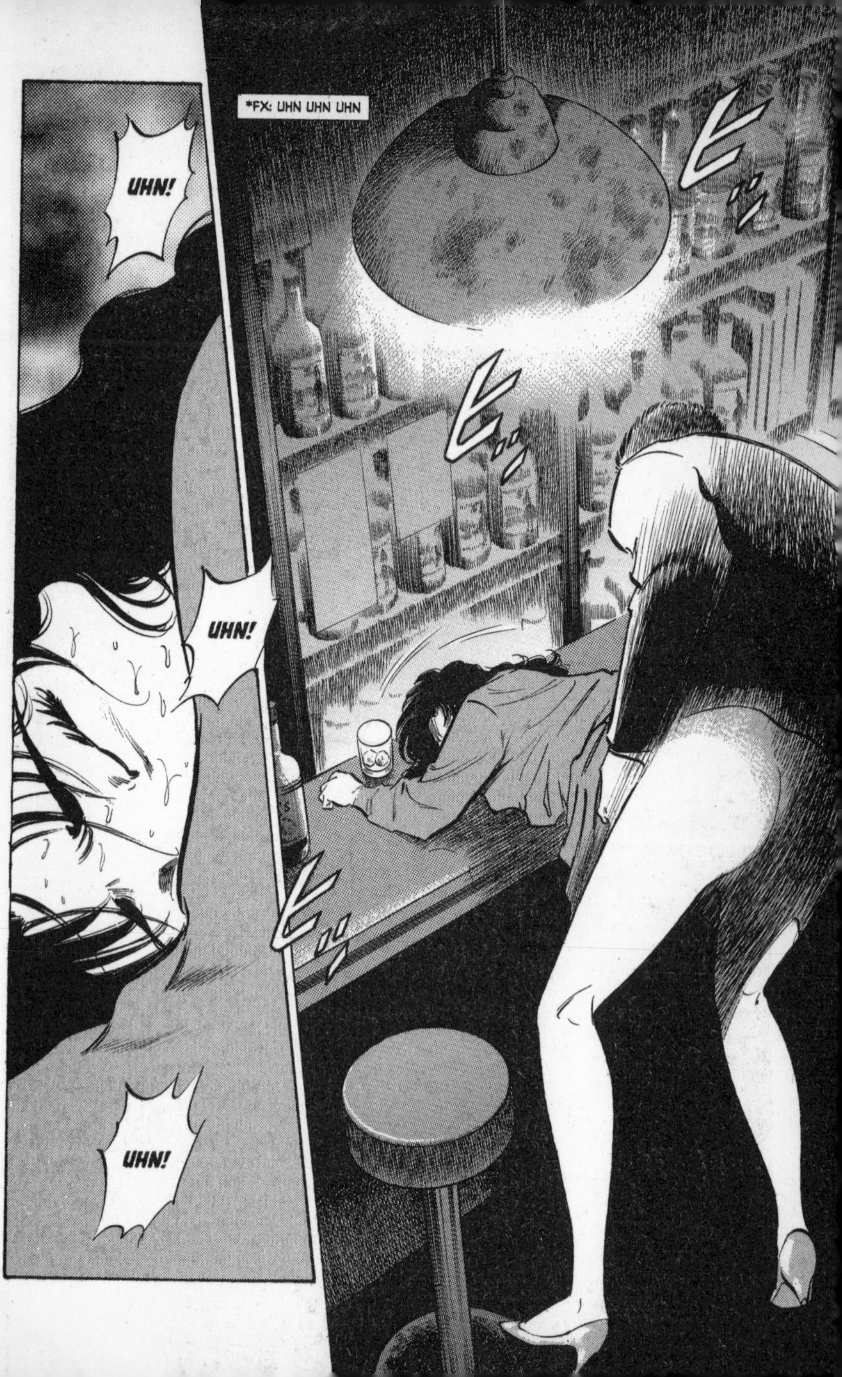
*FX: UHN UHN UHN
UHN!
UHN!
UHN!

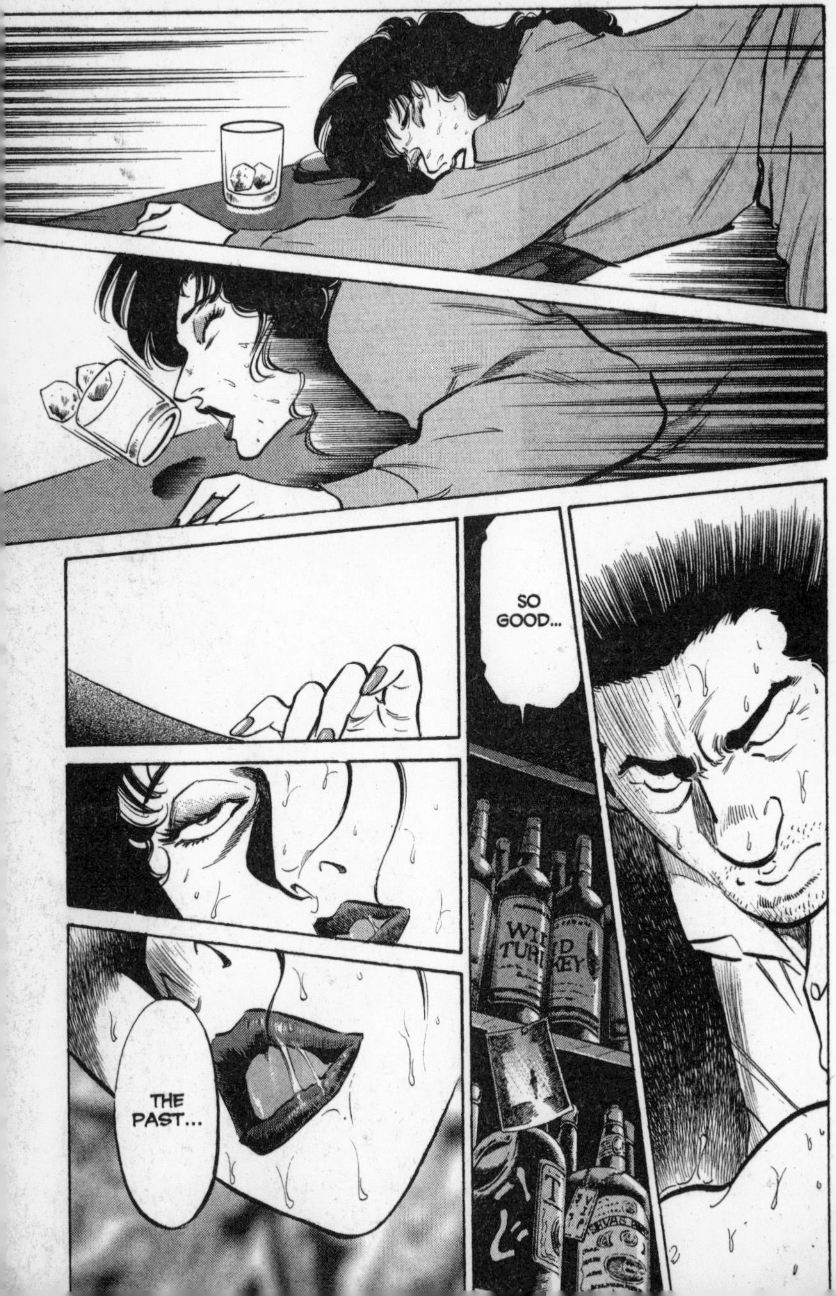
SO GOOD...
THE PAST...

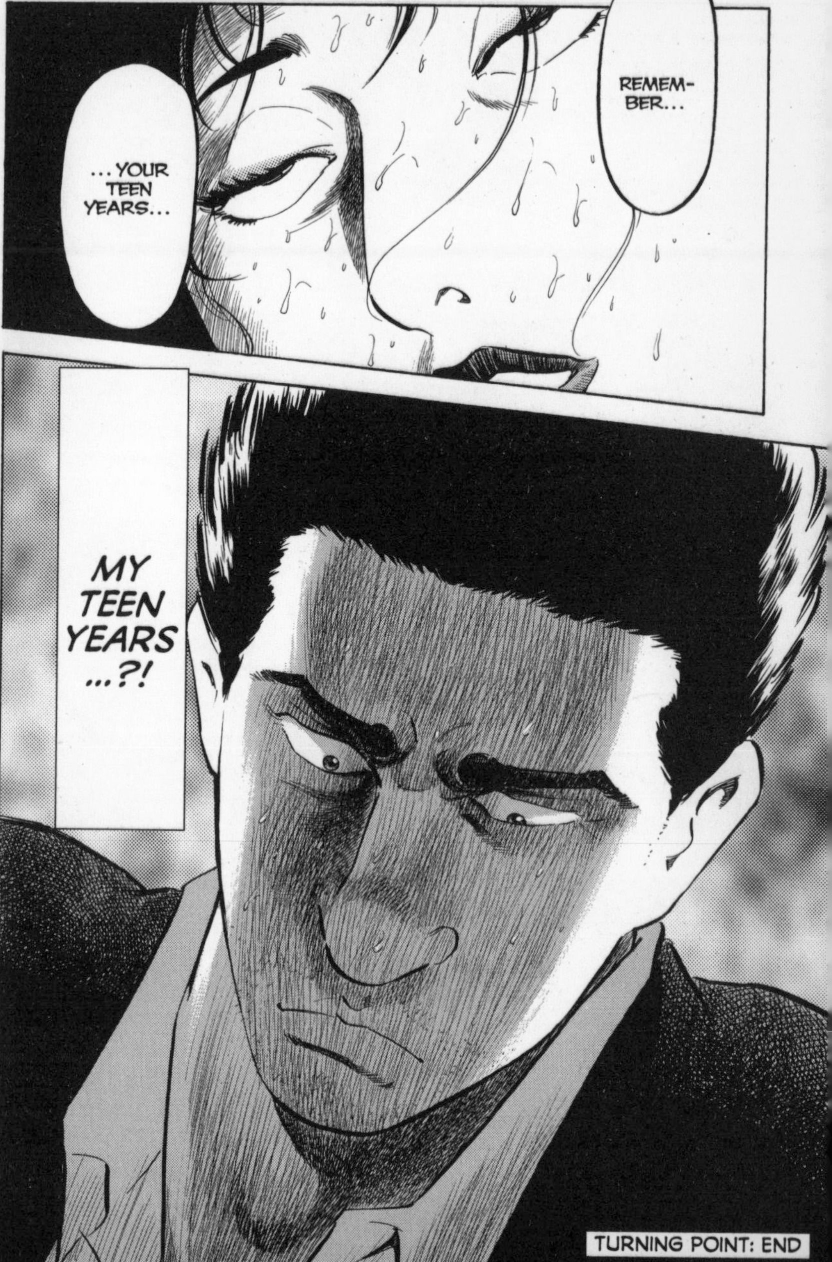
REMEM-BER...
...YOUR TEEN YEARS...
MY TEEN YEARS ...?!
TURNING POINT: END

OLDBOY

Ten years ago, he was abducted and confined to a private prison. He was never told why he was there, or who put him there. Suddenly his incarceration has ended, again without explanation. He is sedated, stuffed inside a trunk, and dumped in a park. When he awakes, he is free to reclaim what's left of his life . . . and what's left is revenge.

This series is the inspiration of the *Oldboy* film directed by Chan-wook Park, which was awarded the Grand Jury prize at the 2004 Cannes Film Festival!

VOLUME 1:
ISBN-10: 1-59307-568-5
ISBN-13: 978-1-59307-568-2

VOLUME 2:
ISBN-10: 1-59307-569-3
ISBN-13: 978-1-59307-569-9

VOLUME 3:
ISBN-10: 1-59307-570-7
ISBN-13: 978-1-59307-570-5

$12.95 EACH!